# The Mammoth Book of

# WOMEN WHO KILL

*Also available*

# The Mammoth Book of
# WOMEN
# WHO KILL

Edited by
Richard Glyn Jones

CARROLL & GRAF PUBLISHERS
New York

Carroll & Graf Publishers
An imprint of Avalon Publishing Group, Inc.
161 William Street
16th Floor
New York
NY 10038–2607
www.carrollandgraf.com

First published in the UK by Robinson,
an imprint of Constable & Robinson Ltd 2002

First Carroll & Graf edition 2002

ISBN 0–7867–0953–7

Printed and bound in the EU

# Contents

# Introduction

Writers about murder, especially male writers, tend to go off the rails when they talk about female killers. They quote Kipling (often inaccurately) about the female of the species being deadlier than the male, they wax lyrical about the excesses of the "fairer" or the "gentler" sex, and often seem to be half in love with their subjects when they write about the "delectable" Madeleine Smith (who callously poisoned her superfluous lover) or naughty Miss Lizzie Borden (who hacked her parents about their respective heads with an axe). Either that or—if the murderesses do not lend themselves to such flirtatious treatment—they tend to talk about "great monsters of history" or of Modern Medusas. One account of the Ruth Snyder/Judd Grey case, a fairly standard suburban love triangle though a particularly vicious one, is entitled "Messalina and the Corset Salesman". It can be entertaining stuff, especially if one has a taste for gallows humour, but it cannot be said to offer very insightful or even particularly accurate explanations of what drives women to kill.

A more recent phenomenon has been the feminist, or at least quasi-feminist, study of women as criminals, offering a great deal more in the way of social background and often casting valuable light on the circumstances that turn women into murderesses; for, these books argue, women have often been *driven* to such extremes of behaviour by their disadvantaged social status or by their own repressed conditions, which now and again explode into violence. Such studies are on the whole very welcome, although in their more extreme or radical manifestations they can be as silly as the other writers, tending to exonerate women from any taint of blame, still less of being bad or—perish the thought—evil, on the grounds that Men drove them to it. Some even advance the dangerous notion of female killers (of men) as feminist heroes and role models—the "Amazon" approach—presumably on the grounds that any woman who destroys men is advancing the cause, though God knows the concept of Lizzie Borden as a pioneering feminist is ludicrous enough.

In editing this collection of forty-nine notorious women I have tried to avoid the worst excesses of both these approaches, though moderate examples of each style are to be found in the pages that follow. Overall, I have tried to choose balanced accounts by good writers offering lively portraits of these women, who range from the very bad to the merely unfortunate. There is, despite the radical feminists and the social theorists, simply no getting away from the fact that in the end some murderers can only be described as evil: of the females, Countess Bathory, Elizabeth Brownrigg, Irma Grese and Jeanne Weber (to name just a few of the ones included here) seem so far beyond compassion or redemption that apologists would have an extremely difficult time accounting for their actions, and we are left with words like *wicked* and *evil* for them. Others such as Ruth Ellis, Edith Thompson and Alma Rattenbury seem to be women caught up in emotional tangles that ran out of control, and they may invite our strong sympathy. Indeed, I should make it clear at this point that by no means all of the women included in the book should necessarily be regarded as murderers; some were never caught or were acquitted at trial—though many have had grave doubts about the innocence of Lizzie Borden, for instance!—whilst others were found guilty and imprisoned or hanged when they may well have been innocent, or unfairly tried. Most people who have studied the case feel that Ruth Ellis, for one, should not have been hanged.

Nonetheless, these are all accounts of women who have been accused of or tried for murder, and having read widely on the subject I would like to be able to offer my own thesis as to what drives women to kill—to present my own theory at this point—but alas I have none. Looking at these appalling or tragic stories convinces me only that women are as diverse and interesting as any other subdivision of humanity, and if once they tended to employ poison rather than weapons of violence, that is no longer the case. The case of Aileen Carol Wuornos suggests that these days women's crimes are not much different from men's, which is equality of a sort if not a very welcome manifestation of it.

To bring things up to date for this new edition I have added my own account of the case of Rosemary West, the most appalling multiple tragedy of recent years. In between, I have concentrated on domestic or "hands-on" murders and tended to exclude political assassins such as Ulrika Meinhof—and, for that matter, Lucrezia Borgia and Catherine the Great—and female gangsters and outlaws like Bonnie Parker and Belle Starr. These considerations apart, I have simply tried to include the most notable and interesting murder cases involving women, and as it turns out there are about fifty that stand out from the crowd. Since the male sex is responsible for 80 per cent of all the crime that is committed (some authorities put the figure as high as 90 per cent), the women who do achieve notoriety in this way are unusual and almost inevitably fascinating. Some will disagree with my selection, pointing to certain omissions, but I found that some cases are very similar to one another (domestic poisonings, jealous women with guns) and have opted for variety and interest rather than encyclopaedic thoroughness. This has, however, enabled me to include some out-of-the-way cases that the reader might otherwise have missed: in particular, I had to look long and hard to find a good account of the aforementioned Countess Bathory, who is credited in *The Guinness Book of Records* as the most prolific mass murderer of all time, male or female, has inspired a number of movies and works of fiction, and seemed essential for a book of this nature. It is surprising that she features in so few true-crime books, and I am glad to be able to include her here—though she is not for the faint-hearted!

In researching this subject I found Mary Hartman's *Victorian Murderesses* and Ann Jones's *Women Who Kill* extremely useful. I would also like to thank Margaret Hallam for her invaluable help in assembling a complex manuscript.

R.G.J.

# The Contributors

The writers, listed below, are identified by initials at the end of their contributions. Details of the works from which the pieces are drawn are detailed in the *Sources and Acknowledgements* on pages 544–7.

A.E.—Andrew Ewart
A.L.—Arthur Lambton

B.L.—Brian Lunn
B. O'D.—Bernard O'Donnell
B.S.—Bill Starr

C.B-J.—Carys Bowen-Jones
C.K.—Charles Kingston

D.D.—Dorothy Dunbar

E.D.R.—Edward D. Radin
E.H.S.—Edward H. Smith
E.P.—Edmund Pearson
E.Q.—Ellery Queen
E.V.—Elizabeth Villiers

F.T.J.—F. Tennyson Jesse

G.D.—Grierson Dickson
Geo. D.—George Dilnot
G.S. Judge Gerald Sparrow

H.M.W.—H.M. Walbrook

J.E.H.—J. Edgar Hoover
J.F.—Janet Flanner
J.G.—John Glaister
J.K.—John Kobler
J.R.N.—Jay Robert Nash
J.S.—Joseph Shearing

M.H.—Michael Hervey
M.J.W. & K.M.—Marvin J. Wolfe and Katherine Mader

N.C.—*The Newgate Calendar*

P.L.—Philip Lindsay
P.Q.—Patrick Quentin

R.E.L.M. & E.L.—R.E.L. Masters and Eduard Lea
R.F.—Rupert Furneaux
R.G.J.—Richard Glyn Jones

T.C.H.J.—T.C.H. Jacobs
T.G. & H.H.G.—Tom Gurr and H.H. Cox

# 1

## AGRIPPINA

### Poison in Ancient Rome

---

When two beautiful women—each ruthlessly ambitious, each utterly immoral—-clash over an Emperor as their prize, someone is sure to get hurt. The fact that the Emperor was a lecherous, misshapen and stuttering half-wit is merely an illustration of how far those delightful creatures were prepared to sacrifice their fair bodies on the altar of power.

Agrippina, born in April in A.D. 16 was a daughter of Emperor Tiberius's nephew, Germanicus, and through him claimed descent from Livia. Tiberius was a dangerous relative for any man. Not only did he arrange the liquidation of Germanicus, who was too popular with the Roman people for his taste, but he deported his widow and imprisoned two of his three sons.

The third son was left alone because of his age (he was in his early teens at the time) which was a great pity for the people of Rome, as his name was Caligula. He showed his maniacal tendencies early by raping all three of his sisters, of whom Agrippina was one.

It is said that when the incidents were reported to Tiberius, he spoke sharply to Caligula and hastily found husbands for the three unfortunate sisters. Thus Agrippina was obliged to marry a worn-out rake 25 years older than she who inspired her only with disgust. She cannot be blamed for seeking consolation elsewhere, although she was careful not to compromise herself too much.

However much she detested her husband, Cnaeus

Domitius, the fruit of their union was an unparalleled disaster for Rome—the monstrosity known as the Emperor Nero, and Agrippina herself recorded in her Memoirs (which are now lost) that her son "came into the world feet first," to the Romans a fearful omen. She invited Caligula and Claudius to the purification ceremony (similar to our Christening) but not, apparently, the father.

Obviously trying to ingratiate herself with brother Caligula, who had been Emperor under a year, and perhaps to take out a form of insurance for her son, she asked Caligula to choose a name for the boy. Instead of walking into the trap, he pointed to the elderly Claudius standing discreetly in the background and shouted in jest: "I'll call the baby after you!"

Agrippina took this as a humiliating slight, as Claudius was then regarded as a laughing-stock and named the future Nero as Lucius Domitius Ahenobarbus.

Of his three sisters, Caligula—unnatural in all things—preferred one named Drusilla and installed her as his mistress, even though he did not ignore the younger Agrippina, taking her to bed with him from time to time. To give Drusilla a semblance of respectability he arranged for her to marry a handsome youth named Lepidus (with whom he is said to have had homosexual relations) and actually named him as his successor, so that his favourite sister would have become empress.

Drusilla spoiled that little set-up by dying prematurely, so Caligula dropped Lepidus. Agrippina at once tried to take her sister's place as her brother's mistress but was rebuffed. She then offered her body to Lepidus and promised to marry him if he managed to assassinate Caligula. She involved the third sister in the plot and set about winning recruits to their cause by offering her favours to all who would give her their pledge to join!

Remember these people were the rulers of the entire civilized world at that time.

Of all the characters in this squalid chain of events, probably Caligula showed up best—he ordered the execution of Lepidus, exiled his sisters and confiscated their possessions, a merciful judgment on them considering that they were plotting against his life. But he could not resist adding a typically macabre condition: Agrippina was forced to travel to Rome clutching to her bosom the ashes of her dead lover in a jar.

Exile did not cure the cancer of ambition in Agrippina, it merely held it in check. In any case her separation from the heart of things lasted only eighteen months. Then the hateful Caligula was assassinated and the family joke "Uncle Claudius" brought off the million-to-one chance and became Emperor.

His first act was to recall his two nieces from exile and restore their property. Agrippina, now 26, was able to snatch back her son, the growing Nero, whom she had left in the doubtful care of her sister-in-law, Domitia.

These two women, described by Tacitus as "equally shameless, violent and of bad repute," had the heartiest possible dislike for each other. A dislike which was intensified when Domitia successfully palmed off her vivacious and sexy little daughter on the ageing but still lascivious Claudius. The girl was just fifteen—her name, Messalina. And Agrippina's feelings turned to jealous hatred when, not long after the marriage, Claudius became Emperor. Even worse, less than a month later, Messalina gave the new Emperor a son. Rome's favourite guessing game was the identity of the father, but Claudius seemed to entertain no doubts.

Agrippina who, as we have seen, would slip into the bed of a brother or anyone else whom she thought might press forward her insatiable ambitions, imagined it would be easy to get into the Emperor's bed especially as she had unrestricted access to him as his niece. She reckoned without Messalina's mother, Domitia. While her daughter was beginning to build up a reputation as the most flamboyant lover-girl of that, or any other age, Mummy was always on the watch outside Claudius's private apartments so Agrippina could not get near him.

The crafty schemer decided on a switch of tactics, looked round for a rich and respectable husband, found one and set about the business of becoming the leading lady of Roman society. She knew that Messalina's wild excesses would bring her downfall sooner or later, and she did all she could to encourage the talk that she herself would be a much more fitting Empress. Let us see how the empty-headed libertine played into the hands of the older and much more intelligent woman.

First Agrippina used her young sister as a stalking-horse, to try out the strength of Messalina's hold over Claudius. This attempt to oust Messalina from the Emperor's bed also was frustrated by the vigilant mother, Domitia, and Agrippina's young sister was sent into exile once more—then discreetly liquidated. Messalina drew a dangerous conclusion from that incident—that she could do no wrong in the ever-loving eyes of Claudius. She went on a wild round of pleasure. Meantime Agrippina concentrated on educating her son Nero and establishing a salon for the illustrious citizens and literary celebrities of Rome.

The Roman Empire was now being virtually ruled by a handful of Levantine slaves whom Claudius had freed many years earlier to administer the family estates. When he became Emperor they merely carried on as before with the Imperial estates. They were all able men and devoted to Claudius. Agrippina decided to woo Pallas, the Imperial Treasurer—she was, of course, always ready to offer herself to gain even her most trivial ends and she became the mistress of the former slave, thus securing herself a spy within the Claudius government. Together they kept tabs on Messalina's extra-marital adventures and saw to it that scandal stories were spread throughout Rome.

Messalina added plenty of fuel to the fires they were stoking. She persuaded the dim-witted but trusting Claudius to give her a separate wing of the palace and there she staged a series of orgies to which she invited a fantastic variety of lovers—the young men about Rome, actors, slaves, ambassadors. Very soon, though, her guests discovered that there was a fatal catch in her party invitations: she had the habit of covering up the traces of her debaucheries by murder. Time and again she made secret reports to the Emperor that an ex-lover who was becoming an embarrassment to her was plotting treachery, and Claudius always obediently ordered his execution.

Of course, she over-reached herself—as Agrippina knew she would. When Claudius went off to campaign in southern England, Messalina really went to town. She challenged the leading harlots of Rome to a non-stop sex bout with the aim of seeing who could sleep with most men in a single night. It is recorded that at dawn after the twenty-fifth engagement, the last whore conceded defeat but Messalina carried on until high noon.

Shortly after this victory in the erotic championship, a new love "not far removed from delirium" (in the words of historian Tacitus) "took possession of Messalina". The object of her insatiable passion was "the most handsome young man in Rome" (Tacitus again) Caius Silius, on whom she showered the most expensive gifts, including furniture from the palace and other Imperial property. Silius was already married but, as we have seen, that was an insignificant detail to determined ladies.

Messalina, who wanted to stamp "mine" all over him, ordered him to divorce his wife and join her in a plot to assassinate Claudius, after which they would marry and he would become Emperor! That was an attractive enough bait for this gallant gentleman, but Messalina was playing the three-card trick all round for, when Claudius returned to Rome, she bamboozled him with a ludicrous tale about an astrologer's prediction that "her husband would die within a month".

To get round the prophecy, she proposed that Claudius give her a temporary divorce so that she could marry a victim of the stars then re-marry Claudius. The poor simpleton agreed to this arrangement, then left on an official visit to the coast. During his absence Messalina staged a marriage ceremony with Silius which turned out to be a prolonged orgy culminating in the bridegroom's carrying his near-naked bride through the streets in procession, followed by roistering guests wearing leopard skins.

This was the chance for which Agrippina and her pliant henchman, Pallas, had been waiting. They sent off a messenger to report the shocking goings-on to Claudius. Immediately he returned to Rome to confront Messalina. She tried to pass the whole affair off as an elaborate joke but, under the influence of drugs supplied by Pallas, Claudius was persuaded to give the order for his wife's execution, as well as decreeing instant death for Silius and the wedding guests

This left a vacancy in the Emperor's bed, and Agrippina's wooing of Pallas, his closest confidant, paid off. There were, of course, obstacles in the way. She had a husband—but he died with indecent haste, poisoned. Then she was the niece of Claudius and, under Roman law, union of uncle and niece was incestuous. A special decree authorizing this marriage was rushed through the subservient Senate.

At last the dream which Agrippina had cherished all her life was realized—she was Empress. At once she let her enemies and rivals know it. She had one beautiful woman, Lollia Paulina, done to death, then insisted that the body be brought to her. The face was disfigured by agony so Agrippina herself opened the mouth to examine the teeth "which she knew Lollia had done in a special way", recorded a shocked historian of that period.

She swept all Messalina's sycophants out of the court and substituted her own creatures. Claudius seemed to succumb to the egotism and authority of this infamous woman who set her sights on a new target—marrying son Nero to Claudius's daughter, Octavia.

The snag was that Octavia was already betrothed. However, Agrippina had taken far more formidable obstacles than that in her stride. She (of all people!) trumped up a charge of incest against the young fiancé and his sister which brought them disgrace and banishment. Octavia and Nero were duly betrothed.

Not content with that success, the voracious Agrippina set about organizing the adoption of Nero into the Claudian family. Claudius had only one son, Britannicus, for whom he felt a deep paternal attachment, but such was the hold Agrippina had managed to fasten on him in such a short time that he allowed himself to be talked into adopting Nero—a most obvious rival for the succession—into his family. Which meant that Nero was now betrothed to his legal sister. No problem at all for the resourceful Agrippina—she had Octavia legally adopted into another family!

The stage was dressed for her great coup—wresting the succession as Emperor from the hands of Britannicus into the grasp of her son, Nero. She neglected nothing to serve that end, putting his education under the direction of the most celebrated philosopher, Seneca, who was under orders to make certain, above all, that the boy would be taught the art of public speaking.

It seems, though, that Nero had no aptitude for oratory. Instead he became obsessed with that combination of poetry, mime, song and music which the Romans called the Cantica. From the age of 12, when his frenziedly ambitious mother was hoping to lay the foundations for his accession to the Imperial throne, the lad was to dream of becoming a great singer. He held Agrippina in awe amounting almost to hypnotic terror, so he was careful to conceal his secret ambition from her.

By the year A.D. 50 Nero was entering his 14th year, which the Romans celebrated as the beginning of manhood—Britannicus was three years younger, Agrippina left nothing to chance and decided it was time to put the pressure on in favour of her son. First she persuaded the compliant Claudius to authorize the toga of manhood for Nero nine months in advance of the legal date. Then she saw that honours were showered on Nero and that he had plenty of opportunities to show off his skill on horseback before the public. At the same time she either cut Britannicus off from the limelight or tried to belittle his standing. She even put about the rumour that the boy was an epileptic.

Her next move was to encourage Nero's training as an advocate, then as a judge in the Forum. When Claudius fell ill, Agrippina prompted her son to offer games in the circus for the Emperor's recovery—all at his own expense, of course. To cap all this she organized the wedding of Nero, then 15. and Octavia, 13, although the bride was below the legal age limit.

There was only one major feat left for her to perform—to get rid of her husband, and have her son proclaimed Emperor. This was inevitably a delicate operation, well worthy of her evil genius. There must be no breath of suspicion and both the Senate and the Army must be prepared in advance so that both would hail herself and Nero as soon as Claudius breathed his last. As poison had disposed so neatly of her previous husband, she decided to use it again. Agrippina summoned to her a notorious professional poisoner, a woman named Locusta.

A sure-as-death concoction was prepared and Agrippina, knowing what a glutton the Emperor was, decided to administer the poison in his favourite dish, mushrooms. She craftily doctored the biggest and most succulent-looking mushroom with the fatal dose, then offered the dish to Claudius, being careful to help herself to one of the harmless mushrooms first. As she had guessed, the greedy old man went for the prime specimen, swallowed it, and immediately lost consciousness. What she could not have guessed was that the unconscious Claudius would be violently sick and, according to Tacitus, "nature in relieving his stomach, appeared to have saved his life".

It was a short-lived respite. Agrippina realized her opportunity must be taken now or never and made it plain to the doctor in attendance that, if he valued his life, he had better see to it that his royal patient did not recover. The physician made use of a goose feather to tickle the Emperor's throat and encourage his vomiting—only this time he tipped it with some of Agrippina's poison and

Claudius died without regaining speech or hearing. She had brought off her major *coup de theatre*.

The news of the Emperor's sudden illness spread beyond the palace and Agrippina issued official bulletins to say that he had passed a comfortable night, condition as well as could be expected, etc. She even brought in a troupe of mummers to give a show before the dead Emperor, who was swaddled in blankets and propped up in bed like an invalid, though, of course, far beyond appreciation.

Only when all was ready to acclaim Nero as the new ruler did she allow the news of her husband's death to reach the public. It is also reasonably certain that she even kept Nero in the dark until the last possible moment. He went through the many ceremonies of that day like a puppet—and a puppet was what Agrippina intended him to remain, with her always there to pull his strings.

She proceeded diabolically to remove by death all possible rival claimants to the throne. Probably it was this reign of terror and revenge which changed his overwhelming awe of his merciless mother into an overwhelming disgust, although it was for his sake that she had turned Rome into a slaughter-house. At any rate Nero defied her for the first time in his life and refused to sign two of her murderous decrees. Soon he decided to dispense with her presence by his side when receiving ambassadors from abroad.

The first real trial of strength came when Nero conceived a violent passion for a freedwoman attached to his wife Octavia's domestic staff. The girl's name was Acte and it did seem a genuine case of love at first sight for Nero because not only did he load her with costly presents, but, to prove the sincerity of his affections, he wanted to send his wife packing and marry Acte at once.

When Agrippina discovered that her precious puppet

proposed to make a serving wench her daughter-in-law she fell into a fit of rage and vituperation. She demanded a private session with her son and it can well be imagined what went on at that interview. Nero held his ground and apparently threatened to abdicate rather than abandon his Acte.

Tacitus then reports that a wind of change blew through the palace . . . "Formerly exceedingly severe", writes the historian, "but now prostrate at his feet, she offered him all her resources which were about as large as his own." She was full of motherly concern for him and even put her apartments at his disposal as a "love-nest."

Agrippina was to learn that power could be as heady a wine for others as it had been for her. Nero still showed her the outward respect of a son but he began to whittle away her favourites and co-plotters at the palace. Pallas, who had done so much to pave the way for her with Claudius, was the first to go.

This was too much for Agrippina—Pallas was not only her right-hand man, he was her lover. She had an even stormier showdown with her son than over Acte. This time she did not fall at his feet. She threatened him with Britannicus, whom she had manoeuvred out of the succession but whom she was ready to prop up again as a rival to this ingrate of a son. Nero took her threat seriously and decided to do something about it before his mother had a chance to get to work. He invited Britannicus to dinner in his private apartments. Well tutored in these matters, he took the precaution of calling in the deadly Locusta first and got her to prepare one of her instant poisons. His problem was how to get Britannicus to take it.

Nero was not his mother's son for nothing. He knew Britannicus had a wine-and-food taster always in attendance so he offered him a harmless dish which was so hot that his guest asked for cold water to be added to it. The poison was in the cold water which, says Tacitus, "circulated so rapidly in his veins that it deprived him of speech and life".

For Agrippina, who was present at the fatal feast, the murder of Britannicus was the Indian sign. She understood that her son had pulled off his velvet gloves and could be as ruthless as herself in gaining his ends. There were other, more personal blows to follow. Nero removed her guard of honour, then all her military protectors, including a special corps of mercenaries. Then she was politely requested to leave his palace.

This tigress could not change her spots. She went to work to find another claimant to unseat her ungrateful son and to foment disaffection among Nero's Praetorian Guards. The plot reached the ears of Nero. His immediate reaction was to order the death of his mother and her accomplices.

Seneca, who was his chief adviser, persuaded the Emperor to send a commission of inquiry to question his mother in her home—but Nero made the Chief Commissioner swear that, if he found her guilty of conspiracy, he would put her to death on the spot. She made a magnificent speech in her own defence and convinced the commission it was all a dreadful misunderstanding.

Having got away with it, she decided to lie low for a year or two, brooding on how to get back to favour—and power. She settled on the most abhorrent and disgusting way of all. As she had lost the authority of a mother over Nero, she would seduce him and become his mistress. It sounds too vile a design even for this abominable woman but their incestuous relationship is vouched for by a historian who was familiar with activities in the palace and this writer declares that the odious union was discussed with horror everywhere in Rome. Here is the version by Tacitus:

> *"In her eagerness to regain power, Agrippina went to such lengths that, at midday, just at the time when Nero was heated with wine and good food, she offered herself several times, carefully arrayed and ready for incest, to the young man. Lascivious kisses and caresses, preludes of the ignominy, attracted the attention of those surrounding them. Seneca, seeking to counter the seductions of one woman by the help of another, sent Acte to Nero. Apprehensive both for herself and for the honour of the prince, she warned him that a rumour of the incest had spread, and that his mother was glorying in it, but that the army would not support an emperor soiled with such a crime."*

Another historian, Suetonius, confirms this account by Tacitus and adds that their unnatural liaison was by no means confined to their private apartments but that they made love in a litter in which they were being carried out of doors. Later writers, seeking to explain such vicious conduct, try to excuse Nero on the ground that it gave him a dominance over his domineering mother before whom he had cowered all through childhood and, having already stripped her of all power in the state, he achieved final mastery of her as a woman. But no one can find the vestige of an excuse for the execrable Agrippina.

When Nero was brought to realize the full shame of such an act he was overcome by self-hatred, and self-pity. His mother was the cause of all the disturbances in his life. Tacitus writes:

> *"He came to the conclusion that wherever she was, she would be a burden to him—and he resolved upon her death."*

It would, however, be no easy matter to dispose of her. She could be executed only for complicity in a plot against his life and he knew she was too wily to lay herself open again. He considered the method that had worked so well for his mother—and himself—in the past; a poison, but he knew she was well on guard against it.

He was still pondering over the *modus operandi* when he went to the seaside to watch an aquatic show. This included a brand-new attraction which gave him the brain-wave he was so desperately seeking. One of the ships taking part in the display suddenly split in half and released a cargo of wild animals from the hold into the water. The thought struck Nero: why not use this device for doing away with his troublesome mother?

Once he had hit on the method he needed only to set the trap for her. So he wrote her a most affectionate letter inviting her to join him on the coast for the spring festival celebrations. She accepted with joy. He met her on arrival and personally conducted her to her villa on the coast with a great show of affection. Then he asked her to a banquet to be held that evening two miles farther along the coast and promised to send a lavishly decorated galley to take her by sea. She nearly wrecked his plan by deciding to go along the coast road in a litter. However, at the end of the banquet, the galley was waiting to take her back home.

"During the feast", Tacitus reports, "he overwhelmed his mother with attentions and had her placed above him at table." He also saw to it that she had plenty of wine. When the time came for farewells Nero conducted her to the seashore. He thought he was sending her to her death and, full of tenderness, he pressed her in his arms, kissed her eyes, and hands, her breasts . . . then said goodbye.

When the ship was well out from shore the captain, acting under Nero's orders, gave the signal for the splitting operation. First a huge weight of lead had to be tipped on to the roof of the dais on which she was sitting so that it would collapse and bury her. If it did not kill her outright it would probably injure her so severely that, when the hold of the galley opened and dropped her into the sea, she would be unable to swim to to safety.

As often happens with the best laid schemes of mice and men, everything went wrong. The roof crashed down all right and killed one of her attendants where he stood. However, the newfangled splitting apparatus failed to function and the hold did not open. Tacitus, who recorded the scene for all posterity, writes that great confusion ensued aboard the ship and the captain ordered all the oarsmen to put their weight on one side so that the vessel would capsize—but this didn't work either.

The quick-witted Agrippina grasped the situation, ordered her lady-in-waiting to impersonate her and to call out "Save me! Save the Emperor's mother!" That unfortunate lady obeyed, not realizing what was going on, and was bludgeoned to death by oars while the real target was slipping overboard and striking out for the shore.

Agrippina was an excellent swimmer and kept going until a boat making for the scene of the accident picked her up, then she was smart enough to persuade her rescuers to go a round-about voyage before landing her near her villa. Back home again, suffering only slight injuries and shock, she had enough presence of mind left to send a messenger to her son with the news that, "The benevolence of the gods and the Emperor's good fortune had enabled her to escape from great danger" and begging him "though no doubt filled with fear at the occurrence, to put off visiting her as she needed rest above all things".

As Tacitus shrewdly remarks: "She understood that the only way to avoid falling into traps was to appear not to suspect them". But before going to bed on that eventful night, she ordered her staff to begin a search for the will of her ill-fated lady-in-waiting as that faithful friend had promised to leave Agrippina all her money!

Nero was beside himself with panic when he found that his intricate murder plot had boomeranged, believing that, when it became known, he would be branded forever. He was also terrified of his mother's vengeance and imagined a party of armed men coming for him the next day. So he abandoned all subtlety and caution, hastily concocted a story that she was plotting to take his life and sent a group of thugs to her villa with orders that she must not waken again.

In the small hours three strong-arm men burst into her room—one of them being the captain of the ship who had bungled his job earlier. She was lying in bed, but wide awake. As they came for her she raised herself and said to them:

> *"If you have come to find out how I am, you can say I am going on well. If you have come to commit a crime, I cannot believe my son to be capable of it—surely he cannot have ordered a matricide."*

Without a word they fell upon her. After beating her about the head one of them drew his sword. Then, or so the historians report, she still found enough strength to pull off her nightdress and present her body to her attackers, saying: "Strike me in the belly!" but it took more than one sword thrust to silence her, and her ambitions, forever.

Her slaves were commanded to prepare a bonfire and her body was thrown on the flames at once—Nero intended that no one should have a chance to examine the tell-tale evidence of murder most foul. Thus in horror and violence ended a life burned up by ambition which, when achieved, no matter how, had to feed on more ambition. Of this woman, if of no other, it can be said with truth: there was not one redeeming feature.

—A.E.

# 2

# MA BARKER
## Matriarch with a Machine Gun

They never came any tougher than "Ma" Barker and her brood, and that goes, too, for the other half of the gang—the hoods led by Alvin Karpis. I should know, for I helped to hunt them and, finally, to eliminate them. Of all public enemies they were unquestionably the vilest—a throng of wanton killers, vicious, depraved and incredibly ruthless. Without a single exception they were monsters, and pity was a word of which they had never heard. They moved in a welter of blood; mail robberies, bank hold-ups, kidnapping and pitched machine-gun battles; they loved nothing better than to kill a police officer, and if some innocent bystander fell to the same hail of bullets that did not matter either. They executed their own traitors, bought over unfaithful police officials, "fixed" paroles and prison breaks. Their anarchy fouled the very roots of law and order.

I remember their heyday and the various impressions I received from the tortuous investigation, the interrogation of witnesses, and the study of reports which came in from special agents all over the country. "Ma" Barker, for instance, renting an apartment from an unsuspecting landlord, knowing that if he looked into her hard eyes he would guess the truth; a drunken doctor shaving the fingertips of a crazed hoodlum no longer under an anaesthetic; Karpis, the slit-eyed killer, explaining how he was going to wipe out top F.B.I. agents in Los Angeles, Chicago, New York and myself in Washington by using automobiles and planes, and hating it like hell because somebody had called him a rat; an afternoon search in St. Paul when we were sure we had the gang dead to rights and a flood of sound unexpectedly broke out—church bells, kids yelling and a dog howling.

Yes, Alvin Karpis, otherwise Francis Albin Karpavicz, had dreams of gunning the F.B.I., and never more vivid than at the moment we grabbed him.

So intensely did the Barker-Karpis alliance live by the gun that it is impossible to give an orderly picture of their stained history. They intertwined murder with corruption, but it is probably right to ascribe to "Ma" Barker the gang's inspiration for organised crime. She was born Arizona Donnie Clark of very mixed blood—Scots, Irish and Indian. She grew up in the Ozarks, the wild, mountainous region of Missouri, and among people who were as stark as the scenery. She is supposed to have coached her four sons, Herman, Lloyd, Fred and Arthur, on the principle of how to do business with bankers—with a tommy-gun. But in the beginning she herself had no criminal experience on which to draw. She indulged them, though, wilfully and wickedly, and it is beyond dispute that the four Barker boys owed their criminal careers to their mother. She was both resourceful and ruthless and they looked to her for inspiration and guidance, if those are terms which can be used in respect to a she-wolf and her vicious whelps.

A theme that repeats itself with great frequency in the Barker-Karpis combination is the strength it derived from friendships that took root in various penitentiaries and Federal prisons. For example, Fred Barker and Karpis learned to understand and admire each other while both were imprisoned in the Kansas State Penitentiary. Karpis, allegedly dubbed "Old Creepy" because of the feeling he inspired in other mobsters with his cold, fishy stare, was smart enough to take advantage of conditions in Kansas. Convicts assigned to the coal-mines there were rewarded for extra production by having days lopped off their time, but Karpis found that working alongside him were a number of lifers.

It did not take him long to figure that for these men there was no incentive. They could, however, be stimulated into more active mining with money and such small services as he was able to render, and soon Karpis was buying the extra coal output of a half-dozen lifers and thus appreciably shortening his own sentence.

It was the kind of trick that appealed to Fred Barker, and their jail friendship was translated into a partnership on their liberation, and they committed their first murder together. It was a cowardly affair. Two days before, they had used a De Soto to pull off a robbery, and when Sheriff C. R. Kelly, of West Plains, Missouri, saw the car in a garage he recognised it as suspect. He walked over to question the occupants and was cut down by a blast of gunfire before he could draw his own weapon.

Fred Barker, Karpis, "Ma" Barker and her paramour, Arthur V. Dunlop (alias George Anderson), occupied a cottage in Thayer, Missouri, but with the murder of the sheriff they fled to St. Paul, leaving behind their latest haul. They took over a furnished house, and had not long settled in when they were joined by William Weaver, known variously as "Phoenix Donald" and "Lapland Willie." Weaver had been paroled from Oklahoma State Penitentiary, where he had been serving a life sentence for murder during a bank robbery, and where he had met "Doc" Barker and Volney Davis, jointly convicted for the slaying of a night watchman.

"Ma" Barker and Karpis were satisfied with Weaver's

credentials, but although the gang lived quietly, and as inconspicuously as possible, it was noticed that whenever they left the house together one of them carried a violin case. All five knew how to play the instrument inside, but it didn't make them musicians!

It was uncanny the way the Barker-Karpis gang, throughout its lifetime, was able to smell danger before it was too late. When the St. Paul police raided their hide-out early one morning it was to find an empty house. It had been a hasty departure, and for some reason we were never able to discover they decided that Arthur Dunlop was a squealer. The day after the gang left St. Paul Dunlop's nude, bullet-riddled body was found on the shores of a lake near Webster, Wisconsin. Close by was a woman's blood-stained glove.

Kansas City was the next stop, and here the gang was reinforced by the addition of Thomas Holden and a fellow mobster, both of whom had escaped from Leavenworth; Harvey Bailey, a notorious bank robber; Larry DeVol and Bernard Phillips, a renegade policeman turned bank bandit. In June a bank at Fort Scott fell to the gang and some of the loot was used to stage an elaborate "Welcome Home" party for a classmate of Fred Barker at Kansas State Penitentiary.

The celebrations had not long been over when late in the afternoon of July 7th, 1932, F.B.I. special agents stepped out from some bushes surrounding the Old Mission Golf Course and put the bracelets on Holden, Bailey and another gangster. The other member of the foursome, Bernard Phillips, happened to be absent when these arrests took place and went streaking with the news to "Ma" Barker. The gang took off in such haste for St. Paul that a raiding party found they had left their quarters just as dinner was about to be served!

St. Paul once more—and another murder! It stemmed from the arrest of Harvey Bailey, who was tried for participation in the Fort Scott bank robbery. He was defended by J. Earl Smith, a criminal attorney of Tulsa, Oklahoma, but the evidence against him was too strong and he was convicted. Shortly afterwards a mysterious telephone call lured Attorney Smith to the vicinity of the lonely Indian Hills Country Club, fourteen miles north of Tulsa. The following morning Smith's body was found, full of bullet holes.

To offset casualties that occurred for one reason or another the gang was ever on the look-out for new recruits, but they had to measure up to tough requirements. During the next few weeks two new comers were roped in, Earl Christman, confidence man wanted in several states, and Frank Nash, who had slipped out of Leavenworth. Christman brought his moll with him. They took part in an audacious daylight raid on the Cloud County Bank at Concordia, Kansas, that yielded over 240,000 dollars.

With all this coin to play with, the Barker-Karpis organisation turned to the task of springing some of its old hands now tucked away. It was successful in getting "Doc" Barker paroled from the Oklahoma State Penitentiary and in securing from the same institution an incomprehensible "two years leave of absence" for Volney Davis. An attempt to secure the release of Lloyd Barker, another brother, doing twenty-five years in Leavenworth for mail robbery, failed.

Looking for Christmas money the gang descended on Minneapolis and murdered three in taking the Third North-Western Bank for a heavy score. Two policemen who got in their way were chopped down by machine-gun fire, and, as they were about to leave, one of the Barker-Karpis mob thought a civilian was trying to memorise the licence number of their automobile. He too died from a stream of hot lead.

It was in Reno, Nevada, that the gang holed up to enjoy the stolen money, and while there Volney Davis made a trip to Missouri to pick up his favourite moll, who had escaped from a Mid-Western penitentiary. She stayed with Davis when the mob shifted its headquarters first to St. Paul and in April of the following year to Chicago, from which city they struck successfully at the Fairbury National Bank, Fairbury, Nebraska.

In this raid, however, Earl Christman was so badly wounded that he was rushed to the home of Verne Miller. He died despite medical care and one night was secretly buried. Christman's mother wanted to know where her son's body rested, but nobody would tell her.

It was about this time that Fred Barker began to yearn for a mate and found one in the widow of a well-known bank robber killed while following his "profession." She had a history that satisfied even "Ma" Barker.

Either Christman's death or a belief that it had got into a rut persuaded the gang that new ideas were needed, and a fling was taken at kidnapping. The first victim was William A. Hamm, Junior, of the Hamm Brewing Company, St. Paul. The ransom collected was 100,000 dollars, and those who played the principal parts in the snatch were Fred and "Doc" Barker, Karpis, Charles J. Fitzgerald and a widely known underworld character—Fred Goetz, alias "Shotgun Zeigler," purportedly a former engineering student and football star at a Mid-Western university.

Wherever the gang moved it cast a shadow of murder, and two further slayings were added in quick succession to the lengthening list. In a stick-up of the Stockyards National Bank, South St. Paul, a police officer was killed outright and another crippled for life; the loot was 30,000 dollars. In Chicago the mob pounced on two bank messengers, but again they got very little, and in fleeing became involved in a minor mishap with their car. Unaware of the robbery which had taken place only a few minutes earlier, Patrolman Miles A. Cunningham approached the bandit car at an intersection on Jackson Boulevard to inquire into the accident. Without warning he was blasted to death with a machine-gun.

By the end of the year the mob, now idling in Reno again, was more motley than ever. "Ma" Barker was there and so, too, was Fred, with the widow of the bank robber, who still stuck to him. A seasoned shoplifter had teamed up with William Weaver and Karpis, Volney Davis and Fred Goetz had their molls with them. Towards the end of the year all of them set out for St. Paul. They had planned to rob the Commercial State Bank, but on the way they got another idea. Instead of a hold-up—the danger was great and the reward uncertain—why not snatch the bank president, Edward George Brenner? The task would be much easier and it would open the bank vaults for whatever sum they demanded.

On the night of January 13th the gang gathered at the apartment of William Weaver and his paramour for a final checkup. Everything had been worked out, and those who were to do the job were soon able to leave. But as they drew away from the kerb another car, containing several men, one of them in uniform, fell in behind them. One of the bandits yelled "It's the cops" and instantly guns began to blaze. The bandit car sped away at last, leaving behind two badly wounded employees of Northwest Airways—the "cops" the gang thought they had spotted.

This fiasco did not upset the original plan, it only delayed it, and four days later five members of the

Barker-Karpis outfit "took" Brenner as he halted his car at a street signal after dropping his nine-year-old daughter at a private school. There followed almost a month of complicated negotiations, with the F.B.I. keeping close watch but deferring to the family wish to effect the bank president's release before taking action. The gang collected 200,000 dollars in five- and ten-dollar bills. Brenner was then released in the vicinity of Rochester, Minnesota.

It was at this juncture that things began to get complicated for the gang. Fred Goetz offended some of his gangland pals and was executed by two blasts from a shotgun which blew off his face. There is no evidence to show if it was the vengeance of the Barker-Karpis mob, but it was certainly effective! Soon the strain of associating with the mob—their unbridled violence and the frenzy of escaping from one hide-out to another to avoid the special agents they knew were hunting them—proved too much for Goetz's moll. She became deranged and was placed in an asylum.

Converting the hot Hamm and Brenner snatch money to clean bills was a problem far from easy to solve, and the tortuous negotiations and fixing that were required almost transcend belief.

First to offer assistance was a suspect Chicago politician and ward heeler known as "Boss" McLaughlin. He was not too bright, though, and our special agents picked him up in quick time. His wife telegraphed both the President of the United States and the Attorney-General protesting against his arrest. Nevertheless, McLaughlin stayed in jail.

Next to be recruited to handle the hot money was a certain Dr. Joseph P. Moran, who had once served time for abortion and of late had looked after any hood who needed his services. In turn Dr. Moran got his nephew to help him, and apparently the arrangement was that Dr. Moran would get hold of enough of the ransom funds to put his nephew through medical school!

Yet a third character emerged in the negotiations. He was a fifty-year-old Chicago gambler with connections reaching all the way to Havana. He managed to exchange nearly 100,000 dollars of the tainted money for Cuban gold, which a well-known bank then converted into one-thousand-dollar American bills at a discount of a quarter of one per cent!

During this time Dr. Moran (he was to disappear later, and according to reliable underworld reports his weighted body was dumped by his "pals" into Lake Erie) operated on Fred Barker and Alvin Karpis in an attempt to obliterate their fingerprints and change their looks. Both realised time was running out, but what they suffered on the operating table did no good. They could not hide their identity as public enemies; they nor other members of the gang for whom there was no escape from justice.

Volney Davis, "Doc" Barker and Harry Campbell also underwent the agonisingly painful Moran "refresher" treatment to no avail. The gang did not stay in one place long. They doubled back on their tracks, dodged to this city and that county, but they could not throw off the pursuit of F.B.I. agents and decided to split up into small units. They then scattered to locations as widely separated as Glasgow (Montana), Allandale (Florida), Las Vegas, Miami, Cleveland and Havana. It was the beginning of the end.

On the night of January 8th, 1935, special agents arrested "Doc" Barker in Chicago. He was traced through a woman with whom he had become infatuated. When the apartment of the couple was searched a sub-machine-gun was found which had been stolen from a guard at the time of the St. Paul payroll robbery.

The same night special agents surrounded the apartment occupied by Russell Gibson and another mobster and their girl friends. Ordered to surrender, all but Gibson complied. Armed with a Browning and a Colt automatic he tried to get out through a rear door, but it was being watched. Gibson fired and missed, and that was the end of him. As his body was carted to the morgue the F.B.I. were collecting a small arsenal inside the apartment.

Oddly enough, it was an alligator which put the finger on "Ma" and Fred Barker! In "Doc" Barker's apartment agents found a map of Florida and a circle round Ocala and Lake Weir. Earlier they had been tipped off that mother and son were hiding out in some southern area that sheltered an ancient alligator known to the natives as "Old Joe." Now they knew for certain, and at five-thirty on a crisp January morning, with the mists hanging over Lake Weir, a picked group of special agents surrounded a cottage on the shore in which "Ma" Barker and her son were holed up.

"We are special agents of the Federal Bureau of Investigation," called out the leader. "I'm talking to you, Kate Barker, and you, Fred Barker. Come out one at a time and with your hands up!"

Further commands were issued, but in the cottage all was silent. The minutes ticked by, and once again the Barkers were ordered to come out singly, unless they wanted to be driven out by tear gas and any other means deemed necessary.

After fifteen minutes "Ma" Barker shouted: "All right, go ahead!" For a moment it looked as if mother and son had decided to throw in their hands, but then a machine-gun began to speak from the house and it swept the surrounding trees and tore into the undergrowth. It sparked off a battle that went on for hours. Tear-gas bombs were tossed into the cottage and a deadly fire from automatics was concentrated on the firing points within. It was a fight to a deadly finish, and when the F.B.I. were at last able to enter the cottage they found "Ma" Barker dead, still grasping a machine-gun in her left hand. Fred was doubled over in death, a .45 Colt automatic beside his stiffening body.

There was enough ironware in the cottage to keep a regiment at bay; two Thompson sub-machine-guns, Browning .12 gauge shotgun, Remington shotgun, two .45 automatics, two Winchester rifles and a .38 Colt automatic, along with machine-gun drums, automatic-pistol clips and ammunition for every weapon.

There was a letter, too, from "Doc" Barker, in which he wrote: "I took care of that business for you boys. It was done just as good as if you had did it yourself. I am just Standard Oil—always at your service. Ha, ha!"

"That business" referred to by "Doc" was, as to be expected, a slight case of murder! The victim, if such a term can be used, was William J. Harrison, who had moved within the orbit of the Capone syndicate before he joined the Barker-Karpis mob. Later his reliability became suspect, and from his Florida hole Fred Barker had ordered Harrison's execution. "Doc" Barker had seen to it. They took Harrison to an abandoned barn near Ontarioville in Illinois on a wild, dark night and shot him. The body, and the barn itself, was then saturated with paraffin and a match was tossed in.

As the F.B.I. ring narrowed, Alvin Karpis and Harry Campbell, with their women, scuttled from Miami to Atlantic City. There a gun battle with the police took place and Karpis and his crony came temporarily to rest in Toledo, Ohio. Meanwhile, Volney Davis was picked up by special agents in St. Louis. He was found to be carrying a counterfeit hundred-dollar bill, and was quick to explain that he "wasn't shoving the queer." He carried the bill with him, he said, to offer as a bribe should he be arrested by law-enforcement officers!

One of the gang surrendered in Kansas after a gun fight, and then William Weaver and his moll were cornered and captured in a house in Allandale, Florida. Although the Barker-Karpis organisation had not merely been split open but virtually destroyed, Karpis and Campbell still had some fight left in them, as can be seen from what followed. It was so fantastic that it is hardly believable.

Karpis picked up a few hoods, among them several ex-convicts, and a gambler who must have believed in his luck. On April 24th, 1935, three heavily armed raiders pounced on a mail truck at Warren, Ohio, and got away with 70,000 dollars and then pulled off a robbery worth 30,000 dollars against the Erie train—Detroit to Pittsburgh. Introduced was a new tactic in robbery—the thieves escaped by aeroplane.

These exploits were followed by an alliance that only a script writer could dream up. Karpis and his crony fled to Hot Springs, Arkansas, where they were afforded protection by the chief of police and the chief of detectives. While an F.B.I. "wanted" poster for leaders of the mob aged and yellowed in the very centre of the jail door at Hot Springs, Karpis and his pals roamed at will through the streets of the spa. Nor was that all, for Karpis bedded up with an adroit woman who not only kept him happy, but also one of the law-enforcement officers as well. She divided her time between the two and owed her vast experience to the fact that she had begun operating brothels at the age of seventeen.

Eventually Hot Springs became a little too warm for Karpis. He was well aware he was being hunted, and in the early part of 1936 he again got on the move. With him was a crony who brought his girl along—a twenty-one-year-old prostitute. This time Karpis's destination was New Orleans, and although he may have thought he had again slipped the net it was in that city he had a rendezvous with justice!

Evil and merciless, Karpis had dealt out so much death that he had every reason to declare, as he had often done, that he would never be taken alive. We knew he was a problem, and planned the raid carefully. It was approximately five-fifteen in the afternoon of May 1st, 1936. Four assistants and myself were to enter by the front door. Other squads were deployed at each side of the building and at the rear. We were about to move in when a man on a horse moved into the lane beside the through traffic.

We waited, anxious to avoid attention, until the horseman had passed down the street. Now was the time for action, but then two men stepped from the doorway and walked briskly down the steps. We recognised Alvin Karpis and his crony. As they made their way towards their car, a little boy on a bicycle scooted between the pair and our vantage-point. We did not want the child hurt, as he might be if shooting started at that moment, so we moved out and hurried forward, calling for the surrender of the fugitives as they were getting into the car.

Perhaps Karpis had come to believe in his own indestructibility. I am sure he had never expected to meet the top G-man and a squad of what he had been pleased to call "sissy" agents. His expression was divided between amazement and fright and his colour was ashen. Neither he nor his shaking companion raised as much as a finger. There was no gunplay, not the remotest chance of any. Like all their breed they derived their courage from getting the drop on their victims. When they were on the wrong end of a gun the fight went out of them—as it does with every hoodlum, who is a coward at heart. Karpis told me that he thought he would never be taken alive—but then Karpis did not know Karpis.

Six days after his arrest we picked up the rest of the gang in Toledo. It was the end of an era of violence.

—J.E.H & K.J.

# 3

# ELVIRA BARNEY
## Laugh, Baby, Laugh

A woman screams. A pistol fires. A man falls dying. The date, May 31, 1932. Time, 4.00 a.m. Place, 21, Williams Mews, Lowndes Square, London.

The dead man, William Thomas Scott Stephen, aged twenty-four, society "hanger-on".

The woman, Mrs. Elvira Dolores Barney, aged twenty-six. Society "beauty", so called.

Their relationship. Lover and mistress.

Her story. He had seized the gun to prevent her from taking her own life. In the struggle the gun discharged accidentally. A story to which Mrs. Barney stuck throughout. A story the police were at first inclined to believe—until they were told that Mrs. Barney had tried to shoot her lover before.

The trial of Elvira Barney for murder was the great society scandal of the nineteen thirties, the day of the "bright young things", the grown up children of wealthy parents. Elvira qualified for this set because her father, Sir John Mullens, was rich, being the government broker. She was separated from her American husband whom she married in August 1929. But, though a leading member of London's smart set, Elvira was neither "bright" nor "beautiful". I remember her as drab, coarse, rather fat and usually drunk. Her marriage had ended in failure after six months and she was living with Scott Stephen, a good-looking young man who vaguely described himself as a dress designer. He had no visible means of support and no home, except Elvira's flat. There he lived as Elvira's kept man as their fierce rows dictated. Thrown out in the early hours of the morning on one occasion, he spent the rest of the night in a greengrocer's van parked in the mews.

Was Mrs. Barney's story of the shooting true? Or did she shoot Scott Stephen deliberately and intentionally as the great Sir Bernard Spilsbury seemed to think? The question of her guilt or innocence turned almost solely on the behaviour of guns and bullets.

At 4.00 a.m. on May 31, Mrs. Barney's respectable neighbours in Williams Mews were wakened by shouts and screams. That was nothing new. Noisy parties, loud quarrels and drunken fights were frequent at No. 21, a two-floored maisonette, which was described by prosecution counsel (who probably never saw it), as extravagantly furnished and decorated. Now the sound of raised voices disturbed Mrs. Dorothy Hall, wife of a chauffeur, who lived opposite. She heard Mrs. Barney, whose voice she recognised, shouting "Get out. Get out. I'll shoot you." Then came a man's voice, which she identified as Stephen's, shouting, "I'm going". This was followed by the sound of a shot, and the man's voice crying, "What have you done?" Then came Mrs. Barney's wail, "Chicken, chicken, come back to me. I will do anything you want me to do". This was followed by a weird, wailing cry of "Michael, Michael". Another woman resident in the mews, Mrs. Stevens, the wife of a taxi driver, heard two shots, one much louder than the other. Neither she or Mrs. Hall took any notice. They had heard shots from Mrs. Barney's flat before. "That's Mrs. Barney firing her pistol again", Mrs. Stevens told her drowsy husband.

At 4.40 a.m. Dr. Durrant, Mrs. Barney's doctor, received a telephone call. Incoherently, between sobs and cries, she told him that there had been a dreadful accident. A man had shot himself in her flat. "He is bleeding to death, come at once," she cried. When Dr. Durrant reached Williams Mews, he found Scott Stephen lying dead on the landing, his back propped against the wall and one leg hanging over the stairs. By his left hand lay a revolver. Mrs. Barney was hysterical, overwrought and frenziedly screaming, "He can't be dead. Why don't you do something for him? I love him so. I love him so". She threw herself on the corpse and kissed its face, crying, "Let me die. Let me die. I can't live, let me kill myself". Dr. Durrant thoughtfully placed his foot on the revolver. Calming down a little, Mrs. Barney told him she and Scott Stephen had quarrelled.

He said he was going to leave her. She said she would commit suicide. He picked up the revolver from the chair on which it was lying. She closed with him. As they wrestled and fought on the landing, the revolver fired. Scott Stephen, she said, staggered towards the bathroom, calling, "Send for a doctor". Then he collapsed by the stairs. Dr. Durrant pointed to a mark on the wall which looked to him like the ricochet from a bullet. Mrs. Barney said it had been made by a bullet she had fired the previous day to frighten Scott Stephen.

Inspector William Winter arrived at 7.30 a.m. having been preceded by a constable. He found Scott Stephen's body still lying on the landing, and he examined the five chambered revolver, in which two cartridges had been discharged. But not in logical order. Their order was: discharged—live—discharged—live—live, an apparently strange sequence which was to take on great significance. When Winter asked Mrs. Barney to tell him what had happened, she raved and shrieked and ordered him out of her flat. On becoming calmer, she said there had been a quarrel. Stephen had taken her revolver. They struggled for it and it went off. Told she would be taken to the police station, Mrs. Barney burst into a paroxysm of rage, violently striking the recently arrived Inspector Campion in the face. "I will teach you to say you will put me in a cell, you vile swine", she cried. Just then her mother, Lady Mullens, telephoned. "Now you know who my parents are", triumphantly exclaimed Elvira.

At the police station she made a statement in which she said that she and Stephen had quarrelled about another woman. He snatched the revolver from the chair, saying, "I am going to take it for fear you'll kill yourself". They struggled with their hands together. The revolver fired. "I did not think anything had happened. He seemed quite all right," stated Elvira.

The police found no sign of a struggle in the flat. In a box they discovered nine cartridges. Sir Bernard Spilsbury, who reached the flat at 1.30 p.m. examined the body, which had not been moved. The bullet was lodged under the left rib, and he formed the opinion that death had followed in about ten minutes. The flow of blood downward indicated that Stephen had been standing when he was shot and had remained upright for some minutes. (Once the heart stops pumping blood, the force of gravity takes over.)

The police soon had good reason to doubt Mrs. Barney's version of the shooting, and she was charged with Scott Stephen's murder.

By the neighbours in the Mews the police were told of what was apparently an earlier attempt by Mrs. Barney to murder her lover. Mrs. Hall declared that on May 19 Scott Stephen left the flat. She saw Mrs. Barney, who had no clothes on, lean out of the window, calling after him, "Laugh, Baby, laugh for the last time". She had something bright in her hand. Mrs. Hall saw a flash, a puff of smoke and heard a shot. Later Scott Stephen told her he was afraid to leave the flat as Mrs. Barney might commit suicide.

The evidence appeared to point to a sordid crime of jealousy. Mrs. Barney, having failed once to kill her lover, had now succeeded. Her story of the fatal discharge of the revolver did not appear to fit the facts as Sir Bernard Spilsbury saw them. In her favour only was Scott Stephen's statement that she might try to commit suicide which seemed to corroborate her story of the struggle and its cause. If her story was true, she was innocent of murder, but she could be found guilty of manslaughter, by causing a death during attempted suicide, which was then a felony.

Mrs. Barney had one inestimable advantage. Her parents' wealth secured her the services of Sir Patrick Hastings, K.C. He had figured in a number of society dramas and he was the right man for the job. Suave and sophisticated, he was well equipped to do battle with the Crown's experts, the witnesses upon whose evidence the jury's verdict would inevitably turn. At Mrs. Barney's Old Bailey trial on July 4, 5 and 6, he was opposed by Sir Percival Clarke. Sir Travers Humphreys, a severe judge of the old school, presided over a court-room packed with celebrities and society women, morbidly eager to enjoy the agony of a member of their own set.

Elvira Barney had shot Scott Stephen deliberately, claimed Sir Percival Clarke. She had tried before and failed. But her second attempt had proved successful. It was practically impossible that Stephen could have caused the injury to himself. Who pressed the trigger?

asked prosecuting counsel. If she did not shoot him, who did? he questioned. He emphasized the couples' frequent quarrels, and Mrs. Barney's behaviour after the shooting, behaviour, which, he suggested, indicated that she was a woman of fierce ungovernable passion, just those ingredients which had led to a murder in jealousy, as the Crown alleged it to be.

By Inspector Winter, two letters he had found in the flat were read to the jury. In the first Scott Stephen wrote:

*"Baby, little Fattable. This little note is to be awaiting your arrival in the place in which I've been happiest of all my life. Be brave, my dear, dear darling, and take care of yourself for me, 'cos you're mine. Don't forget your 'Mickums'. I'll be thinking of you always. Forgive me all the dreadful, horrible things I've done, baby. I promise to be better and kinder so's you won't be frightened any more. I love you, only you, in all the world, little one."*

That, said the Inspector, had resulted in the following reply:

*"My darling baby. I nearly had heart failure reading your letter, it was so divine. I've never been so thrilled over reading anything before. I really do love you, darling. You hand me the biggest thrills I've ever had, my sweet, and all I hope is that we can go on being thrilled endlessly. I adore you when you are so sweet and kind to me as I haven't had a lot of affection in my life, as you have had. So you see it means a great deal. I feel like suicide when you are angry. Don't be jealous with me, baby please, as I*

> *suffer so much from that too. I won't let you down.*
> *God knows why I should when you are so lovely."*

While Elvira's reply establishes for future historians the use of the words "thrill" and "divine" amongst the smart set of the early nineteen thirties, it again expressed the suggestion of suicide, further corroboration to her story that Stephen had seized the gun to prevent her from killing herself.

From Inspector Winter, Hastings extracted a vital piece of information. First he got him to agree that, if either Stephen or Mrs. Barney had held the gun, their fingerprints would be on it. If they had struggled, as Mrs. Barney said, there would be no prints as the weapon might have been twisted about in their hands. "And whose prints did you find?" enquired counsel. "Only those of the police officer who handled the gun", replied the Inspector.

From Winter, too, Hastings obtained the useful information that Scott Stephen had been a strong muscular man and that the medical officer at Holloway Prison, where Mrs. Barney had been taken on her arrest, reported finding marks on her arms and wrists, such marks as might have been made on a fragile woman by a strong man in the course of a struggle.

To make any impression on the jury Patrick Hastings, as he tells us in his reminiscences, *Cases in Court*, realised he had to overcome not only the evidence of Spilsbury, which he knew from the depositions to be damaging, but the incriminating testimony of Mrs. Hall who had witnessed the earlier alleged attempt on Scott Stephen's life. How he adroitly disposed of these dangerous witnesses can be followed in his cross-examination of them and his final questions to Mrs. Barney herself.

Mrs. Hall said she saw Mrs. Barney lean from her window, holding something bright in her *left* hand, and shout after Stephen. Then came a flash, a puff of smoke and a report. Hastings got her to emphasize that the bright object had been in Mrs. Barney's left hand and he drew from her a manual demonstration of the size and shape of the puff of smoke. On this point he contented himself with one question. Did Mrs. Hall know that the cartridges found in Mrs. Barney's revolver were filled with cordite, a smokeless propellant from which there would be no perceptible flash in bright sunlight? The witness, of course, didn't know that, but by his question counsel had thrown doubt on Mrs. Hall's recollection of the alleged shooting incident, the so-called earlier attempt on Scott Stephen's life as he stood in the mews below, the so damaging suggestion which might incline the jury to believe that Mrs. Barney had been successful twelve days later.

In her examination in chief, Mrs. Hall had stated that at 4.00 a.m. on May 31, she heard Mrs. Barney scream, "I'll shoot *you*", before the shot was fired, words which apparently expressed the intention which she then carried out. Hastings could not hope to do more than tone down this interpretation by suggesting that Mrs. Hall might have been mistaken, that what she really heard was, "I'll shoot", meaning that Mrs. Barney intended to shoot herself. The potentially dangerous statement of another neighbour, that she had heard two shots, which appeared to be so strikingly corroborated by the discovery of the mark on the wall and by the presence of two exploded shells in the gun, could be best dealt with, Hastings appreciated, in his cross-examination of the Crown's gunsmith, Robert Churchill.

Churchill gave his opinion that the revolver of American

manufacture was one of the safest he had ever examined. A heavy pull was required on the trigger to raise the hammer and fire the cartridge brought into position by the rotating cylinder. The trigger guard was not big enough to admit more than one finger at a time. While this was highly damaging to Mrs. Barney's defence, the famous gunsmith was forced to agree that it was *possible* for the revolver to be fired in a struggle for its possession. But he made the word "possible" sound very much like "improbable". For the jury's benefit both Sir Percival Clarke and Walter Frampton, junior defence counsel, gun in hand struggled with Churchill to see how the shooting might or might not have happened.

Then Sir Patrick Hastings rose to cross-examine. He concentrated his questions on one fact, the strange sequence of discharged and unexploded shells. How could the firing mechanism have missed one shell? he enquired. Churchill explained that a full pull of the trigger was required to both rotate the cylinder, in order to bring the next cartridge up to the firing point, and to explode it in the breech. Two half pulls could result in the cylinder rotating, and the next cartridge passing the breech, without the revolver firing. In other words, as Hastings put it, "if two people were struggling to get possession of the revolver and the pressure was not enough to fire it at first, the cylinder might spin round". "Yes, it might," replied the gunsmith.

Thus, Sir Patrick Hastings had drawn from a prosecution witness the useful admission that the undischarged cartridge, between two live ones, which seemed to so strongly suggest that the revolver had been fired twice, might in fact confirm Mrs. Barney's story of accidental shooting in the course of a struggle for the gun.

So far so good, but Spilsbury's evidence was yet to

come. The weight of his authority alone could convict Mrs. Barney. In his direct evidence, the ever-sure pathologist stated that he had found no blackening or scorching on the dead man's coat to suggest that the muzzle of the revolver had been held close to him. He had carried out a test, he said, to see if the revolver could have been discharged by Stephen within three inches of his body. This he found impossible for with his wrist bent back, and the dead man's hand holding the butt of the revolver and his fingers on the trigger, "I could not get enough pressure to discharge it at all". If the muzzle had been seized by Stephen, the discharge of the powder would have stained his hand and, stated Spilsbury, no discoloration was found. The wound in Stephen's body, said the pathologist, was horizontal. The bullet had entered at $2/34$ inches below the left collar-bone at a spot 3 inches left of the centre of the body.

Thus, in Sir Bernard Spilsbury's opinion, the revolver could not have fired during the course of a struggle, as Mrs. Barney said. She had been at some distance from Stephen and she had fired straight at him, the revolver being held in a horizontal position and not semi-vertically, as might have happened in a struggle. In 1932 the weight of Spilsbury's authority was immense. He was an impressive witness, precise and certain in his opinions.

Hastings knew, as he tells us, that detailed cross-examination could only make matters worse for it would provide the man of science with the opportunity to be even more emphatic. To overcome this danger, Hastings devised three questions with which to lessen the weight of this damaging evidence. As these questions are famous examples of cross-examination they are set out in full:

*Question I: To quality yourself to give evidence here*

*today that this bullet was fired in a perfectly horizontal position, I gather that you had to examine a skeleton of some person other than Stephen?*

*Answer: I confirmed it on a skeleton of someone else.*

*Question II: Is it a natural supposition that on every human being there is a difference in the formation of the bones?*

*Answer: Yes, there is.*

*Question III: The best way to say whether the passage of the bullet is horizontal is to look at it in the person examined and trace it then?*

*Answer: Yes.*

The logical next question did not come. Hastings sat down, his cross-examination finished. The judge asked it instead:

*Did you look at it? Trace it there?*
*Yes, my Lord.*
*And then form your opinion it was horizontal?*
*Yes, my Lord.*

That ended the prosecution case. The evidence against Mrs. Barney was damaging but not damning. Clearly Spilsbury disbelieved her story and she only could support it by giving evidence herself. In her favour was the fact that she had stuck to the same story from the beginning, and the evidence of her suicidal tendency. The bruises on her arms and the lack of fingerprints on the gun confirmed her story of the struggle in which her lover had lost his life. The unexploded shell, between two live ones, supported it. But in a few fatal answers she could undo all the good her counsel had achieved. Her story called for explanation in the witness-box. She could not avoid the judge's censure, if she failed to take advantage of that opportunity to prove her innocence. The onus was on Mrs. Barney to satisfy the jury that her story was true.

When Mrs. Elvira Barney walked from the dock to the witness-box on the afternoon of that second day of the trial, Patrick Hastings, as he confesses, was anxious. In a few unguarded words she could antagonise the jury, and her behaviour after the shooting hardly suggested that Elvira was capable of being calm in a crisis. But, as she answered his questions, Hastings' anxieties were dispelled. Mrs. Barney made a surprisingly good witness. She was restrained and quiet, soberly dressed, her appearance and demeanour denying the suggestion of brazen immorality conjured up by her long association with the dead man. She repeated her story: her threat to commit suicide, the struggle for the gun. How the revolver came to be fired she didn't know. She went even better: she didn't claim that Stephen's finger was on the trigger, an easy, too easy get out. She denied she had fired previously at him in the mews. She had fired the revolver within the flat to frighten Stephen. Mrs. Hall might have heard the shot but she could not have seen it, a suggestion on which Hastings had already attempted to throw considerable doubt. She had no desire to shoot Stephen, the witness replied to her counsel's question. She had not shot him that night. She had shouted, "I'll shoot", meaning herself, not "I'll shoot you".

Then came the startling end to the prisoner's evidence.

"Place the gun on the ledge of the witness-box", Hastings ordered the court usher.

Amidst a silence in which the dropping of the proverbial pin could have been heard, the usher picked up the gun, walked across the court and set it in front of Mrs. Barney.

"Pick up that revolver, Mrs. Barney," ordered Hastings.

Mrs. Barney did as she was told, picking up the revolver in her *right* hand. Quick-fire came Hastings' two questions and the witness's replies:

"Have you ever picked up that revolver with your left hand?"

"No."

"Are you left-handed?"

"No."

"That is my case," declared Sir Patrick Hastings.

By his final questions, counsel had exposed a weakness in the prosecution case. He had thrown doubt on Mrs. Hall's memory of the earlier shooting incident. The jury, he knew, would recall that Mrs. Hall had said she had seen the metal object in Mrs. Barney's left hand, and they would remember the doubts he had cast—not on her truthfulness—but on her recollection of the flash and puff of smoke.

In his final address, Sir Patrick Hastings branded the prosecution case as "flimsy". Nothing, he said, in Spilsbury's evidence proved that Mrs. Barney's story was untrue. He did not, he told the jury, ask them to give Mrs. Barney the benefit of any doubt. There was no doubt and there was no evidence whatsoever on which she could be convicted of any offence. "I claim that on the evidence Mrs. Barney has of right to a verdict in her favour," he ended.

Sir Travers Humphreys' summing up was not against the accused. He told the jury that they had to be satisfied that Mrs. Barney had fired the shot intentionally and deliberately. It was in her favour, he said, that she had not claimed that Stephen's finger was on the trigger when the gun fired. There was no evidence that her finger had pressed the trigger, and there was no doubt there had been a struggle. The jury could find one of three possible verdicts. Guilty of murder. Guilty of manslaughter, if they believed Mrs. Barney intended to commit suicide, or not guilty of any crime at all.

The jury left the court at 2.55 p.m. and returned at 4.47, finding Mrs. Barney Not Guilty of either crime.

Once again an Old Bailey jury had accepted a story of accidental shooting, for once rejecting the evidence of the "infallible" Spilsbury, which shows that laymen are hard to convince without visual proof of the opinions voiced by experts. The verdict shows, too, that juries are inclined to believe that guns can and do go off by accident in alleged struggles for their possession.

Was Mrs. Barney's story true? It convinced twelve of her fellow citizens. Or did they give her the benefit of the considerable doubts raised by her eminent counsel?

After the trial, Mrs. Barney returned to her old life, to be pointed out in sleazy clubs and notorious pubs as "That's Mrs. Barney", a fame which lasted until her death in Paris a few years later. I once asked her if she shot Scott Stephen deliberately. Mrs. Barney threw a glass at me. I'm sure she threw it intentionally.

—R.F.

# 4

# ADELAIDE BARTLETT
## Corsets and Chloroform

---

The story of Adelaide Bartlett takes us into that farspread coterie of streets and squares lying between Victoria Station and the Thames and rejoicing in the exoteric name of Belgravia. It is a quarter in which all the mansions so resemble each other in size, shape, and colour, that it is easier, even on a clear day, to miss one's way there than in any other part of London. And in none of its avenues is the architectural uniformity more conspicuous than in the long double row of houses called Claverton Street. There, in the year 1885, in a spacious first-floor set of apartments, lived Mr. Thomas Edwin Bartlett, part-proprietor of half a dozen grocery and provision shops in the Herne Hill and Dulwich districts, and his wife Adelaide. There, on the last day in that year, Mr. Bartlett, who had lately been in poor health, suddenly showed signs of recovery, paid a visit to his dentist and had a tooth removed, made a hearty supper of oysters, chutney, cake and tea, and talked with his wife of shortly running down to Torquay for a change of air. And there, at four o'clock on the following morning, New Year's Day, Mrs. Bartlett found him lying dead in bed. A rather delayed *post-mortem* examination revealed the presence in the dead man's stomach of a quantity of chloroform; and on the following 11th of February Mrs. Bartlett was arrested and charged at the Westminster Police Court with having caused his death by administering to him a dose of that anæsthetic. Exactly a week later a young Wesleyan minister, the Rev.

George Dyson by name, who had been an intimate friend of the Bartletts during the two preceding years, was also arrested, on the charge of being an accessory before the fact. Immediately upon this development, the "Belgravia Mystery" became the talk of the town.

Strange indeed was the story subsequently unfolded in the Central Criminal Court. Prior to her marriage, Mrs. Bartlett had been known to her very small circle of friends by the aristocratically sounding name of Mlle. Adelaide Blanche de la Tremouille. Born at Orléans in 1855, she was the natural daughter of an Englishman of good social position (the names of her parents were never divulged) and had spent her early childhood in France, coming later to live in England. In 1875, in her nineteenth year, she married Mr. Bartlett, who was eleven years her senior, the wedding taking place at Croydon. Small, pretty, vivacious, and speaking fluent English with a slight foreign accent which added to the charm, she was destined to enter upon one of the oddest of conjugal existences. In the beginning she hardly knew her husband. The affair had been arranged apparently by her father, and she had only had one interview with her betrothed before meeting him at the altar. She soon discovered that her husband, a quite uneducated man, was very anxious that his nineteen-year-old bride should be a person of culture; with the result that he promptly packed her off to a boarding-school in the north of London, where she remained two years, spending only her holidays at home. After that he sent her for another year to a convent in Belgium for the finishing touches of a Continental education.

Not until the year 1878 did she take up a permanent home life with the man whose name she bore. For a time they lived at Herne Hill, then at Dulwich, and—apart from the consolations of music and reading, to both of which she was devoted—life can have possessed little charm for Adelaide Bartlett. Her husband was away all day looking after his shops. Her father-in-law, old Mr. Bartlett, a builder, had made himself definitely unpleasant to her. Apparently she had no friends. It is said that in a moment of desperation she ran away with one of her husband's brothers, but the main spreader of the calumny was the father-in-law in question, who had to sign a withdrawal of the story and an abject apology. She is also said to have wished to have children—a desire which her husband emphatically did not share. Indeed, one of his contributions to her book-shelves was a volume by an American physiologist called *The Mysteries of Man*, which told married people, among other things, how to live together without having children. In 1881 she had a confinement, but the child was still-born. In short, although she and her husband seemed on excellent terms with each other, a perceptive visitor to their home would probably have discerned the presence of dangerous possibilities.

Late in 1884 or early in 1885 they moved to "The Cottage," Merton Abbey. Here also, for a time, life went on very much as before. In the summer of the latter year they began attending the Sunday services at a small Wesleyan chapel in Merton High Street. The prayers and preaching of the minister, an amiable-looking young man of twenty-seven with a dark curly moustache, evidently attracted them both, and presently he paid a pastoral visit. The Rev. George Dyson had lately taken his B.A. at Trinity College, Dublin, and it is easy to believe that his conversation was somewhat different from the odds and ends of talk to which Mr. and Mrs. Bartlett's parlour walls were accustomed. Once more the husband's ambition for his wife's culture flared forth. He made arrangements with the reverend gentleman that he should call at "The Cottage" from time to time while he was away at his shops and give the wife lessons in Latin, history, geography, and mathematics. Mr. Dyson accepted the engagement with alacrity, and not only called on Mrs. Bartlett at Merton but took her occasionally to his own apartments at Wimbledon, always with her husband's knowledge. In fact he became on the friendliest terms with them both.

There is no sign that he ever took any books with him on his tutorial visits to "The Cottage," but Mr. Bartlett on his return from work in the evening often had the pleasure of finding him still there, and would persuade him to stay on for supper, during which meal his conversation evidently cheered the wearied grocer as his remarks on Latin and mathematics had previously edified the lonely wife. Presently the Bartletts gave up their place at Merton and went to spend a month at Dover. Mr. Bartlett, to whom the young minister's friendship had now become not merely a luxury but a necessity, offered him a season ticket from London so that he might continue his visits. This, however, Mr. Dyson felt compelled to decline. His pastoral engagements at Merton were too many and too pressing. He promised, however, to run down whenever he could. Twice he stayed with them there, the husband paying his travelling expenses. About this time, too, Mr. Bartlett made a will, in which he bequeathed all he possessed to his wife on condition that she remained single after his death; and he nominated Mr. Dyson as one of the executors. From Dover the couple presently moved to London, taking the first-floor set of rooms in Claverton Street to which reference has already been made; and, in order that the young minister should still be able to function as "The Angel in the House,"

Mr. Bartlett presented him with a railway season-ticket between Putney and Waterloo.

In Claverton Street the life of this strange trio proceeded as before—only more so. Mr. Bartlett would leave home at about 8.30 a.m. and be away all day; and Mr. Dyson would arrive sometimes as early as nine or half-past and change his shoes and his clerical coat for a pair of slippers and a comfortable old jacket thoughtfully kept for him in the back drawing-room. A maidservant who now and then entered the room while Mrs. Bartlett and the minister were engaged in their studies observed that the window-curtains had been drawn together and secured by means of a safety-pin. On one occasion she also discovered Mr. Dyson seated in a low chair and Mrs. Bartlett curled up on the floor, with her head cosily resting on the reverend gentleman's knee. This discovery did not seem in the least to discompose the two students. As the damsel subsequently remarked in describing the incident, "They didn't do anything, but just sat on as they were." Presently, however, Mr. Bartlett fell ill. He had been overworking for years, and now, when he was only just forty, the machine had given way. His illness was an ugly one with squalid accompaniments, and he became morbid and talked much of death. The one ray of sunshine in his melancholy state was the devotion of his wife, who won the homage of everyone by her affectionate and self-sacrificing nursing. For three weeks she scarcely had her clothes off. Night after night she took her rest in a chair at the foot of his bed. Her whole behaviour exhibited a spontaneous and wholly unselfish affection.

At last he got better; and according to Mrs. Bartlett's account, one of the signs of his improvement was a proposal to his wife that there should be a full resumption of marital relations between them. To this, for some reason of her own, she inwardly objected. She decided to protect herself from attentions which had become undesirable. And the person with whom she talked it over was her tutor in Latin and mathematics. Whether she revealed the precise nature of her difficulty to that gentleman is uncertain. Apparently all she said was that she wanted some chloroform, to soothe her husband and send him to sleep, and she asked the young minister if he would procure six ounces for her. He engaged to do so, and she handed him a sovereign. That was on the night of Sunday, December 27. On the following day Mr. Dyson paid a round of visits in quest of the anæsthetic. He ordered an ounce from a chemist in Richmond Road, Putney, and when asked for what purpose it was required answered that it was "to take out some grease stains." From another chemist, in Wimbledon, he bought two more ounces, offering the same explanation of the purchase; and finally, in Putney High Street, he procured a further couple of ounces. The cost of it all was between six and seven shillings. On his return to his rooms he emptied the various bottles into one large one and corked it up; and on Tuesday, the 29th, he took it to Claverton Street and handed it to Mrs. Bartlett. Whether he told her how much the contents had cost and handed her the change from her sovereign he could not afterwards remember.

Shortly before midnight on December 31 the wife settled herself for the night's vigil in her usual seat at the foot of her husband's bed. She heard the clocks striking twelve and the customary sounds welcoming a New Year. Her husband had fallen asleep, and presently she also fell asleep. About four o'clock in the morning she awoke, and observed that her husband was lying on his face, curiously quiet. She rose, touched him, turned him over, and tried to administer some brandy. Presently she went upstairs to the bedroom of the landlord of the house and tapped at the door. "Will you come down?" she said, "I think Mr. Bartlett is dead." The landlord put on his dressing-gown and went down. He found his tenant lying with his eyes closed and his body perfectly cold. "Do you think he is dead?" said Mrs. Bartlett. "Yes, he must have been dead some couple of hours," came the reply. "Did you close his eyes?" asked the landlord. "Yes," said Mrs. Bartlett, "I closed his eyes." The doctor, who had already been sent for, then arrived. He also formed the opinion that death had taken place two or even three hours before, but could see nothing to account for it. That day Mrs. Bartlett wrote to Mr. Dyson to tell him with grief of her husband's passing, and on Saturday, January 2, that gentleman called on her and stayed with her during the *post-mortem*. Next day, Sunday, in a visible panic, he took the bottles in which he had brought the chloroform to his rooms and threw them into the bushes on Wandsworth Common on his way to chapel; and on January 4 he had a painful interview with Mrs. Bartlett, in the course of which he reprobated her procedure and cried, "I am a ruined man!" On January 26 the Home Office analyst, Sir Thomas Stevenson, reported that chloroform had been the cause of death, and the arrests of Mrs. Bartlett and Mr. Dyson followed.

The trial opened at the Central Criminal Court on Monday, April 12, before Mr. Justice Wills. It lasted the whole week, concluding at five o'clock on the Saturday afternoon amid scenes of popular emotion. The array of eminent barristers engaged included the Attorney-General of the day (Sir Charles Russell) leading for the Crown; Mr. (afterwards Sir) Edward Clarke for the defence of Mrs. Bartlett; and Mr. (afterwards Sir) Francis Lockwood leading for the defence of the Rev.

George Dyson. The proceedings commenced dramatically enough with the announcement by Counsel for the Crown that there was no case to be submitted to the jury upon which they could properly be asked to convict Mr. Dyson, followed by an intimation from the Judge to the jury that it was their duty accordingly to declare that gentleman "Not Guilty." This instruction the jury obeyed, and the reverend gentleman was discharged, with the intimation, however, that he would be called as a witness. From that time onward the other prisoner occupied a chair in the centre of the dock, a composed, pale, fragile-looking little woman, who directed her gaze from time to time upon every person concerned in the proceedings with one exception—the advocate who with the utmost zeal and ability was defending her, Mr. Edward Clarke. From him she kept her eyes studiously averted. At one point, however, she sent him a little note. It contained a single sentence, and ran as follows: "Monsieur, I am very grateful to you though I do not look at you."

It is impossible in a necessarily brief survey to describe in anything like detail a trial so crowded with incidents. A full report of it, with a preface by Sir Edward Clarke himself, was published in 1886; and in the year 1927 a revised one, with a masterly introduction by Sir John Hall, Bart., soldier and man of letters, and containing a number of portraits and other illustrations, was added to the "Notable British Trials" series. In these two books the reader will find the whole of the legal proceedings—and curious indeed are the lights they shed on what Tennyson calls "the abysmal deeps of personality." Here it can only be stated that the outstanding features were (i) the evidence of Mr. Dyson, (ii) the speech for the defence by Mr. Edward Clarke, and (iii) the masterly charge to the jury by Sir Alfred Wills. As regards the young Wesleyan minister, foolishly and wrongly as he had behaved—particularly as a Christian minister—in his relationship with Mr. and Mrs. Bartlett, it is difficult not to mingle a certain commiseration with whatever other sentiments his record in the case may evoke. He had been the accused woman's friend, and now, as a result of his folly and weakness, he was standing in the witness-box not only, as he had said, a ruined man but with the consciousness that at any moment he might let fall a word which might help to bring her to the scaffold. Thanks in no small degree to the tact of Mr. Clarke he got through his ordeal without definitely incriminating anybody or anything except his own delicacy and common-sense.

The part which Mr. Clarke played in the trial has ever since been recognised as one of the outstanding chapters in the annals of English advocacy. More than thirty years afterwards, in his volume of memoirs, *The Story of My Life*, he described how he had immediately recognised the case as one likely to repay a special effort. He spent, he says, a week or ten days at the British Museum or in his own library studying the best and latest authorities on the qualities and effects of chloroform and its administration, and during the week of the trial he (one of the most ardent of Conservatives) left politics alone and confined his reading entirely to the papers in the case and the relevant medical books. The points upon which he specially concentrated were: (i) that it was extremely difficult to render a sleeping person unconscious by an inhalation of chloroform, and (ii) that it was a physical impossibility to force a sleeping man to swallow such a dose as that from which Mr. Bartlett had died. In the volume just alluded to he stated his belief that the turning point of the trial came in the following series of questions and answers in his cross-examination of the Home Office analyst, Dr. Stevenson:—

*"Now, suppose you had to deal with a sleeping man, and it was your object to get down his throat, without his knowing it, a liquid the administration of which to the lips or throat would cause great pain, do you not agree it would be a very difficult or delicate operation?"*—*"I think it would be an operation which would often fail and might often succeed."*

*"Would you look on it as a delicate operation?"*—*"I should look on it as a delicate operation, because I should be afraid of pouring it down the wind-pipe."*

*"That is one of the dangers you contemplate?"*—*"Yes."*

*"If it got into the windpipe there would be spas-modic action of the muscles, would there not?"*—*"At the stage when you had come to the conclusion that you could do it, when there is insensibility or partial insensibility, the rejection of the liquid by the windpipe would probably be less active than when the patient was awake."*

*"If the patient got into such a state of insensibility as not to reject it, it would go down his windpipe and burn that?"*—*"Probably some might go down his windpipe."*

*"It would probably do that?"*—*"Probably."*

*"If it did so, it would leave its traces?"*—*"I should expect to find traces after death unless the patient lived some hours."*

*"Of course a great many* post-mortem *appearances are changed if the patient lives some hours?"*—*"Yes."*

*"Not only by the chloroform disappearing, so*

> *to speak, but also other changes incidental to a* post-mortem *condition?"*—*"Yes."*
>
> *"And if the* post-mortem *examination had been performed as Mrs. Bartlett wished it to be, on the very day on which death took place, there would have been still better opportunity of determining the cause of death?"*—*"Yes."*

Following as it did the full establishment in court of the fact that immediately after her husband's death Mrs. Bartlett had demanded the *post-mortem* to be made as promptly as possible and to have it conducted by the best available skill, this series of questions and the experts' answers to them form a classic instance of cross-examination at its most effective.

The other memorable feature of the trial was, as has been said, the Judge's summing-up. Sir Alfred Wills was not only a great lawyer but a man of character, wit, high culture, and many interests. In his younger days he had been a great Alpine climber, and his account of an ascent of the Wetterhorn which he made in September, 1854, is among the immortal things of mountain literature. All through the trial of Adelaide Bartlett, his knowledge not only of law but also of humanity, his lofty ethic, and his sense for the neat phrase render his contribution to the proceedings most enjoyable reading. In the course of his cross-examination, Mr. Dyson, replying to a certain question, ventured to remark, "This is a very delicate matter for me." "No, no," interposed the Judge, "we have long outstripped the bounds of delicacy." To one of the doctors, who, in the witness-box, had exhibited rather a tiresome self-consciousness in choosing his words, the Judge drily remarked, "If you did not think so much of the literary effect and would just tell us what happened, it would be better for everybody." The same witness, in another passage of his evidence, remarked lightly to Counsel, "Oh, that goes without saying." "No," interjected his lordship, "nothing 'goes without saying' here. Please to take that as an axiom." In his long charge to the jury he summarised with great precision and absolute impartiality all that had been brought forward against the prisoner. Now and then, too, he allowed himself to express an opinion on matters not strictly judicial, as, for instance, in the following reference to the book, *The Mysteries of Man*, which had been quoted from by the prisoner's counsel:—

> *"It has been my unpleasant duty to look at this book . . . I cannot, sitting here, have such garbage passed under my eyes and then allow it to go forth that an English Judge concurs in the view that it is a specimen of pure and healthy literature. It is one of those books which, in my judgment, under the garb of ostentatious purity, obtain entrance probably into many a household from which it would otherwise be banished. It scatters its poison and does its mischief. The women of the present day are used to strange things—things which would have startled us in the time of my boyhood—and it is such reading as this that helps to unsex them, and to bring them to a place like this day after day to listen willingly to details which, to men of mature life like yourselves and myself, and to men like myself unwillingly steeped in the experience of criminal courts and to knowledge which untainted men would gladly dispense with, are distasteful and disgusting."*

One wonders how the ladies in the Old Bailey court-house in 1886 listened to those bitter sentences.

The jury spent nearly two hours considering their verdict. At five o'clock they at last filed back into their box. To everyone's astonishment, the foreman, on being asked if they had found the prisoner guilty or not guilty, entered upon a summary of the difficulties with which they had been confronted. "We have," he began, "well considered the evidence, and although we think grave suspicion is attached to the prisoner, we do not think there is sufficient evidence to show how or by whom the chloroform was administered." For a moment there was a stillness that could be felt. Then came the voice of the Clerk: "Then, gentlemen, you say that the prisoner is not guilty?" To that, the foreman answered slowly, "Not Guilty." Immediately a great burst of cheering broke forth, speedily followed by another from the crowd in the streets outside. The Judge, pale with indignation, had the greatest difficulty in procuring silence. "This conduct is an outrage," he was at last able to say. "A court of justice is not to be turned into a theatre by such indecent exhibitions."

So Mrs. Bartlett was free! Amid all the surrounding excitement of the moment her Counsel was sitting with his face buried in his hands. As he wrote long after in his memories: "For the first and only time in my fifty years of advocacy the suspense and emotion as I saw my client go from the dock to freedom broke me down, and I found myself sobbing." Afterwards the crowd in the streets gave him an ovation, and his brougham was followed along Holborn by a throng of cheering admirers. That night he was the object of another popular demonstration. His old friend and schoolfellow, Henry Irving, had invited him to the Lyceum, to which all London was then crowding to see the great actor and Miss Ellen Terry as Mephistopheles and Margaret in *Faust*. As Mr. Clarke and his wife entered their private box the defender of Adelaide Bartlett was immediately recognised, and the house rang with applause.

—H.M.W.

# 5

# ELISABETH, COUNTESS BATHORY
## Countess Dracula

---

The blood of six hundred, perhaps more, girls and young women stained her hands, her lips, her entire voluptuous body—for she bathed in this warm and viscous fluid, seeking thus to preserve her famous beauty. The scent of death, torture, and innumerable lesbian orgies hovered about her: a sinister perfume. And even when she was caught in the midst of a murderous debauch, no executioner's axe could touch her white and still lovely throat, for she was the Countess Bathory, widow of Hungary's great "Black Hero," cousin to the Prime Minister himself, kin of princes and kings, bishops and cardinals, judges and governors.

Castle Csejthe, its massive gray stones arranged in walls and towers, turrets and battlements, dominated from its bleak hilltop the thatch-roofed village below. The peasants of northwestern Hungary's county of Nyitra climbed the path to the somber fortress only when imperiously summoned, and then with a fearful reluctance. The Counts Nadasdy, who occupied Castle Csejthe, were traditionally cruel and without mercy, liberal where the lash and the dungeons were concerned, tight-fisted in dispensing rewards to those who toiled endlessly to work their lands.

It was to this feudal chateau, already of hateful reputation, that twenty-one-year-old Count Ferencz Nadasdy, destined for greatness as a warrior, brought his bride, the fifteen-year-old Countess Elisabeth Bathory, already renowned as a prototype of the Hungarian style of beauty: astonishingly white flesh, almost translucent, through which one could see clearly the delicate blue veins beneath; long, shimmering, silken hair, black as the plumage of the raven; sensual, scarlet lips; great dark eyes, capable of doelike tenderness, but sometimes igniting into savage anger, and at others glazing over with the abandoned somnolence of intense sexual passion.

Who can say what course the lives of this pair might have taken had the young Count Nadasdy remained at home, with his ardent and beautiful young wife, instead of galloping off to win on bloody battlefields the acclaim of all Hungary? They were well matched: the same tigerish desires drove them, the same streak of barbarous cruelty surged in their blood. Even Elisabeth's consuming interest in witchcraft, sorcery, and diabolism was one they shared. That despite all separations, all the tests to which it was put, their love for one another endured, is testimonial enough to the powerful bond that linked them.

If the taint of traditional savagery marred the bloodstream of the noble Nadasdy line, no less was it true that hereditary forces found their culmination in the monstrous passions of Elisabeth Bathory. Hers was a curious heritage, wherein distinction and even greatness resided side by side with psychosis, brutality, and extremes of corruption.

Kings and cardinals, bishops and judges, sheriffs and governors bore proudly the name of Bathory. The prime minister of Hungary, Gyorgy Thurzo, was Elisabeth's cousin. The great Sigismund Bathory, Prince of Transylvania, was her kinsman. One of the greatest of Hungary's military leaders, Sigismund was both a genius and a madman, noted for the savagery and instability of his temperament. An aunt, one of the most distinguished ladies of the royal court, was a witch and a lesbian, a notorious corruptor of young girls. An uncle, equally distinguished, was a sorcerer, an alchemist, a witch, and a worshipper of the Devil. Elisabeth's own brother, handsome and brilliant like all the Bathorys, was a satyr, a monster of depravity, whose lusts were so overwhelming and barbaric that neither child nor withered crone could be considered safe from his unremitting and twisted cravings.

As if this heritage were not sufficient, the Countess Elisabeth was exposed from infancy to the vicious teachings of her nurse, Ilona Joo, a woman steeped in black magic, witchcraft, and satanism. Never, throughout her life, was Elisabeth to know freedom from this malign influence: an influence paid its full due by the Hungarian tribunal, which burned the hag alive after putting her to the torture, while others of the Countess' entourage were merely beheaded.

Left in the castle by her warrior husband, Elisabeth, her sexuality fully aroused by the virile Nadasdy, grew ever more lonely and more frustrated. The magic of Ilona Joo could not relieve her anguish. Gradually, she accumulated around her other witches, alchemists, and sorcerers: Darvula, a strange female creature who had practiced her witchcraft in the depths of the forest; Johannes Ujvary, alchemist and black magician, servant and plotter of tortures; Thorko, sorcerer and favorite of Nadasdy, who sometimes accompanied his master into battle, meanwhile formulating evil spells for the Count to send home by courier—tokens of his affection—to his beloved young countess; Dorottya Szentes, witch, lesbian, and sadist; and others of similar qualifications and predilections.

It was still not enough. Elisabeth summoned to the castle a pale young nobleman whose strange black eyes flashed in a head made even more cadaverous by long dark hair that hung thin and lifeless to his shoulders. He was reputed to be a vampire, and perhaps it was this that fanned to flames Elisabeth's smoldering passion. The pair eloped—it was her only infidelity—but soon she returned, alone.

Forgiven by Nadasdy, who could understand the overwhelming force of passions no less demanding than his own, Elisabeth absorbed herself again in witchcraft and—since no man save her husband would again know her embraces—in other practices aimed at easing the aching her body knew in the long lonely nights.

With her two personal maids, Barsovny and Otvos, carefully chosen for their youth, their beauty, and their unscrupled ardor, Elisabeth abandoned herself to all the possible pleasures one woman may know in the arms of another. For a time this, and the occasional visits of her husband, were sufficient to fend off her evil destiny. But always in Elisabeth's ear were the whispers of the crone Ilona Joo, hinting of other, far more perverse, more dangerous, more monstrous pleasures. Long before she succumbed, Elisabeth knew that one day she would put into practice the evil her old nurse suggested. As fully as Ilona Joo, perhaps more fully than the old woman or any other member of her corrupt household, Elisabeth craved the descent into evil. If she delayed, it was from prudence, a fear of the consequences, and not from any want of desire or absence of depravity sufficient to the dark deeds contemplated.

For ten years following her marriage the Countess had failed to conceive, though Nadasdy, strongly desirous of a male heir, strove manfully. At length, the bevy of witches, alchemists, black magicians, and sorcerers was instructed to take a hand in the matter. Perhaps they were successful. At any rate, shortly after her twenty-sixth birthday Elisabeth gave birth to a child, who was followed in quick succession by three others. For a time, the Countess was absorbed by her maternal role. Like a typical mother, she dispatched loving notes to Nadasdy, returned to the wars, advising him of the doings and health of the children. Indeed, up until Nadasdy's death, when she was almost forty, Elisabeth seems to have resisted the more extreme urgings of Ilona Joo and the others. But once her husband, who had been a true lover and companion, was gone, Elisabeth at last cast off all restraints.

Strange and fearful whisperings began to be heard in the village, and at night the peasants locked themselves in their houses and listened in terror to the anguished and agonized screams that sometimes drifted down to them from the hill-top. Despite all precautions, children disappeared, as did young girls, even some of the younger women. Occasionally people came to the village, inquiring after travelers—girls and women—who had last been seen in that vicinity. The peasants were not helpful in such cases. The less said, they surmised, the better.

The maids and former lesbian lovers of the Countess, Barsovny and Otvos, were assigned the roles of pro-curers and kidnappers. If they could not tempt girls and women to the castle with promises of jobs, they drugged them, beat them into insensibility or submission, or otherwise overpowered them. For no less than eleven years the terrified peasants watched from behind their curtained windows and shuddered as the carriage, drawn by black horses and illuminated by moonlight, descended from Castle Csejthe to roam the countryside in search of new victims. On its sides the carriage bore the emblems of the Nadasdys and the Bathorys:

symbols of power no mere policeman would ever dare to challenge.

It was not for the indulgence of her lesbian pleasures only that the Countess required this endless flow of children, girls, and women, not one of whom ever managed to escape the castle alive. Even in middle age, Elisabeth was still a remarkably beautiful woman, seeming far younger than her years. Still, time was beginning to take its toll. It could not be denied—not, at least, by the vain Elisabeth herself. Then, one day, around the time of her husband's death, there occurred an incident that determined to a degree the nature of all the horrors to follow.

Striking one of her maids for some act of carelessness, the Countess noted that where the blood she had drawn fell upon her skin the flesh seemed whiter, younger, softer than before. Obtaining more blood, she bathed her beautiful face in it. Sure enough, or so it seemed, the blood restored the youthful texture and vibrancy to her flesh. After that, she was not long in concluding that complete and regular submersion in blood would restore her entire body to the full bloom of youthful loveliness. It was to appease this requirement, as well as her sadistic and lesbian ones, that Barsovny and Otvos scoured the countryside by night, luring, kidnapping, and overpowering new victims for their insatiable mistress.

Ilona Joo and other witches, magicians, and sorcerers had long been insisting to the Countess that only human sacrifices would enable them to achieve the desired results with their magic. For the alchemical experiments, skulls and other bones, especially those of small children, were urgently needed. Further, all in the castle, from the Countess on down to her lowliest cohort, seem to have been capable of deriving intense erotic pleasure from sadistic orgies of torture and murder. Thus there was nothing but enthusiasm when it became apparent that Elisabeth's blood baths would also make possible the fulfillment and indulgence of the other needs.

In the dungeons beneath the castle, girls and women were chained to the walls and fed like cattle being fattened for market. The fatter they were, thought the Countess, the more blood in their veins; and the healthier, the better the cosmetic effects of their blood when she immersed herself in her gory baths.

The delicacy of the Countess' flesh was such, she thought, that it could not be subjected to drying by coarse towels. Emerging from her tub, covered with human blood from head to toe, she had herself licked by girls, carefully chosen for their beauty and, above all, for the softness of their tongues. If such a girl became ill or otherwise displayed her disgust, horrible tortures and a speedy death awaited her—as each was firmly advised before being admitted into the Countess' bloody presence. If, however, a girl reacted as if with pleasure to the experience, and especially if she lingered long and lovingly between Elisabeth's ceaselessly voracious thighs, she might gain the Countess' favor. Such favor might mean a deferral of the death sentence for a considerable length of time, though it seldom did. The Countess soon wearied of those she exploited for her pleasure, however obliging they might be. And not infrequently she took a particular delight in inflicting the most cruel tortures of all upon precisely those who for a time had been her favorites.

Some of the tortures inflicted by Elisabeth and the others upon their victims are a matter of record, preserved in still-existing (at last word) records pertaining to her trial. At that trial, Ilona Joo and Thorko, along with others, testified that hundreds of girls had been, over the years, kept in the dungeons and milked there, by means of incisions, of their blood, as if they were a kind of human dairy herd. The Countess, these accomplices turned witnesses declared, not only bathed in this blood, but she also drank it, as did some of the others.

Human sacrifices were made, in the course of magical and alchemical experiments and rituals and other practices. Girls were bound with ropes, and these were twisted until they cut into the flesh, after which the veins were opened with scissors, and the blood, as a result of the "tourniquets," spurted forth under great pressure, drenching the walls of the torture chamber as well as the eager bodies of the torturers. Girls were beaten with whips and their flesh slit with knives. Sometimes they were flayed, and after this "frozen" in tubs of icy water. The victims were also, it was testified, forced to hold in their hands metallic objects heated until they glowed. Paper was placed at their toes, and then set afire. Some of the tortures described were "so revolting" that even at that time, when torture was commonplace as a punishment and in the questioning of accused persons, the judges found themselves scarcely able to believe that such things could be. (Eisler insists, taking his information from Von Elsberg by way of another writer, that most of the victims were brought to the Countess' bed and there "bitten to death." But apparently a great many died in other ways, as the trial testimony indicates.)

Rumors of these tortures and murders and reports of kidnappings had reached the ears of the authorities, and even come to the attention of King Matthias of Hungary, years before any action was taken. It was most difficult to proceed against the Countess, whose distinguished family had powerful friends everywhere. Her cousin, the prime minister, was by no means eager to confirm his suspicions about what was going on at Csejthe. But despite all this, it was at last and reluctantly decided that an investigation would have to be undertaken. Once this decision had been made, the inquiry was placed under the personal direction of Prime Minister Thurzo, who took with him to the village the governor of the province. There, they conferred with the village priest, who had lodged a lengthy and specific complaint, as well as with numerous villagers who insisted that the castle was the residence of a vampire. They were more nearly correct in this than either Thurzo or his chief assistant, the governor, suspected.

The raid on Castle Csejthe was conducted on New Year's Eve, when it was hoped the raiding party would be able to approach the castle undetected. This proved to be the case, and the raiders, Prime Minister Thurzo, the governor, the priest, and numerous soldiers and policemen, gained the summit of the hill unnoticed. There, they found the massive doors of the castle ajar, and were able simply to walk in. Grisly surprises awaited them.

In the great hall, not far from the door, lay the pale, lifeless body of a young girl, the blood completely drained from her body. Sprawled grotesquely and pitiably on the floor, a few paces away, lay another girl, still alive. Her body had been pierced repeatedly with some kind of sharp instrument, and a great deal of blood had obviously been removed. Yet a little further on, chained to a pillar, was the body of another murdered girl. She had been burned, savagely whipped, and her blood drained from her body.

Hastening to the dungeons below, which the prime minister recalled from childhood visits to the castle, the party found several dozen children, girls, and women, many of whom had been bled repeatedly by the Countess and her household. Others had not yet been molested, and were fat and in excellent health, for all the world like animals ready to be shipped off to the slaughter-house.

Still, the party of raiders went unnoticed. After freeing the captives from their chains, they made their way to the second floor of the castle. There, they surprised the Countess and the others in the midst of a drunken and depraved orgy, details of which are said to have been too awful to be described. The celebrants were easily overpowered and taken into custody, Countess Bathory being confined in her apartment in the castle under heavy guard, and the others taken away to a nearby jail.

The trial court was convened as quickly as possible, with Theodosius de Szulo of the Royal Supreme Court presiding. The seriousness of the case and the high position of Elisabeth Bathory are emphasized by the fact that no less than twenty other judges, all of prominence, were on hand to assist Szulo.

The corpses, skeletons, and other human remains found by the raiders at Csejthe, along with a mass of additional evidence including testimony of the liberated prisoners, eliminated all possibility that pleas of "not guilty" might reasonably be entered. Instead, having been caught red-handed (an accurate description here if anywhere!), the murderous crew of witches and sorcerers, diabolists and alchemists, competed to see who could provide the court with the most detailed and horrifying testimony, each hoping, by such enthusiastic and unreserved cooperation, to win clemency. Some of that testimony has already been summarized, and to repeat more of it would shed no further light on the case.

Present in the courtroom were all the accused except one: the principal defendant, Elisabeth Bathory. She was permitted to remain in her apartment at the castle, where she was kept under heavy guard at all times. *In absentia,* she was announced convicted along with the rest. All were held to be guilty of at least eighty murders, the number of identifiable cadavers actually found. There were strong indications, however, that the real number of victims was in excess of three hundred, and possibly as high as six hundred and fifty.

After due consideration of the roles played by each of the defendants, the court announced the following sentences, which were without exception carried out.

Ilona Joo: Her fingers will be torn off one by one, after which torture she will be burned alive and her ashes strewn.

Dorottya Szentes: The fingers will be torn off one by one, to be followed by burning alive. (It is not clear why Szentes was singled out to share with Ilona Joo the more extreme punishment.)

Johannes Ujvary, Thorko, Darvula, Barsovny, Otvos: All will have their heads struck from their bodies by the executioner.

Following the solemn reading of these grim sentences, Judge Szulo at once declared the special tribunal adjourned. The reader will note, no doubt, that in reading the sentences Judge Szulo omitted the name of Countess Elisabeth Bathory.

This was not done lightly. King Matthias II of Hungary, whose father had been a wedding guest at the ceremony uniting Elisabeth and Count Nadasdy, was personally interested in the case and, despite many close ties with the Bathorys and the Nadasdys, favored execution. Only the strenuous efforts of Prime Minister Thurzo, who convinced the King of Elisabeth's insanity—and perhaps brought other pressures to bear—saved her from sharing the fate of her childhood nurse and lifelong mentor, Ilona Joo.

In Elisabeth's apartment at Castle Csejthe, the stone masons went to work. Her windows were walled up, save for tiny slits in the stone, left for ventilation. The same was done with the entrance to the apartment, with the exception that there was left an aperture through which food might be passed in to the prisoner. Inside this heavily walled apartment, never to be seen again in life, was Countess Elisabeth Bathory, still a strikingly beautiful and strangely youthful woman, though she was nearing her fiftieth birthday.

The Countess lived for four more years in her solitary confinement, never attempting to communicate with anyone, never uttering a sound that could be heard by the guards always stationed outside the slitlike aperture in the massive stone wall that imprisoned her. Her death, detected only when the food plates went for a long time untouched, is believe to have occurred on the 21st of August, 1614. She was fifty-four.

—R.E.L.M. & E.L.

# 6

# MARTHA BECK

## Trail of the Lonesome Hearts

It was Joseph Fouché, Napoleon's minister of police, who is supposed to have coined the phrase, "*Cherchez la femme.*" And in non-professional crimes of violence to this day the first thought of the police is to hunt for "the woman." More often than not they turn one up.

From this statistical fact a myth has arisen: that the Woman in the Case is invariably fairer-faced than Helen of Troy and more irresistibly constructed than next year's Miss Universe. Nothing could be less true; indeed, it is remarkable how few really beautiful women the literature of murder has been able to record. Case after bloody case revolves about plain, even homely, women.

Obviously these women had something. But what?

Take the case of Martha Jule Beck. Martha Beck was five feet six inches tall and she weighed 230 gross and quivering pounds. If her face would not have stopped the clock, neither would it have inspired poetry or sweet dreams. She had mouse-brown hair and dirt-colored eyes—an altogether unappetizing female. Still, because of this woman, a man who had wooed and won girls and women all over the world permitted himself to be dragged into murder.

Martha was born in Florida, the youngest of a brood of five in a home raucous with parental quarreling. Her introduction to sex and her subsequent sexual history in her teens are too sordid to be specified even in these uninhibited times. Oddly enough, she was a good student. She became a trained nurse.

Throughout her short life this obese and unattractive woman was obsessed with sex. She collected provocative photos of movie stars; she pored over sensational magazines; she devoured books on sex.

Her early marriage to a man named Albert Beck was a fiasco from the start. She divorced him, retaining custody of their two children.

Martha Beck was 29 years old and head nurse at a school for crippled children in Pensacola, Florida when, in November 1947, one of her friends as a joke sent her name in to a Lonesome Hearts club. The first Martha knew of it was when she received a letter from one Raymond Fernandez, apparently a kindred "lonely heart." Martha's obsession drove her to correspond with him. Fernandez joined her in Pensacola. She promptly quit her post at the school, dumped her two children on friends, and went off with Fernandez.

Raymond Martinez Fernandez was no innocent flower of the field. Born in Hawaii, at various times living in the United States, Spain, Gibraltar, he worked occasionally as a seaman or a freight-handler on the docks, but his chief occupation was swindling women. He was small and slight and swarthy with unsavory sideburns, and he was half bald, but he had a way with lonely women which he exercised freely. He had "married," fleeced, and deserted gullible females in a dozen countries. But he met his match in Martha Beck.

Martha did not become his latest victim. She became his partner, his mistress, and his Nemesis. Eventually she dominated him body and soul, and he was as helpless to get away from her as a rat from a snake. She held him fast by carnality, greed, and fear, and she taught him the terrifying pleasures of murder.

Byron Center is a suburb of Grand Rapids, Michigan. On February 28, 1949 the local police were notified by neighbors of Mrs. Delphine Downing, twenty-eight-year-old widow, that Mrs. Downing and her twenty-two-month-old daughter Rainelle had disappeared. Moreover, the neighbors charged, the vinecovered Downing cottage was being occupied by a strange couple.

At the cottage police found a fat, muddy-eyed young woman who said she was "Martha Martin from Long Island" and a swarthy man of thirty-four with sideburns and a toupee, whom the fat woman introduced as "my brother Charles, who is going to marry Delphine Downing." Mrs. Downing and her baby, the "Martins" said, were off visiting relatives.

The police doubted it. In the bedroom they found packed luggage and cartons as for a getaway, a large bundle of paper money done up in a bedsheet, and a list of more than 125 names of women. In the cellar storage bin they found a patch of wet cement. And three feet under the wet cement they found the dead bodies of Mrs. Downing and her baby. They had been murdered.

The "Martins" denied everything. They had not so much as set foot in the cellar, they said. The money in the bedsheet was their savings; the list of women from all over the country were friends or former patients of Martha's—she had been a trained nurse in several states.

The pair was separated and questioned singly. The fat woman stolidly stuck to their story. Away from her. the man broke, almost with relief. He was evidently in mortal terror of her.

"Charles Martin" was an alias, he said; his real name was Raymond Martinez Fernandez. The fat woman was Martha Beck, his "common law wife." Their present home was in Valley Stream, New York. He was a Lonesome Hearts swindler, he said, and the women's names were his sucker-list, gathered from various Hearts clubs. Martha was his confederate.

Fernandez admitted that he had corresponded with Delphine Downing for several months, until she asked him to visit her. Martha had accompanied him as his "sister," their usual technique. She had checked into a hotel in Grand Rapids while he executed a whirlwind three-day courtship of Mrs. Downing. When Delphine promised to marry him, he brought his "sister" to the cottage. They had got the young widow to agree to sell her home and buy a new car—and open a "joint bank account" with Fernandez.

On February 26th the affair had come to a head. He had returned from shopping in Grand Rapids with a new toupee. Delphine became angry; she had not known he was bald. Her anger turned to hysterics and Martha had solicitously given her some "nerve" pills. They were actually powerful sleeping pills, Fernandez said, and Martha had cajoled Delphine into swallowing a heavy overdose.

A few hours later the young widow was still breathing. Fat Martha calmly examined her. "She might even recover," she told Fernandez. "You better do something about it right now."

Fernandez had gone for his gun and, with Martha egging him on, had shot the doped woman in the head. They had then trussed the body with clothesline, carted it down to the basement, dug a hole in the storage bin, dumped the body in, and recemented the floor. After which Martha had "freshened up" and prepared a good dinner. Then, because Fernandez was afraid some neighbor might drop in, he and Martha had taken the baby and gone to a movie.

The next day, February 27th, had been a Sunday. The murdered woman's baby kept crying and calling, "Mommy, mommy." They had taken her for an automobile ride and bought her a puppy. But it frightened the baby, and they took it back.

The next day little Rainelle was ill. Martha became annoyed. She had Fernandez drive over to Grand Rapids and close out the joint account he had opened with Delphine. And that evening Martha Beck had taken the baby down into the cellar, undressed her, and drowned her in a tub of dirty water. Then she directed Fernandez to reopen the mother's tomb, drop the child's body in, and cement the hole over again.

Confronted with Fernandez's confession, the fat young woman laughed. "It's a trap," she said to her inquisitors. "I stick to my story."

Back they went to the demoralized Fernandez. "Tell us about your activities before you and Martha Beck came to Michigan."

"You mean about Mrs. Janet Fay?" Fernandez muttered.

"Yes," the detectives said. They had no idea who Mrs. Janet Fay might be. "Tell us about her."

So Fernandez told them about another of Martha Beck's adventures in murder.

It was in mid-December of the previous year, Fernandez said, that he and Martha had rented an apartment in Valley Steam, Long Island, and furnished it modestly. (New York police later said that the flat was filled with ecclesiastical objects, the property of previous swindle-victims.)

Settled in the apartment, Martha and Raymond had gone through his Lonesome Hearts files to select a fresh victim. They agreed on one Mrs. Janet Fay, a widow of Albany, New York, whose letters to Fernandez claimed that she was 44 years old and financially independent.

Using his favorite alias of "Charles Martin," Fernandez resumed his ardent correspondence with Mrs. Fay and soon had an invitation to visit her. He and Martha drove up to Albany and checked into a hotel as brother and sister.

At Fernandez's first contact with Mrs. Fay he was amused to learn that she was not forty-four but sixty-six. On New Year's Day he brought his "sister Martha" around to meet the old lady. Everything went smoothly. The old woman confided in Martha. She was "in love with your brother Charles." She even took them on a visit to some relatives in the Albany area. On their return to her home she insisted on their staying the night.

The swindling pair had stayed all of the next day, too. The "lovers" talked of marriage, a honeymoon, a "business for Charles." Mrs. Fay would give up her Albany house and live on Long Island. And that night the foolish old woman wrote a check for $2,000, payable to herself, and another for a $1,500 transfer from her Albany bank to a bank in New York City. And the following day she went to her bank and withdrew $3,400 in cash.

Now the unholy couple moved fast. They bustled Mrs. Fay and her luggage into their car and drove to Long Island, Fernandez making love to the old lady all the way. They got to the Valley Stream apartment in the early evening, and by 10:00 p.m. the widow had endorsed the checks over to "Charles Martin," signing her death-warrant. That was January 3rd.

In the small hours of January 4th Mrs. Fay dreamily undressed and got into bed. She was very happy. Her happiness lasted no longer than a lightning-stroke. Martha Beck came silently into the bedroom, walked over to the bed, loomed there over the horror-stricken old lady like some bloated monster in a nightmare. In the fat hand was a hammer. The hammer rose over the old woman's head . . . fell . . . rose . . . fell . . .

"She kept screaming," Fernandez told the Michigan detectives. "I was scared the noise would wake up the neighbors. So I took a scarf and wound it around her neck . . ."

When old Mrs. Fay was dead they tossed her body into a closet. The fat murderess and her lover spent most of what remained of the night trying to scrub the bloodstains from the bed and carpet. The carpet especially was stubborn. About noon they left the flat and bought a new carpet, also a big trunk. They replaced the bloodstained carpet, packed the body in the trunk, and took it to the home of an unsuspecting relative of Fernandez's for "temporary" safekeeping. A week later they rented a house in South Ozone Park, Queens, brought the trunk to the house, dug a grave in the cellar, deposited the body in the grave, and patched up the cement floor.

"I was in a sweat," Fernandez mumbled. "But not Martha. Only a day or so after we killed the old woman Martha went to Albany and cashed one of the checks."

Faced with her lover's story of the Janet Fay murder, Martha tightened her lips and refused to talk at all.

The Michigan police notified the police in Albany, New York City, and Nassau County of the Fernandez confession to the murder of Mrs. Janet Fay. The police of Albany, at least, were not surprised. On January 11th a letter purportedly from Mrs. Fay had been received by her Albany relatives. It was typewritten. But Mrs. Fay had been unable to type. The Fay family had gone to the police with the letter and the story of the "brother and sister" who had visited the missing woman over the holidays.

The New York authorities launched a joint investigation. In the South Ozone Park house they found the body of Mrs. Fay. In the Valley Stream flat they found the bloody furniture and other evidence of the murder.

A jurisdictional conference of the Michigan and New York authorities led to a decision to allow New York to try Fernandez and the Beck woman for the Janet Fay murder rather than have them stand trial in Michigan for the murders of Delphine and Rainelle Downing. There was grim logic behind this decision. New York had an airtight case against the guilty pair in the Fay murder, whereas Michigan's case against them in the Downing murders was not. And New York State had the death penalty; Michigan did not.

Martha Jule Beck and Raymond Martinez Fernandez went on trial before Justice Ferdinand Pecora in Bronx Supreme Court in New York City. On August 22, 1949 they were found guilty of murder in the first degree and sentenced to die in the electric chair. They were executed at Sing Sing prison on March 8, 1951.

The trial unlocked Martha Beck's lips. She tried over and over to take the blame for the murders, saying that Raymond Fernandez was "mixed up." Until the moment she was strapped into the electric chair she kept insisting that she had loved Raymond heart and soul.

As indeed she had; Fernandez confirmed it. Her

demands for his lovemaking had been incessant and insatiable. Was that the secret of the huge woman's fatal fascination for him? Perhaps. But the likelier answer may lie in the Lonesome Hearts swindler's repeated assertions to the various detectives who questioned him. Martha was the only woman who had ever been able to control his actions—she was the only woman, Fernandez said, he had ever been afraid of.

—E.Q.

# 7

# KATE BENDER

## Bumps in the Night

Late in the year 1870, there appeared in Labette County, Kansas, a family of four persons: John Bender and his wife; their son, or reputed son, John, and his sister, Kate. Almost everything about them is in dispute, and it is often said that the younger man was really John Gebhardt, the son of Mrs. Bender by a former husband. It is also asserted that Kate Bender was not the sister, but the mistress of the younger man. Many imaginary but no authentic portraits of the quartette are in existence, and these differ as widely as do the written descriptions of them. One portrait of old Bender shows him as a stolid peasant, not remarkable in any way; another makes him a shaggy-looking monster from a nightmare. The young John is depicted as a commonplace-looking man, under thirty; but, elsewhere, it is said that his face "had the fierce malice of the hyena." Concerning the appearance of Kate Bender, the writers have done their best, with the result that you may read that she was "a large, masculine, red-faced woman"; that she was a rather good-looking red-haired girl; or that she was a siren of such extraordinary charms that one has to call on every famous beauty, from Cleopatra to Mrs. Langtry, for suitable comparisons. She was the most interesting of the family; her father was a poor second; while the elder Mrs. Bender and young John were tied for third place.

From some official descriptions of them, issued by Governor Osborn of Kansas at a time when he was dealing in facts, rather than impressionism, these details are selected: John Bender was about sixty years old, and of medium height. He was a German, and spoke little English. He was dark, spare, and wore no beard. His wife was ten years younger; heavy in frame; had blue eyes and brown hair. There was nothing distinctive about John Bender, Jr.; he was twenty-seven, of slight build, wore a light brown moustache, and spoke English with German pronunciation. Kate was "about twenty-four years of age, dark hair and eyes, good looking, well formed, rather bold in appearance, fluent talker, speaks English with very little German accent."

Everybody agrees on two matters: old Bender was a disagreeable, surly fellow; and Kate was notably attractive to the men of that region; who found her pleasant, vivacious, and a desirable partner at the occasional country dance. She danced well, was a good horsewoman, and went to Sunday school and to "meetin's" in the school house. For a few weeks, in 1871, she condescended to act as waitress in the hotel at Cherryvale. There was about her, however, a more marked peculiarity: she believed in spiritualism, lectured on the subject, and claimed to be a medium, with the power to call up spirits of the dead. Her lectures, in the various towns of the county, caused a mild sensation. This was the decade when lecturing women aroused great curiosity and antagonism; often they were accused, not only of the offence of seeking to vote, but also, like the Claflins, of advocating various degrees of laxity of morals. How much these lecturers actually risked by putting themselves too far in advance of their time, and how far the reports about them were the exaggerations of horrified men, determined to put down the pestiferous creatures, by foul means or fair, it is always hard to discover.

A curious light is thrown upon Kate Bender's character by an advertisement which she seems to have had published in some of the newspapers in neighbouring towns, about a year before she became nationally famous. This was it:

> *Professor Miss Kate Bender can heal disease, cure blindness, fits and deafness. Residence, 14 miles east of Independence, on the road to Osage Mission. June 18, 1872.*

The Bender family moved into their new house near Cherryvale, Kansas in the spring of 1871. It was built in a small hollow at the end of a long vale in the prairie. Near by was a stream, Drum Creek, bordered with thickets of wild plum and of cottonwood trees. The house seems to have had but two rooms, divided by a heavy curtain. The Benders professed to offer entertainment for man and beast: there was a small stock of tinned food and other supplies for sale in the front room; somewhere or other in the house sleeping space was found for travellers who cared to stay all night; while their horses could be sheltered in a stable in the rear. Back of the stable and house were a garden and orchard.

For a year and a half, the Benders seem to have lived the usual life of a family in that region, and to have attracted no especial notice, favourable or otherwise. Many of their neighbours, men and women who were living recently, remember meeting and talking with them. The two younger members of the family were often absent from their wayside tavern for days at a time; John Bender, Jr., on business unexplained, and Professor Miss Kate on her lecturing tours in Parsons, Oswego, Labette, or Chetopa, holding séances for the purpose of calling spirits from the grave; or perhaps exercising her remarkable curative powers upon persons afflicted with blindness, fits, or deafness. It is believed, however, that her most remarkable and permanent cures were effected, not during these visits, but upon patients who came for office consultation and treatment at her residence on the road to the Osage Mission.

It is impossible to determine exactly when it began to be rumoured in the country round about that there was something queer in the Bender ménage. Nearly everything about them and their performances depends upon statements never tested in a court of law; never sifted by cross-examination. Reputable persons can be found making assertions of an exactly opposite nature, and with perfect sincerity. With many people, no form of belief is held so tenaciously as that founded upon nothing more certain than local tradition and impressions acquired in childhood. They simply *know* that certain things are true because they have always been told that they were true. A number of the early adventures of travellers at the Bender house, and a number of fortunate escapes therefrom, sound much like things remembered—with additions—after the event. It is said, probably with truth, that the Benders did not begin their peculiar operations until the autumn of 1872, and that their entire career in the business which made them famous was during a period of about six months. Whatever they did during the autumn and winter of 1872 to 1873 caused no public outcry or investigation. It was not until the disappearance of Doctor York that any general suspicions were aroused.

Early in March, 1873, Dr. William H. York, who lived at Independence, was visiting his brother, Colonel A. M. York, at Fort Scott. On the ninth of the month, he left his brother, intending to ride to his own home. He was well mounted; had a good saddle; and carried a large sum of money and a fine watch. He spent the first night at Osage

Mission, and left there on the morning of March 10th. Some of his friends met him, riding alone, on the road near the Bender house. He told them that he intended to stop for his midday dinner at the Benders'. And that was the last seen of Doctor York.

A considerable time, perhaps as much as two or three weeks, elapsed, and Colonel York was making a determined search for his brother. He traced him to a point on the road a few miles east of the Benders', but could get no farther in his investigations. At Independence he heard rumours of a strange adventure which two other travellers had experienced while dining with the Benders. These men had become convinced that they were about to be attacked; they left the house hurriedly; one of them went to the stable and brought out their carriage, while the other stood with a drawn revolver to cover the retreat. They believed that they were fired at, as they drove away toward the town of Parsons.

Colonel York prevailed upon twelve men from Cherryvale and elsewhere to visit the Bender house with him. They made the call on April 24th and had interviews with all that engaging group. Old Mrs. Bender, it was true, muttered something about a crowd of men disturbing a peaceable family, but the others were affable enough. Young John, who had been sitting by the side of the road with a Bible in his hand, searching the Scriptures, said that he had often been shot at by outlaws near Drum Creek. Doctor York had had dinner with them, Miss Kate had served it; on his departure, he had been foully slain, so the young Mr. Bender believed, by these same audacious bandits. One of the party, believing in spectral aid, asked Professor Miss Kate to consult the spirits, but she replied that there were too many unbelievers present; the spirits would be reluctant to assist. She made an appointment with him for a séance, alone, five days later. The men of the family helped Colonel York and his friends drag Drum Creek and search elsewhere. Altogether, they convinced Colonel York of their desire to aid him and of their ignorance of the fate of his brother. So the Colonel and his followers departed, and came not there again for eleven days.

On May 5th, with a larger number of men, who were still of the opinion that the Benders were somewhat maculate, he returned, to find the neighbours already on the premises. On the day before, May 4th, two brothers named Toles, who lived near by, were passing the Benders' house at eight in the morning. The agonized lowing of a calf attracted them; they found the animal nearly starved in its pen, while its mother was standing outside in as great distress to nourish her child as the calf was to be fed. They turned the two together, and then knocked on the door to see if the folk inside were ill and in need of help. There was no response; they looked in at the windows—the house was empty and in confusion, as if after a hurried departure of the family. This, in fact, had taken place. The Benders left, it is believed, on the night of April 29th, five days after Colonel York's first visit. The house had therefore been abandoned for four or five days.

On Monday, May 5th, when Colonel York and his men arrived, the door had already been broken open and the place was under examination. Aside from the clothing on the floor, household utensils, and "manuscripts" of the lecturer, there was, at first, nothing remarkable to be seen. A trapdoor in the floor of the rear room was opened, and some of the men entered the cellar. This led by a tunnel toward the garden and orchard. On the floor of the cellar were damp spots which seemed to be human blood.

The search had been in progress for some length of time when Colonel York, standing in the rear of the house, and looking toward the orchard, suddenly remarked:

"Boys, I see graves yonder in the orchard!"

They laughed at him, and suggested that he had graves on the brain. Presently others were convinced that there were a number of long, narrow depressions, like graves, in the ground which old Bender had always kept freshly ploughed and harrowed. Soundings were made, with disquieting results, and presently spades were procured and one of the hollows was opened. At a depth of five feet, they discovered the naked body of a man, lying face downward. It was lifted out, and Colonel York's search for his brother was at an end.

Amid great excitement, everybody set to work, and other graves were opened, until the orchard was thoroughly excavated. They found eleven bodies: nine men, a young woman, and a little girl. The skulls of all, except that of the child, had been crushed in one or more places from a blow with some blunt instrument like a sledge hammer. The girl was found lying under the body of her father, and from the absence of any wounds and from other indications, it appeared that she had died by suffocation; had, in fact, been buried alive.

Except for the young woman and one of the men, all the victims were identified, then or later. Three of the men, at least, had been known to be carrying large sums of money. These were a man named McKigzie, and two others, William F. McCrotty and Benjamin M. Brown. The two latter had three thousand dollars between them, so the Benders carried an unknown but considerable amount of loot when they fled. The number of bodies varies in different accounts: to the eleven buried in the orchard are added, by one writer, two or three skeletons afterward discovered in or near Drum Creek and attributed to the work of the Benders. Other authorities set the figure at from seven to ten. The histories of Kansas set the number, conservatively, at seven. The names of the nine in the orchard who were identified are given, however, in more than one published account, so I think that, bearing in mind the counsel of the lady in the play to "be just," we can credit the Bender family with the murders of from ten to twelve persons.

The exact figures did not matter to the men who had carried on the search. When the body was exhumed of Doctor York—a man well liked and respected—and when the pitiful spectacle was revealed of the little girl, evidently put still living into the ground, and buried beneath the dead body of her father, there was an immediate desire for vengeance upon somebody, and the spirit of a lynching mob swept over the group.

The process of the murders became apparent from an examination of the arrangement of the house, together with what could be learned from some of the surviving travellers who had taken a meal there. The diner sat on a bench or chair, with his back to the curtain which separated the two apartments. Sometimes he was entertained with pleasant conversation by whichever of the ladies was serving the meal. This was generally the younger one. One or two of the men of the family, attending behind the curtain with a sledge hammer, could await the moment when the guest, taking his ease, leaned back and showed the outline of his head. Or the curtain was perhaps moved cautiously forward to meet him. The first blow, sufficient to stun him, if not to kill, was then delivered through the curtain. After that, the Benders worked rapidly. The body was dragged to the rear room, robbed and stripped. The trap-door being opened, one of the family cut the victim's throat and tumbled him into the cellar. If this happened by day, all was then secure, until night, when the dead man could be carried to the orchard and buried. Great precautions had been taken to keep the graves from becoming noticeable; these were successful at the time of Colonel York's first visit and nearly successful the second time.

Many stories are told of the part which Professor Miss Kate took, as the meal was served to a traveller. Sometimes she merely charmed him with her good looks, agreeable manners, and light table-talk. If he were docile, and took his chair as she set it, closely snuggled up against the curtain, she became an especially gracious hostess. But if he disliked the arrangement of things, became captious—as we all of us do at times—about the method of seating the guests, she would begin to sulk. Her conversation lost its sparkling qualities, and the dinner was practically a failure, from the point of view of both guest and hostess. One or two suspicious persons had moved to the other side of the table, so as to face the curtain; and two especially nervous gentlemen, who perhaps heard the sound of shuffling feet, and of heavy breathing behind the arras, insisted upon eating their meal standing up—which annoyed the Benders almost to the verge of incivility.

The romantic school, among the Benders' historians, have it that Kate dealt in mesmerism and other psychic methods of allaying suspicion and putting the traveller at his ease. There seems to be little doubt that she conversed with many of them upon spiritualism, and found willing listeners.

The Benders had four or five days' start; they vanished into darkness.

The posse which started in pursuit divided into four

parties; many of these men were veterans of the Civil War; they were skilful, brave, and determined. One party went south toward the Indian Territory: they were seven in number, under command of a former captain in the Union Army. Another party went toward Thayer, Kansas; a third toward Cherryvale and Independence; and a fourth toward Parsons and thence to Oswego. Three of these groups returned in a few days, in the belief that the Benders had escaped. The Captain and his seven men came back from the Indian Territory saying that they had given up the chase. They instantly dropped the subject and would never talk about the Benders again. To some persons, this fact was indication that they had caught and lynched the whole family.

In favour of the theory that they were caught are the character and skill of the men who went in pursuit, the fact that no satisfactory trace of the Benders was ever found again, and the statements of the police chiefs of Cherryvale and Independence. To account for the singular and unnecessary silence about their success, it has been said that when the Benders were captured they were carrying seven thousand dollars. Their captors decided that this was prize money, and after the Benders were "laid under the ground," divided it amongst themselves. To avoid any further discussion about the ownership of this money, they agreed upon complete silence and kept their agreement.

Against the theory of the capture and in favour of the belief that the Benders got away, it may be urged, first, that they had a long start. Second, there was no reason for reticence if anybody did catch the fugitives—lynching the Benders would not have imperilled anybody's popularity. Next, in 1880, the Commissioners of Labette County offered a reward of $500 for proof that they were taken and put to death. The reward was not claimed. Finally, there were found, as late as 1889, a number of reputable citizens, willing to take oath that they recognized two living women as Mrs. Bender and Kate. It is true that they were quite mistaken in this identification, but the fact shows that these persons, who had known the Benders, did not believe that the whole family had been exterminated.

—E.P.

# 8

# LIZZIE BORDEN
## Far from the Old Folks at Home

For sheer Alpine altitude in the illustrative peaks of crime, the blood-stained palm goes to Miss Lizzie Borden of Fall River, Massachusetts, and her inseparable symbol, the hatchet. Nineteenth-century murder without Lizzie Borden is like Heloïse *sans* Abélard, Dr. Johnson minus Boswell, or "Turkey in the Straw" without a fiddle. Lizzie isn't an example of nineteenth-century murder, she *is* nineteenth-century murder—a study in scarlet filtered to a pretty pastel pink by Victoriphobia.

In 1892, Fall River, Massachusetts, was an ugly but productive cotton-mill town of some 75,000 people. There was definitely a right and wrong side of the track, because a foreign-born element had moved in to labour on the business enterprises of the native born. It was one of those towns buttressed with community spirit that might be called nosiness by the uncharitable, and it had its own aristocracy of old Yankee families who defied the contamination of Boston or New York.

One of these families was that of Andrew J. Borden. He was one of Fall River's leading citizens. A home-town boy who made good, he started his business career as an undertaker, and, by a high death rate and caution with the dollar, in 1892 Andrew Borden was worth over a quarter of a million dollars. He was president of a bank, an owner of profitable real-estate holdings. This tall, slightly stooped, white-haired New England magnate was scrupulous and upright in his business dealings, but he was a fatally slow man with the buck. He was not above bringing a basket of eggs from one of his farms to sell in town. Although his one great love affair was with money, he married twice. His first wife obediently produced two daughters and died, and, at forty, Mr. Borden took a second wife—a palpitating, grateful spinster named Abby Gray.

For the past twenty years Andrew Borden had lived in a narrow frame house with the second Mrs. Borden and the two daughters of the former marriage. Ninety-two, Second Street was in a neighbourhood that had seen better days, and Andrew Borden's house was situated on a narrow lot, hemmed in by other narrow houses and set almost flush with a busily trafficked street. Downstairs there was a sitting-room, dining-room, parlour and kitchen, while upstairs there was the master bedroom, a dressing-room for Mrs. Borden, separate bedrooms for each of the two daughters, and a guest room.

Andrew Borden was seventy with a lean, chipped-away, Grant Wood look. Abby Borden was sixty-four, short, and weighed a regrettable two hundred pounds, Miss Lizzie was thirty-two, a plump, unmarried lady with rimless eyeglasses who liked to try recipes, put bird houses in the garden, and read best sellers like *When Knighthood Was in Flower* and *Alice of Old Vincennes*. She was secretary to the Christian Endeavor Society, belonged to the Fruit and Flower Mission, and was active in the Women's Christian Temperance Union. She also taught a Sunday-school class and had made the grand tour of Europe in 1890. And Lizzie was a young lady with a mind of her own who took a very dim view of some of her father's convictions. She wanted to entertain lavishly, and she wanted a modern bathroom. To Andrew Borden the former was extravagant frivolity; the latter was downright decadent. Emma Borden, although nine years older than

Lizzie, was like the negative to Lizzie's positive. She was much less active in church work, her tastes were much simpler, and she was caught up in the apathy of spinsterhood. The fifth resident at 92 Second Street was Bridget Sullivan, the pert, Irish maid-of-all-work.

It was a portrait of New England home life in the nineties. Andrew Borden was one of those I'll-damn-well-have-the-final-word domestic patriarchs. Mrs. Borden, although a stepmother, seems to have gone about her household chores and domestic relations in an aura of unquestioning good will and easygoing plumpness. There was nothing of the "heavy" stepmother about her—except her weight. The two daughters of the house went their rounds of tranquil social life and light domestic duties. If it was a dour household, it was a righteous one, and what the Bordens lacked in humour or gaiety they made up for by relentless virtue and paying their bills on time. But, as in so many cases, this accepted picture of middle-class life had unexpected lights and shadows that blurred the focus, and the home that framed this portrait of domesticity was actually a house divided.

It is unhappy to relate that the two maiden ladies constantly squabbled with their father over property, money, and their standard of living. The girls, particularly Lizzie, wanted luxury—frosting on the cake. Andrew was content with life's necessities. And when Mr. Borden showed signs of helping his wife's stepsister financially, a restrained sort of hell broke loose. Lizzie expressed grim displeasure by ceasing to call stepmother "Mother" and, if forced to speak to her at all, called her "Mrs. Borden". The two sisters took their meals at pointedly different times than the old couple, and Lizzie even referred to the harmless Abby Borden as a "mean old thing" on several occasions, a statement that still stands unsupported, as so many of Lizzie's pronouncements do.

The floor plan of the house further strained relations. The upstairs could be split into two separate parts by closing one communicating door, so that the master bedroom and dressing-room could only be reached by the back stairs, the bedrooms of the two daughters and the guest room by the front stairs. The bad feeling seems to have been unanimous. The bolts were drawn on both sides of the crucial communicating door, permanently.

Late in July 1892, Emma Borden went to visit friends in Fairhaven. Lizzie went to New Bedford for a visit but only remained a few days and returned home. On August third, Fall River was in the middle of a suffocating heat wave, but the sweltering monotony was broken by three interesting events. John Vinnicum Morse, a brother of the first Mrs. Borden, arrived at 92 Second Street for a short visit. He found Mr. and Mrs. Borden recovering from a sick spell the night before. They told him Lizzie had also been mildly affected. Miss Lizzie, in spite of the heat, went out on an errand that afternoon. She went to the pharmacy and tried to purchase prussic acid to clean a sealskin cape. The druggist refused to sell her such a potent dry cleaner, but Lizzie was never one to be easily discouraged. Eli Bence and two other drug clerks later identified Lizzie as the would-be purchaser, but she flatly said she wasn't. Then, Lizzie visited a neighbour and family friend, Miss Alice Russell, and carried on like the voice of doom. She told Miss Russell of the daylight robbery that had taken place last year, of the Bordens' illness of the previous evening. She was afraid the milk might be intentionally poisoned.

She feared her father had enemies, the barn had been broken into twice. She was afraid an anonymous *they* "would burn the house down over us", and her last word on the subject was: "I feel something hanging over me, and I can't throw it off." Miss Russell suggested the barn might have been broken into by boys chasing pigeons. As for the other gloomy forebodings, she had no answer. It was probably too hot to cope with such things. Most of this sounds like conversational heat lightening, but one statement was based on fact, not humidity. There had been a daylight burglary at the Borden home in June 1891. Mr. Borden's desk had been broken open, and he was relieved of eighty dollars in bank notes, twenty-five to thirty dollars in gold, some streetcar tickets, a watch and chain, and some small trinkets. His thrifty soul outraged, Mr. Borden called in the police, who looked helplessly at the ravished desk and nodded sagely when Miss Lizzie said the cellar door was opened and *they* might have come in that way. However, a few days later Andrew Borden told City Marshal Hilliard: "I am afraid the police will not be able to find the real thief." Whether it was some inflection of voice, the curious choice of the word "real", or his uncharacteristic readiness to abandon the inquiry, there was a definite feeling at the local precinct that Mr. Borden was not entirely in doubt as to the robber's identity.

At the trial, Lizzie's lawyer blamed the curious conversation with Alice Russell on her monthly female condition. In the neo-Lydia Pinkham era this was a shrewd gambit, and Lizzie, at the inquest, used her condition as a neat bit of insurance just in case any blood was found on her clothes. The assertions about poison were probably wishful thinking about her disappointment at the drug store. The milk and the stomachs of Mr. and Mrs. Borden all registered negative on poison tests made after the tragedy.

On August fourth, life at 92 Second Street started out in a routine swelter. Mr. and Mrs. Borden and Mr. Morse ate a truly terrifying breakfast at seven, prepared and served by Bridget. There are many elements of horror in the Borden case, but one of the worst was the August fourth breakfast—mutton, sugar cakes, coffee, and mutton broth. Bridget was later ill in the backyard, and if she ate that breakfast she deserved it.

By 9:15, Mr. Morse had left the house to visit relatives. Mr. Borden set out to make a few business calls, defying the heat in an inferno-like, black broadcloth suit. Miss Lizzie had come downstairs and was in the kitchen, sensibly sipping a frugal cup of coffee, while Bridget washed the breakfast dishes. Mrs. Borden asked Bridget to wash the first-floor windows inside and out and said she was going to put fresh pillowcases on the pillows in the guest room. Bridget got her pail, brushes, and cloths and went out through the side door, leaving it unlocked. She talked over the fence to Mrs. Kelly's girl for a few minutes and then started sudsing her way methodically round the house. It took an hour, and, as she washed, she looked in each ground-floor room and never saw anyone. Mrs. Borden and Lizzie were inside, and it is evident from later medical testimony that Mrs. Borden experienced the abomination of foreseeing her own death and knowing her executioner before blood and blackness engulfed her life and her world.

Bridget came in the house, locked the side door, and started washing the windows inside. At about 10:45, Mr. Borden pounded on the front door. He had forgotten his key, and that was no light matter if you lived at the Borden house. It was a veritable Bastille. The side and back doors were wooden and locked and they both had screen doors with hooks on them, the front door had three fastenings—a spring latch, a bolt, and a lock which operated by key—and Bridget had to let Mr. Borden in.

As she fumbled at the three locks, there was a laugh, which has been described in terms running the gamut from "low and amused" to "high and maniacal". Whatever it sounded like, there was no doubt where it came from. Bridget turned around and saw Miss Lizzie standing at the head of the staircase a few feet from the open door of the guest room. Lizzie came down the stairs and told her father: "Mrs. Borden has gone out. She had a note from someone who is sick." Mr. Borden took the key to his bedroom from a shelf, went up the back stairs to his bedroom and a few minutes later came downstairs and went in the sitting-room to rest. He took off his coat and, as further proof that New Englanders are impervious to the weather, put on a cardigan jacket before he stretched out on the couch to rest. He lay on his right side with his congress shoes hanging over the side on the floor. He was in the same position less than an hour later, but he wasn't in such good condition.

In the meantime, Bridget was washing the windows in the dining-room and Lizzie joined her there to start ironing handkerchiefs. Bridget went into the kitchen to wash out her cloths, and Miss Lizzie followed her: "There's a cheap sale of dress goods on downtown. They are selling some kind of cloth at 8 cents a yard."

But Bridget was not to be tempted by the vanities of the world. She had been up since six, she had been sick, and the heat was shimmering in a haze off the street. Bridget decided to go up and rest for a few minutes before lunch. Lunch was to be cold mutton and mutton soup, which makes death lose some of its sting.

Bridget lay down in her attic room and heard the clock strike eleven. Fifteen or twenty minutes later Lizzie called up to her, "Come down quick. Father's dead. Somebody came in and killed him."

Bridget was sent for the doctor. Dr. Bowen, an old friend of the Borden family, found Andrew Borden lying on his side on the couch, his head thoroughly bashed in, blood all over his face. The wounds, it was later proved, were caused by a sharp instrument dealt by a person of ordinary strength and inflicted from behind. But at the moment, the chief fact that struck Dr. Bowen was that the face of his old friend was "hardly to be recognized by one who knew him".

The neighbours, including Mrs. Addie Churchill from next door and Alice Russell, the police, and a curious crowd had gathered with disaster-inspired speed, and Dr. Bowen left to send Miss Emma a wire in Fairhaven. By the time Dr. Bowen returned to the house, Bridget and Mrs. Churchill had found Mrs. Borden, adrift in her own blood on the floor of the guest room. And it was written literally in blood that Miss Emma and Miss Lizzie were inheritors of $175,000 each. Coagulation, and lack of it, showed that Abby Borden went to her reward a good ninety minutes before her husband.

In a montage of curiosity, heated discussion, and growing suspicion on the part of the police, the funeral and the inquest took place. Miss Lizzie, so clearheaded and composed during the nerve-racking morning hours of August fourth, a pillar of strength to those who had come to comfort her, at the inquest, under the questioning of District Attorney Hosea Knowlton, became confused and snappish by turn, and she literally just didn't know where she was on the crucial morning. Seven days after the murders, Lizzie Borden was arrested for the murders of her stepmother and father. And the world became "Lizzie conscious". Coffee and conversation percolated with equal heat at the nation's breakfast tables, and the question was hotly asked and hotly answered, "How could a woman do such a thing?" Some people thought it impossible, but some nasty-minded sceptics thought it was not only possible, it was highly probable. But Lizzie had moral support from Lucy Stone and her following of suffragettes. Mrs. Susan Fessenden and the W.C.T.U. got behind Lizzie, and she had physical as well as moral support from her pastors, Reverend Buck and Reverend Jubb. She usually made her appearances leaning on the arm of one or the other. "Unfortunate girl . . . innocent . . . persecuted . . . harshly treated" were adjectives and phrases that were loosely bandied about, until it seemed as if the Commonwealth of Massachusetts should be indicted and tried for their treatment of Lizzie Borden.

Children in the street chanted, "Mr. Borden he is dead, . . . Lizzie hit him on the head." And one of the barbershop witticisms of the time was: "What did Lizzie Borden say when someone asked her what time it was? 'I don't know, but I'll go axe Father.'"

So Lizzie added variety to an already spicy situation by the quantity of answers she gave to the increasingly pertinent question: "Where were you when it happened, Miss Lizzie?" She always had a ready answer, each one different. She told Dr. Bowen she was out in the yard when she heard a groan. Mrs. Churchill was informed, "I went to the barn to get a piece of iron. I heard a distressing noise and came back and found the screen door open." She told Patrolman Harrington she was in the loft of the barn and heard nothing. The loft was examined and found to contain a pristine layer of dust untouched by human hand or foot. It was so hot in the loft, the patrolman had to leave gasping for air after a few minutes. But "Asbestos Liz" swore she had been there about twenty minutes. To Miss Russell she again gave the "looking for a piece of iron to mend a screen door" version. Now, these variations could be excused on the grounds of excitement and confusion, but at the inquest, Miss Lizzie claimed she strolled in from the barn, casually took off her hat, and accidentally discovered her father's body. There's just too much variation between hearing a noise and running in to find your father hacked to bits and hearing nothing and coming upon the disaster accidentally. Also the point was brought up that if Lizzie thought someone had come in and killed her father as she said to Bridget, it was either extremely foolhardy or extremely courageous to stand in the hall, just a few feet from where fresh blood spilled and reeked, and call up to Bridget. Rushing out on the street, away from the carnage, would have seemed more likely. Her account at inquest of her activities during the time between Mr. and Mrs. Borden's deaths was just as erratic. She gave the lie to the axiom that a person can't be in two places at the same time. She was reading an old *Harper's* magazine in the kitchen, and she was upstairs in her room sewing a piece of tape on a dress.

Then there was the curious question of Miss Lizzie's elastic wardrobe. At the inquest, she testified that she wore a blue-and-white-stripe dress the morning of the murders but changed to a pink wrapper after somebody told her to. (The case crawls with anonymous collective nouns.) Nobody admitted giving this bit of advice. Both Bridget and Emma Borden said Lizzie was in the habit of wearing a cotton dress of light blue with darker-blue figure in the mornings. At the trial, Dr. Bowen confusedly described Lizzie as wearing a drab-coloured calico-type dress. Mrs. Churchill said Lizzie was wearing a light-blue cotton with a darker-blue shape. However, when Lizzie was asked by the police to turn over to them the dress she wore on the morning of the murder, she handed them a dark-blue silk dress which she had been wearing during the morning since the murder. Shown the dress at the trial, Dr. Bowen had no resort to the indecisive word "drab". "I should call it a dark blue." Mrs. Churchill when confronted with the dark-blue silk reluctantly admitted that: "I did not see her with that on that morning."

Then Alice Russell, torn between friendship and conscience, finally told the following story. After a visit Saturday night following the murders from the mayor, who warned Miss Lizzie she was under suspicion, Miss Russell found Lizzie in the kitchen on Sunday morning, burning a lightblue, cotton-cord dress with a dark figure. Emma Borden at the trial said there was paint on it, and she had urged Lizzie to burn the dress. However, police officers who had searched the house said they never saw a dress smeared with paint, and Miss Russell saw no paint on the portion of the dress Lizzie was burning. Lizzie's militant advocates were delighted when the news came out that Lizzie seemed to be the one Borden in the house without blood on her the morning of August fourth. It was proof of her pure innocence. However, the story of the dress could knock the props out of this. Miss Lizzie had some sort of a blue-and-white cotton dress that she was in the habit of wearing in the morning. She was wearing it the morning of the murder, according to witnesses. However, after the murders she changes into a pink wrapper, and for the next few mornings wears a dark-blue silk dress, which she turns over to the police when they request the dress she wore on the morning of the murder. She is found burning a dress that resembles the one she wore on August fourth—after she is told that she is under suspicion. She says she wore the blue-silk dress, which is produced in court. Witnesses say it is not the dress she wore. Emma says the burned dress had paint on it, Lizzie says it had paint on it. Police say there was no paint-stained dress present when they examined the clothes.

The problem of blood could have been easily taken care of after the first murder. There was ample tidying up time, since Bridget was outside washing windows for about an hour. As to the second murder, where time was more tricky, one look at an extant photograph of Mr. Borden's body as it was found gives a pretty adequate idea of what could have happened. The couch on which he was lying was directly to the side of the sitting-room door, against the wall. With Mr. Borden lying on his side, the back of his head would have been to the door and the murderer could merely have reached an arm and an aiming eye around the door and started banging away. If a few spots of blood were later discovered on the sleeve of the dress, they wouldn't have been obvious to excited eyes, but might have been apparent if tested, so the dress was disposed of just in case. The other theories of Lizzie stripped to the buff or Lizzie in some sort of all-enveloping waterproof garment gave colour to the conjectures of the time, but they don't hold water. Even if Lizzie had betrayed her Puritan upbringing by hacking her father to death without any clothes on, she wouldn't have had time to get dressed again, considering what the ladies of the 1890s considered "dressed". Nothing resembling a waterproof garment was ever found.

But whatever theory was believed, there was one certainty in the whole mixed-up matter of Lizzie's dress: Alice Russell was crossed off the Borden Christmas-card list. There was nebulous gossip, too, about Lizzie's lover. The leading candidates were a non-materializing young man she was supposed to have met during her European trip and a shadowy clergyman. But there was never any tangible proof of a romance in Lizzie's life. Like her spiritual ancestress, Elizabeth I of England, she died wearing the righteous if unwelcome crown of virginity, and any tangible lover remained conspicuous by his absence.

There was also the matter of the note Mrs. Borden received. Protestors of Lizzie's innocence were faced with the uncomfortable fact that not only did the sick person never come forward, but the messenger also disappeared from the face of the earth. Lizzie's lawyers never made too much of that. The law takes little notice of anything other than the first, second, and third dimensions, and with the eyes of the town, the country, and the world turned on Lizzie, the sick friend and the messenger boy must have indeed been fourth-dimensional characters not to come forth.

On a warm June day in 1893, the thirteen-day wonder, noted in legal documents and court transcripts as the Trial of Lizzie Borden, opened in New Bedford. It was held in a bare, white-walled room with chairs, desks, and settees. The three superior court judges required by law wore regular business suits and fanned themselves with palm-leaf fans. Thirty or forty members of the press, including representatives from the *New York Sun* and the Boston *Globe*, were poised to rush news to a breathless, waiting world, and finally Lizzie Borden made her entrance in the grand manner. Walking sedately, flanked by Reverends Buck and Jubb, she wore a new, stylish black mohair dress with leg-of-mutton sleeves and a black lace hat with rosettes of blue velvet and a blue feather for properly subdued dash.

Mr. Hosea Knowlton and Mr. William Moody conducted a fair, accurate case for the commonwealth. Under more ordinary, less emotional circumstances they had a case as strong as that which has sent many protesting innocents to their final reckoning with state executioners and the Almighty. The trial revealed little news, although Mrs. Hannah Reagan, the matron of the Fall River Police Station, heard the following conversation between Emma and Lizzie Borden: "Emma," said Lizzie, "You have given me away."

"No, Lizzie, I have not," was the reply.

But Lizzie insisted: "You have; and I will let you see I won't give an inch."

It's cryptic conversation, to put it mildly, and, as it stands so starkly without any context, it is open to all sorts of interpretations. However, Reverend Buck made it seem more important than it actually was, when he visited Mrs. Reagan and tried to get her to sign a statement retracting her story of the conversation. It is gratifying to learn that Mrs. Reagan refused to sign the retraction, and Reverend Jubb, a vehement and vocal champion of Lizzie's innocence, was told by the Fall River officials in no uncertain terms to mind his own business.

A gruesome touch was added when a plaster cast of Mr. Borden's head with appropriate blue marks to indicate the wounds was introduced as part of the medical testimony, and Miss Emma Borden snatched the headlines from Lizzie for one golden moment. Miss Lizzie entrenched herself on her constitutional rights as firmly and eagerly as any object of a twentieth-century Senate investigation, and her sole statement has a familiar ring. "I am innocent. I leave my counsel to speak for me."

The only time Lizzie had really run into trouble was during District Attorney Knowlton's merciless barrage of questions at the inquest. She had withdrawn from this encounter bruised and punchy. She wasn't about to get back in the ring for another sparring session with the question-happy District Attorney, and Emma Borden was an ideal substitute. She could testify on everything that happened before and after the murder, but she could not be cross-examined about the morning of August fourth. Emma came out strongly on her sister's side and said it was she who had urged Lizzie to burn the controversial dress.

The commonwealth based its case not only on the fact that Lizzie had the opportunity and motive but the question, "Was there an opportunity for anyone else?" There was no sign of housebreaking, no struggle, nothing taken. They were hampered by the exclusion of both the pharmacists' testimony on Lizzie's abortive attempt to obtain prussic acid and Lizzie's suspect inquest testimony. The other weaknesses of the Commonwealth's case were the inability to prove that the axe found in the Borden home was the murder weapon, even though it showed signs of recent washings and scrubbings with ashes and fitted the length of the wounds by an exact three-and-one-half inches; and not being able to come up with conclusive evidence that the blue dress Lizzie wore was the same one that met a fiery end in the Bordens' kitchen stove. Otherwise, the prosecution anticipated Dragnet by fifty years and presented the facts, clearly and damningly. It was an appeal to the intellect.

As for the defence, it was more colourful, if less cred-itable, and Lizzie had an ideal legal figure in her lawyer. Ex-Governor of Massachusetts, George Robinson was a shrewd Yankee who knew the value of the cracker-barrel approach on a New England jury. Lizzie was her own worst enemy geographically. She was flitting all over the house that morning—upstairs, downstairs, in my lady's chamber—and yet in this narrow house with its communicating doors and thin partitions, the defence maintained, there was a very tangible messenger of death, slaughtering Mrs. Borden in her own guest bedroom, waiting in a small closet yet leaving no trace of blood or physical presence for an hour and a half until Andrew Borden decided to come home and lie down and take a nap. This hypothetical killer then struck again, took the hatchet down to the basement and got out of the house without being seen by Bridget or Lizzie, then walked down Second Street invisible to all the neighbours and off into some fiendish limbo.

Lizzie's guilt might have violated every Victorian precept of gently nurtured female, but the story of her defence violated every known limitation of time and space. Ex-Governor Robinson's closing speech for the defence typifies his whole argument: "To find her guilty, you must believe she is a fiend. Gentlemen, does she look it?"

The jury looked at her, the tasteful clothes, the rimless spectacles, the air of gentility, backed by her pastors and her family, and they brought in a verdict of not guilty.

After the jury congratulated the vindicated darling of the Women's Christian Temperance League, to a man they headed for the nearest hotel bar to celebrate a job well done.

Lizzie may not have been the most beautiful or the sexiest lady ever to flutter a courtroom, but she was the luckiest: She got acquitted. Today a great gulf yawns deep and wide between the jury that acquitted Lizzie Borden and the lawyers, writers, and crime fanciers who study the case. Faced with the fiction of a church-working spinster who couldn't even have such a thing as murder enter her pure thoughts and the fact that no one else could have done it, the Borden jury bought the whole fiction package. It was dogma in 1892 that a woman couldn't do such a thing, but twentieth-century courts are more sceptical and have been known to hand down verdicts where looks gave way to facts and have indicated that moral turpitude does not guarantee the difference between guilt and innocence on a capital charge.

Anna Marie Hahn looked like a comfortable "Cincinnati Dutch" housewife, but the mortality rate of old men she loved and left landed her in the electric chair. Mr. Chine, the ex-choir singer, appeared like a harmless little man addicted to buttermilk, until he started cremating his wives with undue haste. Major Armstrong was the spit-and-polish image of military propriety, but he bought too much arsenic to take care of his dandelion problems. James P. Watson, alias "Bluebeard"—and that was no courtesy title with sixteen wives unaccounted for—was a mild-spoken, highly successful businessman who was tenderhearted and easily moved to tears. Louise Peete was the epitome of refinement, but corpses kept turning up with embarrassing regularity wherever she lived. And Dr. Alice Wynekoop, well-known doctor, club woman, and social worker, just couldn't account for her daughter-in-law's body in her examining room. None of these ladylike or gentlemanly paragons were acquitted.

There has been no change or developments in the Borden case since the warm June day when the daughter of the house was acquitted to wild cheers and hosannas. There were, indeed, dark hints about a jet-propelled Emma Borden quickly sneaking into her home and then flashing back to Fairhaven. John Vinnicum Morse came in for his share of dark mutterings, but both his alibi and that of Miss Emma were checked and not found wanting. Bridget has been mentioned as a suspect. But she had a good character, was contented with her job, and it was unlikely that she would put such a strain on employer-employee relationships. Also Miss Lizzie was Bridget's alibi, as she could never be Miss Lizzie's.

There was, of course, the usual rash of wild-eyed men, maniacs waving hatchets that dripped with blood in broad daylight, and deathbed confessions—all adding up to a big fat zero.

Miss Lizzie and Miss Emma moved to a larger, more spacious home about a mile and a half from Second Street, and it is to be hoped that it had a modern bathroom after all the sisters had been through. In February 1897, Lizzie hit the front pages again. "Lizzie Borden again. A warrant for her Arrest has been issued. Two Paintings missed from Tilden-Thurber Company's store. Said to have been traced to Miss Borden's Home in Fall River." No more is heard of this matter except that an "adjustment was made out of court". It brings to mind the burglary of 1891.

Lizzie lived on in Fall River in her fine new home. She preferred Washington and Boston, where she was an inveterate theatregoer. She seldom patronized Fall River stores and was not seen on the streets of the town except for brief glimpses of her in her carriage and later her motor car. At any rate, guilty or innocent, it seems that Lizzie, who changed her name to Lizabeth A. Borden, didn't win any popularity polls in her home town. She loved the theatre and seemed to have a school-girl crush on a favourite Boston tragedienne, Nance O'Neil. She shocked Fall River by throwing a big party for Miss O'Neil after a local performance, and there is an even more amazing record that she rented a house at Tyngsboro and entertained Miss O'Neil and her company for an entire week, an almost Roman entertainment for a gentle New England spinster. Evidently, all this was too much for Emma. She left Fall River shortly after this saturnalia and was heard of no more until she and Lizzie got into a legal hassle over the sale of a building from the estate in 1923.

And that's the story of Lizabeth A. Borden, who lived happily until her death in 1927. On 1 June 1927, Lizzie died at her home in Fall River, and on 10 June of the same year, Emma died at Newmarket, New Hampshire. Lizzie left an estate of $266,000 to friends, relatives, and the Animal Rescue League.

Lizzie was not only lucky to get acquitted. She did herself comfortable—to use a local expression—with her home, cars, trips and theatre jaunts, but it all has that "company look" of dutiful smiles and empty conversation. Did the bloodstained images of Second Street ever gibber idiotically at her memory? Did the wet footprints of the past walk through her mind? There's no way of knowing. Her life after the double murder appeared as placid, although more independent and luxurious, as it had been before the one violent eruption in continuity, and the dark truth lies under a tombstone at the foot of Andrew Borden's grave, marked simply Lizabeth A. Borden.

But she belongs to the world, and it has given her an epitaph in poetry, not in stone:

> *Lizzie Borden took an axe,*
> *Gave her mother forty whacks.*
> *When she saw what she had done,*
> *She gave her father forty-one.*

Lizzie is a legend. The axe is immortal, and for those interested in the influence of heredity, Lizzie inherited the right to use the Borden coat of arms from her ancestors, Joan and Richard Borden, who pioneered in the locale of Portsmouth, Rhode Island, around 1638. The coat of arms is a "Lion Rampant, holding a Battle-Axe, proper".

—D.D.

# 9

# CORDELIA BOTKIN
## The Poisoned Chocolate Case

Had she lived in another age and a less restricted society—say, the Court of Louis XIV, or Borgian Rome—Cordelia Botkin of Stockton, California, might have enjoyed glittering triumphs. But Destiny chose to plank her down in the rump-end of the nineteenth century, and, for all her tenacity, she achieved only a friable romance and a convict's cell.

Paltry rewards, they nevertheless reflect her potentialities. Though well across the threshold of maturity, she managed to captivate a cavalier ten years younger and keep his devotion at white heat for six years. For this battle her only weapons were determination, a fine pair of eyelashes, and the type of figure then fashionable, of which it has been said, "One could span her waist with one's hand, but one couldn't place her fundament in a wash tub."

Mrs. Botkin's story properly begins one smiling June afternoon in San Francisco's Golden Gate Park, where, gaily arrayed and in a mood for adventure, she was sunning herself on a bench. Adventure soon appeared in the rakish person of Mr. John Dunning, an Associated Press war correspondent, who, though married only a year, was, like the poet's daughter, not averse. Mrs. Botkin fluttered her gentian-like lashes. Mr. Dunning smiled and raised his dicer. Presently they were sitting side by side.

They exchanged biographies. Mrs. Botkin coyly sliced five years from her age, which was thirty-eight, and introduced herself as Mrs. Cornish. Her husband, she hastened to add, was in England on business. Later, in a splurge of frankness, she admitted that Mr. Botkin—Welcome C. Botkin, to put down the full, happy name—and a grown son were no further away than the next county. Formerly a Kansas City bank official, Mr. Botkin had removed to Stockton. He was neither observant nor suspicious and Mrs. Botkin found ample opportunity for gallant adventures. The Botkins had been married twenty years.

With equal honesty, Mr. Dunning confessed to being a newspaper correspondent, latterly at leisure for lack of a first-class war. The year before he had married Miss Mary Pennington, daughter of Delaware's Congressman John Pennington. There was a baby daughter.

From that informal meeting blossomed a lively romance. Mrs. Botkin agreed to abandon her husband altogether and live in an apartment on Geary Street in San Francisco, which Mr. Dunning furnished. For convenience he took rooms in the same building.

Meantime, Mrs. Dunning began fretting over her husband's absences. Her suspicions were quickened by a letter from the usual "well-wishing friend." Wounded to the core, she swept up her baby and headed East for Congressman Pennington's home in Dover.

Far from distressing her wayward husband, this merely gave him more time to spend with Mrs. Botkin. Their relationship became overt. They showed themselves everywhere, at the races, in restaurants, theaters and cabarets.

So matters progressed for six years before a rift in the lute. At forty-four, Mrs. Botkin's ardor was still at par, but her charms had noticeably declined. By swift, relentless marches she passed from full-blown to over-blown, and her admirer grew restless.

His roving eye began casting about for less ripened companions. Shortly he was seeking a gentlemanly way to break with Mrs. Botkin. But he was soon made to realize that the lady would not give him up without a struggle.

As the situation became critical, the Associated Press came to the rescue with an assignment in Puerto Rico. Secretly rejoicing, but with a convincing show of regret, he bussed Mrs. Botkin good-by. To his dismay she offered to accompany him to the ends of the earth, if necessary. Mr. Dunning perceived the need of brutal frankness.

"I am going alone," he declared flatly. "I do not plan to return to California—ever. As a matter of fact, I hope Mrs. Dunning will have me back."

Let us decently lower the curtain upon the ensuing scene. It raged for days, reaching a fine climactic frenzy on the eve of parting. She pursued him across the Bay like a Fury. On the station platform she made her last stand, releasing him only after a blistering exchange of venom.

As the train finally chuffed away, the decamping lover almost sobbed with relief. He probably felt like a hunter freed from the embraces of a hungry python. But if he fancied that Cordelia Botkin could no longer touch him, he was gravely mistaken.

On the afternoon of August 9, 1898, four months after Mr. Dunning left for the West Indies, John Deane, Congressman Pennington's little grandson by his eldest daughter, pattered down to the Dover post office to fetch some letters and a small package which had arrived by registered mail from California. The package was addressed to his aunt, Mrs. Dunning.

After supper the members of the Pennington household—Mrs. Dunning, her sister, Mrs. Deane, and their children (Congressman Pennington was away)—went out to the cool verandah, and proceeded to open their mail.

The package for Mrs. Dunning contained a small box of chocolate creams wrapped in a silk handkerchief. A note read: "Love to yourself and baby. Mrs. C."

Mrs. Dunning was puzzled. During her unhappy residence in California, she had made many friends, but she recalled no name beginning in C. Assuming her to be someone with a better memory than hers, Mrs. Dunning passed the box to her sister and the two eager children.

As they sat contentedly munching the goodies, two estimable Dover spinsters, the Misses Milligan and Bateman strolled by. Mrs. Dunning invited them to share her gift and each ate two or three chocolates before resuming the evening promenade. The children were restricted to one apiece. But before retiring their mothers depleted the box by half. It was then almost midnight.

Toward dawn Mrs. Dunning awoke with racking stomach cramps. She staggered into the bathroom only to find Mrs. Deane and the children ahead of her. They, too, had awful pains. Before collapsing, Mrs. Dunning managed to summon the family doctor. He arrived with stomach pumps and appropriate antidotes.

Later in the day it developed that the Misses Milligan and Bateman had suffered similar agonies, but their symptoms were less malignant and they recovered. So did the two children. But not Mrs. Dunning and Mrs. Deane. On the 11th they both perished miserably.

The connection between these seizures and the mysterious box of chocolate creams was irresistible. Autopsies revealed huge quantities of white arsenic in the viscera of the departed ladies, while uneaten candies proved to be loaded with the nasty stuff. Plainly the sisters had been murdered, but by whose hand or from what motives eluded the police.

John Dunning's timely return from Puerto Rico cleared

up everything. He glanced at Mrs. C's note, and, convulsed with shame and remorse, confessed his six-year liaison.

"That note," he concluded, "is in Cordelia Botkin's hand!"

Detectives left at once for Stockton, where the lady was once more living peacefully with Welcome Botkin. They booked her for murder and went ahunting more evidence.

Mrs. Botkin had shown an appalling lack of attention to detail. A visit to Mr. George Haas's sweet shop disclosed that a lady answering her description had purchased some chocolate creams ten days before the Dover catastrophe. Mr. Haas remembered her request for a fancy box without the shop's name and her explanation that she wished to wrap it in a handkerchief.

Another oversight had been the price-tag on the handkerchief, so that the detectives easily traced it to a linen shop whose clerks identified Mrs. Botkin.

The most useful witness was one of the prisoner's dearest friends, who testified that during some tea-table chit-chat Mrs. Botkin had asked (1) what was the action of arsenic, (2) must one sign one's name to mail a registered package.

A canvass of San Francisco's drug stores ended in the Owl Pharmacy, whose owner furnished that piquant detail without which no poison mystery is complete: the purchaser's reason for requiring arsenic. A fat volume, a sort of poison-shopper's guide, could be filled with these pretexts. They range from the conventional war on rats to beauty preparations. Mrs. Botkin said she wanted arsenic to clean a hat. The pharmacist suggested less deadly, but more effective compounds. Mrs. Botkin held out for arsenic.

Handwriting experts produced more proof by comparing the note in the candy box with Mrs. Botkin's impassioned letters to Mr. Dunning.

But the clincher was one of those wild happenstances which no novelist would attempt. The clerk at the ferry post office in San Francisco happened to be named John Dunnigan. When Mrs. Botkin handed him a package addressed to Mrs. John Dunning the similarity of the two names so stuck in his memory that he was later able to make a positive identification.

On December 9, 1898 Cordelia Botkin went to trial before Supreme Court Justice Cook. Star witness was the desolated Mr. Dunning, who gallantly refused to divulge the names of his other lady friends and was shunted off to jail for contempt. This affected Mrs. Botkin's situation neither one way nor the other. She was sentenced to hard labor.

Under California's penal system Mrs. Botkin was able to exercise her remarkable latent talents. Prisoners were not compelled to serve sentence in the State Penitentiary, but could remain in any jail within county jurisdiction. Thus, pending her appeal, Mrs. Botkin occupied a cell in San Francisco.

Three months after he sentenced her, Justice Cook was riding on a horse-car when a smartly tailored woman attracted his notice. Turning pale with shock, he stared into the limpid eyes of Cordelia Botkin. Before he could determine whether this creature whom he had personally consigned to prison had escaped or whether he had lost his mind, she signaled the conductor to pull up at the county jail and blithely descended. Justice Cook dazedly watched her mince through the jail gates.

When he had recovered, Justice Cook investigated the conditions which permitted a lifer to take joy rides on public vehicles. He learned that Mrs. Botkin had so charmed her two warders that they had placed at her disposal a suite of cells, supplied her with special bedding, sheets and clothing, allowed her to receive whom she chose when she chose and served her epicurean meals, though she had no money to pay for these attentions. Just what payment this fading siren did make mortified the judge's correct soul.

Her warders allowed she was an enchanting female, but denied that she had ever left the grounds. This Justice Cook bluntly contradicted.

Despite her exposure—and here Mrs. Botkin's resolution became positively Napoleonic—she continued to live in luxury until 1906. In that year occurred an Act of God which stymied even her. The San Francisco earthquake wrecked the county jail. She was transferred to San Quentin, where for once her wiles missed fire. Unable to adjust herself to these harsh conditions after her cushy berth in San Francisco, she curled up her toes and died.

—J.K.

# 10

# MRS BRAVO
## Was it Accident or Suicide?

A gentle-seeming, faded woman, soft of speech, silent of tread, refined in manner, was the most mysteriously sinister figure in this strange story of passion and death—a widow of good birth but poor circumstances who had found herself obliged to seek means by which she might earn her living, and the paths of employment for gentle-women were very restricted in the final quarter of the last century. Therefore this Mrs. Cox decided to become "a lady's companion," a profession that is practically extinct in these days, but which seems to have existed when Queen Victoria was on the throne, and chaperones were needed by all and sundry. Mrs. Cox thought herself fortunate when she secured an engagement with Mrs. Ricardo, a girl in the early twenties who had been newly widowed.

Florence Ricardo, highly strung, emotional, impulsive, was of the merry widow type, out to enjoy life to its full. In contrast to her youth and red blooded vitality the quiet figure of Mrs. Cox, creeping in her footsteps, seemed as a shadow.

As a girl in her teens Florence Ricardo had been wooed and won by a captain in the Guards, a handsome man with whom she had fallen romantically in love before she had left school. They had married and almost at once her devotion had cooled—or was it his? Her own story was that she had loved her husband passionately during the few years they were together, but that he had rewarded her devotion with unfaithfulness and neglect. Be that as it may, he had died in the prime of life, and when little more than twenty years of age Florence found herself a wealthy and very beautiful widow. She and her husband had lived in a house called The Priory, Balham, overlooking *Tooting Bec*, and there she remained after his death, becoming the leader of a social set taking part in all the gaieties of the time, the croquet parties, the lawn-tennis—that had been newly introduced as a game—the dances, the afternoon tea parties and so forth.

Soon she declared she was passionately attached to her companion, and confided an unpleasant secret to her dear Mrs. Cox: she was desperately in love with a man forty years older than herself, she said, a retired doctor who lived on the other side of the common with his wife. Her love was returned, and Doctor Gully had been faithless to his wife, with the pretty widow as his fellow sinner.

How Mrs. Cox received the confidence is not clear.

At any rate she and her employer went away to the seaside for their annual holiday, and when they returned Florence Ricardo had forgotten her elderly lover to all intents and purposes, and was deeply attracted towards another admirer of a very different type.

This was a young lawyer named Charles Bravo, a handsome, polished, wealthy man. All that is known of him shows him a downright good fellow, though he was of violent temper and was weak in his conduct towards the girlish widow he loved devotedly. Of his passion for Florence Ricardo there is no doubt; he loved her as few women are fated to be loved.

Whether she returned his devotion or not from the first is not clear, yet she could not but be touched by his devotion. He was so young, so handsome, so winning in every way, she leaned towards him, and then there came the haunting question "Should a woman tell?" In her dilemma she consulted Mrs. Cox, and the latter—rightly—told her to make a clean breast of the ugly secret. There was a suggestion that in giving good advice Mrs. Cox was not actuated by the highest motives, she wanted to prevent the marriage, fearing she would lose her situation if it took place.

Whatever her reason the smoothly spoken woman did give the best advice, and Florence Ricardo acted upon it. She laid bare the secret of her guilt to the man who loved her, and he, chivalrous and generous to the last degree, replied by begging her to become his wife.

She did not consent at once, but a letter of hers was extant when the mystery was in all mouths, and that letter shows the position between the three people concerned—not to mention Mrs. Cox, who watched and waited.

> "*My dear Charles,—After serious and deep consideration I have come to the conclusion that if you still hope to gain my love, we must see more of each other, and be quite sure the solemn act of marriage will be for the happiness of us both. All I can say is that you have behaved in the noblest manner, and that I have no doubt of being happy with you, but before giving up my present freedom I must be sure it would be for our mutual happiness. Need I tell you that I have written to the doctor telling him I must never see his face again? It is the right thing to do, whether we marry or whether we do not. I shall ever have a deep interest in your welfare and feel a great regard for you, as I know you are a good man. Write and tell me what you think of this letter. With every kind wish, your sincere friend,*
>
> "*Florence Ricardo.*"

After that Mrs. Ricardo apparently managed to avoid her elderly doctor, although he lived only a short distance away, and Mr. Bravo pursued his suit with passionate energy until he had broken down all obstacles and won her promise to be his wife. Both families were delighted at the engagement, everything promised well for the young couple, when for the first time the shadow of Mrs. Cox showed in a sinister light. She had urged Florence Ricardo to confess her guilty secret to her lover, and in that she may have been actuated by the highest motives, but what excuse can be made for her when she approached the bridegroom elect, and suggested he should tell his mother his charming fiancée had been Dr. Gully's mistress?

It is impossible to think she could have had any other motive except the desire to stir up strife.

Charles Bravo refused to do anything of the sort. He said he had given Florence Ricardo his word that the subject should be forgotten, and he would guard her secret far more carefully than if it were his own. Indeed he managed to frighten Mrs. Cox, we may conclude, for she adopted different tactics, so working on Florence Ricardo with the story of her own devotion, that Florence told her lover she could not be parted from "dear Mrs. Cox" even when she was his wife. Here his weakness showed. He consented to Mrs. Cox remaining, a third person in their household when they were married—worse still, he gave way to his lady love's urgent persuasions and agreed to live at The Priory, the house her dead husband had left her, instead of taking her to a new home of their own. The arrangement was the more foolish since Dr. Gully lived so near.

However, the marriage took place, the honeymoon was the usual dream of bliss, and back to The Priory Mr. and Mrs. Bravo came, where Mrs. Cox was installed as housekeeper, the entire charge of the servants and establishment being in her hands. Florence did not lose her jointure at her re-marriage, and Charles Bravo was a very wealthy man, indeed it was estimated that the joint income of the young couple was well over five thousand a year—wealth indeed in those days, when money went so much farther than it does in our own times.

For a few weeks—not more—all went well, then came ugly rumours that Charles Bravo was furiously jealous of his wife's past—or was it of her present? Later the suggestion came that Mrs. Cox had poured the poison into his ear, that the woman was envious of the happiness she saw around, and from sheer love of mischief-making reminded him of what had been. She spied upon his wife, she suggested that Florence and the doctor met still—which was untrue—and took upon herself to call on Dr. Gully with suggestions and advice till he ordered her out of the house.

Those pin-pricks of jealousy, whether they were started by the whispers of Mrs. Cox or not, became raging agony to the young husband, and some of the stories told of him by the end of the first three months after the marriage, suggest he was on the verge of insanity. He would insist on taking his wife for walks past Dr. Gully's house. They would pace backwards and forwards before the garden gate, and he would keep asking her, "Is anyone watching us?" . . . "Did you see that window curtain move?" . . . "Is he looking out for you?" and refuse to be pacified when she declared she saw nothing and did not believe the doctor was at a window at all.

To make matters worse Bravo became "close" in money matters. He wanted to sell a favourite hack on which his wife used to ride, and also suggested getting rid of Mrs. Cox—which was far more sensible, though the idea did not come to anything tangible, and the quietly spoken housekeeper stayed on.

Florence Bravo's health gave way under the strain. She made no secret of the fact that this second marriage of hers, which had promised so well, had proved a failure, and she went away from home to recuperate. While she was away Mr. Bravo made a further effort to get rid of Mrs. Cox. The lady had friends or relations in the West Indies, and Mr. Bravo's father, who had shipping interests, offered her a free passage to Jamaica. She thanked him softly and sweetly but—remained at The Priory.

Apparently absence made the heart grow fonder, for Charles Bravo wrote his wife most affectionate letters while she was away, and she replied in the same strain, yet directly she returned home the old trouble broke out again. During the next few weeks matters went from bad to worse. In all the country there was no more unhappy house than this large, luxurious mansion on the common's side, which was the home of two young, healthy, wealthy, successful people.

Thus things went on until April, 1876, six months after that ill-starred wedding day, by which time Mr. Bravo was in such a state of mental unrest that he was vowing to get rid of Mrs. Cox yet taking no definite steps towards that end, and declaring he loved his wife so deeply, yet distrusting her so much, he would not let her out of his sight if he could possibly avoid doing so. Evidently he had become a very uncomfortable presence in the house from the point of view of each of the women concerned.

On Tuesday, April 17th, he was going to his office as usual and—as had been his custom during these late unhappy days—he insisted his wife should drive to the city with him. This she did, and as the couple sat side by side in the brougham which was used to take the solicitor to and from his office, the coachman heard angry voices—the quarrel was more bitter, more violent than ever before.

Only a few words reached the servant but those he heard repeated many times. Charles Bravo was telling his young wife he could bear no more of this "hell upon earth," that it would be better if they were to separate.

Apparently she tried to reason with him—afterwards her own account of what happened bears this out. She reminded him that she had confessed her infatuation for Dr. Gully before her marriage, that he had heard all and promised he would never allude to it again, that she had avoided her late lover and had proved a faithful if most unhappy wife.

The man was in a state of hysteria by that time, and she could have been very little better. With a sudden change of front he cried he was wrong in doubting her, that she was an angel from heaven, far too good for him, that he loved her and could not bear to part from her. Would she kiss him and say all was forgotten?

Considering the way in which he had been behaving, unbalanced, hysterical, violent, Florence Bravo might be forgiven for refusing to kiss to order after the cruel words he had uttered. The wrangle went on till his office was almost reached, when he was heard to say, "If you don't kiss me now, see what I'll do when I get home to-night."

Apparently the vague threat frightened her into submission. They did kiss and seemed good friends as they parted, he to go into office where he conducted his business as usual, his partner and his clerks seeing nothing wrong, while she drove home to The Priory to throw herself into the arms of her "dear friend" Mrs. Cox and pour into that lady's ears the full story of the ugly squabble. Probably one reason why Mr. Bravo objected to the housekeeper so strongly, was his knowledge that Florence Bravo repeated to her practically every word he said.

After a morning at business Mr. Bravo lunched with his partner, and went back to the office for the afternoon. At the usual hour his groom arrived leading a saddle horse, frequently he would ride home, having a gallop on the common on the way, instead of driving in the brougham. On this particular day he may have ridden more carelessly than usual though there was no suggestion of that in the evidence, but while the hack was crossing the common at a gallop his rider—an excellent horseman—was unaccountably thrown. However, he picked himself up, and though shaken said he was none the worse, and on reaching The Priory scouted the idea of being an invalid, going to his room to dress for dinner as usual, though he said something about the return of his neuralgia, probably the result of the shock.

Dinner was rather a formal, not to say a stately meal, at The Priory, and Mrs. Cox invariably shared it with her employers—indeed excepting when Charles Bravo lost his temper and insulted her, as he had done several times of late, she was treated as an honoured member of the family in every way. The two ladies put on quite full evening dress, and Charles Bravo appeared in "tails," the day of the dinner jacket not having dawned.

Afterwards much stress was laid upon the food served at that particular dinner for three, soup . . . fish . . . an entrée . . . a roast joint . . . and a sweet, rather a heavy meal according to our ideas, but quite ordinary fare for such a household. The cellars at The Priory were good, and on this evening both Florence Bravo and Mrs. Cox drank sherry, while Mr. Bravo had burgundy.

During the meal the cloud which had lowered over the house so long seemed to have lifted. The conversation was quite pleasant, but when the dessert stage had passed, Mrs. Bravo said she had a headache so went straight to her room. Mrs. Cox went away also and Mr. Bravo sat alone for some little time with his cigar and wine. Apparently he was tired that evening, or perhaps was feeling the result of the accident and troubled by the neuralgia, for he went up to bed early. His room was next to that occupied by his wife, with a door of communication between.

He had been in his room only a few minutes when he was heard calling for help in a tone so loud and agonized that the servants and Mrs. Cox, in quite a distant part of the house, heard him and ran to see what was the matter. Mrs. Bravo made no sign. She was only in the next room but had fallen into so heavy a sleep she was unconscious of the commotion. Perhaps she had taken some drug to relieve the headache.

Mrs. Cox found Charles Bravo lying on the floor, and was so horrified by his appearance that she rushed into Mrs. Bravo's room and woke her with difficulty, but directly she heard her husband was ill, Florence Bravo sprang up at once, and hurrying on a dressing gown, rushed to his side. He was in dreadful agony, and it would seem his wife rather lost her head, for not contented with summoning one doctor, she sent for three, one after the other, and when they had all arrived she screamed she wanted other opinions still. In this crisis one of the doctors suggested the best thing would be to call in a consulting physician, and Mrs. Bravo at once said she would like Sir William Gull to be called. Sir William was at the head of his profession, a man of the highest personal character and a doctor of the greatest skill: humanly speaking he had saved the life of King Edward VII (when Prince of

Wales) from that dreadful attack of typhoid. Sir William was a personal friend of Florence Bravo's family, and had been a guest at The Priory on more than one occasion, knowing Charles Bravo fairly well.

In the early morning of the following day, the "fatal Tuesday," as it came to be called, Sir William Gull arrived. He had a discussion with the three doctors there already, and learnt they had agreed their patient was suffering from some irritant poison, though he would tell them nothing. He was quite conscious, though in deadly agony. Sir William walked into Charles Bravo's bed-room, and looking at the suffering man, said impressively:

"Mr. Bravo, you have taken poison."

"I know," Charles Bravo said—his words were to be dwelt upon and remembered later. "I took it myself."

"What have you taken?" Sir William demanded, and the answer came:

"Laudanum . . . I took it for my neuralgia."

Sir William became more gravely impressed. "You are not suffering from laudanum poisoning," he said. "It is some far different drug. Tell me how you took it and why. Remember you may be dying, and if you die from poison some innocent person may be suspected."

Charles Bravo was very ill indeed; he may not fully have understood the questions—he may not have remembered what it was he had taken. He shook his head feebly and muttered under his breath:

"I have taken laudanum—nothing else—nothing else."

Within the next hour he grew much worse. His mother was sent for: the household watched his agonies and knew they were around a dying bed, but he remained conscious, and when his strength rallied he spoke to his mother of his wife—there had been coldness between the two, Mrs. Bravo, senior, blaming her daughter-in-law for the unhappiness of the marriage. Now he told his mother how dearly he loved his Florence, how devoted she had been to him. Most earnestly he begged that all ill-feeling would be forgotten, and that the elder woman would care for and comfort the younger.

Towards the end Sir William Gull spoke on the subject of poison again.

"You are a dying man," were the great physician's words, according to his own account. "There is still time for you to tell all the truth; tell me what other poison was mixed with that laudanum."

In a low voice that yet was very clear, Charles Bravo, the death sweat on his brow, said:

"Before God it was only laudanum."

A little later he died, holding his wife's hand to the last.

A post-mortem examination proved death was due to a large dose of antimony, and that in all probability the poison had been taken in the burgundy he had drunk at dinner, or during the time he had sat alone after the meal.

Florence Bravo was prostrate with the shock, and while she lay ill, other people in that most unhappy house were at war. Mr. Bravo, senior, took upon himself to seal up all his son's effects and papers, saying that the dead man had been poisoned and probably someone in the house was guilty, so everything must be left to the police. Strictly speaking, he had no actual right to do that, of course, but it is difficult to understand why his daughter-in-law should have taken offence at an action whose only object could have been to bring the truth of his son's death to light.

However, take offence Florence Bravo did, and wrote her husband's father a very angry letter, telling him he had been impertinent, and that she hoped he would not enter her house again. Chiefly, however, Mrs. Cox had command of the whole affair. It was she who wrote to the coroner, saying she understood there must be an inquest, but could it be held in The Priory instead of at an hotel; and if so, would he convey to the jury the fact that refreshments would be provided for them? That last statement was brought up against her as a cause for blame afterwards, but surely it was no more than the words of a foolish woman who was quite at sea as to the proper procedure in such circumstances.

The inquest was held at The Priory, and whether that refreshment was enjoyed or not, the proceedings were haphazard, to say the least. The doctors gave evidence, so did Mrs. Cox, but the coroner said as Mrs. Bravo was ill he would do without her. The inquest was hurried over, an open verdict was returned, and the usual certificate for burial issued.

The funeral took place, but directly it was over, Mr. Bravo, senior, and other of the dead man's friends, met and discussed the possibility of re-opening the matter—a most unusual, indeed an unheard of, proceeding in English law. They might not have succeeded, but certain members of the jury came forward to say the hushing-up was against their wishes, and that they had asked certain witnesses might be called who did not appear. In the result a petition was sent to the Home Secretary begging that a fresh inquest might be held, and permission being granted, Mr. William Carter, the Coroner for Surrey (not the coroner who had held the previous inquest), opened the case at the Bedford Hotel, Balham, July 10th.

It is that inquest which makes the Bravo case so celebrated in legal annals, apart from the fascination it must have to all students of human nature or of criminology. To begin with, when a verdict had been duly given, a new inquest was unknown, and in this case the greatest lawyers of the day were ranged on either side, and for almost a month the inquiry went on—it did not conclude until August 11th.

At that time a coroner's jury was obliged to view the body, so the dead man was exhumed for the purpose and hurried back into his grave. The case opened, and continued with much "washing of dirty linen" in public, till the whole of the country was astir with the discussions of what had gone on at The Priory, and the unanswered, unanswerable question, "How did Charles Bravo die?"

No definite charge was made against anyone, so there was no question of a prisoner or prisoners, yet to all intents and purposes two women were on trial for their lives in that room at the hotel. The late Sir George Lewis was the solicitor for Mr. Bravo's parents, while Florence Bravo engaged Mr. Henry James, afterwards Lord James of Hereford, to watch the case on her behalf. Mr. Murphy, Q.C., appeared for Mrs. Cox, and the Crown was represented by the Solicitor-General, and counsel to the Home Office.

At first the case was devoid of any sensational developments. One after another the dead man's friends told of his love of life, his good spirits, his courage. He had not spoken to any save his own folks of the unhappiness at home, and even to his mother he had said little to cast blame on his young wife. All other people had looked on him as a happy husband without a care in the world. After those witnesses—whose evidence was negatively against the possibility of suicide—came the servants with the same story—their master had been a kindly, if hot-tempered gentleman, too fond of life to seek to leave it, and their mistress was a kind-hearted lady they had loved. They knew there had been trouble between the two, but only as vague gossip, and had not paid any serious attention to the disputes.

Yet by degrees it came out that Charles Bravo had taken a violent dislike to Mrs. Cox, and had made up his mind to get rid of her sooner or later, though there again there was nothing tangible to lay hold of. There had been no open quarrel during the last days, no sudden development in his resentment at her being in the house.

All the same, Mrs. Cox was unpopular. Public opinion, rightly or wrongly, saw her as the woman who had made mischief between husband and wife, and in a sense, as the one person in the world who had reason for getting Charles Bravo out of the way. Her influence over Florence Bravo was so complete she might resent the presence of any other person, especially one who was master of the house by right of position if not in fact.

Mrs. Cox knew ugly suspicions against her were gaining ground, though looking back at the case there seems no doubt of her innocence. She realized what was being whispered if not said, and it is charitable to suppose that in her panic she went a little mad.

Quite suddenly she asked permission to make a statement: that permission was given, and in slow, whispering tones, her eyes meekly downcast, she told how, before marriage, Florence Bravo had been on terms of guilty intimacy with the elderly doctor, and added—what no one had known before—that Florence had confided in her that she had faithfully promised to marry Dr. Gully when his wife died.

All this had nothing to do with the matter of the inquest, there was no suggestion that Dr. Gully was in any way connected with the poisoning, but the inquiry turned upon the scandal and much was made of it, though why it is difficult to imagine, since the affair had taken place so long before, and Mrs. Florence Bravo and her one time lover had been strangers since her marriage.

The young widow showed to advantage in the witness-box, which is more than can be said of Mrs. Cox, who had made a poor figure. Florence answered all questions concerning her husband quietly and collectedly, but when counsel reverted to the old scandal, she faced him in desperation, a lovely woman, her pale face in contrast to the blackness of the streaming veil she wore.

"The affair with Dr. Gully has nothing to do with this case," she said. "I will not answer any questions concerning it. Already I have been subjected to great suffering and pain, and I will bear no more. I appeal to the coroner and the jury as Englishmen to protect me."

It was in vain. She was forced to go over the same ground, and the cruel taunts her husband had flung at her time and again were repeated. She had to confess that those were words he had said; her shame was dragged to the open light of day.

How irrelevant were some of the questions is shown by the fact that at one time counsel asked her: "Do you feel towards Mrs. Cox the same affection you had for her before these proceedings opened?"

Again her reply was dignified and controlled. "I thought Mrs. Cox was my friend, but now I think she might have spared me many of these painful questions I have had to bear."

Even more absurd was the evidence of another witness, a coachman who had been in the service of Dr. Gully years before. The man said he had "once" bought two ounces of antimony for his master, who had told him to use it in treatment of a sick horse. Other questions proved that the horse was given a dose and the rest of the poison was burnt!

Then came another excitement. Dr. Gully walked into court and insisted on being heard in his own defence, at the same time protesting very strongly against the absurdity of dragging that antimony story into the case. This gentleman made a good impression all round; indeed if we ignore the ethics of his association with the pretty widow, his conduct shows in the best light of anyone connected with the affair.

He said definitely that his wife was alive, that there was no question of his wanting to marry Florence Bravo, or wishing to get her husband out of the way. With a grave solemnity that could not be doubted, he said:

"On my solemn oath I declare I had nothing whatever to do, directly or indirectly, with Mr. Bravo's death. Since Mrs. Ricardo's marriage I have had no communication with her whatever."

He added, however, that five times Mrs. Cox had been to see him—on what excuse was not clear—but he disliked her so much he had given his servants orders not to admit her.

Another absurd question followed. He was asked: "You knew Mrs. Bravo had given up her honour for you before her marriage, and yet you went on living near her though you must have known your presence would be very painful to her husband."

Naturally enough Dr. Gully returned: "I did not think of Mr. Bravo in the matter. He had come between me and the lady he made his wife, but I bore him no grudge for that. True, Mrs. Cox once said to me: 'Don't you think it would spare you pain if you leave Balham?' But no suggestion was ever made that Mr. Bravo was jealous of me. I don't know that he ever saw me. I certainly never saw him in my life to my knowledge."

The coroner summed up at great length, the jury

retired for nearly three hours, and returned with a rather remarkable verdict.

"We find that Charles Delaunney Turner Bravo did not commit suicide—that he did not meet his death by misadventure—that he was wilfully murdered by the administration of tartar emetic (antimony)—but that there is not sufficient evidence to fix the guilt upon any person or persons."

There the mystery has remained from that day to this.

The dead man's father offered a reward of five hundred pounds for any evidence that would show where the antimony had been bought or how obtained, and the police advertised that two hundred and fifty pounds would be given for evidence that would lead to the conviction of the murderers. But it was in vain.

There was a suggestion that Charles Bravo had dismissed the "third gardener" because of the latter's refusal to carry a parcel to the railway station, and that the gardener might have put antimony in his bedroom water bottle, meaning to make him ill, though not to murder him, but afterwards had been afraid to confess, yet probably that was a rumour started by gossip later on and had no foundation. Trifles light as air were seized upon and gloated over, but proof was absent.

The mystery remains a mystery, and the tragedy was deepened by the fact that within a year Florence Bravo died tragically.

—E.V.

# 11

# ELIZABETH BROWNRIGG
## A Cruel Mistress

The long scene of torture in which this inhuman woman kept the innocent object of her remorseless cruelty, ere she finished the long-premeditated murder, engaged the interest of the superior ranks, and roused the indignation of the populace more than any criminal occurrence in the whole course of our melancholy narratives.

This cruel woman, having passed the early part of her life in the service of private families, was married to James Brownrigg, a plumber, who, after being seven years in Greenwich, came to London, and took a house in Flower-de-Luce Court, Fleet Street, where he carried on a considerable share of business, and had a little house at Islington for an occasional retreat.

She had been the mother of sixteen children; and, having practised midwifery, was appointed by the overseers of the poor of St. Dunstan's parish to take care of the poor women who were taken in labour in the workhouse, which duty she performed to the entire satisfaction of her employers.

Mary Mitchell, a poor girl, of the precinct of White Friars, was put apprentice to Mrs. Brownrigg in the year 1765; and about the same time Mary Jones, one of the children of the Foundling Hospital, was likewise placed with her in the same capacity; and she had other apprentices.

As Mrs. Brownrigg received pregnant women to lie-in privately, these girls were taken with a view of saving the expense of women servants. At first the poor orphans were treated with some degree of civility; but this was soon changed for the most savage barbarity.

Having laid Mary Jones across two chairs in the kitchen, she whipped her with such wanton cruelty that she was occasionally obliged to desist through mere weariness.

This treatment was frequently repeated; and Mrs. Brownrigg used to throw water on her when she had done whipping her, and sometimes she would dip her head into a pail of water. The room appointed for the girl to sleep in adjoined the passage leading to the street door; and, as she had received many wounds on her head, shoulders, and various parts of her body, she determined not to bear such treatment any longer, if she could effect her escape.

Observing that the key was left in the street door when the family went to bed, she opened it cautiously one morning, and escaped into the street.

Thus freed from her horrid confinement, she repeatedly inquired her way to the Foundling Hospital till she found it, and was admitted after describing in what manner she had been treated, and showing the bruises she had received.

The child having been examined by a surgeon, (who found her wounds to be of a most alarming nature,) the governors of the hospital ordered Mr. Plumbtree, their solicitor, to write to James Brownrigg, threatening a prosecution, if he did not give a proper reason for the severities exercised toward the child.

No notice of this having been taken, and the governors of the hospital thinking it imprudent to indict at common law, the girl was discharged, in consequence of an application to the chamberlain of London. The other girl, Mary Mitchell, continued with her mistress for the space of a year, during which she was treated with equal cruelty, and she also resolved to quit her service. Having escaped out of the house, she was met in the street by the younger son of Brownrigg, who forced her to return home, where her sufferings were greatly aggravated on account of her elopement. In the interim, the overseers of the precinct of White Friars bound Mary Clifford to Brownrigg; nor was it long before she experienced similar cruelties to those inflicted on the other poor girls, and possibly still more severe. She was frequently tied up naked, and beaten with a hearth-broom, a horsewhip, or a cane, till she was absolutely speechless. This poor girl having a natural infirmity, the mistress would not permit her to lie in a bed, but placed her on a mat, in a coal-hole that was remarkably cold: however, after some time, a sack and a quantity of straw formed her bed, instead of the mat. During her confinement in this wretched situation she had nothing to subsist on but bread and water; and her covering, during the night, consisted only of her own clothes, so that she sometimes lay almost perished with cold.

On a particular occasion, when she was almost starving with hunger, she broke open a cupboard in search of food, but found it empty; and on another occasion she broke down some boards, in order to procure a draught of water.

Though she was thus pressed for the humblest necessaries of life, Mrs. Brownrigg determined to punish her with rigour for the means she had taken to supply herself with them. On this she caused the girl to strip to the skin, and during the course of a whole day, while she remained naked, she repeatedly beat her with the butt-end of a whip.

In the course of this most inhuman treatment a jack-chain was fixed round her neck, the end of which was fastened to the yard door, and then it was pulled as tight as possible without strangling her.

A day being passed in the practice of these savage barbarities, the girl was remanded to the coal-hole at night, her hands being tied behind her, and the chain still remaining about her neck.

The husband having been obliged to find his wife's apprentices in wearing apparel, they were repeatedly stripped naked, and kept so for whole days, if their garments happened to be torn.

The elder son had frequently the superintendence of these wretched girls; but this was sometimes committed to the apprentice, who declared that she was totally naked one night when he went to tie her up. The two poor girls were frequently so beaten that their heads and shoulders appeared as one general sore; and, when a plaster was applied to their wounds, the skin used to peel away with it.

Sometimes Mrs. Brownrigg, when resolved on uncommon severity, used to tie their hands with a cord, and draw them up to a water-pipe which ran across the ceiling in the kitchen; but that giving way, she desired her husband to fix a hook in the beam, through which a cord was drawn, and, their arms being extended, she used to horsewhip them till she was weary, and till the blood followed at every stroke.

The elder son having one day directed Mary Clifford to put up a half-tester bedstead, the poor girl was unable to do it; on which he beat her till she could no longer support his severity; and at another time, when the mother had been whipping her in the kitchen till she was absolutely tired, the son renewed the savage treatment. Mrs. Brownrigg would sometimes seize the poor girl by the cheeks, and, forcing the skin down violently with her fingers, cause the blood to gush from her eyes.

Mary Clifford, unable to bear these repeated severities,

complained of her hard treatment to a French lady who lodged in the house; and she having represented the impropriety of such behaviour to Mrs. Brownrigg, the inhuman monster flew at the girl, and cut her tongue in two places with a pair of scissors.

On the morning of the 13th of July this barbarous woman went into the kitchen, and, after obliging Mary Clifford to strip to the skin, drew her up to the staple, and, though her body was an entire sore from former bruises, yet this wretch renewed her cruelties with her accustomed severity.

After whipping her till the blood streamed down her body, she let her down, and made her wash herself in a tub of cold water; Mary Mitchell, the other poor girl, being present during this transaction. While Clifford was washing herself Mrs. Brownrigg struck her on the shoulders, already sore with former bruises, with the butt-end of a whip; and she treated the child in this manner five times in the same day.

The poor girl's wounds now began to show evident signs of mortification. Her mother-in-law, who had resided some time in the country, came about this time to town, and inquired after her. Being informed that she was placed at Brownrigg's, she went thither, but was refused admittance by Mr. Brownrigg, who even threatened to carry her before the lord mayor if she came there to make further disturbances. Upon this the mother-in-law was going away, when Mrs. Deacon, wife of Mr. Deacon, baker, at the adjoining house, called her in, and informed her that she and her family had often heard moanings and groans issue from Brownrigg's house, and that she suspected the apprentices were treated with unwarrantable severity. This good woman likewise promised to exert herself to ascertain the truth.

At this juncture Mr. Brownrigg, going to Hampstead on business, bought a hog, which he sent home. The hog was put into a covered yard, having a skylight, which it was thought necessary to remove, in order to give air to the animal.

As soon as it was known that the sky-light was removed, Mr. Deacon ordered his servants to watch, in order, if possible, to discover the girls. Accordingly, one of the maids, looking from a window, saw one of the girls stooping down, on which she called her mistress, and she desired the attendance of some of the neighbours, who having been witnesses of the shocking scene, some men got upon the leads, and dropped bits of dirt, in order to induce the girl to speak to them; but she seemed wholly incapable. Mrs. Deacon then sent to the girl's mother-in-law, who immediately called upon Mr. Grundy, one of the overseers of St. Dunstan's, and represented the case. Mr. Grundy and the rest of the overseers, with the women, went and demanded a sight of Mary Clifford; but Brownrigg, who had nicknamed her Nan, told them that he knew no such person; but, if they wanted to see Mary (meaning Mary Mitchell), they might, and accordingly produced her. Upon this Mr. Deacon's servant declared that Mary Mitchell was not the girl they wanted. Mr. Grundy now sent for a constable, to search the house, but no discovery was then made.

Mr. Brownrigg threatened highly; but Mr. Grundy, with the spirit that became the officer of a parish, took Mary Mitchell with him to the workhouse, where, on the taking off her leather bodice, it stuck so fast to her wounds that she shrieked with the pain; but, on being treated with great humanity, and told that she should not be sent back to Brownrigg's, she gave an account of the horrid treatment that she and Mary Clifford had sustained, and confessed that she had met the latter on the stairs just before they came to the house. Upon this information Mr. Grundy and some others returned to the house, to make a stricter search; on which Brownrigg sent for a lawyer, in order to intimidate them, and even threatened a prosecution unless they immediately quitted the premises. Unterrified by these threats, Mr. Grundy sent for a coach, to carry Brownrigg to the Compter; on which the latter promised to produce the girl in about half an hour, if the coach was discharged. This being consented to, the girl was produced from a cupboard under a beaufet in the dining-room, after a pair of shoes, which young Brownrigg had in his hand during the proposal, had been put upon her. It is not in language to describe the miserable appearance this poor girl made; almost her whole body was ulcerated.

Being taken to the workhouse, an apothecary was sent for, who pronounced her to be in danger.

Brownrigg was therefore conveyed to Wood Street Compter; but his wife and son made their escape, taking with them a gold watch and some money. Mr. Brownrigg was now carried before Alderman Crossby, who fully committed him, and ordered the girls to be taken to St. Bartholomew's Hospital, where Mary Clifford died within a few days; and the coroner's inquest, being summoned, found a verdict of Wilful Murder against James and Elizabeth Brownrigg, and John their son.

In the mean time Mrs. Brownrigg and her son shifted from place to place in London, bought clothes in Rag Fair to disguise themselves, and then went to Wandsworth, where they took lodgings in the house of Mr. Dunbar, who kept a chandler's shop.

This chandler, happening to read a newspaper on the 15th of August, saw an advertisement, which so clearly described his lodgers, that he had no doubt but they were the murderers.

On this he went to London the next day, which was Sunday, and, going to church, sent for Mr. Owen, the churchwarden, to attend him in the vestry, and gave him such a description of the parties that Mr. Owen desired Mr. Deacon and Mr. Wingrave, a constable, to go to Wandsworth, and make the necessary inquiry.

On their arrival at Dunbar's house, they found the wretched mother and son in a room by themselves, who evinced great agitation at this discovery. A coach being procured, they were conveyed to London, without any person in Wandsworth having knowledge of the affair, except Mr. and Mrs. Dunbar.

At the ensuing sessions at the Old Bailey, the father, mother, and son, were indicted; when Elizabeth Brownrigg, after a trial of eleven hours, was found guilty of murder, and ordered for execution; but the man and his son, being acquitted of the higher charge,* were detained, to take their trials for a misdemeanour, of which they were convicted, and imprisoned for the space of six months.

After sentence of death was passed on Mrs. Brownrigg she was attended by a clergyman, to whom she confessed the enormity of her crime, and acknowledged the justice of the sentence by which she had been condemned. The parting between her and her husband and son, on the morning of her execution, was affecting beyond description. The son falling on his knees, she bent herself over

---

* It seems the child was looked upon as the apprentice of the wife, and not the husband; though the husband was obliged to find her apparel: however, accessories in murder are equally guilty, and it is strange that the man and his son should have been acquitted.

him and embraced him; while the husband was kneeling on the other side.

On her way to the fatal tree the people expressed their abhorrence of her crime in terms which, though not proper at the moment, testified their detestation of her cruelty. Before her exit, she joined in prayer with the Ordinary of Newgate, whom she desired to declare to the multitude that she confessed her guilt, and acknowledged the justice of her sentence.

After her execution, which took place at Tyburn, September the 14th, 1767, her body was put into a hackney-coach, and conveyed to Surgeons' Hall, where it was dissected, and her skeleton hung up.

That Mrs. Brownrigg, a midwife by profession, and herself the mother of many children, should wantonly murder the offspring of other women, is truly astonishing, and can only be accounted for by that depravity of human nature which philosophers have always disputed, but which true Christians will be ready to allow.

Let her crimes be buried, though her skeleton be exposed; and may no one hereafter be found wicked enough to copy her vile example!

# 12

# MADAME DE BRINVILLIERS
## the Age of Arsenic

During five centuries between Gilles de Rais and Landru, our method of selection throws up two French cases appropriate for consideration—both women of Paris, both poisoners, both in their forties when, within four years of each other, they were both executed. It might seem that the cases have too much in common to form fair samples. Actually no greater contrast could be imagined than that between the cool, cultured, quick-witted, loose-living aristocrat, Brinvilliers, and the shrewd, plump, lively, bawdy slum-product, La Voisin. They symbolize the two stages—demand and supply—of a traffic in evil which out-venomed the Roman Locusta and out-magicked Gilles de Rais.

Marie Marguerite d'Aubray was born in 1630, daughter of wealthy Antoine Dreux d'Aubray, civil lieutenant of Paris. She became Madame de Brinvilliers on her marriage at the age of twenty-one to Antoine Gobelin de Brinvilliers, Marquis de Brinvilliers and Baron de Nourar. Eight years before her marriage Louis XIV had started his seventy-two year reign, and there had begun the glamorous era of *Le Grand Monarque, Le Roi Soleil, "L'État c'est Moi"* and all that. It was also the era of great wars to win Europe for France, which kept the people interested; and of great mistresses—gentle La Vallière, evil Montespan, prim Maintenon—who kept the King interested; and under the surface it was the era of almost unprecedented devil-worship and mass-poisonings in high places, leading to the torture chambers of the *Chambre Ardente* and called, in an apt phrase, the Age of Arsenic.

Louis was basically an ordinary sort of man, not a genius but not a fool, and he acted much as many another ordinary sort of man might have done on succeeding by the accident of birth to almost unlimited power. He worked hard and played hard, but his industrious signing of endless state papers obtained him less publicity than his blatant and unrebuked immorality. His example spread downwards, and it is a matter of interest rather than of surprise that the hardly adolescent Marie d'Aubray was happy to give her buxom self to any young man who happened to be handy, not excluding her own brothers. She was at that time a short, well-made girl with thick brown hair, blue eyes, and a strangely white complexion which suggested that she was thick-skinned in every sense of the term. She was intelligent, observant, logical, quite indifferent to religion. She wrote well in a bold style of handwriting and staggered her contemporaries by being able to spell. She could have become a very great lady.

It is not clear from the records whether she married for love or convenience, but the latter seems the more likely reason. The Marquis de Brinvilliers is a rather dim character in history, but it seems that quite soon after his marriage he was spending his wife's fortune in gambling, and spending his own time with mistresses. So in 1659 his young, clever, lonely, lustful wife took one of her husband's friends as a lover. He was Gaudin de Sainte-Croix, a handsome, fascinating officer of her own age. Soon they were spending most of their time together, drinking and gambling in the nighthaunts of Paris with no sign of disapproval from the Marquis, who was no dog-in-the-manger. The only person particularly interested by what was going on was Dreux d'Aubray, who greatly objected to his daughter's new notoriety. His official position, roughly similar to that of a present-day Prefect of Police, entitled him to issue *lettres de cachet*, a kind of blank warrant of arrest which became widely misused in private feuds and vengeances. Whether he had any good reason, or was merely abusing his public office for private ends, Dreux d'Aubray scribbled the name of Sainte-Croix on a *lettre de cachet*, and the indignant officer was dragged from the coach of his wealthy mistress in the streets of Paris and flung into the Bastille.

Madame de Brinvilliers spent the fairly brief period of their separation in planning revenge upon the father who had publicly injured her pride. Sainte-Croix spent his time more profitably in studying the trade of a fellow-prisoner, the notorious Italian poisoner, Exili. When Sainte-Croix was released and rejoined his mistress they possessed between them the means and the motive to murder Dreux d'Aubray, whose death would leave them a fortune to spend and freedom to enjoy it without hurtful parental criticism.

Sources differ as to the sequence of events, but the development most likely to have followed the release of Sainte-Croix is that his gay, pleasure-seeking but hitherto harmless mistress began to turn into a monster. The knowledge of poisons which Sainte-Croix had picked up in prison must necessarily have been academic, and now needed to be augmented by clinical experience. So an apparently reformed Madame de Brinvilliers began to appear regularly in the hospitals of Paris with cheery words, wine and luxuries for the grateful patients. One source says that she "assumed the character of one of the Sisters of Charity" to make this novel act more convincing.

She also kept a mysterious little record of the state of health of her various beneficiaries. Sainte-Croix meanwhile seemed also to have reformed, went regularly to church and confession, and even wrote several dull little works on theology which nobody would publish. And when, after varying periods and degrees of suffering, all the invalids who had accepted Madame's goodies died in agony, it was all very puzzling for the doctors and everybody else excepting Madame, who was able to complete certain entries in her little book.

After a few more experiments made on her servants, Madame de Brinvilliers felt sufficiently experienced to embark seriously on her new career. There can be little doubt that she attempted to poison her husband, who was extravagant, unfaithful and generally unnecessary in her scheme of things. An intriguing explanation of the miracle of his survival was offered in one of the contemporary letters of Madame de Sévigné, who wrote: "While the Marquise gave her husband poison, Sainte-Croix gave him antidotes, so that after being tossed like a ball from one to the other five or six times, now poisoned, now restored, he remained alive." It must have been a wearing life. There is no evidence of genuine love between Sainte-Croix and his rich mistress, and he could not have been eager to contemplate marriage with a widow who adjusted all her domestic problems with arsenic.

Early in 1666 Dreux d'Aubray signed his own death warrant by inviting his daughter to stay with him at his estate in Picardy. He became ill, suffered for some eight months, and died in September of that year. Madame de Brinvilliers later confessed to having administered poison to her father twenty-seven times during that period, which suggests that she still had much to learn.

She returned to Paris, and the successful murder of her father without arousing suspicion seems to have completely released the evil impulses within her which

had had to be partially repressed during those experi-
mental dosings of the sick poor in the *Hôtel Dieu*. She
was no longer a student, she was an expert, wielding the
intoxicating power of life and death. Sainte-Croix was
still her lover and father of two of her children, but
she now took others—her husband's cousin the Marquis
de Nadaillac, a cousin of her own, her children's tutor,
Briancourt, anybody. It was quite like her schooldays
again. One source says that at this time she showed "a
demoniac temper and inhuman cunning such as perhaps
no mortal ever exhibited". That seems rather too sweeping
a statement, but she certainly showed her temper by stab-
bing her husband's mistress. She tried, without success,
to poison her own elder daughter, merely because the
girl bored her. And she had another go at the Marquis
which by now seems almost to have become a habit. He
recovered—one pictures a nervous Sainte-Croix dashing
in with antidotes—but was unable to walk properly for
the rest of his life, and had to be helped to his seat when
he went to watch her executed.

Then, impoverished by extravagance, she began to
covet the fortunes her two brothers would leave her,
and Sainte-Croix helped to place an agent named La
Chaussée in the house which the brothers shared. One of
them died after three months of suffering, and the other
a few months later, both during the year 1670. Madame
tired of the young tutor Briancourt, and when she tried
to poison him she was eagerly assisted by Sainte-Croix,
who did not like to feel that he had a rival upstairs in
the nursery. But Briancourt survived his first dose and
fled for safety to the Oratory at Ambervilliers, knowing
enough about his former mistress to make her, and indeed
himself, very nervous. The fact that he and the Marquis
survived, and that Madame's father and brothers so long

resisted her dosings, falsifies the legend that Madame was an expert poisoner, and shows her to have been a hit-or-miss bungler.

But she did have her successes, and during those last reckless years she seems to have poisoned people for the most trivial motives. Among the stories told about her are that she killed a friend who had spilt coffee on Madame's dress, killed another for having made a joke which was not amusing, slaughtered other acquaintances merely because they were boring or unduly facetious. Many of the stories are probably apocryphal, but they indicate what people were saying about her. Then, on 30 July 1672, came tragedy. Sainte-Croix died.

The cause of his death will never be definitely known, but gossip alleged poison, of course. A point overlooked by some historians is that he had visited Italy—home of Exili and most of the historic master-poisoners—a few months before his death. He may have brought back to Paris some intriguing toxicological novelty which was all the rage in Rome that season. His fatal illness was supposed to have been caused by poisonous vapours with which he had been experimenting in his Place Maubert laboratory. The most picturesque version of his end is that told by Alexandre Dumas, who wrote that Sainte-Croix accidentally broke the glass mask he was wearing whilst experimenting with early forms of poison gas. He died, anyway, deeply in debt, and among his belongings was found a casket. Inside the casket was a request that in the event of his death the contents should immediately be sent, sealed and unexamined, to Madame de Brinvilliers; and the note was so worded that suspicion was aroused by the passionate urgency of the appeal. His executors ignored it and opened the contents of the casket. Twelve packets contained poisons in powder and liquid form and recipes. One packet alone contained a pound and a half of corrosive sublimate. Others contained opium and antimony and an unidentified powder. Some of the phials contained vitriol. The authorities made tests of the unidentified substances on animals, with fatal results.

Meanwhile Madame de Brinvilliers had sent La Chaussée to the laboratory to find out what was going on. When he was told about the casket he fled without troubling to warn Madame, but was soon caught and introduced to the torture chamber. It was the widow of Sainte-Croix who gleefully passed the news on to Madame, eager to panic her husband's detested mistress. And the news had its effect. Failing to obtain possession of the casket by bribes, and with a warrant out for her arrest, Madame fled to England.

She had been in England only a few months when Louis XIV began to demand her extradition. Charles II agreed provided that the operation put him to no expense, and—an unusual proviso—that she be secretly abducted by the French Ambassador's servants and smuggled across the Channel. There were hints that she had friends in high places at the Palace of Whitehall, however, and "I shall have much trouble to succeed in this business" wrote unhappy Ambassador De Croissy, who does not seem to have tried very hard. Madame was, after all, an aristocrat like himself. There was a good deal more correspondence, of the trend of which Madame in her hiding-place is supposed to have been kept informed by friends at Court. And some time—for a period of three years the records are more or less blank—she escaped from England, returned almost penniless to the Continent, and after staying in Cambrai, Valenciennes and Antwerp, finally sought sanctuary in a convent in the then neutral territory of Liége. There she was traced by a clever and—rare quality in those days—incorruptible Paris detective named Desgrez, who arrested her in March 1676. This low fellow was not an aristocrat, of course.

The problem of Desgrez, to arrest a titled woman who was not only on neutral soil but in religious sanctuary, was formidable. There is no record that he overtly broke any international or ecclesiastical law, but we know that he arrived in Liége on 22 March, and had Madame safely in custody by the 25th. "I had no need to employ force," he wrote that night in his guarded report to Paris, "which would not have been convenient under the present circumstances of our leaving." It is an intriguing understatement.

Reading between the lines, it seems probable that there was some basis of fact in the well-known but reputedly embroidered story of the arrest which swept through Paris. Desgrez is supposed to have visited the convent disguised as an abbé, to have seemed to fall for Madame's fading charms, and to have made an assignation with her for a moonlight stroll in the countryside that evening. Only by some such subterfuge, indeed, could he have induced her—and he could not have forced her—to leave the safety of the convent walls. We are not here concerned with police methods, however smart, but the significance of this story, which rings true, is to show that even in that dark hour of her life Madame de Brinvilliers, then in her midforties, showed no trace of repentance or even of modesty, and was eager to slip out of the house of God for a while and make love to a strange priest in the fields.

So Madame came out from sanctuary after dark, and met not an ardent priestly lover but a group of very matter-of-fact detectives who bundled her into a waiting coach. The case against her still had loop-holes, but

Desgrez sealed her fate by re-entering the convent that night, still in disguise, searching her cell, and finding an almost incredible document in which she had written out a full account of her many crimes. When she knew that this had been seized she was in wild despair. In the prison at Maestricht, on the way to Paris, she smashed a tumbler and tried to kill herself by swallowing broken glass. Then she tried to swallow a pin, but it was forced out of her throat. She made a crazy attempt to bribe a detective to cut Desgrez's throat. She sent a letter to an accomplice suggesting that the coach be ambushed, a request which Desgrez intercepted and suppressed. And after an unknown man had tried to bribe the guards to let her go, her escort of a handful of detectives was augmented by a hundred cavalry.

In Paris the authorities examined the amazing document she had written in which, with references to "bizarre and monstrous crimes", she had set out a number of such items as: "I accuse myself of having poisoned my father—I accuse myself that a cousin of mine is the father of one of my children—I accuse myself of having given drugs to my husband," and so on. It was her death-warrant and she knew it. One wonders what impelled her to write it in the quiet convent cell at Liége.

But even without that document the authorities had a good deal of evidence against her. Young Briancourt had been willing to talk from the first. La Chaussée had been unwilling but was persuaded. On 24 March, when Desgrez had been lurking in Liége, La Chaussée confessed fully after his shins had been privately pulped by the torture of "the Boot". Then his limbs were publicly pulverized with an iron bar in the Place de Grève, and he was left with his bones in splinters to die whilst the Paris mob licked their lips over further entertainment to come.

In Court Madame de Brinvilliers was cold and scornful, self-possessed even when the old President was in tears. Asked whether Sainte-Croix had helped her to murder her father, she coolly answered, "Well, and what if he did? Why should they have behaved in such a disgraceful manner to him?" Asked whether she had poisoned her brothers, she said, "My brothers were no good . . . They despised me." Only after sentence of death on 15 June did she show signs of responding to the ministrations of the gentle Abbé Pirot. But it is impossible to attach any importance to the frequent last-minute protestations of piety by multiple murderers, who having realized their failure to bamboozle men, think it may still be possible and worth trying to bamboozle God.

French law of those days forbade the torture of persons of rank, but the law was waived in her case as it had been in that of Gilles de Rais, and on 16 June she suffered seven hours of water torture. "Do you wish to drown me?" she exclaimed when she saw the row of great jars arrayed in the torture chamber. "I am so small a person that you can hardly intend to make me swallow all that." Eight jars were administered, but fruitlessly, as the half-drowned woman had nothing to add to her previous statements. So on the following morning she was led out to do penance and die, and she objected with characteristic *hauteur* to be carried in a common cart. She did her formal public penance, but even the kindly old abbé remarked, "There is little appearance that you have been touched by the grace of God." He pleaded with her for an hour, and she only showed signs of repentance when he took the extreme step of threatening to withhold absolution.

Friday, 17 July 1676, was a long, hot day. The ceremonies and exhortations droned on until about six o'clock in the evening, and on the very scaffold the headsman took half an hour to cut off the weary woman's thick hair. More prayers followed, then at eight o'clock her head was struck off with a sword. "Wasn't that a fine stroke, monsieur!" exclaimed André Guillaume, the proud executioner, to the weeping abbé. "I always commend myself to God on such occasions, and up to the present He has never let me down."

One of the most puzzling features to students of penology is the frequent hysterical public reaction in favour of some of the most monstrous murderers. It is the very proper British practice to make justice an impersonal and cold-blooded procedure, unaffected by momentary emotionalism, and leaving no relics to form the basis of some ludicrous future canonization. That the monument to Gilles de Rais should have become a place of pilgrimage was positively blasphemous. Almost equally blasphemous was the immediate reaction of the superstitious scum of Paris after the execution of Madame de Brinvilliers. Almost at the stroke of the headsman's sword, the mob which had been screeching for her blood began, when they saw it spurting, to regard this vile woman as an innocent martyred figure. In a contemporary letter describing the scene, Madame de Sévigné, who was present, wrote: "The next day there was great searching for Madame de Brinvilliers's bones, for people said that she was a saint in heaven."

G.D.

# 13

# CHARLOTTE BRYANT
## Poison in the West Country

---

John Bryant was thirty-eight years of age when he died, a native of Dorset and an ex-soldier. In 1922 he was serving in Londonderry, Northern Ireland, where he became acquainted with Charlotte McHugh, aged twenty, two years younger than himself. She was a woman of doubtful character, little better than a professional prostitute.

Bryant was a good-natured, easy-going man. Either he did not realize the type of woman she was, or she successfully hoodwinked him. When Bryant was due for discharge from the Army she induced him to marry her on the grounds that she was pregnant by him. As their first child was not born until well over a year later this was probably a mere trap. Bryant fell for it. He brought her to England and married her. If he had been unaware of her true nature before, he was not left long in doubt after their marriage.

In 1925 he obtained employment as a farm hand at Over Compton in Dorset and moved into a cottage on the farm. Mrs. Bryant proved herself to be a violent, ill-tempered woman and her loose living caused indignation and disgust among the country folk. In the neighbouring towns she became well known as a prostitute and was called by such names as "Compton Liz" and "Black Bess".

It would appear that Bryant had no control whatever over his wife. Probably he was scared of her violent temper and vicious tongue, which to a man so easy-going must have been something to avoid at all costs. He did nothing to restrain her from the conduct which was earning her such a foul reputation in the neighbourhood, and they continued to live as man and wife.

The farmer employing Bryant was looking for an excuse to get rid of him. Bryant was a good worker, but the woman's misbehaviour was such that the farmer could tolerate it no longer. His opportunity came early in 1934, when a gipsy, a horse-dealer, whose Christian name was Leonard, was taken as a lodger by the Bryants. No secret was made of the fact that Mrs. Bryant lived on the most intimate terms with Leonard, and Bryant, obviously, accepted the situation. But the farmer did not. He objected to the gipsy lodging in his cottage and dismissed Bryant from his employment.

In March 1934 Bryant obtained a job at Coombe, near Sherborne, and occupied the farm cottage which went with it. Leonard turned up again and lodged with the Bryants until November 1935.

Mrs. Bryant was in the habit of accompanying the gipsy horse-dealer on his travels far and wide over the West Country, posing as his wife. On one occasion she visited her sister in Plymouth and introduced Leonard as her husband. The sister did not learn until much later how she had been deceived.

In September 1934 she gave birth to a child, of which the gipsy was admittedly the father. Bryant may, or may not, have been the father of her other four children. When she was off with Leonard she left them with him and he seems to have raised no objection, doubtless glad to be rid of her company.

There can be no doubt that Mrs. Bryant was deeply in love with the gipsy and that she regarded her husband as a poor fool who stood in the way of her marriage to Leonard. One wonders why a woman of her character should have bothered about marriage at all, especially when Bryant did nothing to prevent her intimate association with the man she loved. However, she did, and it was this desire which was unquestionably the motive for poisoning her husband.

On Monday, 13th May, John Bryant was taken seriously ill while at work in the afternoon, vomiting violently, followed by severe diarrhoea. He complained of burning pains in the mouth, gullet and stomach and was in great agony. He was carried back to the cottage and the local doctor called. He at once suspected arsenical poisoning, but, on treatment, Bryant made such a rapid recovery that the doctor believed himself to be mistaken in his diagnosis.

Mrs. Bryant was not at home when her husband was taken ill. She had gone off in the morning with her gipsy lover, taking the baby and her eldest son. The other three children were at school in Sherborne and did not come home at midday. She had left food for Bryant, and he was the only person who would be likely to eat it.

Bryant returned to work the next day, apparently little the worse for his sudden illness.

On 6th August he had another attack of the same nature, but again he recovered quite quickly and was able to return to work in a couple of days.

From August to December he remained in good health, going about his duties as a farm labourer in the normal manner. If he suspected that he had been poisoned he said nothing about it to his friends and neighbours, as far as is known. This reservation is made because in this case, as in many other investigations in rural areas, the police were up against the extreme reticence of the countryman. Much of the vital information which they did obtain was gathered only by patient and persistent questioning.

There is some reason to think that Bryant might have suspected that his wife was poisoning him, because for some time he had been preparing the Sunday meal himself and doing some of the cooking on other days of the week. But this might well have been due to his wife's negligence rather than to any suspicion that she was tampering with the food.

It was on the 11th December that he had his third illness and this time it was much more serious. He was seized with violent pains and prolonged vomiting shortly after breakfast, blood being present in the vomit. But as none of this vomit was available to the doctor when he arrived, and bearing in mind that Bryant had already made two rapid recoveries from similar attacks, the doctor did not have enough suspicion to feel justified in reporting the matter to the police.

Once again Bryant recovered, though not so quickly as before. By 20th December he was wishing to sign off the panel and resume work on the following Monday, the 23rd. His wife was, of course, aware of his intentions.

In the early afternoon of Saturday, 21st, he was taken with another attack, writhing in great agony, with all the distressing symptoms of arsenical poisoning. The next day, Sunday, the doctor had him removed to hospital, convinced now that his original diagnosis had been correct after all, despite evidence to the contrary. Bryant died one hour after admission to hospital, the doctor being present at his bedside. He refused to sign a death certificate and reported the matter to the coroner and the local police.

The coroner ordered an immediate post mortem. The internal organs of the dead man were removed and sent to Dr. Roche Lynch for examination, although it was obvious to the local surgeons that Bryant had died of arsenical poisoning. Dr. Roche Lynch confirmed the cause of death and advised a full investigation into the circumstances.

The Chief Constable of Dorset decided that this was a clear case of murder and applied to the C.I.D. for assistance. Chief Detective Inspector Bell and Detective Sergeant Tapsell were assigned to the investigation by the Commissioner of Metropolitan Police and proceeded to Sherborne on 30th December. It has sometimes happened that the calling in of London officers has been resented by the local police and their task made more difficult in consequence. On this occasion the C.I.D. men established immediate good relations with the Dorset police and worked with them in the utmost harmony. Indeed, it is largely due to this co-operation that the case was brought to a successful conclusion.

Mrs. Bryant was questioned and made a statement, subsequently proved to be almost wholly false. It brought another woman to the notice of the investigating officers, a Mrs. Ostler, and the statement was clearly designed to throw grave suspicion upon her.

Mrs. Ostler was a widow with two children, and in poor circumstances. She had recently moved to a cottage close to the Bryants' cottage and had become acquainted with them. Both Bryant and his wife seem to have helped her with money and food and no doubt she was grateful to them. So that when Bryant was taken seriously ill on the 21st December she responded immediately to Mrs. Bryant's appeal for assistance in nursing him. Mrs. Bryant said that she was no good at nursing and left Mrs. Ostler to deal entirely with the sick man. Mrs. Ostler gave him his medicine, prepared hot milk, and generally nursed him continuously up to the moment he was taken to hospital.

The investigating officers viewed this manœuvre with the utmost suspicion, because to them it appeared as a calculated and cunning attempt to place Mrs. Ostler in the role of poisoner. As the woman had not come to the neighbourhood until October, she could not possibly have had any hand in the previous attempts to poison Bryant. They questioned Mrs. Bryant, but she stuck to her story, and the C.I.D. men did not unduly press her, waiting for more evidence.

Mrs. Ostler and her two children had since taken up residence with Mrs. Bryant and her family of five. Neither woman had any money and they were forced to apply to the Relieving Officer for assistance. The local police were on the best of terms with that officer and he arranged for the two families to be removed to the Public Assistance Institution at Sturminster Newton.

The cottage now being empty, the police could get to work with a free hand.

One of the first things to be done was to make a search of all the poison registers kept by chemists throughout the West Country. Mrs. Bryant had roamed over a wide area of the West Country with Leonard, the horse-dealer, and the task was likely to prove formidable. As it turned out, the search involved nearly all the Forces of the West and many hundreds of officers, but, at first, without success. It was later discovered that Mrs. Bryant could not write or sign her name, and the search began again. This time success came quickly. A chemist was located in Yeovil who on 21st December had sold a tin of weed-killer to a woman resembling Mrs. Bryant. She had given a false name and signed the register with a cross. he recognized her as a customer who had visited the shop on previous occasions and felt safe in serving her with the weed-killer, but when he was asked to pick ou the woman on a identity parade he failed to recognize her, either from her appearance or her pronounced Irish accent. This was a blow to the police, because however certain they might be that they had traced the source of the arsenic, it was useless as evidence.

In the meantime the gipsy, Leonard, had to be found. His true identity was known to the local police, who had a commitment warrant out against him for bastardy arrears. His description was circulated and he was located at Cellompton, Devon. He was brought back and questioned. He admitted freely his relationship with Mrs. Bryant, and it was plain to the C.I.D. men that though he may have been the cause of Bryant's murder he had had no hand in it, and did not even suspect what had been happening. He did, however, admit that on several occasions Mrs. Bryant had asked him if he would marry her if she became a widow. He had told her that he had no intentions of marrying any woman, and this had depressed her. When he had finally broken with her she had hidden his boots and trousers in an endeavour to force him to stay with her.

The gipsy was eliminated from the enquiry and turned over to the Dorset police.

Mrs. Ostler, when interviewed, proved to be a difficult witness. She realized that she had been placed in an exceedingly ugly position. The fact that many of the local people suspected her more than they did the wife did not help the police to induce her to talk. They had to question her with patient persistence time and again before they obtained what they hoped was the fully story.

She said that on the afternoon of 21st December, when she was nursing Bryant, Mrs. Bryant left her to collect medicine from the doctor's surgery in Sherborne. She declared that Mrs. Bryant was away three hours. In Mrs. Bryant's own statement she had said that she was away only one hour. As the police subsequently proved, she went to Yeovil and bought the weed-killer, and Mrs. Ostler's estimate of the length of her absence was correct.

On 24th December Sergeant Taylor called at the Bryants' cottage for the bottle of medicine which the doctor had prescribed for John Bryant. This was required for examination, in case there had been some mistake in dispensing, or the medicine had been tampered with. Mrs. Ostler saw the sergeant and gave him the bottle. Mrs. Bryant did not appear but kept out of the way, although she had overheard the conversation. She seemed anxious about the police visit and asked Mrs. Ostler what they could want with the medicine. Mrs. Ostler replied that something may have been discovered in the body that ought not to be there. This statement appeared to worry Mrs. Bryant and she called her eldest son to the outhouse and set him to clear up the rubbish there. She came back to the cottage and from a cupboard in the living-room she took a weed-killer tin which had been used for paraffin and which had originally come from the farmhouse. Behind this tin was another, nearly full, and bearing the name Eureka Weed-Killer. Mrs. Bryant picked up the second tin and said, "I must get rid of this, too."

Mrs. Ostler was an intelligent woman and she realized that John Bryant's death was not a natural one, but probably the result of foul play. She was frightened, because she saw at once that she could easily be involved in a murder charge. She protested to Mrs. Bryant that if she had done anything to her husband it would look very bad for her as she had nursed him on his death-bed. Mrs. Bryant made light of her protest and told her to keep quiet about the affair. She went out of the cottage and when she returned without the tin she made the significant remark:

"If nothing is found they can't put a rope around your neck."

Some time later Mrs. Ostler pushed the pram into the outhouse and she observed that the copper fire had been lighted and most of the rubbish had been burnt. She did not see the tin of weed-killer again.

On 28th December Mrs. Bryant was unable to get the copper fire to burn properly and asked Mrs. Ostler to look at it. She cleared out the ashes and observed the tin which had been burnt in the fire and which she thought was the Eureka Weed-Killer tin. The paint had been burned off and there was no means of direct identification, but it did impress her as being the same tin. In clearing out the ashes she had thrust her poker through the end and battered the sides of the tin. She threw it, with the ashes, on the rubbish heap, where it was further distorted from its original shape.

All this information was obtained over a series of interrogations, little by little. In all the hundreds of statements which were taken the police had to labour patiently on until they felt satisfied that they had obtained all the information which the person might have. One case is typical of their difficulties, where it took over twenty-four hours, spread over many days, to extract from a fellow farm worker of John Bryant information of vital importance. This man on one occasion, after drinking tea sent out to her husband in the fields by Mrs. Bryant, had been taken violently sick, followed by severe attacks of diarrhoea. It was not that he wished to withhold information from the police—far from it. It was just that he did not remember the affair or realize that it was important. He was, in fact, a man of excellent character and regarded by the police as an honest, convincing witness whose word could be relied upon. It was obvious that as he had been very close to John Bryant he was in a position to know a lot about his private business. So they persisted in their questions until they were satisfied and rewarded by real information.

The police had already taken possession of a number of tins and bottles which had been submitted to Dr. Roche Lynch for examination, but none had revealed the presence of arsenic.

The quest now was for the Eureka tin, as described by Mrs. Ostler. All the old burned and battered tins from the rubbish heap were carefully collected and sent to Dr. Roche Lynch. One, subsequently identified by Mrs. Ostler as the tin through which she had plunged the poker, was found to contain such heavy traces of arsenic that it was obvious that the contents must have been almost pure arsenic. It had been ascertained that Eureka Weed-Killer contained seventy per cent of arsenic, so that this tin was clearly a major discovery.

Evidence of the manufacture of the tin had now to be obtained. There were a number of manufacturers of such tins, but those likely to be concerned were eventually reduced to two. Detective Sergeant Tapsell of the C.I.D. undertook the job and soon ran into a snag. The first manufacturer stated definitely that it was not of his manufacture and gave his reason for being so sure. Sergeant Tapsell tried the second manufacturer with precisely the same result, the same reason being stated, one which concerned the locking of the side seams.

The detective sergeant was not a man to give up. He was quite sure in his own mind that the battered metal he held for identification had been a Eureka tin. He refused to accept failure. After thinking out all the possibilities he went back to the first manufacturer and asked to be shown the actual process of making the tins. Sergeant Tapsell watched very closely and realized that one of his surmises could be correct: that the difference in locking which had caused both manufacturers to reject his tin as one of their own make could be accounted for by the cylinder being accidentally inserted the wrong way on. To test his theory he slipped in a sheet upside down, while diverting the girl operator's attention. The machine took the sheet and turned out a tin locked exactly as the battered old tin in the sergeant's possession.

The manufacturer was surprised, but a further demonstration convinced him and he agreed (and later gave evidence) that the burnt tin found on the rubbish heap at the Bryants' cottage was identical with those made by him for the Eureka Weed-Killer Company.

The police continued with their investigations, taking hundreds of statements, sifting the information, and, where thought necessary, adding to the accumulation of evidence being built up.

Mrs. Bryant lied and hedged throughout. When she came up for trial at the Dorsetshire Assizes, in May 1936, she had a hard time trying to explain away the deliberate falsehoods and contradictions of her evidence, designed mainly to throw the blame on Mrs. Ostler. But the weight of evidence was heavily against her. Mrs. Ostler had not come to the neighbourhood until October 1935, so clearly could have had no connection with the previous illnesses of John Bryant. It was obvious that she had been brought in by Mrs. Bryant with the deliberate intent of implicating her if the crime was discovered.

Dust taken from the shelf where the tin of weed-killer had stood was found to contain arsenic, as did the right-hand pocket of the coat worn by Mrs. Bryant. Dust taken from other shelves did not reveal any trace of arsenic. Soil taken from the garden contained no more arsenic than that taken from other places in the locality. But soil below the rubbish heap contained five times the normal quantity of arsenic.

Coal ash swept from the grate of the cottage contained four portions of arsenic to one million parts of other material, more or less the normal for coal ash. Ashes taken from the copper fire showed fifty times this proportion, as did other ashes from the rubbish-dump fire.

Charlotte Bryant made a very bad impression in the witness-box. When, on the 6th May, she was found guilty of the murder of her husband and sentenced to death, few persons could have disagreed with the verdict of the jury.

—T.C.H.J.

# 14

## CHARLOTTE CORDAY
### The Angel of the Assassination

---

One by one the shops in the open gallery of the *Palais Egalité* opened; shutters were taken down, doors unlocked, the slatternly figure of a street woman, the congested face of a drunkard, appeared for a second behind the tattered curtains of the flats above the shops, the unclean night-birds began to shuffle out of their haunts in search of food.

Mlle de Corday did not know that such people existed, she did not even see them; the strength of her purpose created a supreme isolation round her; she rose, walked along the pavement, already hot, and found among the shops, already beginning to display their wares, what she wanted—at No. 177 in the arcade was what she sought; there a certain Bardin sold cutlery; already the lad had taken down the shutters and there was in the window a shining array of knives.

The cutler was pleased to see this early customer; no doubt a young housewife making her own domestic purchases, as so many gentlewomen were now forced to do—but she only required a knife, a cheap kitchen knife. She selected one of ordinary size, a flexible blade six inches long, with an ebony handle to which were attached two rings to suspend to the cook's waist or a shelf.

She paid forty sous for this common knife and its case and left the shop to saunter again up and down the arcade, now gradually filling with shoppers and idlers.

It was too early for her, under any pretext, to try to see Marat, so she walked up and down, entirely detached from her strange surroundings, the knife in her long pocket with the small amount of money left to her, her gold watch, her passport and her handkerchief.

A newspaper boy came running past with the morning papers; Mlle de Corday bought one for two sous and, returning to her bench in the dusty gardens, opened the flimsy sheets. The first item of news that caught her eye was the condemnation to death the evening before of nine of the twenty-six citizens of Orleans accused of an attempt to murder Bourdon de la Crosnière; they were to mount the guillotine, in the red shirts of murderers, this 13th of July.

The case was peculiarly revolting and such as sufficed to make an Adam Lux, a Charlotte de Corday, wish to quit an earth where such atrocities were permitted.

This Bourdon, a drunken ruffian, was Marat's lieutenant in Orleans (*Commissaire National près de la Haute-Cour d'Orléans*), where he had made himself loathed by his debaucheries and cruelties.

As he passed blind drunk one night before the town hall, the sentinel challenged him; Bourdon replied by firing his pistol, the sentinel thrust at him with his bayonet and wounded him in the arm.

Bourdon raised the cry of a plot to assassinate him and twenty innocent citizens who had never heard of the incident were dragged before the Revolutionary Tribunal of Orleans.

"This little bleeding [*saignée*] must be cured by a larger one," said Bourdon.

Nine men were to die because Marat's creature, by his own fault, had received a slight wound.

Mlle de Corday left her paper on the bench and hastened on her way; she was impatient to accomplish what she had to do; she touched her bodice to reassure herself that her testament, folded in eight and pinned with her birth certificate inside her dress, was safe.

It was nine o'clock; she made her way to a fiacre stand that she had noticed on the Place des Victoires, and, calling the first driver, asked him to take her to Marat's residence.

She did not know the address; neither, to her surprise, did the *cocher*; only after some consultation with his fellows did the man procure this—No. 20 Rue des Cordeliers, near the Rue l'Ecole-de-Médecine. Mlle de Corday in the shabby vehicle, shaken over the rough roads, noted on a scrap of paper she had in her pocket this address and the way that led there; it might be necessary for her to return, and Paris was confusing, so much larger than she had imagined.

She was calm, still detached from everything, still absorbed in what she had to do; only, now and then, the strange sights of the great city aroused her distant unmoved curiosity; her acute intelligence observed all those details that her emotions ignored.

In the same fashion she thought of her late home in Caen—Mme de Bretteville would be rousing, opening her shutters to the Norman sunshine, Azor and Minette stirring, the decorous servants going about their monotonous duties; perhaps one of them would find the little silk embroidery—"Shall I do it?—Shall I not?" which she had forgotten to move from behind her mirror.

She saw this as a dream within a dream—like the little picture revealed by a peep through the wrong end of a perspective glass.

Marat inhabited No. 20 Rue des Cordeliers, a dull humble house, known as l'Hôtel de Cahors, where he had installed the printing press for which Simonne Evrard had paid, and where he lived with her in a squalid apartment, of which she paid the rent of 450 francs, and which had been taken in her name.

The *porte-cochère* was flanked by shops; passing under it Mlle de Corday found herself in a sombre courtyard, with a well in one corner; to the right, under an arcade, was a staircase which led to the first floor, which, the *cocher* had told her, was occupied by Marat.

She was turning up this stairway when the *concierge*, Marie-Barbe Aubain, *mariée Pain*, who occupied the *rez-de-chaussée*, stopped her, asking her her business.

Mlle de Corday turned away without replying and leaving the building walked up the street; she returned at about half past eleven and quickly ran up the dismal stone stairway before the woman Aubain saw her; a circular iron ramp edged this stone stairway and at the top there was a landing giving on the courtyard by two windows.

In front of the stair-head was the door of Marat's flat; the bell-pull had been broken and replaced by an iron curtain-rod to which was attached a cheap handle.

Mlle de Corday rang.

The door was opened by Catherine Evrard, the sister of Simonne; Marat's own devoted sister, Albertine, the maker of watches, had returned to Geneva with another brother; but these women waited on the sick man, the two sisters and a cook named Jeannette Maréchal. Despite these three attendants, Marat's place was carelessly kept; it was one of his affectations to be dirty and stinking, like the gutter ruffians whose cause he espoused; he enjoyed the distress felt even by the least squeamish of his colleagues at his proximity, only Philippe *Egalité* could sit next him on the benches of the Assembly, any other elements of hygiene that he might have learned in his medical career were forgotten; nor did the three women who administered to him trouble him by any insistence on cleanliness or any observance of sanitary precautions; the sombre and neglected apartment was like a foul shrine where squatted an obscene idol—Marat, decaying alive.

When the door was opened to Mlle de Corday, she was offended by the rancid odour of coarse fish frying in cheap oil, and glimpsed a dismal little antechamber, with a rudely tiled floor and a wall covered with a dirty white paper with a design of broken columns; this hall was lit only by the window which opened into the kitchen beyond.

Mlle de Corday asked for an interview with Marat; she declared that she had some "very interesting and important things to say to him."

Catherine Evrard replied rudely that Marat was sick, that no one could see him, and that the visitor could take herself off.

Mlle de Corday asked if she could return—even in three or four days' time?

Simonne Evrard now came up and supported her sister—no appointment could possibly be made for any day, however distant, for no one could say when Marat's health would be re-established. The door was shut in Mlle de Corday's face.

She returned on foot, through the midday heat, to the Hôtel de la Providence, retracing her way along the streets she had so carefully noted; she did not take a fiacre, as she had to hoard what little money she had left.

Her serene calm was not shaken; but it was more difficult, more horrible than she had thought it could be; to slay the beast one had to descend into the slime.

Always, she had imagined the deed being done in the open air, under the sky, or in the grave chamber of the

Assembly, some venue formal, important, where she might meet an instant death that would wipe out even her identity.

But this revolting background, the sordid lodging, the two low women, who appeared to her sluts, wretches, Marat's concubines, perhaps his attendant furies! Never had she, the fastidious gentlewoman, set foot in such a dwelling or spoken to such people, save when, in the blue robe of a *pensionnaire* at the *abbaye-aux-dames*, she had gone on some errand of charity to create herself order and cleanliness.

And Marat himself! What a foul beast it must be who lurked in such a lair.

What must she see or hear that was repulsive, disgusting, loathsome before her task was done?

But her strength did not falter; when so much had been overcome, shrinking nerves, a feminine squeamishness, must be vanquished.

The rebuff, the delay, first shook, then nerved her; it must be done, and done today.

There was yet another sacrifice to make, that of her fastidious integrity; she had never condescended to a subterfuge, not even to please her father and brother last year in the matter of the King's health. But Raynal had written—"One does not owe truth to one's tyrants."

As she ate her simple meal she revolved with her clear Norman intelligence her plan; when the *déjeuner* was over she went up to her room; the heat had exhausted her, the knife was heavy in her pocket, she took it out and laid it on the marble-topped commode.

There was still some of the cheap paper left that the waiter had bought for her; she took a sheet and wrote quickly, in her large, masculine hand:

> *I come from Caen. Your love of your country must make you wish to know the plots that are hatching here. I await your reply.*
>
> > *Charlotte de Corday. Hôtel de la Providence.*

She went out and posted the letter, carefully addressed. How long would it take to be delivered? A few hours, she was told.

She returned to her hotel bedroom to wait. The day drew on, late afternoon, early evening; she sat down and wrote again:

> *I wrote to you this morning, Marat; did you receive my letter? Can I hope for a moment's interview? If you have received it I hope you will not refuse me, seeing how interesting the business is. My great unhappiness gives me a right to your protection.*

She had employed flattery for the first time in her life; surely this sacrifice would not be unavailing? The tyrant's vanity, curiosity, would doubtless be touched; the letter went into the *petite poste*; it would arrive, she was informed, at the *bureau* at the Rue des Cordeliers about seven o'clock that evening. About seven, then, she would return to the sordid apartment. Surely, if she arrived at the same time as her letter, he would admit her to that "moment's interview" which would be sufficient for her purpose.

There were, first, other aspects of her pride to be sacrificed; she, who had never used even the most delicate coquetry towards any of the high-minded gentlemen of her acquaintance, who had not altered her toilette or her manner for a De Tournélis, a Bougran-Maingré, a Barbaroux, adorned herself to seduce the monster. She remembered the gross admiration of the coarse Montagnard in the diligence, she had heard that Marat, black Calvinist, as he was, was fond of women, she remembered the two sisters who had eyed her with instinctive jealousy on the dirty threshold of the apartment, and it occurred to her that if he heard her voice at his door and looked out of his room, he would, if attracted by her appearance, grant her an audience. Judith had curled her hair and poured a delicious perfume over her body in the service of the Lord.

Mlle de Corday took out her most charming gown, a loose white Indian muslin with self-spots, transferred to the pocket her handkerchief, her money, her watch; inside the low bodice she pinned her testament and the last number of the *Bulletin de Calvados*. She exchanged the black cords on her hat for three bright green ribbons; she asked Madame Grollier to send in a hairdresser.

The assistant Person, a lad of eighteen, came round from the *perruquier* Férieux, whose establishment was near by, in the Rue des Vieux Augustins.

He combed, dressed and arranged the brilliant locks in a more fashionable manner than they had ever known before, disposing the natural curls loosely round the beautiful face and gathering them in a knot behind to fall over the shoulders to the waist. On the front he sprayed powder, making the chestnut gold tresses *blond cendré*; he performed his task indifferently, as a matter of routine; as he worked he perceived, without interest, a knife in its case lying on the marble-topped commode.

When Mlle de Corday had paid the hairdresser and he had gone, she took off her dressing-jacket and carefully folded over her shoulders a fichu of a delicate rose-coloured gauze, which passed round her waist and tied behind.

She then placed the knife in her pocket and left the hotel, walking to the fiacre stand, where she took a vehicle and ordered the man to drive to No. 20 Rue des Cordeliers; it was seven o'clock when she arrived; she told the *cocher* to wait, and passed between the two shops across the courtyard; the porter's box was empty, so that it was without being challenged that she reached the door of Marat's dwelling; her delicately gloved hand rang the broken bell. Jeannette Maréchal opened the door, holding a medicine spoon; behind her the *concierge* Pain was folding copies of *L'Ami du peuple* ready for the morning sale.

Before Mlle de Corday could state her business two other people arrived at Marat's door: Pillet, a young man bringing an invoice, and close behind him, Laurent Bas, a street porter employed in the distribution of Marat's paper; he had come to take some copies of the current issue to the War Office, and had brought with him a parcel of paper from the Maison Boichard.

This last issue of *L'Ami du peuple*, No 242, dated July 14th, was of some importance; it denounced the inaction of the Committee of Public Safety and accused Charles Barbaroux of being a royalist and "an enemy of the country"; in brief, this popular journal, which appeared under the ill-chosen motto, *"Ut redeat miseris abeat fortuna superbis,"* demanded more blood.

The young man Pillet went in to Marat and Mlle de Corday advanced into the passage; the woman Pain, with a lewd grin at the seductive elegance of the stranger, stood in her way behind the freshly folded pile of newspapers; having delivered his invoice Pillet came out of Marat's room and left the flat; Mlle de Corday continued to argue with the *concierge*, who was one-eyed; a coincidence, as her own mother and uncle had had the same defect.

Tenaciously and with superb tranquillity the Norman stood her ground: had her letters been received, could she have an interview?

The woman Pain could not, she declared, tell, with the huge correspondence that came to Marat, what letter had or had not been received, but the visitor could not see the citizen deputy, who was ill and in his bath.

Into this altercation came Simonne Evrard; Mlle de Corday turned to her, imploring an interview:

"I have some important revelations to make."

"Now, it is impossible, perhaps in two or three days——"

Marat, having heard the argument, called out from his room. Simonne went into him and Mlle de Corday remained, resting against the wall covered by the paper with the broken columns, staring down at the one-eyed woman folding the papers that were to carry the denunciation of Charles Barbaroux all over Paris.

Simonne came out, sullenly obedient to her master; Marat would see the citizeness from Caen.

Jean-Paul Marat was seated in his bath in the tiny room adjoining, by means of another little closet, his bedchamber, which gave on to the passage and was lit by two windows which opened on to the street; beyond these chambers was a *salon*; these rooms, with the kitchen, composed the poor apartment, which was miserably furnished and poorly kept, the ignorant mismanagement of stupid women adding to the unavoidable squalor of poverty.

The few pieces of furniture that the place boasted had been bought with Simonne Evrard's small capital, added to by what petty pilferings Marat had been able to make in the accounts of the *Comité de Surveillance*; he was extremely poor and harassed by debts; *L'Ami du peuple* did not make much profit from the sous of the *sans-culottes* and Marat had no other means; despite Barbaroux's flamboyant gibes about *les misérables engorgés d'or dans leurs superbes voitures*, the Montagnards had not gained worldly wealth by their political triumph, not that they were averse from pillage, but by the time they gained power there was nothing left to pillage.

Mlle de Corday entered the bathroom and the two disciples of Jean-Jacques Rousseau, having come by such different ways to this meeting, were face to face: the woman of twenty-four, the man of more than twice her age, separated by nationality, he the Southerner, she the Norman; by religion, he the Calvinist, she the Roman Catholic; he of the people, of obscure and mean descent, she of noble blood, untainted and proud for generations; she so fair and pure, healthy and delicate as a rose, he dying, foul, corrupt and hideous.

The scene that Mlle de Corday beheld had all the horror of an hallucination; never had she imagined such a spectacle as this; Marat was seated in his bath which was sabot-shaped, which had been painted fawn colour and was nearly black from dirt; he was nude to the waist, an old dressing gown thrown across his shoulders. Across the bath was a plank of wood that served as a desk, on this were paper, a pen, a common bottle of ink tilted by a billet of wood. Marat's huge head, so disproportionate to his meagre body, was bound by a napkin dripping vinegar that hung in the clotted masses of his heavy, greasy black hair.

The face itself was terrible beyond even what Mlle de Corday had supposed; the features were swollen and crushed, the frightful humid lips and the sunken cheeks were the same livid hue, the ghastly tint that the olive complexion of a Mediterranean native takes on in mortal sickness; this lead-coloured tint was disfigured by scabs and sores, the sparse hairs of ragged eye brows, the coarse stubble of a half-shaven beard, the naked body was scaled as if by leprosy, and beneath the shrunken flesh showed the pitiful undeveloped frame bent by rickets.

From this almost inhuman mask looked out two piercing yellow-grey eyes, infected with bile and blood, but serene and formidable.

Behind the bath was a map of France nailed to the wall underneath a shelf on which were a pair of pistols, a placard showing the one word *Mort*; on the dirty floor was a copy of *L'Ami du peuple*; on the sill of the small window stood two plates of brains and sweetbreads, ready for supper.

The closet was so small that there was only room for two people; near the door into the passage was a kitchen stool; the other door leading into the cabinet of the bedroom was open.

Without replying to Marat's greeting Mlle de Corday sank down on the stool. He surveyed her curiously, wistfully; with her brilliant beauty, heightened by a superhuman emotion, her loose white summer dress, her rose-coloured gauze over her lovely bust and shoulders, her green ribbons, the powdered curls and elegant air, the girl resembled the aristocratic ladies with whom he had once mingled when he was in the employ of M. d'Artois, and whom he had coveted, and loathed because he coveted. Since he had become the demi-god of the mob the grim Calvinist had had his gallantries, which had been, however, circumscribed by his person and his purse, but no such dainty gentlewoman as this had ever entered the lodging presided over by Simonne Evrard, no such fragrant creature had ever come to one of Marat's rendezvous; and he was not without his appreciation of beauty, he had written love verses in his time which were at least as good as those composed by the seductive Barbaroux.

He spoke to her gently, in that sonorous male voice that came oddly from a feeble body—what was her errand and what could he do for her?

Charlotte de Corday knew that the supreme moment had come; her energy sank down a second before flaring up to the final climax; she turned her blue eyes to the map of France to give herself courage—had not even Judith paused to utter a prayer? "Lord God, strengthen me."

Below the map was the word *Death* on the placard; she had only to think of the massacres committed—nine innocent men that morning—of the massacres planned, to stifle any rising surge of pity for the monster who at near sight was a feeble, sick, defenceless man; but the effort to maintain her calm brought a nervous sob to convulse her throat. The closet was so disgusting, the air so foul. Marat comforted her, asking her to tell him her trouble, her danger; he was flattered that this lovely aristocrat should have run to him for protection.

The sound of her lover's voice using gentle tones to another woman brought Simonne Evrard into the room; the excuse for her intrusion was a carafe of water flavoured with almond and in which floated small cubes of ice; a favourite remedy of Marat's against his feverish thirst; Simonne poured out a glass of the mixture and Marat drank; she asked if it was to his taste? He replied that she might, next time, increase the flavour.

With that the woman retired sullenly, taking with her the two plates of brain to re-heat; she closed the door behind her; Mlle de Corday now remained alone with Marat, who continued to press her gently as to her business. She came from Caen? Well, what was happening at Caen?

She had recovered from her moment of agony and answered calmly, giving him the details he desired on the movements of the Girondists, the rising of the citizens, the number of armed men, the names of their leaders.

Marat pushed aside the proof he was correcting, seized a piece of paper, and noted down question and answer.

He demanded the names of the deputies in Caen; the movements of the refugees were not well known in Paris.

She gave them to him, Pétion, Louvet, Guadet, Buzot, Barbaroux . . .

Marat's eyes shone with pleasure; this news came opportunely for his yet unpublished article attacking the handsome Provençal; he felt the approach of a gratified hate—an especial hate for men like Buzot and Barbaroux, these seductive heroes of romance, these elegant gentlemen, young, healthy, charming, who were all that he would have liked to have been.

Mlle de Corday had risen and approached him; she had her hand in her pocket as if she sought for her handkerchief; her lovely presence was soothing to him in his torment.

"—Buzot, Barbaroux; well, I shall send them all to the guillotine in a few days."

Charlotte de Corday took her hand from her pocket; Marat, stooping over his writing, had allowed the old robe to fall off his shoulders; his bare torso was exposed; the girl leaned forward; she had drawn the knife from the pocket, from the sheath; with one passionate movement she drove it home, straight downwards through the naked breast, up to the hilt, then drew it out and cast it down on the plank where lay the list of proscribed Girondists.

With a raucous cry Marat fell backwards; the door was instantly thrown open by the three women folding the papers in the passage outside, Simonne Evrard, Jeannette Maréchal, the one-eyed woman Pain; they saw Marat stiffened in agony, his eyes staring, his tongue protruding and blood gushing from the gash above his heart.

With yells of horror the cook, Maréchal and Simonne Evrard began to drag the dying man from the bath, while Pain the *concierge*, rushed downstairs, shrieking, to rouse the neighbourhood.

Charlotte de Corday passed through the closet and the antechamber, came out into the passage and advanced to the outer door; she had told the fiacre to wait, she had thought there might be a chance, a wild chance, that she would be able to escape in the confusion, escape at least from the first blind fury of the monster's underlings.

Laurent Bas, the street porter barred her way; she backed before him and he drove her into the *salon* and knocked her down with a chair, holding this over her to keep her prostrate; she struggled to rise, again he knocked her down and struck her; another lodger in the building, one Cuisinier, a lemonade-seller, came running in at Bas's cries of "Help! Help!"

These two men tied the girl's hands behind her back with their handkerchiefs and mounted guard over her; resigned and impassive, she leaned against the mantelpiece.

—J.S.

# 15

# MARY ANN COTTON
## Britain's Mass Murderess

A modest reckoning of the multiple murders of Mary Ann Cotton is that she poisoned four husbands and twice as many children and the heart of the mystery is not that she was able to follow her homicidal inclinations for so long without being detected, but that she ever murdered at all.

She used arsenic, and a hundred years ago the symptoms were so unfamiliar to doctors that she was able to bury her victims without an eyebrow being raised. If there is enigma here it is in the character of Mary herself. She grew up into a God-fearing young woman of impeccable character and it was not until she married her first husband that she began her mad rake's progress in murder—it was an incredible metamorphosis.

She was the daughter of Michael and Mary Robson, working-class people who lived in the mining village of East Rainton, between Sunderland and Durham. The little Wesleyan chapel there was the spiritual retreat of the Robson family and they enjoyed going there. Sunday school was never a penance for Mary, nor was any religious activity. When she was fourteen Mary's father was killed in a pit accident and it was a sad day for a little family which always had been united. There was no gentler child in the neighbourhood than Mary and with her father's death she became more than ever attached to the work of the chapel and found consolation in the Scriptures.

At sixteen Mary went into service at South Hetton,

while her mother—with a family to support—started a village school. Mary stayed in her first job for three years and then came back home to help her mother with the school. Children liked her immensely and she herself seemed happy and contented. Her life and conduct, so far as her friends could judge, were unexceptional.

When she was twenty Mary fell in love with William Mowbray, a young miner, and married him at St. Andrew's Church, Newcastle-on-Tyne. He left the pit to better himself and took on various jobs in Cornwall and in Durham but after five years the couple returned to South Hetton. During that time Mary had given birth to four children. Three of them had died and so, too, did the fourth shortly after Mary and her husband reached South Hetton. Gastric fever had supposedly claimed each victim.

Mowbray subsequently went to sea as a stoker and made several trips abroad. When he came home from the last of these voyages he was taken suddenly ill with a violent sickness and diarrhoea and died in agony.

Mary, now a childless widow, draped herself in deep mourning and drew the insurance money. She became tired of South Hetton and moved to Seaham Harbour, where she got to know a certain Joseph Nattrass who lived there with his two brothers. Mary was greatly taken by the handsome appearance of her new friend and was disappointed when she heard that he had married. It was perhaps fortunate for Nattrass that he was, but nevertheless, he was destined to meet Mary years later and his luck changed as will be seen.

With Nattrass out of the running Mary got a job as a nurse in the fever wing of Sunderland infirmary and among the patients who came under her care was George Ward who promptly fell in love with her. As soon as he recovered he married his ministering angel—of death. He had always been strong and healthy, but Mary had not long been his wife when he was laid low by an illness ominously similar to that which had carried off husband Mowbray and all the little Mowbrays.

Before George joined this company of the dead, he had thoughtfully bequeathed to his wife everything that he possessed and to assuage the grief at the loss of her second husband Mary took a little holiday. She returned to Sunderland and it was not long before she became acquainted with James Robinson, foreman in a shipbuilding yard, and a widower and father of four children. They became man and wife in June, 1867, and the year had not run its course before all four children, two girls and two boys, of whom the youngest was only ten months, had succumbed to gastric fever. As death smote the household Mary, too, bore her third husband a child, but it survived only a few weeks.

Mary, the Lucretia Borgia of the North, had of course been busy with arsenic and the fatal symptoms were identical in each case but it was not until much later in her murderous career that she became suspect and was ultimately revealed as an arch poisoner.

Robinson would assuredly have been marked out for death if he had not discovered that Mary was tricking him. She had pawned some of his belongings and he found out, too, that she had held on to some money he had given her to pay bills and in his rage promptly turned her out of the house. By doing so he undoubtedly saved himself from following his children to the early grave.

Mary was of good appearance and spoke well and these qualities must have impressed those who appointed her as matron to Sunderland penitentiary. She didn't hold this post long because she met a ship's officer and became his house-keeper. The association was quite brief and during her lover's absence in the Mediterranean Mary helped herself to everything saleable in his house and decamped. She then got a job with a Dr. Hefferman of Spennymoor, but if she had any plans which included her new employer they were never allowed to mature. One day the doctor discovered that several sovereigns were missing from a drawer in his bedroom and he sacked her.

Mary had always displayed a hankering for the pit villages of the North and she went to Walbottle in Northumberland. She had an eye for the next man and he proved to be a young widower named Frederick Cotton. He had a family, a fact which did not greatly trouble Mary, nor did she consider it an obstacle that when Cotton asked her to marry him he was unwittingly inviting her to commit bigamy. Third husband Robinson, by the grace of God, was still alive as Mary well knew. It made no difference and she chose St. Andrew's, Newcastle, for the ceremony—the church in which she had married her first husband and at whose altar she had knelt before murder had stained her soul.

To Frederick Cotton Mary bore a son who was fondly named Robert Robson Cotton, the Robson being a gracious reminder of Mary's maiden name. The little newcomer was Mary's sixth—if Cotton had known it. They were living at Newcastle at the time and Mary was apparently not in the least troubled by the proximity of husband Robinson in nearby Sunderland.

But for a reason which needs no explanation Mary did not get on very well with her neighbours and persuaded her doting husband to move to Bishop Auckland. They took the children with them, Cotton's sons aged eight and ten by his first wife, and the new arrival.

Thoughtfully, Mary insured her little family, everybody, that is, excepting herself. She had no reason to anticipate her own death, but with the children and her husband one could never tell. And it was about this time that Mary met Joseph Nattrass for the second time in her life. He was working as a miner in Bishop Auckland and told her that he had lost his first wife and had not married again. Mary understood from the conversation that Joseph found her just as attractive as ever and when she left him, after arranging a further meeting, she began to think about her husband—which had always been a fatal preoccupation.

One morning Frederick Cotton left his home in good spirits and excellent health, but on reaching the pit, where he worked, he was seized with excruciating pains, sickness and diarrhoea. He was brought back home and a doctor was called, but he was beyond human aid and Mary duly collected the insurance due to her.

Cotton's murder marked the last phase in the monstrous career of a woman with whom marriage meant the kiss of death. When Nattrass came to lodge at her house she quickly liquidated the eldest of the Cotton children, her own child, and then Nattrass himself, for whom Mary picked up £30 in insurance. It is really astonishing that with the hearse continually at her door nobody could interpret the sinister signs.

Quite miraculously Cotton's youngest son had survived and it is inexplicable why Mary did not murder him too at the same time. She eventually did but by then she had betrayed herself and signed her death warrant which was long overdue. It seemed that rather than kill the child Mary tried to get him admitted into the workhouse. She was told by the master, a Mr. Thomas Riley, that children were not taken in except with their parents and she answered tartly, "I could have married again but for the child. But there, he won't live long and will go the way of all the Cotton family."

And that is exactly what happened. The young boy died of gastric fever and Mary would have been free to choose her next victim if the workhouse master had not heard of the child's end and remembered the mother's sinister prophecy. He passed on his suspicions to Dr. Kilburn and, as a consequence, the little body was exhumed and was found to be riddled with arsenic. So, too, were other bodies which were dug up when the police discovered how many of Mary's husbands, children and step-children, had been carried off by gastric fever.

At Durham Assizes on May 6th, 1873, Mary Cotton was arraigned for the murder of eight year-old Charles Edward Cotton, the last of her many victims. Her dark hair was neatly arranged and she remained calm as she heard the clerk of assize read out the charge. Her demeanour changed, though, when she heard the prosecutor suggest that in order to prove system evidence should be heard in respect of the deaths of Nattrass, Frederick Cotton and Robert, the prisoner's last child. It was a great blow to her when the judge, Mr. Justice Archibald, agreed.

Nevertheless, her counsel, Mr. Campbell Foster, put forward an ingenious defence. He drew the attention of the court to the fact that the room in which the victims had died was papered in green wall-paper known to contain arsenic. The room, explained counsel, had been washed out with soft soap which possessed an arsenical base. As the soap dried it had created a poisonous dust which the victims had inhaled and died from. Never before had any court listened to such a startling defence, but it failed, and Mary Cotton was sentenced to death.

She who had hovered over the death-bed of so many victims and remained unmoved by their suffering, could not face the prospect of her own end. When the judge pronounced the verdict she cried out, "Oh no, oh no!" and promptly fainted. She was carried out of the court by a matron and two warders. On the eve of her execution the death watch saw her kneel and offer a prayer for James Robinson, her surviving husband.

When her hour approached Mary was anxious that the hangman should not find her untidy. She borrowed a hand mirror and brush from one of her gaolers and carefully brushed her fine black hair until it gleamed with life. "Now I am ready," she said and walked slowly but firmly to the gallows.

—B.O'D.

# 16

# MRS DONALD

## The Aberdeen Child Murderer

On 20th April, 1934, an eight-year-old girl, Helen Priestly, residing at 61 Urquhart Road, Aberdeen, was sent by her mother to the Co-operative Stores for a loaf of bread. The child reached the stores at about 1.30 p.m. She was served with the bread and given the usual voucher, which bore the number 21567. She was seen to leave the shop and should have reached home some ten or fifteen minutes later.

61 Urquhart Road was a tenement house, consisting of four storeys, with two flats on each floor, eight families being resident.

Mrs. Priestly was waiting for Helen on the landing of the first floor and must have seen the child if she had come up the stairs from the ground floor, but she would not have been able to see her enter the house.

When Helen did not return Mrs. Priestly became alarmed. She went to the Co-operative Stores and learned that the child had been there and left again with the bread. Search was made in all the likely places, without result, and the police were informed.

Enquiry in the area between the shop and the house disclosed that Helen had been seen to pass No. 59, the house next door, after which all trace of her was lost. A boy came forward to say that he had seen Helen being dragged into a car by a rough-looking man, and gave most convincing details, all of which were entirely false and existed only in his imagination. Unfortunately, the boy was at first believed and the police lost a lot of time following up this line of investigation.

The search for the missing girl was continued until midnight, when it was called off until five o'clock the following morning.

On the ground floor were two families, the Topps living on the left side of the entrance passage and the Donalds on the right. The passage ran through the house to a door giving on to a yard common to all the occupants of the eight flats. Close to this rear door was a water-closet, common to the two ground-floor flats, and immediately leading into the W.C. was a recess.

At about 1.30 a.m., Mr. Topp, who had been taking part in the search, had occasion to go to the W.C. At 4.30 a.m. he was up again ready to continue with the search and again went to the W.C. There was nothing unusual there at that time. At five o'clock the child's body was found in a sack in the recess leading to the W.C., so that it must have been placed there between 4.30 and 5 a.m.

Post-mortem rigidity was fully established when Dr. Richards, the police surgeon, made his preliminary examination at 5.30 a.m. The sack and the child's clothing were quite dry, but her hat and knickers were missing. It looked, from the external injuries, as if this was a case of savage rape upon the poor little girl.

The body was photographed and later removed to the mortuary, where a post mortem was performed by Dr. Richards and Professor Shennan the same morning.

From about 8 p.m. the previous night it had been raining heavily. There were no footprints on the ground-floor passageway or on the concrete "surround" outside the rear door. The yard was not concreted or paved, but was of bare earth, sodden with rain and very soft. Anyone walking over it must have left footprints, but there was none.

As the police considered the evidence they were forced to discredit the information given by the boy and concluded that this was an inside job. They already had a statement from a slater, working in the backyard, that at 2 p.m. the previous afternoon he had heard a scream which he thought came from No. 61 and sounded like the cry of a frightened child. It had not been repeated and he had done nothing about the matter, thinking that perhaps he had been mistaken.

The body had been found in the recess on the ground floor and had either been carried in from some other place outside the building or had been in the tenement all the time. The extreme improbability that the murderer had entered by the front door, carrying the sack with the dead child's legs protruding, cut out investigation along these lines. There had been a number of persons in the street and actually passing in and out of No. 61 during the night. Entry to the yard at the rear could only be made through other yards and would have necessitated crossing the soft ground, where he must have left footprints. It was clear that he had not come that way. So the evidence pointed to the murder having been committed in the house.

In view of Mrs. Priestly's evidence that she had been waiting on the first-floor landing for her daughter's return, suspicion naturally fell on the Topps and the Donalds, who occupied the ground floor. Helen could have come in at the front door without her mother seeing her, but she could not have come any further than the stairs to the first floor without being seen.

All the occupants of the six flats above the ground floor could provide the police with complete alibis, which were checked and found to be correct. But so could Mr. Topp and Mr. Donald. The only person in the entire building who could not give a reliable statement of her movements between 1.30 and 3 p.m. was Mrs. Donald. She told the police that she had been out of the house and returned home at 2.15 p.m., a statement which was found to be false. This looked very suspicious, but did not necessarily mean that she was guilty of murder. She might well have had some good reason for making a false statement, maybe not wishing her husband to know where she had been. Indeed, the very nature of the horrible crime seemed to exclude the possibility that a woman could have been responsible. It appeared to be a case of rape by a sex maniac.

The result of the post mortem, however, showed the possibility that a woman could have done the murder. This finding on the part of the pathologists altered the whole police outlook on the case, for it was obvious that what had been previously believed to be a case of rape was not, and could have been murder done by a woman. Suspicion hardened against Mrs. Donald, who was regarded as a most unsatisfactory witness.

The cause of death was asphyxia due to manual strangulation, coupled with the inhalation of vomited matter. (The child's dress was thickly stained with vomit.) All the shocking injuries had been inflicted while the little girl was alive.

The time of death was placed at about 2 p.m., probably a little later, if anything. This made the scream which the slater heard very significant. The state of the stomach contents were a big factor in settling the exact time of death. At 12.30 p.m. Helen had eaten a meal of beef and potatoes, and these were identified with the stomach contents. They showed only the first changes of digestion and the lacteals just beginning to fill, indicating that death had taken place about ninety minutes after the ingestion of the meal.

The examination of the child's clothing and the sack in which the body had been concealed led to further important discoveries.

The combinations were found to be grossly contaminated with coliform bacilli and other bacteria, including the entero-coccus. Moreover, the coliform bacilli differed in many respects from the common types of this bacilli, which would be additional confirmation.

When the sack was examined, a quantity of washed cinders was found, together with a small quantity of dust and fluff-fibres and a few human hairs. These latter were at first thought to be from the head of the little girl, but on microscopic examination they were found to be of a different colour and very much coarser. They showed, too, that the lumen bulged and narrowed in a remarkable irregularity of contour, due to artificial waving of the hair.

The fluff, under the microscope, was shown to be characteristic of ordinary household fluff, with fibres of wool, cotton, hair and jute from carpets and clothing and other articles. Fibres showing an alternate pattern of red and pink were most numerous.

With all this information in their possession the police arrested Mrs. Donald and charged her with the murder of Helen Priestly. She was the only person who could have committed the crime in the house and at the time it was decided the murder had taken place.

When the Donalds' flat was searched evidence began to build up fast. The only place in the building where any sacks were found was in this flat, and here seven were discovered, all bearing a characteristic hole in the corner, similar to the sack in which the body had been hidden. In addition, on three of them were found black stains from kitchen pots identical in size and colour-staining with those of the fatal sack.

Attempts to trace the origin of the sacks failed, as has happened in almost every murder case in which a sack has figured. These were ordinary jute sacks with the letters B.O.S.S. painted on them in red. They had originally come from Canada with a wheat shipment, but had passed through the London agents and on to Glasgow agents, who had sent a number of the sacks of wheat to Aberdeen. But when the sacks had been emptied they had been sold to a dealer, who in turn had sold them to other dealers. Similar sacks were found on a farm near the place where Mrs. Donald's brother worked, but could not be traced any better than the others. But as it transpired the sack itself was not of any great consequence in the evidence. It merely represented many weary hours of routine work for the police.

In their search of the Donald flat the police had several things which they had to look for in particular. The instrument with which the internal injuries had been inflicted was likely to be the handle of a brush, or a stick used for stirring porridge or kneading clothes. From the measurements taken of the tears a reasonable estimate of the diameter of the instrument had been made. These were subsequently found to be remarkably accurate.

In addition, there were the child's hat and woollen knickers, traces of blood, urine and vomit, the loaf of bread and the Co-operative Stores cheque, together with specimens of hair and household dust.

All these the police found. There were bloodstains on two newspapers, a packet of soap powder, the linoleum of the kitchen, the doorhandle of the sink cupboard and on two washing-cloths and a scrubbing-brush. When these were tested in the laboratory they agreed with the blood group, O, of the child and differed from those of the accused. Serum cultures were made from one of the washing-cloths and revealed the same uncommon form of coliform bacilli as had been found on the torn combinations. The bloodstains were identical in detailed biological characters, fermentation tests, indol reaction and haemolysis. The odds against their not being from a common origin, the child's body, were enormous.

Hairs taken from Mrs. Donald's hairbrush were identical in every detail with those found in the sack and there could be no doubt that they were from her head.

The fluff taken from the kitchen floor yielded no less than twenty-five definite points of similarity with the fluff found among the cinders in the sack. Moreover, certain fibres were identified with a strip of carpet by the kitchen sink, the red and pink fibres.

Among the cinders from the fireplace was a piece of paper which was identical in structure and microscopical appearance with the paper used in the Co-operative vouchers and had, too, the same green line printed on the reverse side.

The cinders from the Donald house were submitted to the Department of Mines, where they were examined and X-rayed, ashed and subjected to examination by the spectrograph and micro-chemical analysis. But there was nothing peculiar about them which would have led to their being identified with those from the sack. The only evidence here was that Mrs. Donald was the only person in the building who was in the habit of washing cinders.

On the linoleum beneath the kitchen sink was found the impression of a rectangular mark where the cinder-box was normally kept. This box was missing. A cinder had been found pressed between the lips of the dead child and it was thought that the body had been placed in the recess under the sink for some time, but that the cinder-box had become so contaminated with blood that it had been destroyed. No trace of the box was ever found.

Why the cinders had been deliberately placed in the sack is a mystery, unless it was some sort of crazy burying ritual. It could be that they were thrown in with the idea of absorbing vomit and blood. Whatever the reason, they provided excellent material evidence against the accused because of the fluff which had gone into the sack at the same time.

The scrubbing-brush and washing-cloths had been used to wipe up the blood and vomited matter, but these were not properly cleaned afterwards and so remained vital pieces of evidence.

What actually happened on that fatal afternoon will never be known. What probably happened is this. The woman was either waiting for, or met, Helen Priestly as she came in at the front door. She silently lured the child into her own flat and closed the door. Little Helen, of course, knew Mrs. Donald well and would have no suspicion of her intentions. Mrs. Priestly, waiting on the landing above, could not have seen her small daughter from that position. Probably Mrs. Donald did not speak, but merely beckoned Helen in. She then gripped her by the throat and rendered her unconscious, but thinking that she had killed her, she put the body under the sink and lying on the sack and began to think what she should do next. It was probably at this time that the child passed the urine which soaked into the sack and caused the dye from the lettering to stain her clothes.

Shortly afterwards, the terrible injuries were made. It is possible that Mrs. Donald may have had it in mind to simulate a rape, but, if so, she grossly overdid it.

The child was not dead and the frightful agony of those injuries restored her to full consciousness. She screamed, and this was the scream heard at 2 p.m. Immediately after she vomited. She probably tried to scream again as the awful torture was continued. Scared lest the agonized cries should be heard, the woman seized her by the throat again and strangled her, this time with fatal results.

She then hid the body in the kitchen cupboard and got rid of the vomit and bloodstains, together with the ash-pan. The disposition of the post-mortem stains showed that the body had been lying on its left side for many hours after death.

At some time between 4.30 and 5 a.m. the next morning she had smuggled out the dead child, partly concealed in the sack, and dumped it in the recess along the lower passage where it was found.

When she came up for trial it took a Scottish jury less than twenty minutes to find her guilty of this vile murder.

What the motive for this crime might have been is a mystery.

—T.C.H.J.

# CHRISTIANA EDMUNDS
## A Mad Woman in Love

To plan and carry out with great deliberation and even greater cunning a cold-blooded murder in order to prove that one is incapable of committing murder connotes a wickedness, folly and insanity of super-devilish abnormality, and yet it was an educated Englishwoman in comfortable circumstances who was convicted of such a crime in 1872.

The woman who committed this extraordinary crime was representative of a fairly common type, the middle-aged maiden lady reluctantly and sullenly growing old. Christiana Edmunds lived with her mother in apartments at Brighton, where they had few friends and where each day consisted of so many meals, walks on the front, and spasmodic discussions unpleasantly enlivened by railings against fate by Christiana, who bitterly resented their loneliness. Altogether a most unattractive personality, her plain features, uncertain temper, infectious disagreeableness and acidulated manner kept at bay even the most charitable, and her mother was beginning to fear that she had inherited her father's insanity when everything was changed by the appearance on the scene of Dr. Beard.

There was nothing romantic about his entry—Christiana had a headache and wished to see a doctor—and he was called in—but that apparently innocent meeting was destined to have ruinous consequences for both of them. It is impossible to say with certainty exactly when Dr. Beard became indiscreet. He later made out a strong case for himself, and we can believe his assurance that it was his ordinary professional bedside manner which the overwrought, hysterical woman mistook for a deeper and more personal interest. Christiana, whose chief complaint was that no one ever sympathized with her, was so delighted and fascinated by his sympathy and geniality that before he left the room she was in love with him.

The immediate effect on her was revolutionary. Believing that at last romance had come her way and that the handsome doctor was in love with her, she became deliriously happy. There were moments of depression when doubts assailed her, but these were swept away along with the obstacle created by the fact that the doctor was a married man. Had this happened fifty years later Christiana would have attempted to dignify her passion by referring to Dr. Beard as her soul-mate, but she knew nothing of these verbal aids to self-deception, and this Victorian maiden lady could only be unashamedly human when gripped by an uncontrollable passion.

On the occasion of his second visit Dr. Beard knew the full extent of his conquest, and it would have been well for him had he there and then abandoned the rôle which the crazy brain of a romantically-minded woman had assigned to him in a farce which might at any moment become a tragedy. Afterwards he explained that he would have done so had it been possible, but that when she let loose the pent-up flood of emotion of more than twenty years and revealed her very soul to him he realized that if he refused to humour her she would lose her reason. It may be true enough that the affectionate letters he wrote in response to hers were inspired by a quixotic chivalry, but when read in the cold light of a police inspector's office they conveyed the impression that their author was merely a combination of fool and knave.

But those letters were treasured by Christiana, who saw in them further proof that her romantic dreams had become a reality, and she read into them hints that Dr. Beard was waiting only for his wife's death to propose immediate marriage to her.

We know that insanity can breed a cunning which makes of madness a paradox and almost convinces the ordinary person that its victim is too methodical to be wholly irresponsible. It was so in the case of Christiana Edmunds, and it was responsible for the agitation which was the sequel to her reprieve. For from the time she got the impression that Dr. Beard had only to be freed from Mrs. Beard to marry her she began to look about for a plan whereby to enable the doctor to achieve what she conceived to be his romantic ambition. Christiana early on recognized that it would be futile to leave to Nature the sole duty of removing Mrs. Beard, for besides being younger than herself the doctor's wife was plainly healthier and stronger. She therefore decided to assist Nature, and with the aid of an obliging and unsuspecting shopkeeper she obtained a supply of strychnine from a local chemist, signing the book "Mrs. Woods, Hill Side, Kingston, Surrey."

Her next visit was to a confectioner's, where she purchased a box of chocolates and having carefully opened the box, and impregnated several of the chocolates with strychnine, she went on to tea at Mrs. Beard's.

Now Mrs. Beard was not in the habit of eating chocolates at afternoon tea, and when the box was pressed on her declined, but seeing that her guest would be offended if she refused further she took a chocolate cream and put it in her mouth. The instant it broke, however, she detected a bitter taste and spat it out. Christiana pretended to be surprised, and Mrs. Beard pretended to be unsuspicious, but when her husband returned and she described what had happened he expressed the opinion, which she shared, that it had been a deliberate attempt to poison her. What was more, when he had the opportunity he repeated the opinion to Christiana, and wound up a violent harangue by informing her that in no circumstances would he and his wife have anything more to do with her.

It may be assumed that any normal person would have considered herself fortunate in having to pay no higher penalty for so serious an offence as attempted murder, but Christiana Edmunds was not normal, and she was so much in love with Dr. Beard that when he had gone she had a fit of hysteria which left her weak and helpless for days. And it was when lying in bed that she made up her mind to prove to Dr. and Mrs. Beard that if the chocolate had contained poison it had not been placed there by her. With the cleverness of madness she had concocted a scheme whereby he would be convinced that she had been the victim of a confectioner's blunder, and the scheme involved the murder of some one unknown to her!

The plan she conceived for her rehabilitation was so novel that it may easily have been the reason why she carried it out unhesitatingly and unflinchingly, for its unique nature may have struck her as likely to guarantee success. She had protested to Dr. Beard that she had not put the poison in the chocolate, but she had not been able, of course, to produce proof of her statement. It was to provide this proof that she decided to smuggle poison into the stock of a Brighton confectioner, wait until one of his unfortunate customers bought the poisoned sweets and died, and then either go to Dr. Beard and point out the injustice he had done her or wait until he had read proof of her innocence in the reports of the tragedy and come to her to do penance. As the victim would be a person of whose existence she could have had no knowledge, it would be obvious enough that she could not be the murderer. So the woman who had been driven mad by the first and last great passion of her life resolved to commit murder in order to prove that she was incapable of attempting murder!

There was only one method of procedure open to her and she practised it at once. Selecting one of the most popular sweet shops in Brighton, she sent a small boy whom she had accosted in the street to buy half a pound of large chocolate creams, in which she cleverly inserted strychnine before sending him back with the box to inform the confectioner that they were not exactly the sort of chocolates she required. The obliging assistant returned the sweets to stock and supplied others. A few days later she had a similar experience and commented on it to her fellow-assistants, but it was, of course, quite impossible for her or anyone else to suspect the truth, and accordingly the stock of the unfortunate tradesman was further reinforced with poisoned goods.

It was the last week in March 1871, when she made her first purchase of poison, but it was not until June 12th that the tragedy she had been daily expecting occurred. During the interval some customers of the confectioner's had complained of the bitter taste of certain chocolates bought from him, and once he had been interviewed by a strange lady—actually Christiana Edmunds herself—who informed him that a friend of hers had been poisoned by chocolates bought from his shop. It was not, however, until June 12th that a little boy was given a chocolate cream by his uncle and died within twenty minutes of swallowing it, and when the newspapers published details of the startling event Christiana Edmunds believed that her complete vindication was at hand.

The news that a child of four had been poisoned by sweets bought from a reputable confectioner alarmed not only Brighton but the country. We all know how easy it is to create a panic by talking of poisoned food-stuffs, and in the Brighton case it did seem that there was good cause for panic, for there was something too absurdly improbable in the notion that it was not a pure accident, and the only explanation was that the manufacturers of the chocolate had by some extraordinary and unlucky concatenation of circumstances mingled strychnine with this particular consignment to their Brighton customer. The latter's chocolates was at once analysed, and when some of the creams were found to contain strychnine the whole stock was destroyed. At the inquest the confectioner was the principal witness, but he could throw no light on the mystery, and the police were so pestered by busybodies that when a middle-aged lady in black offered to give evidence they declined to call her. The jury's verdict was accidental death, and in recording it they exonerated the unfortunate confectioner.

Meanwhile the police were searching the poison registers in Brighton and by dint of intensive inquiries they were able to satisfy themselves about all the entries save one, that of a "Mrs. Woods, Hill Side, Kingston, Surrey." They were not, however, inclined to attach serious importance to this or to expect anything from it; but when the chemist informed a detective that shortly after the inquest a messenger had called at his shop with a letter purporting to come from the coroner and requesting the loan of the book to verify a statement in a case with which the chemist had no connection whatever, the inspector's suspicion was aroused. It became something more than suspicion, when the chemist pointed out that during the absence of the poison register from his shop the leaf immediately preceding that containing the entry, "Mrs. Woods, Hill Side, Kingston, Surrey," had been torn out. And the mysterious Mrs. Woods became of paramount importance when it was proved that the letter purporting to be written by the coroner was a forgery.

Working rapidly and with great secrecy the police soon identified Christiana Edmunds as "Mrs. Woods," and by writing a letter containing some innocent inquiry obtained a specimen of her handwriting, which when compared with the entry in the poison register proved the latter's authorship. The assistants at the confectioner's were able to describe fairly accurately the small boys who had been employed during the weeks Christiana Edmunds had been busy transferring the poison from her bag to the chocolate creams, and by a series of wholesale interviews with the small boys of Brighton three of the crazy woman's messengers were found. Questioned unknown to each other and in such a manner as to put them at their ease and encourage them to tell just what they knew, each of them told practically the same tale. How the lady had stopped him, promised a few chocolates or coppers if he did what she told him, and how he had been ordered to return the chocolate creams because they were unsatisfactory.

Christiana Edmunds was arrested and sent to the Old Bailey for trial, advantage being taken of the special Act of Parliament passed in Palmer's time to guarantee her a fair trial when she appeared before a judge and jury on January 15th, 1872. But the only defence was insanity, and even when the jury refused to accept it and the judge had to pass sentence of death nearly everybody expected that a reprieve would follow and that the prisoner would go to Broadmoor and not to the scaffold.

Ballantine, who prosecuted, described her crime as "totally unparalleled in the records of any criminal court of justice," and unparalleled it remains.

At Broadmoor she lived to a querulous old age, and down to the day of her death was the least popular person in that strange institution. Affecting the airs and mannerisms of the grand lady, she elected herself leader of its Society—after all the term is merely relative—and with tyrannical haughtiness ruled her little court of mad women, for right to the end there was method in her madness, and no suburban lady could be more particular than this poisoner was as to whom she mixed with and thereby admitted to the ranks of gentility.

—C.K.

# 18

# RUTH ELLIS
## Jealous Woman with a Gun

In this century, up to 1956, the English have executed fifteen women. Most of these female murderers killed by poison or for gain. Ruth Ellis was hanged because she was a jealous woman who happened to have a gun in her hand. The crime of passion, the unwritten law which excuses in some degree murder committed in the frenzy of emotion, is not officially recognised in England but, usually, a reprieve mitigates the harshness of the legal axiom that an eye shall be extracted for an eye and a life taken for a life.

The hanging of women who kill in emotional frenzy is not an English custom. The execution of Ruth Ellis in 1955 set a new degree of ruthlessness; other nations drew back in horror at the barbarity of the English.

Ruth was born in Rhyl in 1927 and brought up in Manchester. During the war she was a munitions worker, a waitress and a dance band crooner. In 1944 she had a son by an American soldier who, she said, was killed the same year. In 1950 she married a dentist, by whom she had a daughter, but the marriage was dissolved. In 1953 she met David Blakely, a racing motorist, a Public School boy and the son of a Sheffield doctor, aged twenty-nine.

The girl from the wrong side of the tracks and the man born with a silver spoon in his mouth, began a tempestuous love affair which ended two years later in the man being shot down in the street, and the girl having her neck broken by the public hangman.

Some people hold that love is only chemistry. If that is true, the Great Alchemist must have laughed at the mating of Ruth and David for their passion, the merging of their bodies into one, produced not life, but death. Love and hate were the fruits of their desire. The merging of their chromosomes gave birth to jealousy. And jealousy consumed them.

Soon after Ruth and David met in June 1953, she became hostess at a club in Knightsbridge, and she went to live in the flat above the club. After two weeks David came to live with her, although Ruth was still married and David engaged to a girl in Huddersfield. He slept at the flat every night from Monday to Friday, going home to his mother's house at Penn each weekend. "At this time I was not very much in love with David," Ruth said at her trial. In December she had an abortion; David offered to marry her, but she preferred to get herself out of trouble. Ruth says she refused to take the affair with David seriously as long as he was engaged to another girl. She told him that their friendship was not good for business, and he did not like it at all.

In June, 1954, David went to race his car at Le Mans, and while he was away Ruth went to bed with another member of her club. When David returned he was suspicious, but the affair continued. He urged Ruth to marry him and he broke his engagement. "I thought he was devoted to me, and I became more affectionate," says Ruth. But she didn't trust David. He stayed away one night and the next night she found love-bites over his back. When she asked him about them, he told her that someone had bitten him while he was playing darts. She ordered him from the flat. Next day he telephoned and asked to be back. He came to the Club, falling on his knees, crying, "Please marry me." Ruth suggested, "I don't think your mother or family would agree to that," but she let her divorce go through undefended so that she could marry him.

According to Ruth, she supported David financially, paying for the flat herself, and settling his drink and cigarette bills at the Club. She didn't mind because she knew he was spending £10 a week on the development of a racing car. She decided to end the affair, because due to her association with one particular man, her earnings at the Club, where she was on a commission basis, were deteriorating. David was drinking heavily: he became violent and he hit her with his fists and hands. The scenes became unbearable, and in December Ruth moved into another man's flat. David arrived on Christmas night and there was a scene. She went to an hotel with him, and moved into a flat he had taken in Egerton Gardens in Kensington. "I was in love with David," Ruth says and she made no further effort to part from him, but within a few weeks she became suspicious that he was sleeping with other women. When she accused him he hit her, giving her bruises, a black eye and a sprained ankle. She had to go to hospital to have the injuries attended to. While she was there David sent her flowers with a card saying, "Sorry, darling. I love you, David." They made up the quarrel, but Ruth's jealousy continued.

David gave her cause. She learned that he had a girl in the country. Her reaction? She persuaded another man to drive her there. She stayed all night outside the house and saw David leaving in the morning. Ruth surprised him as he got into his car, which he had hidden behind a public house. "It was my turn to be jealous now," she said, and she told him that all was over between them. But she took David back because she still loved him, she said.

In March, she was pregnant again. David hit her in a quarrel and she had a miscarriage. When he learned that she had been going to have a baby, he was sorry; sometimes he said he wanted a child, at others he remarked, "I can just about afford seven shillings a week." In April, they talked again of marriage, and he gave her a photograph of himself, inscribed, "To Ruth with all my love, from David."

On April 6 David went to Hampstead where a garage owner was building his racing car. Ruth became suspicious that other purposes were being served, and she got a friend to drive her there. She rang the bell of the flat but there was no reply. From it came the sound of female giggles. David's car was outside and she broke a window. The police arrived, called by David from the flat.

Next day she went to the flat again. She thought that something was going on. She hid in a doorway opposite, from where she observed a party was being held in the flat. About 9.30 p.m. David came out with a woman. She was dark and attractive. Ruth heard David say, "Let me put my arm round you." They went off in his car. David was up to his tricks again, she knew. She went home to her flat. "I had a peculiar idea I wanted to kill him," Ruth said at her trial. Next day she telephoned David at Hampstead. The garage owner who answered the phone, asked at her trial, "Was it obvious that she was in a considerable state of emotional disturbance?" replied, "I did not get that impression."

On Easter Monday, April 10, 1955, Ruth went again to Hampstead. Waylaying him in the street, she shot David Blakely six times with a revolver, five times at point-blank range as he and a car salesman named Bertram Clive Gunnell, came out of the *Magdala* public house. At the trial Gunnell said, "I came out first, carrying a bottle. I went round to the car but the door was locked, so I had to wait for Blakely. I heard two bangs and a shout of

'Clive,' I went round the back of the car and saw David lying on the ground. Mrs. Ellis was firing a gun into his back. I ran to Blakeley and heard Mrs. Ellis say, 'Now call the police.' One bullet had been fired into David's left shoulder from a distance of less than three inches."

When Detective Inspector Davies saw Ruth that night, he was impressed by her composure. There were no signs of passion. She told him that Blakely saw her outside the public house but turned away. She took the gun from her bag and shot him. He ran a few steps and she thought she had missed him. She shot him as he was running. As he lay on the ground, she shot him again.

At her trial Ruth said, "I did not know why I shot him. I was very upset," and in reply to Prosecuting Counsel's one question she said, "It is obvious. When I fired the revolver at close range I intended to kill him."

That Ruth Ellis killed David Blakely, and that she intended to do so, there could be no doubt. The only question at her trial was whether she had provocation. There was no question of her sanity; she knew what she was doing was wrong and against the law.

But, said her counsel, Mr. Melford Stevenson, Q.C., on her behalf, malice was absent. He asked the jury to return a verdict, not of wilful murder, but of manslaughter. He told the ten men and two women, "She is charged with murder, and one of the ingredients of that offence is what lawyers call malice. The law of England provides that if a women has been subject to such emotional disturbance as to unseat her judgment, then it is up to you to say that the offence of which she is guilty is not murder, but manslaughter."

He said that Ruth had found herself in the emotional prison, guarded by Blakely, from which she could not escape. He had treated her brutally; he went off with other women, but he ultimately came back to her and she always forgave him. "There is no question in this of any unwritten law," Mr. Stevenson told the jury. "You may take the view that this young woman was driven by the suffering she had endured at the hands of this young man to do that which she did." It was in these circumstances, driven by a frenzy which for a time unseated her judgment, that she committed the crime.

A psychiatrist, Dr. Duncan Whittaker, said that a woman was more prone to hysterical reaction than a man in the case of infidelity, and in such circumstances could lose her critical faculties and try to solve the problem at a more primitive level. "The situation was intolerable to her," declared Dr. Whittaker. "She both hated and loved him." Over the weekend there was a build-up of emotional tension, and she was impelled to violent action to relieve that suppressed emotion.

In the witness-box, Ruth said she had found the Smith and Wesson revolver in her suitcase. It had been given her by an American service man for a bad debt. On April 10, she took it with her and went to Hampstead by taxi.

The Judge, Mr. Justice Havers, overruled defence counsel's submission that the charge could be reduced to manslaughter by provocation. "The jealous fury of a woman scorned is no excuse for murder. That is the law of England," he instructed the jury. There was an intention to kill, he said. He reminded the jury that Ruth Ellis had said directly after the crime, "I thought I had missed him, so I fired again." To prosecution counsel's one question she had answered, "I intended to kill him." She fired the shots at Blakely deliberately. Finally he warned the jury, "I have felt constrained to rule in this case there is not sufficient evidence, even on the view of the evidence most favourable to Mrs. Ellis, to reduce this killing from murder to manslaughter. It is my duty to direct you that the evidence of this case does not support a verdict of manslaughter on the grounds of provocation."

Inevitably, Ruth Ellis was found guilty of the wilful murder of David Blakely. According to law, jealousy was no defence, even if she knew her lover was committing misconduct with another woman, so that she could not control herself.

That was the law of England in 1955. Since 1957, the new Homicide Act has extended the scope of provocation, which can now be induced by words alone. In 1955 for provocation to reduce murder to manslaughter, the threat or fear of extreme violence was required, or the provocation received had to be "gross". In the case of adultery, the actual sight of a spouse caught in the act was necessary, but such provocation was allowed only to married people. It did not extend to lovers and mistresses. Mere confession of adultery was not sufficient to reduce the crime from murder to manslaughter.

Sufficient time had elapsed between deciding to go to Hampstead, and reaching there, for Ruth's anger to cool.

Ruth Ellis refused to appeal, so the question raised by her counsel, a new point of law, that a woman thwarted in love is more irresponsible than a man, could not be argued.

Major Lloyd George, the Home Secretary, found himself unable to intervene, and Ruth was hanged at Holloway Gaol, while a thousand people knelt and prayed outside. As nine o'clock struck, a street musician played, "Be Thou with me when I die". All over the world people criticised the barbarity of the English.

In *The People*, January and February, 1956, the claim was made that Ruth Ellis was given the gun and driven to Hampstead by a man. Forty-eight hours before her execution, she had told a prison officer that the man had promised to educate her ten-year-old son if she kept silent. She shielded this man because she thought her son's future would be assured. If this story is true, it means that Ruth Ellis's crime was not entirely wilful. She may have been incited to commit murder.

The execution of Ruth Ellis shocked the people of England. Not since the execution in 1922 of Edith Thompson (see page 399) had such a wave of anger and incredulity swept the nation. It was one of the factors that led to the majority vote in the House of Commons in 1956 to abolish hanging, which was rejected by the House of Lords.

Because Ruth Ellis was hanged in 1955, other women who now kill in emotional frenzy may be sent only to prison. If Ruth hadn't had the gun handy, she would probably have done no more than slap David's face.

The significance of the case lies in the way the English people treated Ruth Ellis. She killed in emotional frenzy. She was hanged for calmly premeditated murder.

—R.F.

# 19

# MADAME FAHMY
## *La Crime Passionel*

In 1923 the world was still young. Britain and her allies had emerged victorious from the most dreadful war in history. Everyone wanted to be gay again. Unwise marriages became more common than usual. This perhaps led to a very lovely Frenchwoman from Paris marrying an Egyptian, Fahmy Bey, who was wealthy and travelled in Europe under the name of Prince Fahmy. This marriage in its early months was rose-coloured. The Prince loved his beautiful French acquisition and she loved him. But very soon Prince Fahmy reverted to his Moslem code and commenced to "discipline" his foreign wife and this led to anguish and great unhappiness.

Now at this point I am afraid we have to admit a fact of life at this period of the British story. Englishmen, generally speaking and with notable exceptions, regarded Egyptians as plausible, totally untrustworthy rogues and prone to all sorts of undesirable practices in love, in business and in life. Even so what happened when Princess Fahmy shot her husband—three times—in the chest and stomach in the early morning of the night of 9 July during a horrendous thunderstorm in their suite at the Savoy Hotel, London, was the cause of considerable surprise as well as rejoicing.

Sir Edward Marshall Hall, the greatest advocate of his day, appeared for Madame Fahmy and the case against her, as it appeared in the brief marked 650 guineas with a 100 guineas a day "refresher", delivered to Marshall

Hall's chambers by the late Mr. Freke Palmer the solicitor, seemed damaging in the extreme.

Marshall's great gifts, and the generous and romantic nature of the man himself, were never more willingly and effectively employed then they were in 1923 when he was briefed to defend Madame Fahmy.

The murder, if murder it was, had been preceded by a remarkable and curious incident. The evening before the Prince's death, the couple had dined in the restaurant at the Savoy at a table near the band to which, with many a discreet whisper of "Altesse" and many a bow, they had been seated. The leader of the orchestra, attentive to his wealthier and titled patrons, approached Madame Fahmy, bowed and enquired whether there was any piece of music she would especially care to hear played. She looked up, her eyes tragic, and said: "Thank you, no. My husband is going to kill me. I am not in the mood for music." The leader of the orchestra bowed gravely and withdrew. The remark made no deep impression on him at the time. Many of the beautiful women who stayed at the hotel were temperamental. They seemed always to be in or out of love. When they were irritated they often tried to embarrass their escorts. No doubt Madame Fahmy's remark was of this type—nothing that a little love, or perhaps a necklace, could not overcome.

The night of 9 July and the early morning of 10 July were memorable for a thunderstorm of unusual ferocity, almost Eastern in its violence and intensity, which broke during the night coming from the west and thundering over the city and lighting the sky with startling flashes—a strange terrifying storm.

The roar of the storm did not prevent a porter, wheeling luggage on a rubber-wheeled trolley along the passage that passed the Fahmy's suite, from hearing and recognizing three revolver shots that rose, distinct and in rapid succession, above the fury of the storm. He immediately entered the Fahmy suite. The Prince was lying in his pyjamas on the floor, blood trickling from his mouth. Madame Fahmy still had a revolver in her hand. Three empty cartridges were on the floor. The Manager was roused. He came very quickly. To him Madame Fahmy, sobbing, said, "What have I done? I fired three times. Oh, sir, I have been so wretched."

Marshall Hall read the brief, then re-read it. Mr. Freke Palmer asked him if he could secure a verdict of manslaughter. Marshall Hall replied, "Don't let us bind ourselves. Let us see how the cards play."

Marshall Hall, as was his custom when briefed in a capital case that captured his imagination, returned all other work, and began to study from every conceivable angle the facts of the case. At first sight, there seemed to be virtually no defence.

However, the character and habits of Prince Fahmy, which were most exhaustively inquired into, were to provide a defence—a defence which seemed, at first, only such as might reduce the verdict to manslaughter but leading in the end to a complete plea that Madame Fahmy had fired in defence of her life. When the morning papers came out with the news of this sensational killing, it was clear that the Press had not even conceived of the possibility of an acquittal. However, some of the material which the more sensational papers published was of help to Marshall Hall. In particular a Cairo paper had published a cartoon, in which three figures appeared: the Prince, his secretary Said Enani, and the secretary's bodyguard. The cartoon was captioned "The Light, the Shadow of the Light, and the Shadow of the Shadow of the Light." If Prince Fahmy was notorious in a city with such catholic views on sexual relations as Cairo, then it seemed probable that he had a considerable history. Exhaustive inquiries revealed the real character of the Prince. He was perverted and sadistic to an extent that it might well be said that no ordinary woman could bear him.

The case did not come on until the first week in September before Mr. Justice Rigby Swift, who was Lord Birkenhead's first appointment as Lord Chancellor, to the High Court Bench. Mr. Percival Clarke, a son of the great advocate, appeared for the prosecution.

The secretary, Said Enani, was one of the vital witnesses for the prosecution, for the shooting itself was admitted. Everything turned on the amount of terror and revulsion which the dead man had inspired in Madame Fahmy.

Had she in fact been terrified by him? Was she in fear of her life? This was the one and only point and throughout the trial Marshall Hall hammered at it, building up the terror until, at last, its cumulative effect pervaded the Court and communicated itself to the jury.

Although fear and terror were the qualities that Marshall Hall, throughout the long trial, sought to prove, there was in the defence an additional element. The pistol used by Madame Fahmy was an automatic. It had been given her by the Prince to protect her jewels. She had never fired it before that fatal night. Pistols of this type are dangerous. The movement required to empty the magazine and the pressure required to fire repeatedly are very similar. Mr. Robert Churchill, the gunsmith, was cross-examined by Marshall Hall on this point with the greatest skill. Marshall Hall's intimate knowledge of firearms stood him in good stead and Mr. Churchill made a fair and even generous witness.

As the trial proceeded, there was no doubt that the jury

were reluctant to accept the theory that Madame Fahmy had made a mistake when she fired her pistol. They were far less reluctant to accept the theory that she had killed her husband in fear of her life.

Marshall Hall was at his best in this task. He could not afford to attack the character of the witness. This would have entitled Mr. Percival Clarke to attack the character of Madame Fahmy, who had been a Parisian woman of sophistication. But the character of the dead man had, of course, to be torn to shreds to establish the defence.

There were three main channels along which Marshall Hall, with the greatest skill, was able to navigate his defence.

First of all he cross-examined the secretary, Said Enani. Said Enani was devoted to his master, but he was not unfair as a witness. Here are some of the pertinent questions put to him.

> —"Do you remember a very serious scene between the Prince and the accused on February 21st?"
> —"I do not recall it especially."
> —"Did he swear on the Koran to kill her?"
> —"I do not know."
> —"Two days later, did he take his yacht to Luxor?"
> —"Yes."
> —"Were there six black servants on board?"
> —"Yes."
> —"Was he persistently cruel to her?"
> —"He was rather unkind."
> —"From being a gay and entertaining woman did she become a frightened, wretched, broken person?"
> —"They were always quarrelling."

Said Enani left the box. Marshall Hall had not once

examined him as to his own character. Madame Fahmy was assured that when her ordeal came, she could only be questioned about the death of her husband, not about her own past.

Mr. Churchill was then called, but perhaps the prosecution witness who helped the defence most was a Doctor Gordon who had been called by the Hotel Manager to the scene of the tragedy.

The day after Fahmy's death, Gordon had attended Madame Fahmy to administer a sedative, and she had told him the cause of their last and fatal quarrel. Madame Fahmy was in great pain and had to undergo a serious operation. In spite of this, her husband had pestered her to satisfy his abnormal lust. She had begged him for money so that she might go to Paris (she believed that only in Paris were the best surgeons to be found) but he had refused and had said that she must satisfy him first—then he might send her. Dr. Gordon went further and said that certain marks which Madame Fahmy bore on her neck, arms and other parts of her body were consistent with savagery and ill-treatment by the Prince. The efforts of Mr. Percival Clarke to rehabilitate his witness were not successful.

Finally Marshall Hall called the prisoner. She had the help of Mademoiselle Odette Simon, an attractive member of the French Bar, whom Mr. Justice Rigby Swift allowed to act as her interpreter. In this way, her answers lost none of their tragic quality and the nuance of every word was conveyed to the jury who, by this time, had become enthralled by the terrible story of the prisoner and the Prince.

Marshall Hall guided her through her meeting and marriage with Fahmy. Letters of the dead man were produced to show that his whole outlook on marriage was grotesque and cruel by Western standards. He had written to a friend: "I am disciplining her. I leave her now suddenly without explanation. I expect instant obedience. At first she resented this, but, gradually, I shall break her."

The picture mounted in terror and intensity.

Still there was the shooting to be explained. This is how Madame Fahmy, in the witness box, explained it. Sobbing pathetically, she gasped out her account.

> "*He crouched to spring on me, saying, 'I will kill you.' I lifted up my arm and without looking, pulled the trigger. The next moment I saw him on the ground. I did not realise what had happened. I did not know how many times the pistol had gone off. I did not understand anything. When I saw Fahmy on the floor, I ran to him and took his hand and said, 'Sweetheart, it is nothing. Speak, oh speak, to me.'*"

Mr. Percival Clarke, unable, because of Marshall Hall's prudence, to say a word to discredit the accused, was unable to break down Madame Fahmy's story in any important particular. Some of his questions had the reverse effect to that intended. When he asked her whether she had not been ambitious to become the Prince's wife, she replied simply: "Ambitious? No, I loved him."

In planning and delivering his final speech for the defence, Marshall Hall had to be careful. The newspapers had been saying that Madame Fahmy should have shot her husband in Paris where the *crime passionel* is an acknowledged institution, but not in London where the law is the law. So Marshall Hall kept the rhetorical appeal in check. He was, he said, basing his defence on the admitted facts only. On them alone he would ask the jury to acquit the prisoner.

Up to then it had not been clear that the defence would go all out for an acquittal rather than taking the safer road that would have led to a manslaughter verdict. Marshall Hall had been immensely encouraged by the evidence of the prisoner and by her brave survival of cross-examination. He sensed the jury were looking for legal grounds on which they could legitimately free his client. Along these lines he argued.

It was a tense and graphic scene. The judge, cherubic but adroit, watching Marshall Hall, who had often led him as a junior. Percival Clarke, the epitome of prosecution propriety. Marshall Hall himself, rising to his great height to address the jury, speaking in that fine voice of his that was vibrant with conviction.

As he came to the end of his final speech, it was impossible not to believe that Madame Fahmy, who at the outset had seemed doomed had, in fact, shot her husband in a desperate attempt to save her own life.

Only in the last moment did Marshall Hall allow himself an emotional appeal.

"Open the gate so that this Western woman can go, not into the dark night of the desert, but back to her friends who love her . . ."

Then he did a clever and effective thing. He quoted Mr. Percival Clarke's father in a famous trial. "I don't ask for a verdict. I demand it at your hands."

The jury, after hearing a summing-up of exemplary fairness from the judge, were out for sixty-five minutes.

The Clerk arose and asked whether they found the prisoner guilty or not guilty of murder.

In an intense silence the answer came. "Not guilty."

A storm of cheering, which neither the judge nor the

Court ushers could control, broke out. When at last order was restored, the Clerk rose again and asked the foreman of the jury whether they found the prisoner guilty or not guilty of manslaughter.

Again, across a silence that could almost be heard, came the answer. "Not guilty."

Madame Fahmy collapsed, sobbing hysterically, and the great advocate, who had saved her life, slipped quietly out of the Court.

It was a great acquittal.

Is it just conceivable that Englishmen are as susceptible as Frenchmen? Is it possible that both the English and the French in their distrust of foreigners are extremely alike? And do you rejoice, as I did, that Madame Fahmy was free to go back to the friends who loved her?

We are all human, but some of us are more human than others.

—G.S.

# CHRISTIANA EDMUNDS
## A Mad Woman in Love

To plan and carry out with great deliberation and even greater cunning a cold-blooded murder in order to prove that one is incapable of committing murder connotes a wickedness, folly and insanity of super-devilish abnormality, and yet it was an educated Englishwoman in comfortable circumstances who was convicted of such a crime in 1872.

The woman who committed this extraordinary crime was representative of a fairly common type, the middle-aged maiden lady reluctantly and sullenly growing old. Christiana Edmunds lived with her mother in apartments at Brighton, where they had few friends and where each day consisted of so many meals, walks on the front, and spasmodic discussions unpleasantly enlivened by railings against fate by Christiana, who bitterly resented their loneliness. Altogether a most unattractive personality, her plain features, uncertain temper, infectious disagreeableness and acidulated manner kept at bay even the most charitable, and her mother was beginning to fear that she had inherited her father's insanity when everything was changed by the appearance on the scene of Dr. Beard.

There was nothing romantic about his entry—Christiana had a headache and wished to see a doctor—and he was called in—but that apparently innocent meeting was destined to have ruinous consequences for both of them. It is impossible to say with certainty exactly when Dr. Beard became indiscreet. He later made out a strong by many women as a blessing. After the hectic period through which they had passed, during which sex instinct had been unbridled, the return of the more sober conjugal life proved irksome, and the former love for the husband turned to a desire to be rid of him.

Mrs. Fazekas, the midwife, was a widow. From the beginning, her tendencies had been criminal and she had turned her attention to procuring abortion. Aggrieved at the advent of a rival practitioner in the village, she made plans for her removal by becoming the sweetheart of the rival's brother. Later this rival met with a violent death. But Fazekas outlived the gossip which followed. She did not confine her attention to abortion-mongering, but expressed herself as willing, for a consideration, to remove unwanted husbands or children. She fixed prices for the performance of the crime of poisoning, the amount varying with the social position of the interested parties. Arsenic was the instrument chosen to kill and it was obtained by extraction from fly-papers (as was alleged in the Seddon and Maybrick cases). In the preparation of the poison she was assisted by two friends. The grocer of a neighbouring town was able to testify that more fly-papers were sold in the midwife's villages than in the rest of the country. The extracts from the fly-papers were tested for strength on animals, which were found to die soon after drinking contaminated water. The fee for the crime was demanded at any time up to six months after burial. If the relative of the deceased refused to pay, that person was threatened with denunciation. Sometimes the poison was added to water, sometimes to food, and on other occasions to medicine. According to the official enquiries, the poisonings commenced in Nagyrév in 1911, and in Tiszakürt in 1917. The last case reported from Nagyrév was in 1924, and the last from Tiszakürt in 1929.

The son of Fazekas' rival, convinced that his mother had died through Fazekas' agency, endeavoured to seek confirmation from neighbours. But the midwife, determined to thwart his purpose, associated herself with certain persons in this remarkable community who were willing to set fire to the houses of anyone who gave information about the murder. During the period between 1908 and 1921, Fazekas was indicted for abortion on no fewer than six occasions, but was never actually convicted. She became more confident than ever, and, as her income from abortion was insufficient in her estimation, she decided to augment it by poisonings. She was relatively secure since her chief enemy, the son of her murdered rival, was in prison as a result of an unsuccessful attempt to shoot her.

The death of her first victim, who was already very ill, was stated to have been due to natural causes. His wife, acting in conspiracy with Fazekas, placed his arsenic-contaminated medicine in the coffin where it was discovered at exhumation nineteen years later. The wife of the dead man in this case did not seem to realise the enormity of her offence since, when asked why she had taken part in the poisonings, she is reported to have replied that "she wished to be freed from her husband and thought that perhaps others might similarly desire freedom". When she was short of arsenic solution, she borrowed some from Fazekas. The poisonings continued until 1924. In 1924, a wealthy but infirm peasant died. When his sudden and acute illness commenced, his wife sent for the family physician who diagnosed the ailment as bronchitis. A week later, the doctor was visited by her when she stated that her husband had died, and requested a death certificate. The doctor refused to give the certificate. He called and made an inspection of the body. Still dissatisfied, he filed a declaration to the

Attorney requesting an autopsy. This request was refused since it was based only on the grounds of suspicion. The same year, an anonymous letter was received by the authorities (Nagyrév Office) to the effect that poison was being used extensively in the village of Nagyrév, and that certain persons, who were named, had been poisoned by others who were also named. No attention, however, was paid to this letter.

In February, 1928, the body of a woman was recovered from the river Tisza, and she had been poisoned by her daughter who confessed. The daughter was sentenced to death, but the sentence was subsequently commuted to one of penal servitude for life. The next stage was the delivery of a letter to the local prosecutor. This alleged that certain women of Nagyrév were responsible for the crime of poisoning, and although the letter was sent through certain official channels, no practical action was taken. In 1929, a second anonymous letter reached the Attorney-General at Szolnok, naming three Nagyrév women and their alleged crimes. Resultant investigation did not produce tangible results except that the writer of the letter, following identification, was sentenced for slander since he was unable either to give further information or to furnish additional proof. Anonymous letters continued to pour in, and in them many persons were accused. One of them explained the part played by the woman Fazekas and, in one instance, how she had exchanged an arsenical preparation for a hundredweight of wheat, and how successful the preparation had been in practice. In the final phases of the whole of this case, two women made a full confession of their misdeeds to the police, including the part played by the midwife, Fazekas. Fazekas, on learning that all was lost so far as she was concerned, and on the eve of being arrested, committed suicide by drinking a caustic alkali. In spite of medical treatment, she died, thus bringing to a close the life of the most notorious female poisoner of modern times.

Dr. Beöthy estimates that in this case the minimum number of deaths by arsenical poisoning was over fifty, and he points out the high incidence of mistaken diagnosis in these cases. As the result of the anonymous letters, the investigations disclosed eighty-six cases in the village of Nagyrév in which twenty-six women were implicated. Three women committed suicide and one died while on trial. In the village of Tiszakürt, fifteen persons were detected, of whom one committed suicide and one was certified insane. Altogether, and covering both villages, six were sentenced to death, seven to penal servitude for life, and seven to periods of imprisonment which varied from five to fifteen years.

During the investigations twenty-nine bodies were exhumed. Beöthy points out that, "It is of interest to note that one of the culprits, fearing exposure, travelled to Budapest during the exhumations to enquire at a chemical institute whether arsenic was detectable in a body after twenty years. On being assured that it was, this woman travelled back to her village and there committed suicide." He adds that the fact that arsenic was not discovered in a particular body did not necessarily prove the innocence of a given woman. This was indicated by the fact that the solicitor of a woman, hastening from Budapest to Nagyrév to tell her that the chemical examination had yielded only negative results, was met by her funeral cortège. She had hanged herself during the lawyer's absence.

—J.G.

# 21

# IRMA GRESE
## "We Have No Pity"

Working on a farm and later as a nurse, Irma Grese was to become the epitome of Adolf Hitler's vision for young German womanhood, resolute, unyielding, and devoid of compassion. She was also the epitome of inhuman sadism, torture beyond belief, and extravagant murder. Embodied in everything Irma Grese did were the words of Hitler, "We are a race of savages and have no pity."

Irma came from a good, hardworking family and, at an early age, was shocked by the licentiousness of the corrupt Weimar Republic, a directionless and doomed democratic government that had brought Germany to financial chaos following World War I. Like many well-intentioned but unthinking German youths, Irma joined Nazi youth groups in defiance of her father's wishes, believing Hitler would set a sound moral leadership for her country. She soon became immersed in her politics and the military superiority of Germany, obsessed with the half-baked theories of the Nazis, replacing a normal sex life with her fanatic activities in the party. It would be later pointed out with justifiable reason that Irma, when in absolute charge of more than thirty thousand helpless female prisoners at Auschwitz, manifested her sexual urges in the form of the most bestial sadism and killings committed by any woman in this century.

She was initiated as a concentration camp supervisor in Ravensbruck in 1942, then moved on to Auschwitz. (On the one occasion that she returned home during this period, her father beat her senseless after learning that she worked in these death camps.) The plain-looking, bigboned Irma arrived at Auschwitz at the height of the Nazi commitment to eradicate the Jews. She attacked this problem with unswerving fanaticism. Rising promptly at 7:00 A.M., seven days a week, Irma dressed in her man's SS uniform, slipping on heavy hobnailed boots. She strapped on a pistol and snatched up a whip. She was ready for work.

Even the mental torture Irma worked on prisoners was excruciating. She obtained lists of those scheduled to be sent to the gas chambers. Knowing full well when the prisoners would be sent to their death, Irma toyed with the inmates. She would say to one, "You're lucky—you have another two weeks." When the woman or child would appear relieved, Irma would smile and order the inmate killed at once. She dangled doom like a worm before a trout, telling another, "Your turn comes on Friday, so think about it."

She played barbarous games to amuse herself. At dawn Irma would place a shovel or pick outside the barbed wire enclosing a sand pit where hundreds of Jewish women labored each day. When the women were at work Irma would point to one and order her to retrieve the tool on the other side of the loosely stranded wire; she was always careful to select a woman who did not understand German. When the inmate would step through the wire to get the tool, the guard in the tower would shout a warning in a language the inmate did not understand. When the prisoner did not respond but went blindly to retrieve the tool, the guard shot her to death. On these frequent occasions, Irma's laughter rattled along with the deadly bursts of machine-gun fire.

Constant companions of this nightmare figure were two

savage Alsatian hounds. Irma ordered these dogs, which were kept half starved, to attack and kill any prisoner who displeased her. As the dogs pinned the prisoner to the ground, Irma would jump on the inmate's stomach full force, then literally kick the woman or child to death. Often as not she whipped prisoners to near death in a wild frenzy which would burst from her without warning at any moment.

Though she later claimed that her pistol was never loaded, she was seen on numerous occasions to shoot prisoners to death at will. When spotting one woman staring at prisoners being unloaded from trucks, Irma took out her pistol, walked up to the woman, smiled, asked if she was enjoying the view, then blew away her face. Two young girls refused to leave their barracks while others were lining up in front of gas chambers. Irma dragged them screaming from beneath their beds. The girls leaped from windows and began running wildly across the concentration camp compound. Irma shot both dead in their tracks.

When seeing a woman sobbingly talk to her little daughter through barbed wire, Irma rushed to the woman and beat her to death. Like the hellish Ilse Koch, Irma followed the perverse fad of having the skins of murdered prisoners made into lampshades. Reported Gerald Sparrow, "In her own house Irma had had the skins of three victims made into the most attractive lampshades, because she discovered that human skin, though it was tough and durable, also let the light through in a most pleasing way."

In 1945 Irma Grese was transferred briefly to another horror camp, Belsen, and was captured by Allied troops at the close of the war. Survivors of the death camps came forward in scores to testify against her at her war crimes trial. She faced her accusers stoically, calmly telling her judges, "Himmler is responsible for all that has happened, but I suppose I have as much guilt as the others above me." But she displayed no regret, no remorse: To her all the inmates of the satanic camps in which she ruthlessly murdered were nothing more than subhuman "*dreck*." Her philosophy was that of another war criminal, Hermann Göring, who proclaimed, "I have no conscience. My conscience is Adolf Hitler."

The reality of the woman's incredible sadism was clearly revealed as the damning testimony spilled forth. She listened but did not react as survivors of her brutality told how she delighted in selecting female prisoners with large breasts and how she would then cut their breasts open with her whip. She would next take these bleeding women, according to historian Raul Hilberg, writing in *The Destruction of the European Jews*, "to a woman inmate doctor who performed a painful operation on them while Irma Grese watched, cheeks flushed, swaying rhythmically and foaming at the mouth."

A British court, many of its members nauseated at the horrifying testimony, condemned the bestial Irma Grese to death. She was hanged on December 13, 1945, in Hamelin, Germany.

JRN

# 22

# BELLE GUNNESS
## Love with an Axe

---

Of all the many women who have killed for profit, Belle is perhaps the most efficient and the most bloody. We know of at least eight killings to her credit and there were probably at least four others, and doubtless many of which we have not so much as a hint. She was a Norwegian, born at Trondhjem about 1860, who, when young, migrated to the United States where she worked as a servant in Chicago until she married a fellow-Norwegian named Max Sorenson. Shortly afterwards, the husband died and, although there were no suspicions at the time, in view of Belle's later activities, we might be forgiven for wondering whether this demise were natural, particularly as it brought the widow a decent little sum of money. Later, when her achievements were spread wide in the newspapers, it was suggested that he had been poisoned in a glass of stout, but this is purely supposition without any proof. We will never know, Belle being strict in not telling the truth; but I am certain that she did not kill him.

Years later, her puzzled sister said that Belle had begun to change after Sorenson's death. "She began to get morose," she said, "—mean. She scraped and saved every penny that she could, and even stinted her own children of the clothes they really needed. Not that she spent the money on herself. She didn't! She simply hoarded it and seemed to want more and more."

Belle was determined not to risk poverty again: that was

her prime motive. The shock of her husband dying and leaving her alone in the world frightened her. A peasant with a peasant's dread of poverty coming through no fault of her own, by drought or heavy storms, she swore she would not risk a miserable old age. Husbands could not be relied on to keep her: they might die; on her own strength and cleverness must she depend if she would make a success of life against a hostile fate.

At heart, she was not a cruel woman, although a bloody murderess. Her sister told of her extreme love of children. "I have seen," she said, "as many as ten or a dozen of them running about her home. She would play games with them and treat them with the utmost kindness. She loved to spend money on them and was simply adored by every child in the neighbourhood."

From Austin, Illinois, where she and her husband had been living, she moved back to Chicago and invested her savings in a boarding-house which was shortly afterwards burnt to the ground. Her assets swollen with the insurance money, she bought a confectionary shop, with, before long, a similar result. This time the insurance company became suspicious. Although they had to pay up, apparently unable to find any proof of arson, they refused to have any further dealings with her; and, being thus warned, Belle considered other means of making easy money.

In Indiana, she bought a small farm at a place called La Porte, a pretty little shack perched on a hill. Here, with her three children—she was a most devoted mother—she settled and soon married again, choosing the Mr. Gunness whose name she was to make resound through time, who was shortly afterwards killed by a hatchet. As the widow explained to the sympathetic police, he was in the cellar when the hatchet slid from a high shelf, blade outermost, and stuck in his head. The kindly jury took her word for it and Mrs. Gunness collected the insurance money.

Belle was no fool. She had learned how suspicious insurance companies can be and decided that, even in this isolated and trustful community, it might be risky to marry too many husbands who afterwards conveniently died. Yet the idea was attractive, the work she had found to her taste, and she did not want to relinquish it. So she decided to kill without taking on the responsibility of marriage. In the newspapers began to appear the following seductive advertisement: "RICH, good-looking widow, young, owner of a large farm, wishes to get in touch with a gentleman of wealth with cultured tastes. Object: matrimony." That touch about "culture" was truly admirable; but perhaps she was using it in the later Goering sense.

Carefully she read the many answers, rejecting any that suggested that her possible prey might have relatives liable to become suspicious; and at last she settled on a commercial traveller whose disappearance might not be missed. His other important qualification, his bank-balance, was disappointing, being merely a little over, in English money, about a thousand pounds.

We cannot possibly ignore her letter to this man. It is a little masterpiece of psychology, from which I have deleted only some unimportant passages while telescoping short paragraphs. She wrote:

> *Dear Friend, I have been overjoyed by your answer to my advertisement, because I feel sure you are the one man for me. I feel that you will make me and my dear babes happy, and that I can safely entrust you with all that I possess in the world. But I will be candid with you and tell you exactly how I stand.*

*There must be no concealment on either side. Now as
to the farm. There are seventy-five acres of land, and
also all kind of crops—apples, plums, and currants.
All this is pretty nearly paid . . . I lost my husband
by an accident five years ago . . . I am getting tired
of this, and find it is too much to look after things and
manage the children as well. Anyway, my idea is to
take a partner to whom I can trust everything. As we
have no acquaintances ourselves, I have decided that
every applicant I have considered favourably must
make a satisfactory deposit of cash or security. I
think that is the best way to keep away grafters who
are always looking for an opportunity. I am worth at
least twenty thousand dollars, and if you could bring
five hundred just to show you are in earnest, we could
talk things over . . .*

It is astonishing how gullible are many men in their
conceit of themselves. Instead of hurriedly burning such
a suspicious letter as this asking them to visit an unknown
woman with a large sum of money in his pocket, her dupes
were impressed by her appearance of common sense and
her promise of security, passion and affection. She wrote
like an honest woman comfortably off who was fretting in
her widowhood. This was a prospect which many a small
business man would welcome.

Her first applicant was seen to arrive but never to
depart; and her advertisement continued to appear. A
second applicant arrived; and he, also, did not depart.
Profitable business had opened at the farm. Belle must
have been a shrewd judge of character for she varied her
invitations to suit the susceptibility of her victims-to-be.
Some were written to in the above business-like fashion,
others were fed with treacle. To one she wrote: "You are

my king. I love and respect you. I know from your letters you have a loving heart, honest and faithful. Come to me. Your bride awaits you. We shall be as happy here as a king and queen in the most beautiful home in Northern Indiana. My heart would break if you failed me now."

For all this gush, she never failed to mention the subject of money. Wrapped in sugary phrases, in a whirl of passionate promises, she slipped in the essential request that her beloved should bring his money with him. Then, before he would have time to spit out this piece of grit in her honey, on would she hurry to bedroom chatter. "I am glad to think you were never married in all these years" (she wrote to one man). "You were waiting for the one woman you could truly love. I dream of you, my love, and await your coming." Which she did, with an axe.

Such good luck could not go on forever; but, of course, Belle never considered that. The time had to come when some friend or relative would pause to consider why Tom, Dick or Harry had not been seen about as usual. The brother of a missing Andrew Holdgren had begun to worry. He knew that Andrew had hurried off to bliss with a strange woman—"Come, prepared to stay for ever," the widow had honestly written—and since then he had not sent so much as a postcard. The brother wrote to the Indiana farm and in reply received a despairing letter from Belle. "I would do anything in the world to find him" (she wrote). "He left my house seemingly happy, and since that time in January I have not seen him. I will go to the end of the world to find him. I love him, and will help you."

She must, indeed, have been a skilful letter-writer, for she almost seduced this brother into following in Andrew's steps, into selling everything he possessed and, in her company, roving the United States in search of the vanished man. Meanwhile, Belle was busy at her profession and buried another suitor beside poor Andrew who lay at the bottom of the garden.

What follows must be largely guess-work. Unfortunately, Belle never stood her trial, trials being invaluable episodes which often throw a bright light into dark corners. One of her worms turned, and, doubtless to her indignation and astonishment, she lay murdered in her shack. This particular worm was her farm-labourer, Roy Lamphere, who, having spied on her at her toil, was heroic enough to try to blackmail the amazon.

That is the most plausible theory. It is also possible that on accidentally discovering her activities he became panic-stricken lest he, in his turn, be murdered and therefore he got in first. What we do know as fact is that the house, which the newspapers inevitably dubbed "Murder Farm", was burned down and that the bodies of Belle and her three children were found amongst the ashes. Lamphere was arrested and charged with arson just in time for Holdgren's brother to be able to unpack his bags when he had been about to set off on what would have been his last journey. Fearing lest his brother had been indoors when the farm burned down, he informed the police and they set to work, with spades.

About Belle's methods we can only guess, but it is suggestive that one of her ground-floor rooms had hollow brick walls with sawdust in between, thus making them more or less sound-proof, while the door had two enormous locks and iron bars were over the windows. She was making certain that she would not be interrupted in her sport; and perhaps like others, she starved her suitors, until they were too feeble to resist a determined woman; or perhaps she drugged them and killed them while they slept. She had no neighbours to over-watch, to listen and pry. But she did have occasional servants who might have proved inquisitive, one of whom finally slew her in her turn.

Her apparent motive was, of course, money; and it is curious that, as if she had a premonition of her imminent end, she bequeathed a large part of her fortune to a Chicago orphanage for Norwegian children, dousing any pricks of conscience with the reminder that she was a good woman who murdered largely for charitable purposes. Although adoring children, after her husband's death, she grew to hate men because she was not beautiful and was therefore reduced to using cash and not her appearance as bait for lovers who had to die, remaining always hers and no other woman's.

She was sincerely pious and taught in the local Sunday school amongst the children she adored. To a woman such as her, men were purely fathers who, like certain male insects, were killed once they had satisfied the female's need. Being unattractive, she sought revenge on mankind for her failure as a woman. It has been said—with what truth, I know not, although I would like to believe the tale—that when as a girl she had worked in a factory, her especial friend, a particularly lovely girl, hooked a millionaire. If this tale be true, we need seek no further after Belle's unconscious motives, the satisfaction of an ego which must have quivered with envy at her friend's good fortune, and to a determination to outrival her by making even more money by the use of sex with an axe.

—P.L.

# 23

# MYRA HINDLEY
## Suffer Little Children

It started with a telephone call from a kiosk in Hattersley, a new housing estate near Manchester, to Hyde police station at just before 6.10 a.m. on the morning of Thursday, 7 October, 1965. The caller was David Smith, aged seventeen. He was accompanied by his nineteen-year-old wife, Maureen, and he was carrying a knife and a screwdriver for "self protection". Smith, a shocked and exhausted young man, was reporting a murder. He had been up all night, had witnessed the killing and had been obliged to assist in cleaning up the mess after another young man of his own age, Edward Evans, had received fourteen blows on the head from an axe.

A patrol car arrived at the telephone kiosk within a few minutes, and David Smith and his wife were taken to the police station to tell their story. As a story it was gruesome enough, but it was merely the prelude to an even more horrific story that was to emerge during the course of the subsequent police investigation—a story involving two other child murder victims, and the possibility of even more. But at first the police regarded it as a fairly straight-forward single murder inquiry.

What, then, had happened during the pre-dawn hours of that Thursday morning in October, 1965? First it is necessary to look at some of the people involved, and the events leading up to this final act of evil which shocked a country in which capital punishment had only recently been abolished.

David Smith was born in January, 1948, an illegitimate child. At the age of eleven he was charged with wounding with intent; at fourteen, charged with assault causing bodily harm; at fifteen, charged with house-breaking and larceny. He married Maureen Hindley in shotgun-wedding style because she was pregnant. Maureen, two years older than him, was the sister of Myra Hindley.

Esther Myra Hindley, born July, 1942, was an attractive blonde shorthand typist who looked much older than her twenty-three years at the time of the Evans murder. Her father, a former war-time paratrooper, was an invalid after an injury while working on a building site. Her early life and career were unremarkable; she and her family had lived in Gorton, Manchester, all their lives. There was one traumatic experience—at the age of fifteen she befriended, in a motherly fashion, a lively boy of thirteen named Michael Higgins. One hot summer afternoon, when he wanted to go swimming in a local reservoir she declined to join him. He was drowned. She was present when his body was recovered from the slime, and the shock stayed with her for a long time.

In January, 1961, at the age of nineteen, she changed her job and went to work at Millwards Ltd, an old-fashioned chemical company in Gorton, and there she met Ian Stewart Brady, an order-clerk—an odd young man with whom she was to find herself living within a year or two, around about the time of the Great Train Robbery in 1963 and certainly before Kennedy's assassination on 22 November, 1963. It was on the following day, 23 November, that Ian Brady committed his first murder, and one wonders whether the killing of the American President might have triggered a psychopathic mind into imitative action.

Ian Brady, born in January, 1938, was tall and pale,

with wiry brown hair. His eyes were large and grey, and invariably cold. He had high cheek bones and pouting lips. He was the illegitimate son of a waitress in Glasgow named Maggie Stewart, but was adopted by a Sloan family in the Glasgow Gorbals slum district.

There is a story which throws some light on subsequent behaviour: at the age of ten he found a starving cat in a bombed house in Glasgow, put it in a carrier-bag and buried it alive in a graveyard. The cat was later released by passing schoolboys. By the age of twelve he had started collecting Nazi souvenirs—knives, a German cap, a photo of Eva Braun and Hitler. When he was fourteen he was bound over for two years for robbing a gas meter, and soon afterwards was bound over again for the theft of 25s. In 1954 he obtained a job with Harland and Wolff for a few months, then left and joined a butcher as an errand boy.

Then, in November of that year, aged sixteen, he was arrested for house-breaking and, by order of the court, returned to the care and control of his real mother. She had changed her name from Maggie to Peggy, had married an Irish labourer, and was living in Moss Side, Manchester. And so Ian Brady travelled to Manchester to resolve his future career.

He went through a number of short-lived jobs, was arrested for theft, was sent to Strangeways prison and then to Borstal at Hatfield, Yorks. After his release in 1957 he took some casual jobs, but was mainly unemployed and on the dole. Around this time the Brady family moved from Moss Side to Longsight in Manchester.

It was there that he finally landed a relatively stable job as a stock-clerk at Millwards Ltd, although his truculence often caused trouble; and it was there, during his seven-year stay, that he met the new company shorthand-typist—the blonde Myra Hindley, with whom he was soon to live in her grandmother's home (Mrs Maybury, aged seventy-seven, regularly taking sleeping tablets and so hearing nothing during the violent nights). And it was during this period that he started collecting his vast library of books on Nazism, war crimes, torture, sex and sadism, including some of the better-known works of the notorious Marquis de Sade.

From 1963 onwards there were a number of missing children in the Manchester area. The bodies of some were eventually discovered; others have not yet been traced, and may never be. The record runs like this:

12 July, 1963—Pauline Reade, aged sixteen, of Gorton, Manchester. She left home at 7.30 p.m. to join a girl friend at a "jive session" at a social club half a mile away. She never arrived and has not been seen since.

23 November, 1963—John Kilbride, aged twelve, of Ashton-under-Lyne, near Manchester, the eldest of six children (three brothers and two sisters). Visited a cinema and a market in Manchester. Disappeared on his way to the bus-station to return home.

16 June, 1964—Keith Bennett, aged twelve, of Eston Street, Manchester. Set out in the evening to visit his maternal grandmother half a mile away. He was escorted by his mother across a busy main road. He never arrived at his grandmother's home and was never seen again.

26 December, 1964—Lesley Ann Downey, aged ten, of Ancoats, Manchester. Only daughter, with three brothers. She visited a nearby fair on Boxing Day with her brothers and some small friends, but separated from them at some point and was never seen alive again.

6 October, 1965—Edward Evans, aged seventeen, of Ardwick, Manchester. Family living in condemned house and due to be rehoused in the new year. Went into town

for a beer, and then to the Central Station buffet for a bite to eat. Never seen alive again.

In all but the last three "missing persons" cases (since the Edward Evans murder was reported by David Smith soon after it had happened) the police mounted massive searches and investigations. Thousands of people were interviewed, thousands of hand-bills and posters were distributed, canals, rivers and reservoirs were dragged or searched by frogmen. The police chiefs in the area, who included Superintendent Robert Talbot and Detective Chief Inspector Joseph Mounsey—a stubborn, determined man destined to be involved some years later in the Sewell case—pursued their inquiries in a mood of grim single-mindedness, but to no avail. The missing children remained missing.

One remarkable incident happened during the intensive search for John Kilbride. A clairvoyant (Mrs Anne Lansley) was reported to have said that she "saw" the missing boy out in the open, some way down a slope with the skyline completely barren, with a road on the right and near a stream. In the event, she was almost right, but her clairvoyance did not help the police at that time, and John Kilbride's body was eventually found by methodical police investigation, while that of Lesley Ann Downey was discovered almost by accident.

At 11.30 p.m. on 6 October, 1965, Myra Hindley took the dog for its usual nightly run. She and Ian Brady had driven by car to the centre of Manchester earlier in the evening, had visited an off-licence to buy some wine, and then Brady decided to pick up some beer in the Central Station buffet. When he arrived he found it closed, and he had also found young Edward Evans standing by a milk-vending machine. Evans was dark and slim, wearing a suede jacket, suede shoes and tight jeans. He looked as if he might be homosexual; whatever the truth, Evans accepted Brady's invitation to go back to his home for a drink. He introduced Myra Hindley, who was driving the car, as his sister.

After Myra had taken the dog out, Brady drank wine while Evans apparently did not drink anything. That there was some conspiracy at this stage was evident, for Myra in fact went to the home of David Smith, ostensibly to make arrangements for her mother to bleach her hair the following evening. The time was 11.40 p.m. She asked if David Smith would escort her home as she was "scared in the dark".

So David Smith set off with Myra, reaching the Brady home around 11.50 p.m. Myra asked Smith if he would like to come in for some miniature bottles of spirit and liqueurs. Smith agreed, but Myra insisted on going in first just in case Brady was "taping a record". Brady was a great tape-recorder and camera enthusiast, though by no means an expert.

In the event the door was opened by Brady himself, who took Smith into the kitchen and produced three miniature bottles. Brady then went back into the sitting-room, leaving Smith in the kitchen with the door ajar. At that point Smith had no reason to believe that a visitor, Edward Evans, was on the premises.

A few moments later there was a terrified scream. Then Myra shouted: "Dave, help him!" Smith, imagining that Brady was being attacked by an intruder, rushed into the sitting-room, grasping a stick which he had brought with him. To his astonishment Brady seemed to be holding a flabby dummy by the neck and striking its head with an axe. The dummy was lying face down on the floor and Brady was astride it, crouching down and striking the head of the dummy with the side of the axe and not the sharp edge. As he struck, Brady was shouting obscenities. But it wasn't a dummy at all, because Smith could see blood and bone and flesh matted with dark hair flying in all directions.

After fourteen blows to the skull, young Edward Evans died. Brady dragged a cushion cover over the victim's head to contain the flow of blood. Grandmother, in an adjacent room, was awakened by the disturbance and called out, but Myra assured her that it was only the dog. If the neighbours heard any screams, they did not intervene—people seldom do.

The next stage was clearing up and washing up. Smith, who felt sick, was told by Brady that he would have to help, as he was in it "up to the waist". All three cleaned up with hot water and detergents—the walls, the lino, the rugs, furniture and clothing. Brady commented: "That was the messiest yet."

Brady had, in fact, boasted to David Smith on previous occasions that he had murdered a number of people and that one day he would demonstrate to him how it was done. The night of 6 October, 1965, was the night of the grisly demonstration. It was necessary to do something about the body, still lying on the floor. Myra produced a sheet of polythene, a white sheet and a blanket. The polythene was tied round the crushed head with electric flex to hold in the blood, then the body was "jack-knifed" and bundled into the sheet and blanket and tied up in the shape of a large rectangular parcel.

Finally, Smith and Brady dragged the package up some stairs into an unused room where it was dumped under the window, ready for disposal the following morning. During the exertion of getting the corpse up the stairs, Brady quipped: "Eddie's a dead weight, isn't he?"

David Smith finally went home around 3 a.m. and was

then physically sick. He woke his wife and told her what had happened. For the first time Maureen realized that her sister was living with a killer who had claimed more than one victim. By dawn they had decided to go out to a telephone kiosk and call the police.

The arrest of Ian Brady at around 9 a.m. on the morning of 7 October, 1965, was very much a matter of routine. However, because Smith had told the police that Brady had two loaded guns (which he had), two dozen police and six plain-clothes men in half-a-dozen patrol cars were deployed around No. 16 Wardle Brook Avenue. The operation was under the command of Superintendent Robert Talbot, who, unarmed, decided on a subterfuge to gain access to the Brady house. He borrowed the white coat of a local baker's delivery man to cover his uniform and also carried a basket of bread over his arm.

In such a way he gained access to the house when Myra Hindley answered the door to his knock soon after 8.30 a.m. Brady was still in bed, writing a letter to his employer saying that he would be away from work for a day or so as he had hurt his ankle. Searching the rooms of the house, Talbot came upon the blanket-wrapped bundle and felt the stiff outline of its contents. He called in the police photographer and pathologists and forensic scientists.

All that had to do with the murder of Edward Evans. What Talbot and his colleagues did not even begin to imagine at that stage was that in due course the murder by Brady of other children would emerge from the inexorable process of checking and cross-checking.

Some time later, while carrying out a detailed check on Brady's Mini-Countryman car, the police found a wallet containing, among other things, three sheets of paper on which had been written abbreviated tabulated instructions for disposing of a (or perhaps "the") body—instructions such as *Bury head; destroy poly.; inspect car for spots; clean and polish all buttons and clasps; wear glov.; Packamac?* And *for hatch, paper bag*—where "hatch" clearly stood for hatchet, or axe.

At a three-minute hearing on Friday, 8 October, 1965, Ian Brady was formally charged with the murder of Edward Evans. But there was more to come, and Myra was still free.

Meanwhile, checking through papers and note-books in Brady's home, Superintendent Talbot came upon a slim school exercise-book. It contained drawings, doodlings, sums, accountancy exercises and, on one page, a list of names—some film stars, some clearly fictitious, and Ian Brady's own name. Just a random list of about twenty or so names. But among them were the following: *John Sloan, Jim Idiot, Frank Wilson, John Kilbride, Alec Guiness, Jack Polish, etc.*

None of the names seemed relevant to the inquiry, but suddenly one particular name rang a bell in the mind of Superintendent Talbot. *John Kilbride*. A schoolboy aged twelve when first missed on 23 November, 1963, and not seen since. This could be it! Talbot passed a photostat of the page to Detective Chief Inspector Mounsey who was in charge of the Kilbride file.

There were other things as well—albums containing photographs of Myra and friends and Brady himself and bleak shots of the Yorkshire moors, and Myra posing against featureless moorland. David Smith was helpful. Yes, the Bradys used to picnic frequently on the moors, somewhere near Penistone, and sometimes they slept the night there, in the car or outside wrapped in blankets. He had been with them on occasions, and it always seemed to be the same area. But although he went with the police in patrol cars on the moorland Penistone Road travelled by Brady and Hindley he was never able to identify the actual stopping place.

Chief Inspector Mounsey ordered big enlargements of all Brady's out-door moorland photographs in the hope that it might be possible to obtain visual identification of a particular area. Meanwhile, Ian Brady, when questioned about David Smith's suggestion that Brady had killed people and buried them on the moor, denied it, though he tacitly admitted that he had said it—"it was all part of a fiction to impress him".

When a detective put to Brady that Smith had said that he had once been on a grave where Brady and Myra had buried a body, Brady merely said "it was to build up an image". But there was more than an image involved. By 12 October it was decided to start digging operations on the moors. Fifty police were detailed, and assistance was sought from any local inhabitants such as farmers and shepherds who knew the terrain. But the task was virtually impossible in such a vast area of grass and stone. Nevertheless, it gave rise to intriguing newspaper headlines such as "Police in mystery dig on moors" (*Manchester Evening News*). But the dig went on to no avail. The police even dug up the front and back gardens of Brady's house, with no result.

The stalemate was finally resolved during *another* detailed methodical check of the contents of Brady's house (there had been many before). A detective went through all the many books one by one, page by page, shaking them in case there were slips of paper contained therein, folding back the covers and inspecting the hollow cavity of the spine binding. A thankless task, perhaps, but in this case his patience was more than rewarded. Inside the spine of a prayer-book he found a Left Luggage Office ticket, No. 74843, Manchester Central Station, for two suit-cases.

The real horror was now about to unfold.

Superintendent Talbot opened the suit-cases on the desk of his office. The contents were more or less as expected: pornographic books, gun ammunition, more photographs and photographic albums, coshes, and magnetic tapes. He placed one tape on a recorder, and listened to snatches of pop music, recordings from television, and so on. The other tapes he ignored for the moment.

And then he found a tin box containing a set of photographs—nine of them in all. They were pictures of a terrified little girl in various pornographic poses, gagged with a scarf and naked apart from shoes and socks. He knew immediately that he was looking at photographs of Lesley Ann Downey who disappeared at the age of ten on Boxing Day, 1964. In the final photograph the little girl's hands were raised in an attitude of prayer below the gagged mouth.

Meanwhile on the moors another day of digging had come to its uneventful end. The police and civilian helpers were gathering in the coaches to return home from an area known as Hollin Brown Knoll. A late policeman, coming over a rise in the ground, saw something protruding from the peat—something white, resembling the bone of a small forearm. He called to Chief Inspector Mounsey who was by the coach, waiting to depart: "I think it's Kilbride's body."

The departure of the coaches was delayed. The photographers, pathologists and forensic scientists were again called in to carry out their grim work behind canvas screens in the high wind. Only one point of detail was incorrect. The decomposed body that was carefully recovered from the ground was not that of John Kilbride, but were the human remains of little Lesley Ann Downey. John Kilbride was not far away, but he had not yet been located.

In his office Superintendent Talbot was still working on papers, and now playing the remaining tapes, which he listened to with half an ear as they were mainly music and the kind of rubbish that people record and forget about. And then, suddenly, a new tape presented a different noise. Sounds of movement, bumps, subdued murmuring. And then a scream—the voice of a little girl screaming . . . And the quiet background voice, and another scream and the frantic appeal: *"Don't—please, God help me . . ."*

The tape went on and on for sixteen minutes. Talbot listened to it in a state of virtual petrification, staring at the rotating spool. Less than twenty-four hours after the body of Lesley Ann Downey had been recovered from the grave on the moors, he found himself listening to her defilement, torture and murder. That tape was destined to become one of the most terrifying exhibits in any murder trial, and Mrs Downey, the mother, was to hear it too, in order to identify her deceased daughter's voice—and hear that voice calling for her mother in desperation. The mother had already identified the body, which had lain nearly a year in the ground.

At the end of that tape, after the screams and cries had faded into silence, came Christmas music—*Jolly Old St Nicholas* and *The Little Drummer Boy*. When asked in court during his trial why he had preserved the tape, Brady replied: "Because it was unusual."

Hyde Police Station now became a major operations headquarters, with a Press-room that was attended by about fifty journalists from all over the world. Headed by Detective Chief Inspector Joseph Mounsey, the police were making an all-out effort to find the grave of John

Kilbride on the moors, for they were convinced that it lay in the areas depicted in the photographs taken by Brady, but so difficult to identify. New professional photographs were taken in the vicinity so that they could be enlarged and compared with the inferior Brady pictures, most of which featured Myra Hindley or himself against an indistinct background. The Brady prints were re-processed to improve definition and compared with the landscape shots taken from known points by official police photographers.

In the end Mounsey's patience was rewarded. He was able to match two of Brady's snapshots with one of the police photographs. The background was the same, and so were the stones in the foreground and the nearby water. The assumption was that Brady and Hindley, in their macabre way, had been standing on or near a grave when the pictures were taken. And so the digging started again, but this time with a geographical centre established by photographs.

On 21 October, 1965, at Hyde Police Court, Ian Brady and Myra Hindley were finally charged with the murder of Edward Evans and of Lesley Ann Downey. At this stage there was no charge relating to John Kilbride as the body had not yet been found. But there was not long to go. That same day, in the early afternoon, police probes finally penetrated the patch of ground that Myra Hindley had appeared to be staring at in one of Brady's photographs. One probe encountered something about two feet below the surface of the ground. The tip, on withdrawal, bore the characteristic smell of putrefaction. John Kilbride's grave had finally been found.

Once more the canvas screens were erected and the pathologists called in, while the police formed a cordon round the site to control the mass of people who were now converging on it. The work of excavation went on as night fell on the moors. Light was provided by naked acetylene flares. Finally the remains were lifted and transferred to a metal stretcher for transport by van to the mortuary.

The trial opened on 19 April, 1966, in the Assize Court at Chester. Ian Brady and Myra Hindley pleaded "not guilty" to charges of murdering Edward Evans, Lesley Ann Downey and John Kilbride. Hindley was additionally charged with comforting, harbouring and maintaining Brady, knowing that he had murdered John Kilbride.

Brady admitted killing Evans—it was due to a quarrel, he implied. He maintained that Lesley Ann Downey had left the house safely after the photographs had been taken, and he knew nothing at all about John Kilbride.

The all-male jury returned a verdict of guilty on all three counts. Brady received three concurrent sentences of life imprisonment, and Hindley two, plus seven years for "receiving, comforting and harbouring". They disappeared to their separate prisons.

As for the other two missing children—Pauline Reade and Keith Bennett—they have never been traced or found, nor is there any evidence to suggest that they met a similar fate and are still buried on the moors. There is only the coincidence of time, place and age-group. All were between ten and sixteen years of age, all lived in the Manchester area, and all vanished suddenly between the years 1963 and 1965—the year when Brady was arrested for the murder of Evans.

One can't help wondering whether, if David Smith had kept his silence as Brady expected him to, there might by now have been many more missing children in Manchester, perhaps lying in new graves on the bleak moors.

—C.E.M.

# 24

# HÉLÈNE JEGADO
## Mass Murder in Brittany

Hélène Jegado, a Brittany poisoner, left corpses at almost every spot on which she settled for long. As an orphaned child, she had been taken into service and employed as a cook; and it was not until she was about thirty that she awoke in horror to the realization that she would most likely remain both a maid and a cook forever with none of the freedom and pleasures of her betters above stairs. After this discovery, she took to poisoning as a substitute for love and riches, and, within three months, she had poisoned seven people in the house, including her own sister. Like Anna, she showed herself a devoted, tireless nurse and her patient devotion to the dying and the dead was such that the authorities could not bring themselves to believe that she could possibly have been a murderess.

After wiping out one household, Hélène sought service in another; with the same result. As if a plague had swept into the house on her skirt-hems, everybody, except herself, rapidly died. Continually was she on the move, that being one of the occupational necessities of her chosen profession. She had to keep moving, she explained, because otherwise somebody might actually suspect her of having had a hand in these extraordinary deaths. She was a wretched creature, she moaned, who seemed to carry with her an evil influence. "Wherever I go," she wailed, "people die."

To escape this curse which dogged her movements, she entered a convent, only to be expelled for theft.

In another convent, she was charged with concocting soups and potions which produced death. Not wanting any scandal, the convent dismissed her; and off Hélène plodded again with her packet of arsenic, and people continued to die about her; for now, like Anna, she was unable to stop had she even wished to, of which urge there is no evidence whatever. Here was her sole method of taking revenge on life and of asserting her personality. During these wanderings, between 1833 and 1841, we can more or less safely assert that at least twenty-three murders and uncountable thefts might more than possibly have been proved against her.

Monotonously on goes the record, although for a while we lose track of her, until in 1849 we encounter her in the city of Rennes, employed by a M. Rabot who, catching her stealing, sent her out of his house. Whereupon his entire family was stricken with excruciating pains, although none of them died. Like Jehovah warring with the Egyptians in silence had Hélène struck.

At her next position, she was accused of pilfering brandy, and almost immediately the youngest child fell into convulsions—believed by the simpletons to be an attack of croup—and, shortly afterwards, died. Next we discover her at an inn where, after quarrelling with an upper-servant, the upper-servant died; then the landlady died. Finally, she was dismissed for stealing wine.

Then came her last performance, in the household of a M. Bifard in Rennes where she poisoned a fellow-servant, and for the first time she was to encounter an intelligent doctor. This man became suspicious and he took his suspicions to the police. When the examining magistrate called at the house, Hélène suddenly lost her courage. She screamed that she was innocent. "Of what?" asked the magistrate. "Nobody has accused you." Resulting from thus having involuntarily betrayed herself, her past was investigated. And, in December 1851, she found herself standing trial for her life.

As this trial took place during the Napoleonic *coup d'état*, many important witnesses were unable to attend and the expert evidence was unconvincing, while—most important of all—no arsenic had been found in Hélène's possession: neither could any be traced to her; and this triumphantly she pointed out in court. Nevertheless, the circumstantial evidence proved too strong and, despite her protests, her outbursts of fury during the trial, she was sentenced to death. And calmly, as though to sleep, she laid her neck under the blade.

Difficult is it for normal folk to detect any reason in such seemingly aimless murders, but there is nothing aimless in the acts even of lunatics. In appearance, Hélène was a stupid, sullen woman, repulsive to look at and with dull eyes which showed light only when she was angry or watching the convulsions of one of her victims. She was also deeply and undoubtedly sincerely pious, regularly attending mass either before or after each murder; and when accused of her crimes, she obstinately, pugnaciously insisted on her innocence.

The secret of her deadly pilgrimage must lie in that repulsive appearance which denied her love. If she could be not loved, she might reason, she would at least be feared and hated while she took revenge on women more fortunate than herself in possessing good looks and a happy family-life. Frustration, the impossible-to-be-satisfied craving for love, sent her out to kill. Suddenly, after living quietly, unambitiously for years, she looked aghast at her spiritual desolation and sought revenge for it.

—P.L.

# 25

# WINNIE RUTH JUDD
## Trunks for Two

In November, 1952, when Winnie Ruth Judd fled for the sixth time from the Arizona State Hospital, she was only continuing the flight she began some twenty years earlier with the discovery of this country's most celebrated trunk murders. Her flights, both real and fanciful, have led psychiatrists to disagree, have caused conflict among judges and grand juries, and confused investigators to such a point that one remarked, "The only thing we can be sure of it that it was a crime of passion, but the question is what passion or passions?"

That same question had been asked repeatedly over the years. Actually, the motive is not obscure, the confusion arising mainly from the different statements made by Winnie Ruth Judd. What most observers have overlooked is the simple fact that she varied her stories in an attempt to win her freedom; she had no interest in revealing the complete facts. Enough information has come to light by now to indicate not only what happened, but why.

At the time of the murders, Winnie was an attractive blonde in her mid-twenties, her face dominated by unusually large and beautiful blue-grey eyes. There was no indication in her fully developed figure that she once had been tubercular, and it is interesting to note that she frequently posed for photographers with her knees crossed, giving full display to her long, slender and shapely legs. She possessed a captivating personality, and was able to charm both men and women—so much so, that hospital authorities are convinced that she had help in many of her escapes.

Since Winnie had spun fanciful tales and spread confusion from her childhood on, it is not surprising that her case has caused much controversy. Yet the basic facts are clear.

When Southern Pacific Train Number Three arrived in Los Angeles on its overnight run from Phoenix on Monday morning, October 19, 1931, the baggageman reported to the district supervisor the two trunks had smelled up his car. One was a large packing type, the other a smaller steamer size. Some brownish liquid was oozing from a corner of the large one.

Since the deer season had just opened in Arizona, both men assumed that a hunter was sending home his kill despite regulations against the shipment of game. The two trunks were set aside.

About noon that day an attractive blonde woman, accompanied by a younger man, presented claim checks but the supervisor refused to release the trunks until he could examine the contents. The woman, wrinkling her nose with distaste at the odour, remarked, "I wonder what's inside?" After explaining that her husband had the keys, she said she would be back shortly, and drove off with her companion in an old battered roadster.

Some four hours later, when she failed to return, police were notified and the two trunks opened. Jack-knifed into the larger one was the nude body of a woman. The steamer trunk contained the head and parts of the dismembered torso of a second woman. Both had been shot in the head, with additional gunshot wounds in the breast and right hand of the second woman. Later, the missing pieces of the torso were found in a suitcase and hatbox which had been abandoned in the women's rest room at the depot.

The assorted luggage was a veritable treasure trove of clues. The larger trunk was stuffed with snapshots of the two women, letters, assorted personal papers, clothing, books, a ten-inch curved saw-tooth knife, a set of surgical instruments, and a piece of blood-stained carpet. Several discharged .25 calibre cartridges were in two purses. The hatbox yielded a .25 Colt automatic.

Some of the letters were addressed to Mrs. Agnes Anne LeRoi, the others to Miss Hedvig Samuelson, both at the same address of 2929 North Second Street in Phoenix. Many of the snapshots were labelled *Anne and Sammy*, making the identification of the two women even easier, and police were able to determine that it was Miss Samuelson's body that had been butchered.

As the victims had been shipped from Phoenix, authorities there were notified and began an immediate investigation, while Los Angeles police started searching for the unknown blonde.

At the railroad station in Phoenix, detective learned that the trunks had been shipped Sunday night by a woman who had signed *B. J. McKinnell* to the claim checks. The local address she had given turned out to be non-existent.

Any doubt as to the identity of the victims was removed when police went to the North Second Street address and learned that Mrs. LeRoi and Miss Samuelson shared a duplex bungalow apartment there and had not been seen since Friday night. Mrs. LeRoi, a nurse employed at the Grunow Memorial Clinic had not reported for work on Saturday. Instead, Dr. Percy Brown had received a telephone call, supposedly from her, informing him that Miss Samuelson's brother was ill in Tucson and she had to accompany her roommate there. Because it upset him to be without an assistant to take X-rays, he had demanded that she report for work, but the caller hung up on him.

Suspicious because he had not recognized the voice, Dr. Brown sent his wife to the bungalow. She found the doors locked, nobody answered her repeated rings, and a glance into the bedroom windows showed the twin beds made up. She told her husband that both women were gone.

Police searched the bungalow and at first glance everything appeared to be in order; all furniture was in place, and the refrigerator was well stocked with fresh food. A thorough inspection turned up several small bloodstains on the wall alongside one of the beds. Underneath it, several square feet of carpet had been laboriously cut away with a small pair of manicure scissors left on the floor. The missing carpet matched the bloodstained piece in the trunk. When the officers turned back the covers on the twin beds, both mattresses were missing. Two spots of dried blood also were noticed on the sidewalk in front of the bungalow.

One of the local trucking services had picked up a trunk at the bungalow late Saturday night. A pretty blonde had admitted the expressmen and instructed them to take the trunk to the station. It was so heavy that three men were needed to lift it. They had rested it momentarily on the sidewalk where the blood spots were found. The foreman advised the woman that it was too heavy to go as baggage and she gave him an address on Fast Brill Street, telling him to leave it there in the garage. Winnie Ruth Judd occupied the apartment at this address on Brill Street. Her landlord, H. U. Grimm, said he had taken two trunks to the station for her on Sunday afternoon. It was obvious to police that the large trunk originally had held the two bodies.

Winnie also was employed in the Grunow Clinic, but as a secretary. She had reported for work an hour late on Saturday morning after telephoning that she would be delayed. Her call had come in shortly after the one supposedly made by Mrs. LeRoi, and the telephone operator at the clinic said both calls had been made by the same woman. Mrs. Judd had spent Saturday at the clinic typing menus, a point that was to assume importance later. On Sunday, she entered the clinic, her hand bandaged and left word that she had to leave for Los Angeles because her husband was very ill, but had arranged for a substitute to take her place.

Meanwhile, the trail in Los Angeles also was leading to the name of Winnie Ruth Judd. A baggage clerk had jotted down the licence number of the roadster in which the blonde left the station and this was traced to Burton McKinnell, a student at the University of Southern California, who told police that his sister Winnie had appeared unexpectedly on the campus shortly before noon and had asked him to drive her to the depot to pick up her luggage. After the supervisor refused to hand over the trunks without inspecting the contents, she told her brother that she was in trouble but refused to explain. She got out of his car in the downtown shopping area, borrowed his last five dollars and walked away.

The time of the murders was established at about 11 p.m. Friday. Several neighbours reported hearing shots at that time. Evelyn Nace, a friend of the victims, said she had been at the bungalow all evening until about ten o'clock when her sister stopped by to pick her up. Mrs. LeRoi was preparing for bed and had just put on a pair of pink pyjamas, while Sammy, who was tubercular and allowed to sit up only a few hours a day, already was in bed. "Both girls were perfectly cheerful as they said good night," she told detectives. No other visitors had been at the bungalow that night before she left.

The search for Winnie was extended to Santa Monica where her husband, Dr. William C. Judd, who was ill, was living with a sister. He was surprised to learn that his wife had been in Los Angeles and had failed to get in touch with him. He knew both Mrs. LeRoi and Miss Samuelson and said Winnie was one of their best friends, the three of them rooming together at the bungalow until the previous month when his wife took an apartment in anticipation of his coming back to Phoenix.

Dr. Judd, who was forty-eight, was some twenty-two years older than Winnie. They had met when she was eighteen and had joined the staff of the State Hospital for the Insane at Evensville, Indiana, where he was supervising physician. He had been kind to the shy girl when she first came to work there as a matron; then found himself falling in love with her. They were married after a brief courtship. Some time later she became ill and thought she had a heavy cold. Dr. Judd, however, recognized the early symptoms of tuberculosis, resigned his post, and took her to Mexico, but she failed to make any progress and he brought her to a sanatorium in Pasadena where after eighteen months the disease was arrested. From there they moved to Phoenix. As a result of war wounds, Dr. Judd was unable to work for long stretches and Winnie went to a secretarial school to prepare herself for a working career.

Describing her as "demure and sweet," Dr. Judd refused to believe that she could have been responsible for the two murders. He said he had received a letter from her only that morning. Dated and postmarked Saturday afternoon, which was after the murders, it was a chatty letter and contained no hint of the crime. It read:

*Dear Doctor:*

*I start so many letters and then have to do something else and destroy the letter and simply do not get one mailed.*

*Thank you very much this time for writing me whether I write to you or not. I am busy. I don't seem to get things done . . .*

*Doctor, I am lonesome. I will be so glad to have you here. I love you, oh, so tenderly with arms of love. I am usually so tired I can't write how much I love you. Then after I have rest for awhile, I long for you. I will be glad if you are here Tuesday or Wednesday. I need you and have for some time, but we needed money so badly when someone took $15 of my money.*

*Everybody is going hunting down here. Four of the clinic doctors went, and ever so many people. The deer season is open now. Some of the nurses over at the hospital are going out . . . They want me to go about 3:30. It will be an outing for me so maybe I will go. I would like to.*

*It is much cooler here now. Come home soon. It isn't a pretty home. Doctor, but again, we ain't got barrels of money, maybe we're all ragged and funny but we will travel along singing a song "Side by Side," because we love each other.*

*Ruth*

Dr. Judd showed the officers another letter he had received from her in August in which she wrote: *For the last few years we have had an awful time, that is, breaking away from the "stuff" and never completely getting away from it . . . Doctor you are just part of my life . . . I am sitting here writing and crying so that I cannot see the letters on the typewriter. Doctor, I can't sleep, and I can't do my work*. Asked what she meant by the "stuff", the physician explained that he frequently had to take drugs to relieve the pains of his war wounds and had become addicted. Since then he had rehabilitated himself.

Although he described his married life with Winnie as very happy, he said that she had longed for a child but he opposed it because of his health and their precarious financial position. Her yearning became so strong that at one point she began speaking of a mythical son and accused him of causing the baby to disappear.

The letters Winnie wrote to her husband and the story he told police provide an important key toward understanding the motive, as will be shown later.

Although Dr. Judd protested that his wife must be innocent, officers by now were convinced that she was responsible for the trunk murders, but they ran into difficulty in trying to establish a motive. The first lead was the discovery that Winnie had moved out of the bungalow. Friends of the three women said it was not because Dr. Judd might return to Phoenix but because Winnie and Mrs. LeRoi were unable to get along together. This was substantiated by an unfinished letter Sammy had started to her sister in which she wrote, *Anne and I have moved away from Mrs. Judd, and we are much happier by ourselves, as she and Anne clashed on so many things and their quarrels were sometimes violent*.

But opinions differed on the cause of the quarrels. Some thought that Winnie had tried to drive a wedge into the unusually close frienship that existed between Mrs. LeRoi and Miss Samuelson. The two had met in Alaska where Sammy was teaching school and the other was supervising nurse of a small hospital. When Sammy became ill with tuberculosis, generous Juneau residents contributed money to send her to Phoenix, and

Mrs. LeRoi gave up her post to accompany her friend and live with her. She took a job at the clinic and acted as nurse for Sammy when she came home at night.

An extrovert who liked people, Mrs. LeRoi made friends easily and brought each new acquaintance home to meet Sammy. These included not only nurses and doctors but businessmen in Phoenix, and they became very fond of the schoolteacher, who was always cheerful even though she was bedridden most of the time. Mrs. LeRoi who was a divorcee, had met Winnie after she obtained a job at the clinic. Winnie had moved in with Sammy in August when Mrs. LeRoi went home to Portland, Oregon, for a visit with her family. She cut her trip short after receiving the following letter from Mrs. Judd:

> *I suppose you know that Sammy and I are together, waiting every day for our dear little Anne to return to the fold. Sure, I think we can get along fine, the three of us, until I go to the Doctor. We talk a lot about our Anne and how she is going to behave herself when she comes back. Sammy is flirting as per usual. I went to Bisbee on Saturday, and Sammy moved over to the house on Sunday night . . . Well, at 5 A.M., Sammy heard someone come in the back door and she got up and ran out to meet the milkman! He was terribly surprised and started to run. Then Sammy told him she thought it was me. I don't know what to believe. Anyhow, the milkman is as sweet as pie and doesn't run any more . . . Sammy also flirts with the iceman . . .*

Several weeks after Anne returned, Winnie moved out and took the apartment on East Brill Street.

Other friends, however, thought that Winnie and Anne

had quarrelled over a man. A nurse, who knew both of them, said that she had attended a dinner at Winnie's apartment on Thursday, the night before the murder. John Halloran, a well-known Phoenix business man, was there with two companions. They had brought the food and wanted to invite Anne and Sammy to the dinner. Winnie protested but went along with the others when Halloran drove them over to the bungalow. She refused to leave the car, however, and Halloran went in alone. "Winnie saw him kiss Anne and Sammy when he went into the bungalow and she was furious and upbraided him when he returned to the car," the nurse told police.

Halloran, a married man, denied being in love with Mrs. Judd or having an affair with her. He admired the plucky fight Sammy was making to regain her health and his admiration also extended to Mrs. LeRoi for her unselfish devotion to her friend. He had met them through Mrs. Judd. In view of the letters Winnie had written to her husband, detectives were inclined to accept Halloran's statement that he was nothing more than a friend of all three women.

Meanwhile, Winnie had disappeared. Police of Arizona and California conducted an intensive search and Dr. Judd issued a public appeal for her to surrender. On October 23rd, she telephoned her husband and arranged to meet him with an attorney. After a two-hour conference with her, Dr. Judd notified police.

Her left hand was still bandaged and she said she had been shot by Sammy. She had surrendered because she feared lockjaw. Taken to a hospital, a bullet was removed from the fleshy part at the base of her third finger. Doctors said that her body was badly bruised.

She told police that she shot in self-defence, but refused to answer any questions on advice of counsel.

The following day, however, scraps of an 18-page letter, written on telegraph blanks, were found in the drainpipe of a Los Angeles department store. When the scraps were pieced together, it appeared to be a confession to the murders that Mrs. Judd had written to her husband. The first part was rambling, frequently incoherent, and in it she admitted that she had falsely accused a man of raping her and causing her to be pregnant when she was sixteen. *I lied then and was a virgin when I married you*, the statement said. She also admitted that her stories about having a baby which Dr. Judd had spirited away were false. *I'm crazy on that line*, the letter read. *And aside from that and occasionally a rage that I get into, I seem quite bright.*

When the letter came to discussing the two deaths, Winnie wrote that she had stayed overnight at the bungalow with Anne and Sammy, and the following morning while they all were still in pyjamas they had started quarrelling. She wrote that Anne and Sammy were angry because she had introduced a nurse to a businessman in town and they threatened to tell him that the nurse was being treated for a venereal disease. Winnie said she told Anne that she had no right to reveal information contained in hospital records.

This portion of the letter read:

> "Well," Ann said, "He certainly won't think much of you doing such a thing. You've been trying to make him like you, and Mr.—too, getting him to move you, and when I tell them you associate with and introduce them to girls like that, they won't have a thing to do with you, and . . . he won't take you hunting either."
>
> I said, "Sammy, I'll shoot you if you tell that." We were in the kitchen just starting breakfast. She came

*in with my gun and said she would shoot me if I went hunting with this friend. I threw my hand over the mouth of the gun and grabbed the breadknife. She shot. I jumped on her with all my weight and knocked her down in the dining-room. Ann yelled at us. I fired twice, I think, and since Ann was going to blackmail me too . . . and hand me over to the police, I fired at her.*

*There was no harm introducing this nurse who is very pretty to the men . . . but they were going to kill me for introducing her . . . Doctor, dear, I am so sorry Sammy shot me. Whether it was the pain or what, I got the gun and killed her. It was horrible to pack things as I did. I kept saying: "I've got to, I've got to, or I'll be hung." I'm wild with cold, hunger, pain and fear now. Doctor darling, if I hadn't got the gun away from Sammy, she would have shot me again . . . I killed in self-defence. Love me yet, Doctor.*

There was no signature to the letter. Ruth at first said she had written it and then denied it. A handwriting expert testified she had written the letter.

Officials, at first, were delighted with the find, but as they studied the letter they began to back away from it. Winnie had placed herself in the bungalow Friday night and said the fatal shots were fired Saturday morning. All evidence indicated that the murders had occurred Friday night and Winnie had not been in the bungalow when the victims went to bed at 10 p.m.

She had been labelled the "Velvet Tigress" by reporters and in this statement she had clawed the reputation of several people. The nurse she had named in the letter was the same one who had told police about Winnie's quarrel with Anne, and there was little doubt that the man in the letter was Halloran. Thus she had smeared the reputations of both possible witnesses against her.

With the letter made public, Winnie began to talk. She said that after she left her brother, she had entered a department store and concealed herself in a drapery department on an upper floor, remaining there overnight. The following morning she slipped down to the first floor, bought a package of black dye and changed the colour of her dress in a wash-room. That afternoon she walked out with a group of women and started toward Pasadena. She got a lift from a truck-driver who let her out near the sanatorium where she once had been a patient. She knew that there were vacant cottages on the grounds and she hid in one of them, remaining there until her fear of lockjaw drove her to seek out her husband. To disguise herself for her return trip, she sneaked into an occupied cottage and helped herself to a dress and coat. She admitted that she had written the letter found in the drain-pipe on her return to Los Angeles before her surrender.

"You know the rest," was all she would say about the murders.

Several days later Winnie furnished a new motive in a story she sold to a newspaper. She now claimed that Anne and Sammy were perverts and the quarrel started when she accused them of it. In this new version she said the struggle took place in the kitchen where she shot both of them, later carrying them into the bedroom. It wasn't until Saturday evening when she returned from work that she dissected one body because both would not fit in the trunk.

District Attorney Lloyd Andrews of Phoenix said her second statement, like her first, was a "fanciful fabrication" intended to form the basis of a self-defence or insanity plea.

"She still has not told the real motive," he said to newsmen. "I believe it to be something far more important than the quarrel she described."

He pointed out strong flaws in Winnie's two statements. Although she claimed she had been shot in the hand Saturday morning, she wore no bandage when she reported for work at the clinic and had spent the day typing, an almost impossible task if she had been wounded in the left hand. The physician for whom she worked told investigators he would have noticed it if her hand had been injured. The prosecutor said flatly that she had shot herself in the hand to build up a self-defence alibi. Her story of dissecting the body hours after the shooting was disputed by medical evidence which showed that disemberment had taken place almost immediately after death. The doctors dealt an even more severe blow to her version when they said the path of the bullets through the body proved conclusively that both women had been shot while asleep in bed.

Anticipating an insanity plea, the prosecutor obtained a court order for several psychiatrists, including Dr. Joseph Catton, to examine Winnie. Her attorneys also employed psychiatrists for the same purpose.

Friends of the murdered women denied the perversion charge. Mrs. LeRoi had been engaged to be married and had many men friends. She had encouraged visitors to drop in at any time as part of her plan to keep Sammy cheerful and was visibly pleased when callers came.

Winnie was placed on trial on January 19, 1932. The evidence consisted largely of the facts so far set forth here. One woman testified that Winnie told her that she had a "boy friend." A streetcar conductor said that she had boarded his car at about ten o'clock on Friday or Saturday night—he wasn't certain as to the exact night—and got off near the bungalow. At 11:25 that same night, while he was on his return trip, she again boarded his car, getting off near her home.

For several days Winnie sat quietly between her elderly mother and her father, a minister in Illinois, as the evidence piled up against her, but her temper flared when Dr. Catton came over to speak to her during a court recess.

"Get out of here," she screamed at him. "I won't talk to you. You promised not to tell anything I told you, but you go down to pool halls and talk about me. Get away. Get away."

The reason for her outburst became clear when Dr. Catton took the witness stand. He had questioned Winnie for several hours while she was awaiting trial and she had admitted to him that she was in love with another man and wanted to have a baby by him. She indicated that the other man was Halloran. At one point he asked her if she had been drinking on the night of the murder and Winnie replied, "Nobody was drinking but Halloran." She hurriedly clapped her hands over her mouth and remained silent for a while. Dr. Catton said he asked her whether she had ever cut up a human being under any conditions and she replied, "I am going to say I did," and then added, "I have never even cut a chicken."

The psychiatrist testified that in his opinion Winnie was a frightened woman, but sane. He thought she was above normal intelligence and crafty. "She showed normal love feelings when she told me about her affair with the other man," he said on the stand. "However, she is very remorseful about everything that has happened, and regrets extremely that her husband had to know about it."

Other doctors called by the prosecution also testified that she was sane. Although the defence used the letter found in the drainpipe to plead self-defence, their entire case was built on proving Winnie insane. Her mother took the witness stand and described how Winnie had disappeared from home once and was found several days later in a barn, clad only in a nightgown and gunnysack. It was at this time that she had raised her rape and pregnancy charge. Even after medical examination disproved her story, she continued making baby clothes. Her aged father exposed family secrets when he testified in a trembling voice that his grandmother and an uncle and two other relatives had died insane. Several defence psychiatrists said that Winnie was suffering from dementia praecox and an endocrinologist testified that she had a gland disorder that affected her mentality.

An all-male jury found Winnie Ruth Judd guilty of first-degree murder and voted the death penalty which, at that time in Arizona, was the gallows.

Although Winnie had appeared almost disinterested in her case during the trial, she became alert once she had entered prison. When her appeal for a new trial was denied by the State Supreme Court, she went before the Prison Board and spoke clearly and lucidly for three days as she argued for a commutation of her death sentence.

When this was denied, Winnie announced that she now was ready to tell the full story of the murder. Brought before a grand jury, she repeated that she had shot in self-defence, but this time brought in Halloran as the one who had packed the bodies in the trunk. She claimed that Halloran came calling at her apartment just after she arrived home from the bungalow. She had planned to telephone her husband for advice, but Halloran would not let her do it. He brought her back to the bungalow where the bodies still were on the kitchen floor. While she cleaned up the blood, he packed the bodies. He sent her home before he was through and telephoned her the next day telling her the bodies were in the trunk and that she should ship them to Los Angeles. She said that he had taken away the mattresses. If he would only produce them now, she insisted, the bedding would show that the women had not been killed in bed and that her story was true.

A sympathetic grand jury not only indicted Halloran but also issued a statement urging the parole board to commute her sentence to life imprisonment, which in Arizona means a term of 15 to 20 years.

At a preliminary court hearing for Halloran, Winnie said, "I'm not here for the purpose of clearing him. He had a chance to clear me at my trial and didn't. He is responsible for the deaths of those girls," indicating that he was the cause of the fatal quarrel, which was her original story in the drainpipe letter. Halloran repeated under oath that he knew nothing about the murders.

The court dismissed the charge against him, stating that if Mrs. Judd's story was true and she shot in self-defence, then she had not committed murder, therefore no crime had been committed and Halloran could not be an accessory. This unusual reasoning was interpreted by many to mean that Winnie was innocent.

When the Arizona Pardon and Parole Board refused to accept the grand jury recommendation and ordered the death sentence carried out, defence attorneys requested a sanity hearing before a jury. Winnie constantly interrupted the hearing before a jury with wild shouts of laughter and hysterical screams. She made several dashes toward windows as if to jump out, and tore strands of hair from her head. Dr. Catton testified that he was uncertain as to whether she had developed prison neurosis or was faking. He added that she would recover quickly once the threat of the gallows had been removed.

Only three days before her scheduled execution date the jury, composed mainly of farmers and ranchers, ruled that Winnie was insane. When she was taken to the Arizona State Hospital the next day, she was all smiles and no longer clutched at her hair or stared blankly at walls. The death sentence was deferred until she regained her sanity.

At the hospital, she quickly became one of the most popular inmates and studied to be a beautician. When she began to give permanents to nurses in the hospital, beauty parlours in town protested. Winnie made her first escape shortly after the state abolished the gallows and opened a gas chamber for executions. A ruling was requested as to whether the changeover affected her death penalty, since she had been sentenced to be hanged. The State Attorney General ruled that it did not.

Winnie was free for five days, part of the time visiting with her parents who had moved to Arizona. Back in the hospital she was placed in solitary confinement for five weeks. Resentful at this treatment, she escaped again and left two notes addressed to the Governor. In one of them she asked for a new trial and this time claimed that a physician had assisted Halloran in dismembering the body. When she was captured 12 days later in Yuma, she had a 12-page statement ready for reporters in which she expanded on this same theme, meanwhile still claiming she had killed in self-defence. A grand jury ignored her latest story.

Meanwhile, Winnie had not been without friends. A citizen's committee was formed in Phoenix and asked the pardons board to hold public hearings to determine if the death penalty was delaying her recovery. The committee wanted the death sentence commuted.

This was finally done in May, 1952. Winnie Ruth Judd

no longer faces the death penalty and if she is able to prove herself sane, she probably will gain her immediate release in view of the years she has served in the State Hospital.

We now come to the question of motive. Although Winnie was in love with her husband (he died in 1946), her letters to him indicated that it was more the affection of a younger girl toward an older man whom she admired and respected. While she frequently mentioned the word *love*, she rarely used the kind of terms of endearment that would be natural in such personal letters. Her salutations invariably began "Dear Doctor," and she continued to use that title in the body of her letters, never using his first name. If anything, she still was in awe of him, and she apparently never got over the relationship that existed between them when she was a young frightened girl on her first job and he was the physician in charge of the hospital.

Her longing for a child was deep-rooted with her sex desires. It began with her false accusation when she was sixteen and continued years later when she was married and invented a baby. She was frustrated sexually and admitted to Dr. Catton that because of her husband's fears of having a child they had never completed a sex act during their entire married life. At the time of the murders, Winnie was a normal, healthy woman, physically attractive to men. She and her husband had been separated most of the time. It was quite likely that she had been telling the truth when she confided to a woman friend that she had a boy friend.

Whether it was Halloran is another matter. If she was in love with him, all evidence indicates that it was largely in her mind and was not reciprocated, but her imagination could have made it seem real to her. Dr. Catton had characterized her as crafty and it is rather odd that, after successfully fencing with police, prosecutors and other officials for weeks, she should have made a slip and mentioned Halloran's name. Her coy clapping of her hands over her mouth after the slip appears to have been play acting and she may have deliberately used a wrong name to cover up the identity of the man she actually loved and with whom she was having an affair. It is possible that this man assisted her in dismembering Miss Samuelson's body when she telephoned him in a panic after the murders. Autopsy surgeons said the dissection was crudely done and showed no signs of any medical skill. Mrs. Judd was seen riding in a car with a man on Sunday, hours before she left for Los Angeles. This man was not Halloran and he never has been identified. The mattresses could have been disposed of at that time.

We know that Dr. Judd was planning to return to Phoenix in several days. We know that Mrs. LeRoi and Winnie did not like each other, and it is quite possible that Mrs. LeRoi knew the identity of Winnie's secret lover and threatened to tell Dr. Judd about her misconduct. The one bullet hole in Mrs. LeRoi's head indicates that she was shot first; it was her mouth that Winnie wanted to seal. The shot awakened Sammy who grabbed for the gun and was shot in the hand. During the struggle the second shot caught her in the chest. Winnie then delivered the *coup de grâce* in the head when Sammy fell back on the bed.

Winnie's love affair was threatened and she took positive steps to eliminate the threat. This situation has served as a motive for murder since the beginning of mankind.

—EDR

# 26

# ILSE KOCH
## "Merely a Housewife"

Born and bred in Dresden, Germany, Ilse Koch began working in a cigarette factory at age fifteen, giving half her wages to her impoverished family. Two years later she went to work in a bookshop. A voluptuous blue-eyed blonde, by then, she was enthralled by Hitler's storm troopers and had joined the Nazi Youth Party. The bookstore was an official branch of that party and the elderly owner pandered to the racist tastes of the Nazis. He told the naive Ilse that he would introduce her to classic literature but instead gave her obscene books to read to heighten her passions for the young storm troopers who visited the store to purchase Hitler's *Mein Kampf* and other party-approved dogma. (This tactic, of course, was in keeping with Hitler's program in the mid-1930s to promote youthful marriages, which in turn would produce more babies for the Third Reich.)

Ilse had many affairs with SS men but was singled out by Heinrich Himmler, the dreaded leader of the SS and Gestapo, for marriage to his then top aide, Karl Koch. Himmler entered the bookstore with Koch in 1937, spotted the oversexed Ilse, and ordered Koch to mate with her. Himmler himself arranged for their marriage later that year.

A thick-set, bullet-headed man with the manners and morals of a pig, Koch assumed command of the new Buchenwald concentration camp outside Weimar. After his wedding, he took his youthful bride to a magnificent villa near the camp and promptly forgot about her—except to produce two children through their union in compliance with party dictates. Koch then began indulging in orgies with women at Weimar, staggering "sex feasts" costing fortunes. Ilse was left to her own diversions.

At first she spent her time riding to the hounds in Brandenburg. Then she flirted with Koch's junior officers, finally having affairs with a half dozen at a time, staging her own orgies where she would drink with several SS officers until taking them all into her bed. Her appetite for sex was insatiable, and her desire for perversion and sadistic acts obsessive. The prisoners at Buchenwald became her playthings.

Not until the war was in full progress did Ilse give vent to her incredible depravities. Ilse also took particular delight in sunbathing naked at her villa, where potential SS lovers would ogle her, and close to the camp, where she could tantalize the prisoners. She would greet all incoming trucks and trains standing semi-nude next to lines of male prisoners, mostly Jews by then, wiggling her hips, fondling her large breasts, and making lewd remarks. If one prisoner dared look up at her, he was beaten senseless. On one such occasion, guards noticed three prisoners glance up from the ground to stare at the "Bitch of Buchenwald." Two were beaten to death on the spot with clubs, the other was pushed face first to the ground, a guard standing on his neck grinding the man's face into the mud until he suffocated to death. Smirking, Ilse filled out a report that these men had been executed for giving her lascivious looks.

For sport, Ilse Koch encouraged the guards to participate in random mass slayings. One day, at her urging, guards opened up with pistols, shooting at prisoners as one would scurrying turkeys in a barnyard. Ilse was beside herself with ecstasy and grabbed a pistol, helping to murder many of the twenty-four prisoners killed that day.

Ilse brought a young female relative to live with her in her camp villa and ordered the girl to watch for attractive male guards newly arriving at Buchenwald and arrange orgies for her mistress. Ilse also forced the girl to participate in these acts.

One afternoon Ilse spied two male prisoners working without their shirts. Both had livid tattoos on their backs and chest. She ordered that the prisoners be killed immediately—they were taken to the camp hospital and murdered by injections that night—and their skins prepared and brought to her. Thus began one of the most heinous hobbies the world had ever known. Ilse's fascination for human skin, particularly that bearing tattoos, never abated. She had lampshades made from the skin, with which she adorned her living room. Skin from other selected victims went to make up pairs of gloves which Ilse proudly wore on her delicate hands.

Ever inventive, Ilse ordered the heads of executed prisoners to be severed and, in an elaborate process, shriveled down to grapefruit size. Dozens of these grotesque human trophies decorated the sideboards of Ilse's dining room, where she dined each day with her children.

At the close of the war, Ilse Koch was arrested and tried as a war criminal, although she fared far better than her counterpart from Belsen, Irma Grese. She was placed on trial in 1947–48 in Nuremburg before an American military court and sentenced to life in prison, a judgment that prompted deep resentment the world over. A U.S. review board, headed by the military governor of the U.S. zone, General Clay, ordered her release two years later. The world-wide protest to *that* action was of hurricane proportions. President Truman ordered a special investigation, but authorities finally declared that offenses by one German against other Germans could not be considered a war crime.

It was left to the German people to judge the woman. She was placed on trial again in 1950–51 in Augsburg, Bavaria, charged with murdering 45 prisoners and being the willing accomplice in another 135 concentration camp homicides. The woman standing in the dock was anything but beautiful. Her Titian hair was now a straggly dirty blonde, her features were bloated, her body a lumpy sack. She had no defense, really, and blamed her husband for everything, which was convenient in that Karl Koch had long ago been executed by the Nazis for embezzling party funds to pay for his orgies.

Ilse stood in the dock terrified, her eyes darting to the open windows. Outside, hundreds were screaming incessantly, "Kill her! Kill her!" She appealed for mercy from the court, stating the tired excuse that she had no knowledge of what went on at Buchenwald. "I was merely a housewife," she sobbed. "I was busy raising my children. I *never* saw anything which was against humanity!"

When confronted with photos showing mounds of corpses at Buchenwald, Ilse screamed, "Lies! All lies!" She had seen nothing, she had done nothing. The dozens of camp survivors who testified against her were impostors, actors, she said, playing out roles assigned to them by the Allies.

Halfway through the proceedings, Ilse Koch pretended to go into an epileptic state, forcing her body to twitch uncontrollably, responding to nothing, a blank stare masking her emotions. Doctors who examined her told the court that she was in perfect health. In her cell, Ilse laughed at one physician, telling him that he was enjoying her "First-class comedy act."

Yet Ilse persisted in the pretense, faking illness that prevented her from leaving her cell bed to hear the court declare her guilty of all the charges. She was to be imprisoned for life, and that decision too, caused this horrible woman to convulse with laughter; she had, unlike Irma Grese and others, escaped the headsman. Her eerie cackle was stilled by her death in 1971.

—JRN

# 27

# MADAME La FARGE
## A Cake as Large as a Plate

The story of Madame Lafarge, who was tried in France for the murder of her husband in 1840, is a strangely romantic one.

Marie Fortunée Cappelle was the daughter of a captain in the Imperial Artillery. Her parents died in her child-hood, and she was placed in the care of an aunt, who, at the earliest opportunity, determined to relieve herself of the burden of her support by negotiating a marriage for her. While still a girl, through the instrumentality of a matrimonial agent in Paris, an alliance was arranged between Marie Cappelle and one Monsieur Charles Lafarge, who was a widower and an iron-master of Glandier.

The marriage, which was purely a commercial transaction, took place in Paris on August 15, 1839, after which, Lafarge and his young wife set out for his old and gloomy seigneurial mansion in Glandier.

From statements made afterwards, Madame Lafarge became disgusted with her husband's brutality before the honeymoon was over. After they reached their own house, however, they were reconciled, and there seemed to be every possibility of their spending a happy wedded life together.

Besides the newly married pair, there lived in the family mansion the mother and sister of Lafarge, and his chief clerk, one Denis Barbier, was a frequent visitor at the house, and had liberty to walk through the place without restriction.

In a very short time Madame Lafarge discovered that

both she and her relatives had been deceived as to the position of her husband, and that instead of being a man of considerable fortune, he was straitened for means. On his representations she bestowed upon him all her fortune, and even wrote letters at his dictation to some of her wealthy friends, asking them to aid him to find money to develop a new method he claimed to have discovered for smelting iron. With these letters of introduction, Lafarge set out for Paris in December, 1839, to raise money to start his new project.

While he was thus away, his wife had her portrait drawn by an artist in Glandier, and determined to send it to her absent husband. She therefore packed it in a box, with some cakes made by his mother, together with an affectionate letter, and despatched them to Paris. This box, which contained nothing but the five small cakes, the portrait, and the letter, was packed and sealed by Madame Lafarge in the presence of several witnesses.

When it reached Paris and was opened by Lafarge, it contained only *one large cake*, after partaking of which he was suddenly taken ill, and was eventually compelled to return home, where he arrived on January 5, 1840. His sickness continued and increased in severity, and nine days afterwards he died.

Shortly after his death his mother and friends, who were well aware how the widow disliked them and her husband also, who had made her life so unhappy, at once imputed the cause of death to poison administered by his wife in the cake she had sent to Paris, and Marie Cappelle Lafarge was arrested on suspicion.

When the house of the deceased man was searched, certain diamonds were found which were supposed to have been stolen from the Vicomtesse de Léotaud by Madame Lafarge before her marriage.

The unfortunate woman was therefore charged with the double crime of theft and murder.

Though arrested in January, 1840, the trial of Madame Lafarge did not commence till July 9 of the same year, and the charge of theft was first proceeded with in her absence, and she was found guilty.

While this judgment was still under appeal, she was brought to trial on the graver charge.

The evidence for the prosecution went to prove that the illness of Lafarge commenced with the eating of the cake received from his home. As already stated, when the box arrived in Paris the seals had been broken, the five cakes had disappeared, and *a single cake "as large as a plate"* had been substituted for them. It was alleged by the prosecution that this single cake had been prepared by Madame Lafarge, and secretly placed in the box; but no evidence could be brought to prove that she ever tampered with the box after it had been sealed. Lafarge's clerk, Denis Barbier, made a clandestine visit to Paris after the box had been despatched, and he was with Lafarge when it arrived in Paris, yet no notice seems to have been taken of this suspicious fact. It transpired, it was he who also first threw out hints on his master's return that he was being poisoned by arsenic, and told a brother employé that his master would be dead within ten days. There was ample proof, however, that there was a considerable quantity of arsenic in the house at Glandier. It was found that Madame Lafarge had purchased some in December, stating she required it for destroying rats; Denis also stated in evidence, that Madame had requested him to procure her some arsenic. He bought some, but did not give it to her. It was further stated that Madame Lafarge was seen to stir a white powder into some chicken broth which had been prepared for her husband, the remains of which, found in a bowl, were said by the analyst to contain arsenic.

The medical men who conducted the post-mortem examination gave it as their deliberate opinion that the deceased man had been poisoned by arsenic, of which metal they professed to have found considerable quantities. The friends of the accused then submitted the matter to Orfila, the famous toxicologist, who, on giving his opinion of the methods and manner in which the analysis had been carried out, said that owing to the antiquated and doubtful methods of detection employed by the medical men, it was probable they fancied they had found arsenic where there was none. Thereupon the prosecution asked Orfila to undertake a fresh analysis himself, which he consented to do, and, on making a careful examination of the remains, stated he discovered just a minute trace of arsenic.

This apparently sealed the doom of the accused woman, and served to strengthen the bias of the jury. But now another actor appeared in the drama in the person of Raspail, another famous French chemist, who had watched the case from the beginning with interest. On hearing the result of Orfila's examination, he had taken the trouble to trace the zinc wire with which Orfila had experimented, to the shop where the great toxicologist had procured the article, and he found on analysis that the *zinc itself* contained more arsenic than Orfila had detected by his examination. Orfila had used Marsh's test, which is infallible so long as the reagents used are free from arsenic themselves.

Raspail, having placed the result of his discovery of arsenic in Orfila's reagent, at the service of the defence, was on his way to Tulle, where the Assizes were being held, when an unfortunate accident delayed his progress, and the unhappy Marie Cappelle Lafarge, after a trial which lasted sixteen days, was found guilty meanwhile, and condemned to imprisonment for life with hard labour, and exposure in the pillory. Raspail, however, would not let the matter rest, and at once set to work to save the condemned woman. He at length got Orfila to fairly admit his error and join him in a professional report to the authorities to that effect.

After being imprisoned for twelve years, in the end the sentence on this unhappy woman was reduced to five years in the Montpellier house of detention, after which the Government sent her to the Convent of St. Rémy, from whence she was liberated in 1852, but only to end her wretched life a few months afterwards.

There appeared in the *Edinburgh Review* for 1842 a careful examination of this interesting case from a legal point of view, in which the writer states the strongest evidence indicated Denis and not Madame Lafarge as the perpetrator of the crime. It was proved this man lived by forgery, and assisted Lafarge in some very shady transactions to cover the latter's insolency. He was further known to harbour a deadly hatred for Madame Lafarge. He was with his master in Paris when he was seized with the sudden illness, and it transpired that out of the 25,000 francs the ironmaster had succeeded in borrowing, from his wife's relatives, only 3,900 could be found when he returned to Glandier. On his own statement he was in the possession of a quantity of arsenic, and he was the first to direct suspicion against his master's wife. Yet all these facts appear to have been overlooked in the efforts of the prosecution to fasten the guilt on the unfortunate woman. That Lafarge died from the effects of arsenical poisoning there seems little doubt, but by whom it was administered has never been conclusively proved, and the tragedy still remains among the unsolved poisoning mysteries.

—C.J.S.T.

# 28

# MARIA MANNING

## The Fashion in Black satin

---

Manning was a retired railway guard. Mrs. Manning was of Swiss extraction—by name Marie Le Roux—and had been lady's maid to the Duchess of Sutherland. Manning's father kept the "Bear Inn" at Taunton, and his son is said to have been implicated in the great bullion robbery while he was in the employ of the Great Western Railway.

At first, the son, like his father, elected to become a publican, and acquired "The White Hart" at Taunton, but the rumours anent the bullion robbery became so obsessive that he was compelled to quit. He and his wife then became proprietors of a beer-shop in Hackney, but subsequently they levanted with most of the property. This is said to have been due to the persuasions of Patrick O'Connor, who combined the duties of a gauger with—to his cost—the pleasures of paying attention to Mrs. Manning. This he supplemented by usury at extortionate interest, and he was reputed to be worth ten thousand pounds.

At the time of the drama the Mannings were residing at No. 3 Minver Place, Bermondsey. From that address on August 8, Mrs. Manning wrote:

> *"Dear O'Connor,—We shall be happy to see you to dine with us to-day at half-past five o'clock. Yours affectionately, Marie Manning.—P. O'Connor, Gauger, London Docks. Wednesday morning."*

O'Connor did not dine at Minver Place on the Wednesday, but on the next afternoon he was seen at the Mannings', smoking and talking to Mrs. Manning. On that same day, Mrs. Manning, who was a frequent visitor to O'Connor's rooms in Greenwood Street, Mile End Road, called there at a quarter to six in the evening, and remained there about an hour. And on the following day she called again, and seemed very excited.

Now on that day (August 10) O'Connor was absent from duty at the docks for the first time, and when on the following Tuesday there was still no trace of him, the police and detectives called at Minver Place, as everybody knew how intimate was the missing man with the Mannings.

To all enquiries Mrs. Manning gave calm and collected replies. But on August 17, when the police again called, the house was literally empty, as all the furniture had been sold *en bloc* to a broker in the neighbourhood. The police then made a thorough investigation, and one of the officers fancied he detected traces of tampering with a flagstone in the back kitchen, and on probing the mortar with his knife, he found it quite soft.

Upon removing the flags and the earth they discovered the body of O'Connor. It lay doubled up in a small oblong hole, filled with quicklime. So rapidly had this agent done its work that O'Connor was only recognizable by an unusually prognathous chin and a set of false teeth. Yet for a week Mrs. Manning, who kept no servant, had gone about her household duties as usual, and cooked the meals within a few feet of the victim.

Whether O'Connor was shot or bludgeoned to death will never be known. The body was a mass of wounds. It was proved that the Mannings were desperately hard-up, and that O'Connor had stated that he had left everything to his "Maurid Rhua," which is the Erse for "Red Mary." Moreover, Manning had enquired from a medical student named Massey who lodged with them, "what drug was most useful to cause a person to put his hand to paper," and if "just behind the ear" was the most vulnerable part of the skull. Manning also enquired of Massey about the capabilities of an air-gun, and it was proved that as far back as July 11 he had purchased a crowbar, and when he bought it he was indiscreet enough to vouchsafe the information that it was "to lift heavy things up, such as stones." Lastly, it had been suggested that the Mannings had taken the house with a view to carrying out their scheme.

Mrs. Manning was traced to Edinburgh, where she was arrested. While there, she had called on a firm of stockbrokers with a view to realizing some foreign railway shares and investing some five hundred pounds which she had in cash—the result of her second visit to O'Connor's rooms, after her abortive search on the Thursday evening.

Manning fled to Jersey, where he put up at an inn. There, fired by frequent potations of brandy, he was extraordinarily indiscreet, speaking of Massey by name, and even divulging the fact that his own name was Manning. Upon arrest, he put all the blame upon his wife, and asked: "Is the wretch taken?"

Very shortly afterwards, both husband and wife appeared in the dock at the Old Bailey. The Lord Chief Justice, Sir F. Pollock, presided, the Attorney-General, Mr. J. Jervis, prosecuted, Sergeant Wilkins and Mr. Charnock defending Manning, while Sergeant Ballantine (as he afterwards was) and Mr. Parry appeared for Mrs. Manning. The case created extraordinary interest, and those on the Bench included ambassadors and some of the greatest noblemen in the country.

There is no doubt that Sergeant Wilkins was right in contending for Manning that he was the mere dupe of his wife and that the whole crime was due to her instigation; and, although Sergeant Ballantine deprecated this "unmanly" line of defence, Manning can scarcely be described as being very "manly" at any time, as all along he had acted as *maquereau*, and connived at his wife's liaison with O'Connor.

The jury were only absent three-quarters of an hour, both prisoners were found guilty and both sentenced to death. Manning made no comment, but Mrs. Manning addressed the Court vehemently, and in a strong foreign accent, repeating again and again:

"Base and shameful England."

After conviction, Manning made a confession to the chaplain to the effect that his wife induced O'Connor to go down to the kitchen and wash his hands, and that while he stood by the open grave prepared for him, she placed a pistol close to the back of his head and shot him. (But against that, the one bullet found had lodged in the skin over the eye.) She then fetched Manning, whom she had plied for some considerable time with brandy, and on their perceiving that O'Connor still lived she induced her husband to finish him off with the crowbar.

The execution took place before fifty thousand people at Horsemonger Lane Gaol. It is noteworthy because husband and wife have rarely appeared together on the scaffold. Then, so disgraceful was the behaviour of the crowd that it drew from Dickens, who was a horrified spectator, his famous letter to *The Times*. Yet it took him another twenty years to procure the abolition of public hangings, although Thackeray wrote in the same strain when he attended the executions of Müller and

Courvoisier. (On that latter occasion several people were trampled to death.)

As all the world knows, Mrs. Manning sent black satin out of fashion for fully forty years by electing to be hanged in that material.

—A.L.

# 29

# MRS MAYBRICK
## Cruelly Wronged

For many years I, as a crime writer, have been fascinated by Mrs. Florence Maybrick. Of all the women famously convicted of murder, she has seemed to me the most probably innocent and certainly the most cruelly wronged. She intrigues me far more than any fictional lady in distress that I have created myself. I would love to have met her.

It is ironic, therefore, that once I actually offered her a ride in my car without having the faintest idea who she was.

It happened in July, 1940, 51 long years after the trial at which Florence Maybrick was sentenced to hang, by a mad judge, for the murder of her husband. I was driving to visit some friends in South Kent, Connecticut. As I passed the campus of the South Kent School for Boys, I noticed a little old woman trudging along the street. She was shabbily dressed, almost a hobo; her grizzled head was bare; and over her shoulder she was carrying a bulging burlap sack which seemed to be stuffed with newspapers.

As I drew the car up alongside of her, she turned to look at me. Her face was wrinkled as a walnut and her eyes gazed with sunken vagueness. Her lips parted as if she were going to speak and I noticed that two of her few remaining teeth were bizarrely tied together with a piece of string.

"Want a ride?" I asked.

Slowly she shook her head, turned away, and started plodding forward again along the road.

When I reached my destination, I mentioned the little old woman to my hostess.

"Oh, that must have been Mrs. Chandler," she said. "She's been living here for years in a tumble-down shack with dozens of cats. She hangs around the school campus. She's quite an institution there. The boys call her The Cat Woman. She's perfectly harmless, but, of course . . ." She put a finger significantly to her head.

I forgot the old woman until, just over a year later, I read in the paper that a South Kent milkman had found the little 79-year-old recluse, Mrs. Chandler, dead in her bed, surrounded by hungry, wailing cats. From documents discovered in the squalid shack, Mrs. Chandler was disclosed to have been Mrs. Florence Maybrick.

Mrs. Florence Maybrick, that name which once had been familiar to millions of people all over the world! Mrs. Florence Maybrick, the bent little woman with the burlap sack who had refused to ride with me!

I put down the newspaper, looking back to one of the most bitterly lost opportunities of my life . . .

Florence Maybrick was the victim of a disastrous marriage. At 18, the pretty, convent-raised daughter of a wealthy and aristocratic Alabama family, she met James Maybrick on a transatlantic liner. He was a coarse, new-rich cotton merchant from Liverpool, England, and was old enough to be her father. It is impossible at this late date to know what attracted her to him or why her charming, worldly mother, married for a second time to a German baron, allowed so obvious a misalliance. But Florence married James Maybrick, and after a brief stay in Norfolk, Virginia, the couple went to live in Battlecrease House, Garston (a suburb of Liverpool).

At that time "Society" in English provincial manufacturing towns was extremely narrow and insular. Immediately, Florence was eyed with suspicion as a foreigner. Her husband's two brothers were hostile to her. The dowdy neighboring ladies, envious of her youth and her smart clothes, looked down their noses. Even the servants, snobbishly aping their "betters," made it plain that they despised their imported American mistress.

To make it worse for Florence, her husband, once back in his own setting, showed himself in his true colors. He both tyrannized her and neglected her, and soon reverted to his old bachelor habits of drinking parties, race meets, and affairs with the local tarts.

And that was not all. He had yet another and secret vice. He was not only a hypochondriac; he also took dope. His unusual tastes ran to strychnine and arsenic. Arsenic, he claimed, "picked him up" after his many debauches.

For eight years, in which she bore her husband two children, Florence Maybrick endured this lonely, humiliating existence without complaint or rebellion. But she never became absorbed in the Liverpool way of life. She remained the outsider, a predestined victim for mass hysteria, if ever an opportunity came to arouse it.

The opportunity came. Early in 1889 Mrs. Maybrick met a young Texas cotton dealer named Alfred Brierly. Little is known of this relationship except that at one time they were both registered at the same hotel in London. Her accusers twisted this fact into proof of a sordid affair. This may or may not have been true. It is certainly true that some sort of "indiscretion" must have occurred between them and that Florence Maybrick felt she had at last found a friend, a chivalrous champion.

It must also be true that this new friendship brought

the strained Maybrick domestic drama to some kind of a crisis.

On March 29, 1889, a few days after Mrs. Maybrick's return from London, the Maybricks attended the Grand National Steeplechase at Aintree. Brierly too, it was claimed, was there. The Maybricks had their first public quarrel. Later, when they had returned home, James, in front of witnesses, struck Florence in the eye. Florence went immediately to pack her bags. She would have left the house forever if Maybrick's relatives and friends had not dissuaded her "for the sake of the children."

From that moment on Florence Maybrick was lost. Accident and malice conspired together to destroy her. She herself struck the first nail into her own coffin. On April 24 she bought a dozen arsenic-coated flypapers from a local chemist. On April 26 one of the familiar packages of "medicine" arrived for James from his London dealers. He took some and next morning became violently ill. He blamed the attack on the "strychnine" in his medicine but was well enough to go to the races at Wirral. That evening, however, he felt worse and summoned the family physician, Dr. Humphreys, who confirmed his patient's diagnosis and put him to bed. On April 29 Florence Maybrick bought two dozen more flypapers from another chemist. On April 30 Alice Yapp, the children's nursemaid, saw the flypapers soaking in a basin of water.

These flypapers virtually convicted Mrs. Maybrick of murder. But she had her own innocent explanation for their purchase. Arsenic, in those days, was universally used as a beauty aid. She claimed she had bought the flypapers as an ingredient for a face lotion she wanted to prepare because she had to attend a charity ball with her husband's brother, Edwin, on April 30.

In any case, she went to the ball with her brother-in-law. James improved and returned to work on May 1. On the 3rd, however, he had another attack, suffering from pains in the legs and severe thirst. Dr. Humphreys put him back to bed.

A trained day nurse was hired, but for the next five days Mrs. Maybrick helped attend her husband, bringing him the many prescribed medicines and invalid's foods and, for all we know, surreptitiously providing him with his private "White powders" which, unknown to her, were strychnine and arsenic. James Maybrick did not improve, and slowly, the hostile, excitement-hungry servants smelled Murder. On May 8 Alice Yapp told two neighbors, Mrs. Briggs and Mrs. Hughes, about the soaked flypapers. That was enough. "Mrs. Maybrick is poisoning her husband." The news spread like wildfire. The older Maybrick brother, Michael (composer, as "Stephen Adams," of such song successes as the still popular "The Holy City"), was summoned from London. Edwin Maybrick hired a second nurse and expressly forbade Florence to enter the sickroom.

It must then have been clear to Florence that she was under suspicion. She lost her head. She wrote a hysterical letter to Brierly and handed it to Alice Yapp, who, instead of mailing it, passed it on to Edwin Maybrick. At its most damning, this letter only showed guilty fears at some past indiscretion and the need for someone to cling to, but it contained the words "M. is sick unto death." This was all Edwin Maybrick needed.

When his brother arrived, they both confided their suspicions to Dr. Humphreys and to another family doctor. Immediately every sickroom bottle that Florence had touched was analyzed. Nothing was found except a faint, unlethal trace of arsenic in a bottle of Valentine's meat-extract. Later, Michael Maybrick saw Florence pouring the contents of one bottle into another. He snatched the bottles from her for analysis. The result, once again, was negative.

Meanwhile, James Maybrick grew steadily sicker and, on the evening of May 11, he died.

Naturally enough after her ordeal, Florence Maybrick collapsed. Instantly, every member of the household started a hysterical search of her room. They hit the jackpot. Alice Yapp found a sealed package, marked "Arsenic—Poison for Cats," and a candy box containing two bottles. The next morning Mrs. Briggs found two hat boxes. In one of them was a wooden box containing three bottles and, beside the box, a bottle of meat juice. In the second box was a glass of milk and a rag. Analysis showed that there was enough arsenic in all these items to kill at least 50 people.

Since James Maybrick had been a steady and furtive arsenic addict, these caches might well have been secreted by him or by his unsuspecting wife at his own request. But even if the arsenic had belonged to Florence Maybrick, arsenic turned out to have nothing to do with the case. For the post-mortem showed no more than a tenth of a grain of arsenic in the dead man's organs. Such a small amount could not possibly have killed anyone, let alone the arsenic-habituated James Maybrick.

But the lynching was on and there was no turning back. On May 14 Superintendent Isaac Bryning of the Liverpool police arrived to arrest Florence. She was too ill to be moved. Frightened and half out of her wits, Florence moaned that she had no money, no one to turn to. The neighboring Mrs. Briggs, who was with her, sarcastically remarked, "What about your friend Brierly?" With pitiful naïveté, Florence wrote him a second note. "Your last letter is in the hands of the police. Appearances may be against me, but before God I swear that I am innocent."

This letter, too, was given to the police, and as soon as possible Florence was taken to the Liverpool jail. In spite of the medical evidence, the coroner's jury found that James Maybrick had died from an irritant poison administered by his wife. She was charged before a Grand Jury on July 26 and brought to trial five days later.

She never had a chance. The prosecutor's Victorian thunder against the woman taken in adultery was shockingly abetted by the judge, Mr. Justice Stephen, who constantly referred to Florence from the bench as "that horrible woman, the epitome of all that is loathsome and evil."

One year later Justice Stephen was shut up in a lunatic asylum. But that was too late for Florence Maybrick. After a mere 45 minutes, the jury found her guilty as charged. Mr. Justice Stephen put on the Black Cap and sentenced her to be hanged.

The verdict became public scandal. Many people believed that James Maybrick had died of gastroenteritis and had never been murdered at all. Public protest grew so strong that the Home Secretary had finally to commute the sentence to life imprisonment.

But there the matter stood. In spite of world-wide indignation, appeals to the Home Secretary and to Queen Victoria herself, in spite of the efforts of Florence's mother, who spent her entire fortune on a fruitless attempt for a pardon, Florence served her 20-year term, including a nine-month period of solitary confinement.

In 1905 she was released and, still courageously using her married name, returned to the States where she lived for a while in Highland Park, Illinois, and in Florida.

Her mother had died. She had no friends. Except for a small pension, she was penniless. Notoriety dogged her wherever she went.

Finally, in 1920, she started a new life, under her maiden name of Chandler, in South Kent where she became the little shack-dwelling recluse with her cats and her shy appearances on the South Kent campus.

I hope, after all she had suffered, that she found some peace in those last 20 years. I know that I wish her well. And, beyond anything, I wish she hadn't walked away from my car, so that I could have taken her hand and said:

"Good luck to you, Mrs. Maybrick."

—P.Q.

# 30

# SARAH METYARD

## "The Blood of Innocence"

A single year had not elapsed since the public example made of Elizabeth Brownrigg [see page 135], and to which the public indignation was yet alive, when these two, if possible, more cruel women, were torturing their apprentices to death.

Sarah was a milliner, and the daughter her assistant, in Bruton Street, Hanover Square, London.

In the year 1758 the mother had five apprentice girls bound to her from different parish workhouses, among whom were Anne Naylor and her sister.

Anne Naylor, being of a sickly constitution, was not able to do so much work as the other apprentices about the same age; and therefore she became the more immediate object of the fury of the barbarous women, whose repeated acts of cruelty at length occasioned the unhappy girl to abscond. Being brought back, she was confined in an upper apartment, and allowed each day no other sustenance than a small piece of bread and a little water.

Seizing an opportunity of escaping from her confinement, she got unperceived into the street, and ran to a milk-carrier, whom she begged to protect her, saying, if she returned, she must certainly perish, through the want of food, and severe treatment she daily received. Being soon missed, she was followed by the younger Metyard, who, seizing her by the neck, forced her into the house, and threw her upon the bed in the room where she had been confined; and she was then seized by the old woman, who held her down while the daughter beat her with the handle of a broom in a most cruel manner. They afterwards put her into a back room on the second story, tying a cord round her waist, and her hands behind her, and fastening her to the door in such a manner that it was impossible for her either to sit or lay down. She was compelled to remain in this situation for three successive days; but they permitted her to go to bed at the usual hours at night. Having received no kind of nutriment for three days and two nights, her strength was so exhausted, that, being unable to walk up stairs, she crept to the garret, where she lay, on her hands and feet.

While she remained tied up on the second floor the other apprentices were ordered to work in an adjoining apartment, that they might be deterred from disobedience by being witnesses to the unhappy girl's sufferings; but they were enjoined, on the penalty of being subjected to equal severity, against affording her any kind of relief.

On the fourth day she faltered in speech, and presently afterwards expired. The other girls, seeing the whole weight of her body supported by the strings which confined her to the door, were greatly alarmed, and called out, "Miss Sally! Miss Sally! Nanny does not move." The daughter now came up stairs, saying, "If she does not move, I will make her move:" and then beat the deceased on the head with the heel of a shoe.

Perceiving no signs of life, she called to her mother, who came up stairs, and, having ordered the strings that confined the deceased to be cut, laid the body across her lap, and directed one of the apprentices where to find a bottle with some hartshorn drops.

When the child had brought the drops, she and the other girls were ordered to go down stairs; and the mother and daughter, being convinced that the object of their barbarity was dead, conveyed the body into the garret. They related to the other apprentices that Nanny had been in a fit, but was perfectly recovered, adding, that she was locked into the garret lest she should again run away; and, in order to give an air of plausibility to their tale, at noon the daughter carried a plate of meat up stairs, saying it was for Nanny's dinner.

They locked the body of the deceased in a box on the fourth day after the murder; and, having left the garret door open, and the street door on the jar, one of the apprentices was told to call Nanny down to dinner, and to tell her that, if she would promise to behave well in future, she would be no longer confined. Upon the return of the child she said Nanny was not above stairs; and, after a great parade in searching every part of the house, they reflected upon her as being of an untractable disposition, and pretended that she had run away.

The sister of the deceased, who was apprenticed to the same inhuman mistress, mentioned to a lodger in the house that she was persuaded her sister was dead; observing that it was not probable she had gone away, since her shoes, shift, and other parts of her apparel, still remained in the garret.

The suspicions of this girl coming to the knowledge of the inhuman wretches, they, with a view of preventing a discovery, cruelly murdered her, and secreted the body.

The body of Anne remained in the box two months, during which time the garret door was kept locked, lest the offensive smell should lead to a discovery. The stench became so powerful that they judged it prudent to remove the remains of the unhappy victim of their barbarity; and, therefore, in the evening of the 25th of December, they cut the body in pieces, and tied the head and trunk up in one cloth, and the limbs in another, excepting one hand, a finger belonging to which had been amputated before death, and that they resolved to burn.

When the apprentices were gone to bed the old woman put the hand into the fire, saying "The fire tells no tales." She intended entirely to consume the remains of the unfortunate girl by fire; but, fearing the smell would give rise to suspicion, changed that design, and taking the bundles to the gully-hole in Chick Lane, endeavoured to throw the parts of the mangled corpse over the wall into the common sewer; but, being unable to effect that, she left them among the mud and water that was collected before the grate of the sewer.

Some pieces of the body being discovered about twelve o'clock by the watchman, he mentioned the circumstance to the constable of the night. The constable applied to one of the overseers of the parish, by whose direction the parts of the body were collected, and taken to the watch-house. On the following day the matter was communicated to Mr. Umfreville, the coroner, who examined the pieces found by the watchman; but, supposing them to be parts of a corpse taken from a churchyard for the use of some surgeon, he declined summoning a jury.

Four years elapsed before the discovery of these horrid murders, which at length happened in the following manner:—Continual disagreements prevailed between the mother and daughter; and, though the latter was now arrived at the age of maturity, she was often beat, and otherwise treated with severity. Thus provoked, she sometimes threatened to destroy herself, and at others to give information against her mother as a murderer.

About two years after the murders a gentleman of the name of Rooker took lodgings in the house of Metyard, where he lived about three months, during which time he had frequent opportunities of observing the severity with which the girl was treated.

He hired a house in Hill Street, and, influenced by compassion for her sufferings, and desirous of relieving her from the tyranny of her mother, he invited the girl to live in his family in the capacity of a servant; which offer she cheerfully embraced, though her mother had many times violently opposed her desire of going to service.

The girl had no sooner removed to Mr. Rooker's house than the old woman became perfectly outrageous; and it was almost her constant daily practice to create disturbances in Mr. Rooker's neighbourhood, by venting the most bitter execrations against the girl, and branding her with the most opprobrious epithets.

Mr. Rooker removed to Ealing, to reside on a little estate bequeathed him by a relation; and, having by this time seduced the girl, she accompanied him, and lived with him professedly in the character of his mistress.

The old woman's visits were not less frequent at Ealing than they had been at Mr. Rooker's house in London; nor was her behaviour less outrageous. At length Mr. Rooker permitted her to be admitted into the house, imagining that such indulgence would induce her to preserve a decency of behaviour; but he was disappointed, for she still continued to disturb the peace of his family.

On the 9th of June, 1762, she beat her daughter in a terrible manner; and during the contention many expressions were uttered by both parties that gave great uneasiness to Mr. Rooker. The mother called Mr. Rooker "the old perfumed tea dog;" and the girl retorted by saying, "Remember, mother, you are the perfumer; you are the Chick Lane ghost," alluding to the body of Anne Naylor having been kept in the box till it became intolerably offensive, and then thrown among the mud and water in Chick Lane.

The mother having retired, Mr. Rooker urged the girl to explain what was meant to be insinuated by the indirect accusations introduced by both parties in the course of the dispute; and, bursting into tears, she confessed the particulars of the murders, begging that a secret so materially affecting her mother might never be divulged.

Mr. Rooker imagined that the daughter could not be rendered amenable to the law, as she performed her share in the murders by the direction of her mother; but we pretend not to say that he would have suppressed the discovery, had he supposed that making the horrid transaction public would have endangered the girl's life. Mr. Rooker wrote concerning the affair to the overseers of Tottenham parish, whence the girls were put out apprentice; in consequence of which the elder Metyard was taken into custody.

On the day of the examination Mr. Rooker, the younger Metyard, and two children, apprentices in the house when the murders were committed, attended at Sir John Fielding's house in Bow Street. The evidence against the prisoner left no doubt of her guilt, and she was committed to New Prison, Clerkenwell, for re-examination; and the girls were put under the protection of the overseers of St. George's, Hanover Square.

Upon the prisoner being examined a second time she was remanded for trial; and, some circumstances having arisen to criminate the daughter, she was ordered to stand at the bar; and, the evidence against her being recapitulated on oath, she was committed to the Gate House.

On the trials of these offenders, which came on at the ensuing Old Bailey Sessions, they bitterly recriminated each other, and their mutual accusations served to confirm the evidence of their guilt. The younger Metyard pleaded pregnancy; on which a jury of matrons was summoned, who pronounced that she was not with child; after which they were both sentenced to be executed on the following Monday, and then to be conveyed to Surgeons' Hall for dissection.

The mother being in a fit when she was put into the cart, she lay at her length till she came to the place of execution, when she was raised up, and means were used for her recovery, but without effect, so that she departed this life in a state of insensibility. From the time of leaving Newgate to the moment of her death the daughter wept incessantly. It is true she joined the Ordinary in prayer; but such was the distracted state of her mind, that there is but too much reason to fear that she died without that sincere repentance which alone can avert the terrible decree denounced against those who impiously arrogate to themselves the power of the Almighty, and imbrue their hands in the blood of innocence. They were executed at Tyburn July the 19th, 1768. After hanging the usual time the bodies were conveyed in a hearse to Surgeons' Hall, where they were exposed to the curiosity of the public, and then dissected.

# 31

# THE PAPIN SISTERS
## The Housemaid's Revenge

When, in February 1933, the Papin sisters, cook and housemaid, killed Mme and Mlle Lancelin in the respectable provincial town of Le Mans, a half-dozen hours from Paris, it was not a murder but a revolution. It was only a minor revolution—minor enough to be fought in a front hall by four females, two on a side. The rebels won with horrible handiness. The lamentable Lancelin forces were literally scattered over a distance of ten bloody feet, or from the upper landing halfway down the stairs. The physical were the most chilling details, the conquered the only dull elements in a fiery, fantastic struggle that should have remained inside Christine Papin's head and which, when it touched earth, unfortunately broke into paranoiac poetry and one of the most graceless murders in French annals.

On the day he was to be made a widower, M. Lancelin, retired lawyer, spent his afternoon at his respectable provincial club; at 6:45 he reported to his brother-in-law, M. Renard, practicing lawyer at whose table they were to dine at 7 *en famille*, that, having gone by the Lancelin home in the Rue La Bruyère to pick up his wife and daughter Geneviève, he had found the doors bolted and the windows dark—except for the maids' room in the attic, where, until he started knocking, there was a feeble glow. It had appeared again only as he was leaving.

Two lawyers this time set off for the Lancelin dwelling, to observe again the mansard gleam fade, again creep back to life as the men retreated. Alarmed (for at the least a good dinner was drying up), the gentlemen procured a brace of policemen and a brigadier, who, by forcing Lancelin's window, invited Lancelin to walk into his parlor, where he discovered his electric lights did not work. Two of the police crept upstairs with one flashlight and the brother-in-law. Close to the second floor the trio humanely warned the husband not to follow.

On the third step from the landing, all alone, staring uniquely at the ceiling, lay an eye. On the landing itself the Lancelin ladies lay, at odd angles and with heads like blood puddings. Beneath their provincial petticoats their modest limbs had been knife-notched the way a fancy French baker notches his finer long loaves. Their fingernails had been uprooted, one of Geneviève's teeth was pegged in her own scalp. A second single orb—the mother's, this time, for both generations seemed to have been treated with ferocious non-partisanship—rested shortsightedly gazing at nothing in the corner of the hall. Blood had softened the carpet till it was like an elastic red moss.

The youngest and third policeman (his name was Mr. Truth) was sent creeping toward the attic. Beneath the door a crack of light flickered. When he crashed the door, the light proved to be a candle, set on a plate so as not to drip, for the Papins were well-trained servants. The girls were in one bed in two blue kimonos. They had taken off their dresses which were stained. They had cleaned their hands and faces. They had, the police later discovered, also cleaned the carving knife, hammer, and pewter pitcher which they had been using and put them neatly back where they belonged—though the pitcher was by now too battered to look tidy. Christine, the elder (Léa, the younger, was never after to speak intelligibly except once at the trial), did not confess; she merely made their mutual statement: they had done it. Truth took what was left of the candle—the short-circuiting electric iron had blown out the fuse again that afternoon and was at the bottom of everything, Christine kept saying, though the sensible Truth paid no attention—and lighted the girls downstairs, over the corpses, and out to the police station. They were still in their blue kimonos and in the February air their hair was wild, though ordinarily they were the tidiest pair of domestics in Le Mans.

Through a typographical error the early French press reports printed the girls' name not as Papin which means nothing, but as Lapin which means rabbit. It was no libel.

Waiting trial in the prison, Christine, who was 28 years of age and the cathartic of the two, had extraordinary holy visions and unholy reactions. Léa, who was 22 and looked enough like her sister to be a too-long-delayed twin, had nothing, since the girls were kept separate and Léa thus had no dosage for her feeble brain.

Their trial at the local courthouse six months later was a national event, regulated by guards with bayonets, ladies with lorgnettes, and envoys from the Parisian press. As commentators *Paris-Soir* sent a pair of novelists, the Tharaud brothers, Jean and Jérôme, who, when they stoop to journalism, write of themselves as "I" and nearly even won the Goncourt Prize under this singular consolation. Special scribes were posthasted by *Détective*, the hebdomadal penny dreadful prosperously owned by the *Nouvelle Revue Française*, or France's *Atlantic Monthly*. *L'Œuvre*, as daily house organ for the Radical-Socialist Party (supposedly friendly to the working classes till they unfortunately shot a few of them in the Concorde riot), sent Bérard, or their best brain.

The diametric pleas of prosecution and defense facing

these historians were clear: either (*a*) the Papins were normal girls who had murdered without a reason, murdering without reason apparently being a proof of normalcy in Le Mans, or else (*b*) the Rabbit sisters were as mad as March Hares, and so didn't have to have a reason. Though they claimed to have one just like anybody else, if the jury would only listen: their reason was that unreliable electric iron, or a mediocre cause for a revolution . . . The iron had blown out on Wednesday, been repaired Thursday, blown again Friday, taking the houselights with it at 5. By 6 the Lancelin ladies, in from their walk, had been done to death in the dark—for the dead do not scold.

While alive, Madame had once forced Léa to her housemaid knees to retrieve a morsel of paper overlooked on the parlor rug. Or, as the Tharauds ponderously wrote in their recapitulation of the crime, "God knows the Madame Lancelins exist on earth." This one, however, had been rare in that she corroborated Léa's dusting by donning a pair of white gloves, she commentated on Christine's omelettes by formal notes delivered to the kitchen by Geneviève—both habits adding to the Papins' persecution complex, or their least interesting facet. Madame also gave the girls enough to eat and "even allowed them to have heat in their attic bedroom," though Christine did not know if Madame was kind, since in six years' service she had never spoken to them, and if people don't talk, how can you tell? As for the motive for their crime, it was again the Tharauds who, all on the girls' side, thus loyally made it clear as mud: "As good servants the girls had been highly contraried" when the iron blew once. Twice "it was still as jewels of servants who don't like to lose their time that they became irritated. Perhaps if the sisters had been less scrupulous as domestics the horror which followed would never have taken place.

And I wish to say," added Jean and Jérôme, without logic and in unison, "that many people still belong to early periods of society."

Among others, the jury did. They were twelve good men and true, or quite incompetent to appreciate the Papin sisters. Also, the trial lasted only twenty-six hours, or not long enough to go into the girls' mental rating though the next forty or fifty years of their lives depended on it. The prosecution summoned three local insane-asylum experts who had seen the girls twice for a half-hour, and swore on the stand that the *prisonnières* were "of unstained heredity"—i.e., their father having been a dipsomaniac who violated their elder sister, since become a nun; their mother having been an hysteric "crazy for money"; a cousin having died in a madhouse, and an uncle having hanged himself "because his life was without joy." In other words, heredity O.K., legal responsibility 100%.

Owing to the girls' weak, if distinguished, defence— high-priced French lawyers work cheaply for criminals if bloody enough, the publicity being a fortune in itself—their equally distinguished psychiatrist's refutation carried no weight. Their lawyer was Pierre Chautemps, cousin to that Camille Chautemps who, as Prime Minister, so weakly defended the French Republic in the 1933 Boulevard Saint-Germain riots; their expert was the brilliant Parisian professor, Logre, whose "colossal doubt on their sanity" failed to count since under cross examination he had to admit he had never seen the girls before even for five minutes; just knew all about them by sitting back in his Paris study, ruminating. He did, too, but the jury sniffed at the stuck-up city man.

Thus, they also missed Logre's illuminating and delicate allusion to the girls as a "psychological couple," though they'd understood the insane-asylum chief's broader reference to Sappho. Of paramount interest to twelve good men and true, the girls' incest was really one of the slighter details of their dubious domesticity. On the jury's ears Christine's prison visions also fell flat. Indeed it was not until six months after she was sentenced to be beheaded that these hallucinations were appreciated for their literary value in a scholarly essay entitled *"Motifs du Crime Paranoïaque: ou Le Crime des Soeurs Papins,"* by Docteur Jacques Lacan, in a notable surrealist number of the intelligentsia quarterly, *Minotaure.*

In court, however, Christine's poetic visions were passed over as a wilfull concoction of taradiddles that took in no one—except the defence, of course. Yet they had, in the limited data of lyrical paranoia and modern psychiatry, constituted an exceptional performance. Certain of the insane enjoy strange compensations; having lost sight of reality they see singular substitutes devoid of banal sequence, and before the rare spectacle of effect without cause are pushed to profound questions the rest of us are too sensible to bother with. "Where was I before I was in the belly of my mother?" Christine first inquired, and the fit was on. She next wished to know where the Lancelin ladies might now be, for, though dead, could they not have come back in other bodies? For a cook she showed, as the Tharauds said, "a bizarre interest in metempsychoses," further illuminated by her melancholy reflection, "Sometimes I think in former lives that I was my sister's husband." Then while the prison dormitory shuddered, Christine claimed to see that unholy bride hanging hanged to an apple tree, with her limbs and the tree's limbs broken. At the sad sight Crazed Christine leapt in the air to the top of a ten-foot barred window where she maintained herself with muscular ease. It was then that Léa, whom she had not seen since their incarceration six months before, was called in as a sedative. And to her Christine cried with strange exultation, "Say yes, say yes," which nobody understands to this day. By what chance did this Sarthe peasant fall like the Irish Joyce in the last line of *Ulysses* on the two richest words in any tongue—those of human affirmation, *Yes, yes* . . .

Thus ended the lyrical phase of Christine's seizure, which then became, maybe, political. At any rate she hungerstruck for three days, like someone with a cause, went into the silence, wept and prayed like a leader betrayed, traced holy signs with her tongue on the prison walls, tried to take Léa's guilt on her shoulders, and, when this failed, at least succeeded in freeing her own of her strait jacket.

"Wasn't all of that just make-believe?" the prison officials later asked her. (All except escaping from the strait jacket, of course, or a reality that had never occurred in French penal history before.) "If monsieur wishes," said Christine politely. Both the girls were very polite in prison and addressed their keepers in the formal third person, as if the guards were company who had just stepped in to the Lancelin's parlor for tea.

During the entire court proceeding, report on visions, vices, and all, from 1:30 after lunch of one day to 3:30 before breakfast of the next, Christine sat on the accused bench with eyes closed. She looked like someone asleep or a medium in a trance, except that she rose when addressed and blindly said nearly nothing. The judge, a kind man with ferocious mustaches, was, in his interrogation, finally forced to examine his own conscience, since he couldn't get Christine to talk about hers.

"When you were reprimanded in your kitchen, you never answered back but you rattled your stove-lids fiercely; I ask myself if this was not sinful pride . . . Yet you rightly think work is no disgrace. No, you also have no class hatred," he said with relief to find that he and she were neither Bolsheviks. "Nor were you influenced by literature, apparently, since only books of piety were found in your room."

(Not that printed piety had taught the girls any Christian mercy once they started to kill. The demi-blinding of the Lancelins is the only criminal case on record where eyeballs were removed from the living head without practice of any instrument except the human finger. The duplicating of the tortures was also curiously cruel; Christine took Madame in charge, the dull Léa followed suit by tending to Mademoiselle; whatever the older sister did to the older woman, the younger sister repeated on fresher flesh in an orgy of obedience.)

As the trial proceeded, the spectators could have thought the court was judging one Papin cadaver seen double, so much the sisters looked alike and dead. Their sanity expert had called them Siamese souls. The Papins' was the pain of being two where some mysterious unity had been originally intended; between them was a schism which the dominant, devilish Christine had tried to resolve into one self-reflection, without ever having heard of Narcissus or thinking that the pallid Léa might thus be lost to view. For, if Christine's eyes were closed to the judge, Léa's were as empty in gaze as if she were invisible and incapable of sight. Her one comment on trial for her life was that, with the paring knife, she had "made little carvings" in poor spinster Geneviève's thighs. For there, as her Christine had said, lay the secret of life . . .

When the jury came in with their verdict Christine was waiting for them, still somnambulant, her hands clasped not as in prayer but as if pointing down into the earth. In the chill predawn both sisters' coat collars were turned up as if they had just come in from some domestic errand run in the rain. With their first effort at concentration on Léa, whom all day the jury had tried to ignore, the foreman gave her ten years' confinement and twenty of municipal exile. Christine was sentenced to have her head cut off in the public square of Le Mans which, since females are no longer guillotined, meant life—a courtesy she, at the moment, was ignorant of.

When Christine heard her sentence of decapitation, in true belief she fell to her knees. At last she had heard the voice of God.

—J.F.

# 32

# PAULINE PARKER and JULIET HULME

## "Let's Kill Mother"

---

The crime of the Murdering Girls struck Christchurch (New Zealand) with cataclysmic force.

One was sixteen years of age. The other was fifteen. They wore the white blouses and blue tunics that were the uniform at Christchurch Girls' High School. Different as they were in family background, in appearance, and in manner, they were close friends, bound together, it seemed, in one of those intimacies which are so common among adolescents, which seem so tremendously important at the time, and which invariably end with schooldays. But this was no ordinary friendship. It was deep and dark, and it was to become terrible.

Pauline Yvonne Parker was the sixteen-year-old one, a dark and dumpy girl, five feet three inches tall, with cold brown eyes gleaming watchfully from her olive-skinned face. She walked with the suspicion of a limp. When she was five years old, she contracted osteomyelitis, as a result of which she spent several months in hospital, and for which, over a period of three years, she had a series of operations. While other little girls of her age were laughing and playing in the sunshine, little Pauline Parker had to lie in bed, weary month after weary month, and watch them through the window.

Because of her slight lameness, Pauline Parker at sixteen was unable to participate in the tennis and the running and the other sports at the girls' high school. Her friend and classmate, Juliet Hulme, owned a pony and often rode it when she came to visit her, and so Pauline had developed an interest in horses. Lameness did not matter, she said, when you are in the saddle. For some time, she had been pestering her parents for permission to keep a pony, so that, like her friend Juliet, she could become a member of the Horse and Pony Club.

Pauline's father and mother said "No". Their daughter was becoming a constant worry to them. In the house she often pointedly ignored them. ("Pauline kept me out of her life," the father said sadly.) She was constantly writing novels. One night, sitting before the fire, she volunteered that she was writing an opera. This was a rare kind of admission for her to make, but on this occasion, burning with the creative urge, she could not repress the information.

Then there was Pauline's friendship with Juliet Hulme. Pauline was crazy about Juliet, could not stop talking about her, seemed perpetually to be in her company. Pauline's mother and father could see all the factors which were responsible for their daughter's lack of progress at school. Possession of a pony, concentration on yet another craze, would result in marks even lower.

But Pauline had a pony! She kept it secretly in a paddock, had been keeping it there for weeks, ever since, with the advice of her good friend Juliet, she had bought it with money she obtained nobody knew where. That was typical of the slyness of the lame Pauline, who among other forbidden things had for a time been sneaking into a boy's bedroom at night.

When the news about the pony was broken to them by the dark and determined Pauline, her parents shrugged their shoulders in a resigned manner and agreed to let her keep it, seeing she had had it so long, and seeing, of course, that if they did not agree Pauline would metaphorically tear the house down.

And all Pauline's parents wanted was a happy home. They had been through so much trouble together during their twenty-three years as man and wife, had had so many difficulties to overcome.

In the first place, they were not married. The obstacle to the performance of a formal ceremony of marriage was not stated during the progress of the Christchurch case. Whatever the reason, the parents of Pauline Parker, in an extraordinary gesture of honesty, proclaimed the irregularity of their union for all the world to see. On the front door of the near-white painted house in a Christchurch suburb, the ground floor of which was their home, there was a carefully lettered notice: "Mr. Rieper . . . Mrs. Parker."

Herbert Rieper, a gentle, pipe-smoking, carpet-slippered little man, owned a reasonably successful wholesale fish business in Christchurch city. Honora Mary Parker had been a good and loving wife to him. They had had four children. The eldest was eighteen-year-old Wendy, who had been no trouble at all to them, and who was an affectionate daughter. Then there was Pauline, over whom they had had all the worry and expense when she had the bad time with osteomyelitis as a little girl, and who, now that she was sixteen and had her head full of strange ideas, was still a worry.

There had been two others, and they didn't like to think about them. One had been a mongoloid, a flat-faced, drooling imbecile, who had been placed in an institution. And the fourth child had been born a "blue baby", with a congenital heart defect. Mercifully it had died.

Pauline's schoolmate, Juliet Hulme, was the biggest worry of all for Herbert Rieper and Honora Mary Parker. The two girls were crazy about each other. They used to sprawl on the lawn of the Hulme home and write "books" together. They had all kinds of secrets. It seemed they could not bear to be away from each other. Their mutual affection was so intense that it seemed to be abnormal. Mrs. Parker had taken Pauline to Dr. Bennett, and while their daughter waited in the consulting room had told him all about the friendship. The doctor had had Pauline into the surgery, and had examined her and talked to her.

When the mother suggested that Pauline should leave the high school, and go to another school where her progress might be better, Pauline surprisingly agreed.

And then, one day, Juliet's father called at the house, and said he was leaving New Zealand and was taking Juliet with him. This was the happiest news that Herbert and Honora Mary had heard for many a day. To Pauline, it meant disaster.

Juliet Hulme. Fifteen years of age. Tall for her age, five feet seven inches, and slim. Shoulder-length light brown hair. The clear pink-and-white complexion of an English hedge rose—Juliet was an English girl, bomb-shocked in the blitz at the age of two. Slanting grey eyes, the clear eyes of youth; high forehead; a slim and graceful body, and a confident air. Now she was intelligent and attractive. Soon she would be intelligent and beautiful.

Juliet Hulme (pronounced, in the English manner, Hume) was an intellectual, born and bred. The tall and stooping figure of her father, bespectacled, forty-six-year-old Dr. Henry Rainsford Hulme, had been a familiar one during World War II in the corridors of the War Office. One of England's leading mathematical scientists, he was one of two "boffins" who worked out the degaussing method which countered the German magnetic mine.

After the war, young Dr. Hulme was being regarded as

one of England's bright minds in the atomic era when he dismayed his colleagues by announcing that he was going to New Zealand to the £2,200 a year post of Rector of Canterbury University College at Christchurch, and to membership of the Senate of New Zealand University. Hulme was not running away from his work in atomic research because of ideological or any other reservations. He was leaving for the single and simple reason that his elder child, Juliet (there was a son, Jonathan, five years younger), was threatened with active tuberculosis. Doctors felt that the clear air of "the colonies", away from industrial smog, would benefit the girl tremendously. With his coolly aristocratic wife, Hilda Marion, and the children, Hulme arrived in New Zealand in 1948.

Early in 1953 they put Juliet in hospital. After four months' treatment she was discharged, but not as cured.

If there is any overseas city in which an expatriate Englishman can feel at home, it is surely the cathedral city of Christchurch. Dr. Hulme lived in a sixteen-roomed stone mansion with extensive grounds, called "Ilam". His salary, by New Zealand standards, was a good one. His wife, Hilda, was prominent in welfare work and in cultural movements.

And his position as Rector of the university college established him in the front rank of the honoured citizens of Christchurch. The Anglican Bishop was one of his best friends.

Then Walter Andrew Bowman Perry, another Englishman, arrived in Christchurch, and the relationship between Henry and Hilda Hulme was never the same again.

Big, moustached Perry was an engineer, and a man of considerable charm. He was in Christchurch on a prolonged business visit, and, like the Hulmes, was interested in sociology. He promised to assist them in the conduct of a marriage guidance bureau. When the

Hulmes suggested he might be more comfortable in a self-contained flat which was part of "Ilam", he was glad to move in. At the beginning, they were all friends together, the donnish Rector, the calm and queenly Mrs. Hulme, the lively young Jonathan, and Juliet. The latter could quote pages of the classical poets, knew something about good music, could model in clay like a born artist, could embroider like a maiden aunt or a ship's captain, and also wrote. A brilliant girl, Juliet. All of a sudden, like other brilliant people, this fifteen-year-old girl lost one of her enthusiasms: she had decided that riding no longer interested her, and wanted to sell her horse. The obliging Perry was glad to buy it for £50 from his little friend, who now had a secret reason for getting all the money she could.

Then, one afternoon, Juliet found her mother and Walter Andrew Bowman Perry in bed together. And, shortly afterwards, Dr. Hulme resigned the rectorship of the university college to return to England, where his outstanding scientific talent was required in the British atomic research team led by Sir William Penney. He would, he told friends, take Jonathan with him. Mrs. Hulme, however, would remain with Juliet: "The girl's lungs aren't too strong, you know, and the English winter . . ."

Then the Hulmes, who had been aware of, and disturbed by, their daughter's obsession with her friend, the daughter of the fish-shop proprietor, made an alarming discovery. Juliet and the dumpy Parker girl, who often came to stay with Juliet at weekends, had written what they called "novels". Well, adolescents did things like that. But the alarming fact was, the girls had decided to go to America to sell their novels there. And, as everybody knew, they were two very determined young ladies. Their friendship could be quite unhealthy. Twice, Dr. Hulme had called on that quiet fish-man, Rieper, and talked to him about it. In the circumstances, it would be an excellent plan to separate the girls before something embarrassing happened.

And so, Dr. Hulme told Juliet he intended to take her with him and Jonathan as far as South Africa. She could return alone to her mother in Christchurch. (Looming over this father-daughter discussion was the affair between Perry and Mrs. Hulme, which the father guessed at, and the daughter, on the evidence of her own eyes, knew about. But neither admitted it to the other. The relationship between a forty-six-year-old father and a bright fifteen-year-old daughter is not always an easy one.)

Juliet's reaction was a flat demand. Her friend Pauline must go to South Africa with her. Impossible, replied Dr. Hulme tetchily. Impossible, said Honora Mary Parker, firmly, when the two girls put it to her.

For Honora Mary Parker, impossible was a fatal word. Her daughter and her daughter's intimate friend were already planning her murder, with all the enthusiasm and excitement which two high-school girls might display in arranging the details of a school dance.

At 3 p.m. on June 22nd, 1954, a grey winter's day, Honora Mary Parker, Pauline Parker and Juliet Hulme left a refreshment kiosk in Victoria Park, on the Cashmere Hills on the outskirts of Christchurch. Topcoated against the cold, they walked down the track.

Juliet Hulme hurried along in front. Her hand in her pocket clutched part of the plot—a collection of brightly coloured pebbles, picked up by the roadside during the preceding few days. When she had rounded a bend in the track and was out of sight of the Parkers, she scattered the pebbles.

Pauline Parker, walking by her mother's side with that suggestion of a limp, also had her hand in her coat pocket, and also clutched part of the plot—half a brick, which Juliet had brought from her home to the Parkers' at noon that day. Pauline had slipped the piece of brick into the foot of an old stocking, thus making an effective sling-shot.

Juliet was sixty jards in front, and still out of sight down the track, when Honora Parker caught sight of a pink pebble, and Pauline remarked how pretty it was. Honora bent down to pick it up. Behind her, Pauline pulled the sling-shot from her pocket, braced her legs, and swung. The brick crashed on her mother's head, and she collapsed.

And that was the moment when Pauline wished it hadn't happened. But some force possessed her, drove her on, some inner voice which commanded: It is too late to stop! She struck again, and again, and now Juliet, panting from a sprint along the track, was kneeling beside her, and swinging the sling shot. Blood was spurting from twenty-four wounds in Honora Parker's face and head. Sobbing hysterically, the girls looked at each other and at their victim. The blood was only trickling now. They had beaten Honora Mary Parker to death.

The plan had to be completed.

Blood was dripping from their hands when they ran the four hundred yards back to the kiosk. "It's Mummy!" gasped Pauline to the proprietress, Mrs. Agnes Ritchie. "She's terrible! I think she's dead. We tried to carry her. She was too heavy."

"Yes, it's her mother!" Juliet burst out. Her voice was breaking with hysteria. "She's covered with blood!"

Pauline pointed down the path, in the direction in which the body lay, and as she made the gesture Mrs. Ritchie saw that blood was spattered upon her face. "Don't make us go down there again!" Pauline breathed.

And then: "We were coming back along the track. Mummy tripped on a plank and hit her head when she landed. She kept falling, and her head kept banging and bumping as she fell."

"I'll always remember her head banging," cried Juliet dramatically.

While Mrs. Ritchie called her husband, the girls went to a sink to wash the blood off themselves, and Mrs. Ritchie heard them laughing hysterically as they did so.

Kenneth Nelson Ritchie ran down the track. Under a tall pine tree by the track, and lying on a bed of pine needles, was the battered body of Honora Mary Parker. Ritchie hurried back to the kiosk and telephoned the police and the ambulance. The police took the girls away, and the ambulance took the body away. Doctors counted forty-five separate wounds upon it.

Three weeks later, a magistrate committed Pauline Yvonne Parker and Juliet Marion Hulme for trial on a charge of having murdered Honora Mary Parker.

The trial was the most tremendous event in the history of Christ church. In a city where Rugby Union Football seems to challenge Anglicanism as the popular religion, it drew to the court-room, on one day of the hearing, a crowd of beribboned supporters of the opposing teams in an inter-provincial match, Canterbury *v.* Waikato, who remained in court until within a few minutes of the game.

To the reporters who had flown in from Australia, to the Crown Prosecutor and the defence, to the jury, and to the people of New Zealand, stirred as they never had been before by human tragedy, one single exhibit was the core of the case. It was Pauline Parker's diary, and its contents, together with medical evidence and legal argument, were to decide the vital question: Were Pauline Parker and Juliet Hulme sane?

Most decidedly they were, Crown Prosecutor Alan W. Brown told the jury. Furthermore, they were dirty-minded little girls. The motive for the murder, the Crown Prosecutor said in measured tones, arose from the opposition of Mrs. Parker to the girls' plan to go overseas together. Their friendship was one of intense devotion. They spent a good deal of time in each other's beds (but the Crown Prosecutor did not add there was no real evidence of any immoral physical relationship between them). They scribbled, said Mr. Brown scornfully, what they called novels (so, the Crown Prosecutor did not see fit to remark, have thousands of adolescents, some of whom eventually have become novelists, some of whom have become lawyers).

"You may feel pity for these girls, but pity and sentiment have no part in British justice," declaimed the Crown Prosecutor to the twelve in the jury box.

And so, clearly and dispassionately, Crown Prosecutor Brown described the crime, and the confessions of Pauline Parker and Juliet Hulme, made shortly after its commission, to Senior Detective Macdonald Brown. Revealing passages of these statements to the police were:

From Juliet Hulme's: "I gave the brick to Pauline . . . I know it was put in the stocking . . . I wasn't quite sure what was going to happen when we went to Victoria Park. I thought we might have been able to frighten Mrs. Rieper [Parker] with the brick, and she would have given her consent for me and Pauline to stay together. I saw Pauline hit her mother with the brick in the stocking. I took it and hit her, too. After the first blow was struck, I knew it would be necessary for us to kill her. I was terrified, hysterical."

From Pauline Parker's: "I killed my mother. Had made up my mind to do it some days before. I don't know how many times I hit her; a great many, I imagine."

The Crown Prosecutor produced the diary which had been found in Pauline's bedroom. It was a bound book, with a space for every day in the year, of the kind so many business men used to jot down in outline the record of their activities. The entries were written in ink, in clear, adult calligraphy. The story they told was one of the strangest ever read in a court of law; it became a phantasmagoria; the twisted shapes of a disordered imagination seemed to swirl visibly in the heavy air of the court-room. And the two adolescents sat in the dock and listened to its recital with calm detachment, Pauline with a brown felt hat shielding her cunning brown eyes, Juliet, a pale green Paisley scarf tied round her fair hair, staring coolly from her slanted eyes at one person in court after another. From time to time, Juliet leaned across the wardress who sat between them, and spoke to dumpy Pauline, who did little more than nod in reply.

The diary was not put in as evidence in its entirety. But, as the prosecution and the defence introduced passages from it, the diary was revealed as one of the strangest and most terrible exhibits in criminal history.

The diary referred to Juliet by the pet name of Deborah, and revealed that Pauline was affectionately known to her friend as Gina. Mr. Brown read these extracts:

"February 13th, 1954: Why could not Mother die? Dozens, thousands of people are dying. Why not Mother, and Father too? Life is very hard."

"April 28th: Anger against Mother boiling inside me as she is the main obstacle in my path. Suddenly, means of ridding myself of the obstacle occur to me. If she were to die . . ."

"June 20th: Deborah and I talked for some time. Afterwards, we discussed our plans for moidering Mother and made them clear. But peculiarly enough, I have no qualms of conscience. Or is it peculiar? We are so made."

(The term "moider" had apparently been acquired by the pair in reading crime fiction. It is the Brooklyn pronunciation of the word "murder".)

"June 21st: Deborah rang and we decided to use a brick in a stocking rather than a sandbag. Mother has fallen in with plans beautifully. Feel quite keyed up."

"June 22nd: I felt very excited last night and sort of night-before-Christmas, but I did not have pleasant dreams. I am about to rise."

And the top of the page for June 22nd was headed in printed letters: "The Day of the Happy Event."

While his daughter was in custody awaiting trial, Dr. Hulme left for England and his new career, taking the boy, Jonathan, with him. Mrs. Parker lay in her grave in a Christchurch cemetery. And so the parents who were left to stand the ordeal of the gaping crowds in court, and the verbal probing of the barristers, were self-effacing Herbert Rieper and cool, composed Hilda Marion Hulme. She, however, had a bulwark to lean upon: the sturdy Walter Andrew Bowman Perry.

Rieper had two significant pieces of evidence to give: at lunch on the day of the murder, Pauline and Juliet were in high good humour, laughing and joking; and in

1953 Pauline had been interested in a boy (later identified by the name Nicholas) who had been staying with them. Rieper had had to send the boy away.

At this time, the mention of Nicholas did not appear to have any particular impact upon Juliet Hulme, who was engaged in a habit she developed through the police court hearing and the trial, of trying to out-stare the occupants of the Press box, one after the other . . . But soon there was to be a violent reaction.

A sensitive and demanding girl was her Juliet, Mrs. Hulme told the court in her serene English accents. Because of the active threat of tuberculosis, she explained, Juliet had had to spend quite a lot of time resting in bed. Her friend Pauline would keep her company, sitting at the bedside. Oh yes, she had read one of the books Juliet had written, and considered it quite ordinary, certainly not over-exciting.

When Dr. Reginald Warren Medlicott, of the southern and Scottish city of Dunedin, was called to give evidence of his psychiatric examination of the accused, there began the real battle to decide the fate of Pauline Parker and Juliet Hulme. He had talked to the girls, but the diary was the basis on which the prim and precise doctor had formed his views.

Juliet, he said, had told him that Pan was the favourite god of Pauline and herself. The girls believed they lived in "a fourth world", and their god was a more powerful version of the humans' God, having greatly magnified powers.

The girls, said Dr. Medlicott, had extraordinary conceit. A poem written by Pauline Parker was an example. It was called "The Ones I Worship". The second verse:

*I worship the power of these lovely two,*
*With that adoring love known to so few,*
*'Tis indeed a miracle, one must feel,*
*That two such heavenly creatures are real,*
*Both sets of eyes though different far,*
*Hold many mysteries strange,*
*Impassively, they watch the race of man decay and*
*    change,*
*Hatred burning bright in the brown eyes for fuel,*
*Ivy scorn glitters in the grey eyes, contemptuous*
*    and cruel,*
*Why are men such fools they will not realise,*
*The wisdom that is hidden behind those strange*
*    eyes,*
*And these wonderful people are you and I.*

How did the girls feel after the murder? Pauline, said the doctor, showed signs of remorse only when she told him that she now tried always to sleep on her left side. When she slept on the right, her mother "seemed to come back". However, the girls believed that by their own standards what they had done was morally right. Pauline had told him that she and Juliet were sane. Everybody else was off the mark. The views of Juliet herself were much more logical and sensible.

Early in January, said Dr. Medlicott, Pauline wrote in the diary about Juliet having tuberculosis of one lung, and added: "I spent a wretched night. We agreed it would be wonderful if I could get TB, too."

On January 29th, Pauline wrote excitedly about the latest scheme. "We have worked out how much prostitutes should earn, and how much we should make in this profession," wrote the enthusiastic Miss Parker. "We have spent a really wonderful day, messing around and talking about how much fun we will have in our profession."

An illuminating episode occurred at this stage of Dr. Medlicott's evidence. The doctor was being questioned by the Crown Prosecutor about the diary's relations of Pauline making repeated nocturnal visits to the bed of the boy Nicholas. According to Pauline, said the doctor, the boy had had sexual relations with the girl only once.

Sexual relations . . . Juliet Hulme, sitting calmly in the dock, her grey eyes gazing calmly at the official court reporter, suddenly became aware of what Dr. Medlicott was saying. She looked as if she had been struck across the face! Hands clenched, eyes flashing, face suffused, teeth bared, she leaned across the wardress and hissed, rather than whispered, to the dark and impassive Pauline. It was the reaction of a mother who has found her young daughter in bed with the butcher boy.

The motivation of the murder, as the psychiatrist in the witness-box saw it, was the girls' decision to go to America together to have their novels published. The first reference to the planned death of Honora Parker appeared in the diary on February 12th. In March Pauline was visiting shipping companies. On April 30th (and this was one of the most important entries, in retrospect, in the entire case) she told Juliet that she intended to kill her mother. Early in May, the girls began a campaign of shoplifting to get money towards their projected American trip. On May 27th, Pauline set out alone, in the early hours of the morning, to rob the till in her father's fish shop, but the sight of a policeman on the beat caused her to go home to bed.

The diary rose to a febrile crescendo. On June 19th Pauline wrote: "Our main idea for the day is moider."

(Always the Brooklyn rendition of the terrible word which Pauline could never bring herself to write.) "We have worked it out quite clearly."

Now the Crown Prosecutor, who was most ably following his brief, which was to prove that the girls were sane murderers, referred Dr. Medlicott to an entry in the diary of April 17th. Mrs. Hulme had been "perfectly beastly to Deborah". It seemed that Juliet had gone to Perry's rooms and taken a gramophone record. Juliet had had to apologise, and this made the friends feel very cross, so they went to a field, sat on a log, and watched members of a riding club. "We shouted nasty jeering remarks to every rider that passed. About fifty did. This cheered us up greatly, and we came back and wrote out all the Commandments so that we can break them."

Now back to the deadly month of June. Passages from the diary: "We are both stark, staring mad." And "Dr. Hulme is mad—mad as a March hare."

Then there were the Saints, to which the diary referred several times. They were creatures of the imagination, based on film stars, of whom Mario Lanza was one, and the girls had spent a delirious night in bed, imagining encounters with seven of them.

Did the girls know the legal penalty for the killing of Honora Parker, Dr. Medlicott was asked?

In the dock, Juliet Hulme answered him. She drew her finger across her slim throat, and Pauline Parker looked at her from under the brim of her brown felt hat and smiled.

The girls, said Dr. Medlicott, were mad. They suffered from a form of insanity in which two persons were joined in their instability—*folie à deux*. They were a couple of paranoiacs, as all the evidence had gone to show.

And in support of Medlicott, the calm and cogent

Dr. Francis O. Bennett went into the witness-box. Of all the expert witnesses, he knew best the characters concerned. He was the Rieper-Parker family doctor, and he agreed that Pauline and Juliet were paranoiacs who were cases of *folie à deux*. Seven months before the murder, both Dr. Hulme and Mrs. Parker had consulted him about the close attachment of the two girls. He had thought that there was a homosexual relationship between them, and naturally had suggested that they be separated. The next time he saw them was in prison.

"They suffer from paranoia," said Dr. Bennett, "and follow delusion wherever it is. They become antisocial and dangerous. They think they are superior to the general race of man. Intellectually they are a little higher than girls of their own age, but they are not intellectual giants. They had delusions of grandeur, formed a society of their own, and lived in it. In this society they were no longer under the censure and nagging of mothers."

Again the diary; For April 3rd, 1953. Dr. Bennett quoted Pauline: "Today Juliet and I found the key to the fourth world. We saw a gateway through the clouds. We sat on the edge of a path and looked down a hill out over a bay. The island looked beautiful, the sea was blue, and everything was full of peace and bliss. We then realised we had the key. We know now that we are not genii, as we thought. We have an extra part of the brain, which can appreciate the fourth world."

The girls, Dr. Bennett related in his steady professional voice, had bathed together, gone to bed together, had dressed up and acted together on the lawn in the moonlight. They had made a little cemetery, and in it they had buried a dead mouse under a cross. When the Queen visited Christchurch, they made no attempt to see Her Majesty.

The Crown Prosecutor: "Is their relationship homosexual physically?" . . . "I don't know. I'm inclined to think not."

The girls believed in survival after death. Heaven was for happiness, paradise was for bliss. There was no hell, Juliet had told him in the remand prison. The idea was "so primitive". "The day we killed Mrs. Parker," Juliet had added, "I think she knew beforehand what was going to happen. And she did not bear any grudge."

The Crown now called its own medical witnesses, first the senior medical adviser of Avondale Mental Hospital, Auckland, Dr. K. R. Stallworthy, who had examined each girl four times in remand prison, who had read the diary, and who was quite sure that neither girl had a disease of the mind, and that each had known the nature and quality of her act. They had written down what was going to happen. They had given clear accounts of what they had done. They knew it was wrong to murder, they knew they were murdering somebody, they knew it was against the law. A primary request for paranoia was the presence of delusions, which he did not admit with these girls. Juliet's mental calibre was that of a highly intelligent person of much greater age. Pauline's intelligence was considerably above average.

Dr. Stallworthy had no doubt there had been a physical homosexual relationship.

Dr. James Edwin Saville, medical officer at Sunnyside Mental Hospital, had interviewed each girl five times. They were sane now, and they were sane when they killed Mrs. Parker, he said.

Dr. James Dewar Hunter, superintendent of Sunnyside, echoed Saville: Five interviews, same conclusion. Both sane then, and now.

In his final address, Crown Prosecutor Brown pithily

summed up his submission: "These girls are not incurably insane. They are incurably bad."

For Pauline Parker, Dr. A. L. Haslam, a brilliant pleader, traversed the evidence of "this rottenness, this disease" which had made killers of two paranoiac girls. And for Juliet Hulme, Mr. T. A. Gresson followed the same line. He told the jury that in "this appalling case" the girls were incapable of forming a moral judgment of what they had done.

The jury was out for two hours and thirteen minutes. The girls returned to the court-room simultaneously with the jurymen, and they smiled and laughed with the gallant disdain of the daughters of French aristocrats arraigned before Fouquier-Tinville. They took the verdict of "Guilty" calmly. With an air of indifference, they heard themselves sentenced to imprisonment during Her Majesty's pleasure.

The crowd streamed out of the grey stone court-house.

At his home, Herbert Rieper sat by the fire and smoked his pipe and sighed. Dr. Hulme, having taken his son Jonathan off the liner *Himalaya* at Marseilles, had reached England by a circuitous route. And in Christchurch, Mrs. Hulme was changing her name by deed poll to Mrs. Perry.

They sent Pauline Parker to Arohata Borstal, near Wellington, New Zealand's capital city, and Juliet Hulme to Mount Eden, the grim prison at Auckland where all New Zealand's hanging is done, and where, in her first year of sewing uniforms, there were four evening executions on New Zealand's portable steel scaffold.

At Arohata, Pauline Parker studied for a year under the Government's correspondence school scheme. In her cell, she sat for the school certificate, marking graduation from high school, and passed.

On her first day in Mount Eden in her prison dress of blue denim, Juliet Hulme was introduced to the sewing machine, and to enable her to operate it more efficiently a prostitute prisoner was kind enough to clip her long, well-cared-for finger-nails. Alone in her cell, Juliet knits, writes, according to competent judges, brilliantly, and studies languages. When she refers to the murder, which seems to be fading from her mind, she explains that she participated in it out of loyalty to "Gina"—her dark friend, Pauline.

And, though "Her Majesty's pleasure" is generally accepted as a sentence of twenty-five years, it would not be surprising if that of the two Christchurch girls, Juliet Hulme will be the one who will serve a short sentence; and it is possible that, under another name, the world in time will recognise a writer of talent.

This assumes that Juliet Hulme's tuberculosis (a disease found often in cases of sexual divergence) has been subdued, if not conquered; that the New Zealand prison system provides psychiatric treatment of a kind which, extended in 1953 to both Pauline Parker and Juliet Hulme, could have taken them out of the nightmare world they were making for themselves.

When Mr. Justice Adams passed sentence, a man in the public gallery called "I protest!" An Australian editorial writer heard in the minds of thousands of others an echo of this cry against the sentence, but for a different reason: "It is that two young human beings should ever be in such a way the victims of a dark conspiracy of circumstance so evil in its purpose and so appalling in its outcome.

"The psychiatrists will explain it all, however, and contradict each other in the explanation. Less knowing people will ponder upon the fact that it was the same world of the normal child's imagination which Pauline Parker and Juliet Hulme extended into a universe of sinister fantasy and gross design. They had vicious and depraved tendencies, and without each other they might have remained problem children; but their coming together, as if by the magnetism of some strange force in the hinterland of their minds, was a fatal conjunction of abnormality.

"Sane, legally, the girls may have been when, threatened with separation, they committed the murder, but it was surely the kind of sanity that mocks at all reality. The normal mind shrinks from the implications of this tragic story. In many other crimes, lessons of some sort or other are to be found. Here there is little but horror, sadness, and bafflement."

TG & HHG

# 33

# MRS PEARCEY
## Strong Nerves

At dusk on October 24, 1890, a policeman's attention was attracted to a bundle lying on the ground at Cross field Road, Hampstead. On examination he was horrified to find that it was the corpse of a woman lying in a pool of blood, the latter fact being accounted for by the condition of the head, which was almost completely severed from the body. This was wrapped in that species of waistcoat known as cardigan.

A doctor and the inspector of police were summoned with all speed, and the former pronounced the murder to have taken place within an hour or two as the body was still warm.

About the same time as the gruesome find at Cross field Road a second policeman made another discovery, which, if not so alarming as the first, was at least curious. This was no less than a perambulator, and on his taking it to the police-station (where, incidentally, as was only to be expected, he underwent a battery of good-natured chaff from his colleagues) he pointed out to the inspector that on the cushions was a quantity of blood, and also to them were adhering woman's hairs.

Then came a third discovery, not by a policeman, but by a member of John Bunyan's profession, that is to say, a tinker. Here, however, was no allegory but brutal fact. This tinker had encamped in nomadic fashion on a piece of waste ground at Hampstead, and in the morning (October 25) he had been startled to find the dead body of a baby lying in some furze bushes. The little body was, on the information of the tinker, removed to the police-station, and pronounced to be that of an infant from a year to eighteen months old.

It transpired that a Mrs. Hogg had gone out with her baby in a perambulator on the afternoon of October 24 and had not returned. At first, Mr. Hogg, who was a furniture remover, attached no importance to his wife's absence as her mother was very ill, and he concluded that she had gone to visit her, but he speedily became alarmed when a niece of his burst in upon him with the news that she believed the murdered woman was her aunt because of the description of her clothes, a black dress trimmed with astrachan.

Hogg, it must be admitted, all through showed himself to be a weak, hysterical, lachrymose creature who did little else but weep, and it was entirely owing to his niece (by name Clara Hogg) that the skein began to be unravelled.

The first step taken by Clara Hogg was to call on a friend of her aunt's—Mrs. Pearcey—and to her she made the same communication as she had to her uncle. Mrs. Pearcey poo-poohed the idea, but at length, because of her importunity, consented to accompany Clara Hogg to the mortuary.

Arrived there, Mrs. Pearcey seemed about to collapse, exclaiming: "It's not her! It's not her!" and her companion likewise failed at first to recognise her aunt, but she did recognise the garments and the perambulator.

Later on, at the request of the police, Clara Hogg again entered the mortuary, and the dead woman's face having in the interim been carefully laved, this time Clara Hogg declared the corpse to be that of her aunt.

Meanwhile, the police had been so struck with Mrs. Pearcey's demeanour that they determined to embark on a searching expedition. The first thing that they discovered was a key upon Mr. Hogg's person. Under pressure, the husband of the murdered woman confessed that this key gave access to Mrs. Pearcey's house, and that, unbeknown to his wife, he was in the habit of visiting her.

The next search the police made was of Mrs. Pearcey's house.

Mrs. Pearcey had distinct claim to good looks. Slightly built (to which I shall again refer presently), she possessed attractive brown hair, light blue eyes and good teeth.

When the police came to search Mrs. Pearcey's house they discovered nothing incriminating until they came to the kitchen. There among other things they noticed that not only much of the furniture, but much of the glass was broken.

Upon the kitchen dresser blood was found, and in explanation of this Mrs. Pearcey declared that the place was mice-infested, and that she had been killing these little rodents. But blood was also found in other places where mice are not generally found. For instance, on the walls, on the broken glass and at the back of the hearth.

A more likely place for mice to patronise, the carpeted floor, was also blood-stained. Also were discovered blood-stained clothes soaking in water, broken china, and disarranged kitchen utensils. Blood, too, was upon a chopper and two carving-knives.

And attaching to a poker in addition to blood were woman's hairs that corresponded to those adhering to the cushions of the perambulator. Lastly, the police noticed that there were deep scratches upon Mrs. Pearcey's hands. Upon all this incriminatory evidence Mrs. Pearcey was arrested.

Then commenced the usual foolish volunteered statements that go so far to assist the hangman in fastening the noose round the neck. To the police on the way to the police-station she stated that Mrs. Hogg had called that afternoon to borrow two shillings, but she never entered the house. "She ought to have mentioned this before."

But when on being searched at the station her

underclothes were found to be smeared with blood she told quite another story. She said Phœbe Hogg had had tea with her and had irritated her by some remark.

At the inquest the woman who lived next door to Mrs. Pearcey testified that on the afternoon of October 24 she heard piercing feminine shrieks and the sound of broken glass coming from Mrs. Pearcey's house, but very shortly afterwards absolute silence prevailed.

On the same night another witness who knew Mrs. Pearcey well was astonished at her cutting her dead in the street, and still more astonished to see her wheeling a perambulator. On thinking it over, Mrs. Pearcey seemed to be in a sort of trance and deadly pale, and probably had not noticed the witness.

Then two lodgers swore that when they were going through the hall of Mrs. Pearcey's house the latter accosted them with the warning that they must be careful not to collide with the perambulator stationed there.

Then a lad named William Holmes stated that on the same afternoon Mrs. Pearcey had given him a penny to take a note to Mrs. Hogg at the latter's house.

Then we had the truth about the Pearceys and the Hoggs. Mrs. Pearcey's real name was Wheeler. Mr. Pearcey, a man of means, was her protector, not her husband. But the protection had ceased because of the liaison with Hogg.

It must be conceded that not the least curious feature of this case is May Eleanor Pearcey's infatuation for Hogg. At the funeral of Mrs. Hogg and her baby only a large force of police thwarted the efforts of the crowd to lynch him.

In weighing all the evidence and sifting all the circumstances, I have no doubt that the murder was premeditated. The note that the boy Holmes delivered at the Hoggs' house was undoubtedly an invitation to tea, and as opposed to Mrs. Pearcey's first statement to the police, Mrs. Hogg did enter

Mrs. Pearcey's house and to such purpose that she never left it alive. Probably arrived there, the visitor found tea all prepared, and then, while seated at the table, she and her baby were attacked from the rear with the poker.

But all the signs of a terrible struggle were demonstrated, and, with our knowledge of the overpowering instinct of maternity, we suggest that the murdered woman would put up an extra desperate fight when she realized that not only was her life at stake, but that of her offspring.

That ablest of solicitors, Mr. Freke Palmer, took up the defence, and at once seized upon the point that no slightly built woman could have wheeled a perambulator all that way laden with at least 130 lb.

And that is where the mystery lies. Had Mrs. Pearcey an accomplice? Was anybody an accessory either before or after the fact? In a moment, I think, I can make it clear that there was tremendous force in Mr. Freke Palmer's contention.

The trial took place at the Old Bailey on December 1 before Mr. Justice Denman. It lasted three days. Mr. Forrest (afterwards Sir Forrest) Fulton and Mr. C. F. Gill were for the Crown, and Mr. Freke Palmer entrusted the defence of his client into the hands of Mr. Arthur Hutton.

But whether or no Mrs. Pearcey had an accomplice, she herself was a murderess, and the jury had little hesitation in finding their verdict. One of the most damning pieces of evidence was when Mr. Pearcey swore that he owned the cardigan waistcoat found wrapped round the head of Mrs. Hogg.

The Judge, who had summed up dead against the prisoner, in pronouncing sentence of death, said that lust had been the demon that had caused her to commit this awful crime. In expressing his opinion of Hogg his lordship merely expressed the opinion of everyone both in and out of court. In answer to the usual question, Mrs. Pearcey declared her innocence. She was then sentenced to death.

The love letters written by Mrs. Pearcey to the unusually unattractive and contemptible Hogg give one to think furiously, and are only another proof that woman is an inexplicable being and that only too often they love unwisely and are bad judges of men. The letters were those of a woman beside herself with love. But where Mrs. Pearcey alienated all sympathy was in including the baby in her scheme of jealous revenge. For all the world loves a baby (except Mrs. Pearcey and a very few others), and it is well that it should be so.

Mrs. Pearcey was hanged on December 23. Her last words were that the sentence was just, but the evidence false—spoken, of course, to the chaplain. But in her last interview with Mr. Freke Palmer she asked him to insert the following notice in the leading Madrid newspapers: "M.E.C.P. Last wish of M.E.W.* Have not betrayed."

Here is a reproduction of it! Does it not look odd amidst all the Spanish? And who was M.E.C.P.? And why the Madrid newspapers?

Does not this lend very considerable support to the theory that Mrs. Pearcey had an accomplice? And I must not conclude without paying tribute to her wonderful nerve.

Fancy remaining in that house, a house in which there were other inmates, for such a length of time, when in the hall was stationed a perambulator, its drawn hood concealing its gruesome secret, till at length it becomes sufficiently dark for the removal of its ghastly freight. Indubitably one of the stock instances of nerve in the whole of criminology.

—A.L

* May Eleanor Wheeler.

# 34

# LOUISE PEETE

## Dr Jekyll and Mrs Hyde

---

She wasn't beautiful, not really, but she radiated a most compelling aura, a highly refined sexiness. Men were fatally attracted. All four of her husbands committed suicide. She shot and killed at least two other men and abused a third to a bitter end. But then she murdered a woman and was strangled by the law in a noose fashioned from the skeins of her own silken lies.

Lofie Louise Preslar was born in Bienville, Louisiana, in 1883. She was given the best New Orleans education her newspaper publisher father could buy. Louise was a classic Southern belle, cultured and refined. And Louise was unscrupulous, voluptuous and promiscuous. The combination caused her expulsion from an elite finishing school and brought about a marriage at age 20 to a traveling salesman, Henry Bosley.

Bosley soon found her in bed with a New Orleans oilman. Less than 48 hours later he took his own life. Louise sold or pawned Bosley's meager possessions and moved to Shreveport. She excelled at her new profession: call girl. "I'm expensive, but 'guaranteed,'" she confided to a friend.

After acquiring some working capital, Louise moved to Boston, appropriated a wealthy and respected name—Gould—and practiced her amorous trade among the scions of Beacon Hill. And among the *pères* and *grands-pères* or anyone else who could pay the price. She took to visiting the mansions of the rich—in

Madam's absence. And she took any of Madam's small valuables that might be lying about. One day she very suddenly and very prudently took a train to Waco, Texas.

There she made the acquaintance of free-spending, diamond-bedecked wildcatter Joe Appel. She shot him in the back of the head and his diamonds mysteriously vanished. Louise was arrested, and appeared before a grand jury. In her best Louisiana accent she told an eloquent and moving tale of attempted rape. She was an innocent, a well-bred Southern lady of quality, and Appel, a horrid Yankee carpetbagger, had attempted to force himself upon her protesting self. So she took his gun and shot him. In self-defense. The grand jury ordered her released. They applauded her as she grandly left the jail.

In 1913, she turned up in Dallas, broke. She quickly married Harry Faurote, a hotel clerk, and went back to whoring, the work she knew best. She went at it, with her usual gusto, in Harry's own hotel. He soon hanged himself in the basement.

She went to Denver in 1915 and married Richard Peete. They bought a small house. Louise bore a daughter in 1916. But Peete, a door-to-door salesman, would never make the money that Louise wanted. In May 1920 she picked a fight with him, packed a bag, took a train. She headed for the bright lights, for the quick score. She headed for Los Angeles.

There she found Jacob Denton, a millionaire businessman, a worldly widower. He owned an English Tudor mansion near the Ambassador Hotel on booming Wilshire Boulevard. He was preparing to take an extended trip east; he wished to rent out his house. Peete moved in on him, moved into his house and into his bed. Soon she proposed marriage. Denton was enraged—but not for long.

Sometime around the end of May, Denton disappeared. Peete told the caretaker that Denton wished to have a ton of topsoil removed from the garden and placed in the basement. He was fond of mushrooms, said Peete, and she would show him how to grow them.

Denton's absence was soon noted. Peete had explanations, many different ones. She was incredibly inventive, never at a loss for an answer. Though many of her tales were plainly incredible, her elegant, cultured manner, her unflappable composure and the tightly-woven fiction of her background deceived nearly all. An attractively plump, mature woman, she was at all times utterly charming and utterly believable, an utterly sympathetic figure.

A business associate complained that Denton had missed an appointment. Louise said Denton had received an urgent telegram and left immediately for San Francisco. An insurance agent arrived for an appointment with Denton. Denton had gone to the beach, Louise explained, but had asked her to handle this matter. Would the agent be kind enough to add her to his auto policy, since she would be driving his car while he was absent?

The agent assented. Denton had another appointment with Hudson salesman Hal Haydon. Denton had ordered a new car, which he would pick up in Michigan, and he wished to trade in the old. When he failed to bring it in, Haydon came to Denton's house.

Denton, Louise told Haydon, had gone to Arizona, had returned, and then left for San Francisco. And he had somehow been wounded in the right arm. The wound had become infected. "Mr. Denton is ashamed of the wound," Louise told Haydon. "He doesn't want people to know about it." By the middle of June, said Louise, the arm had to be amputated. There would be no trip East. So he had left instructions for the new car to be delivered to his home. Louise returned the old one to the dealership.

Now her story became more ambitious, more inventive, more convoluted. And less believable. Louise said Denton had given her power of attorney to sell his house, and to take a $3,000 commission on the asking price of $27,500. Louise was inventive, she was creative, she had vast, perhaps unlimited, stores of moxie. She sometimes even convinced herself that her inventions were truth. But Louise wasn't nearly as smart as she had believed. Had she bothered to inquire, she would have learned that most reputable realtors would have charged only about half that much.

On June 5 she went to the Farmer's & Merchant's Bank. She had the key to Denton's safety deposit box and a check made out to her for $300 on his account. Another check to her for $450 had been cashed elsewhere. Neither of the signatures matched Denton's signature card. What was going on? Louise told her new, improved story to a bank official. Denton was in Seattle. He had gone to Missouri, but would return. His arm had been amputated above the elbow. Out of the goodness of her heart, she was helping the poor man with his affairs. She was helping him by writing checks and by signing his name. He held on to the end of his pen with his other hand, she said, so it was legal, wasn't it? The banker appeared puzzled. He couldn't honor Denton's checks, but neither could he bring himself to call the police about this dear, sweet woman.

And then Louise added a dramatic flourish. The Spanish Woman. The Spanish Woman was a mysterious figure who first turned up with Denton in May, or perhaps it was early June. She and Denton were an item, said Louise, but they quarreled, often violently. The Spanish Woman was in some way connected with the loss of poor Denton's arm, Louise hinted.

The charade continued through the hot days of summer. Louise rented out rooms and collected rents. Denton was in and out of town, but was so ashamed of his disfigurement that he would see no one except Louise. He telephoned from time to time but spoke only with Louise. Louise continued to act as though Denton had charged her with keeping his affairs in order. Small checks came by mail. Endorsing them with his name, she cashed them. She forged a lease agreement giving her the right to occupy the property. She charged a few dresses to Denton's account at Bullocks. She had a few of his silk shirts altered into blouses for her own use. Louise gave away a few of Denton's clothes, pawned one of his rings. But the big score eluded her.

In mid-August she leased the mansion to a couple named Miller, and made a show of her return home to Denver. But she continued to write to Los Angeles realtors and auto dealers, making minor ripples in Denton's financial affairs. Denton was still nowhere to be found.

On September 23, Denton's family hired an attorney, Rush Blodgett. He hired a private detective, A.J. Cody. Cody and Blodgett came calling with spades. They found Jacob Denton at home. His body lay on the floor of the basement. Some of the dirt Louise had ordered had been loosely shoveled on top of him. The coroner used an X-ray photo—at the time, a new and daring forensic innovation—to reveal the cause of death: a .32 caliber bullet fired at close range into the back of his neck. The bullet came from Denton's own gun, which now lay in an upstairs drawer with one spent cartridge still in its chamber.

Los Angeles Chief Deputy District Attorney William

Doran was fairly certain Louise Peete had killed Jacob Denton. But he also knew that Peete was in Colorado and that she was extremely persuasive. Extradition in that era was far from foolproof. Doran thought it likely that Louise could convince Colorado authorities not to turn her over to California. Or she might simply flee.

So Doran decided to turn Louise Peete's own method against her. He concocted a fiction, a story designed to lure Louise back to California. He sent a man to Denver to ask her to help Doran find Jacob Denton's killer. Louise, as everyone knew, was Denton's good friend. No one knew as much about his final days as she. Wouldn't she come to Los Angeles and help her good friend and strong supporter, the assistant district attorney, solve this mystery?

Louise took the bait. With her husband in tow, she boarded a train for Los Angeles on October 2. But Doran had an arrangement with the Santa Fe Railroad and the train made an unscheduled stop at the summit of Cajon Pass, in the San Bernardino Mountains. Doran persuaded Louise and an increasingly reluctant husband to leave the train for a car he had provided. They drove to a remote resort hotel, Glenn Ranch. Doran kept Louise comfortable and well-fed, but isolated from her friends—and most especially from the press—and he began his game of cat and mouse.

Doran's probing produced one incredible story after another. Louise claimed that if the man in the basement was Denton, then the man who lost an arm, the man who slipped back into town only to see Louise, the man who took up with the Spanish Lady—this man must have been an impostor. Find him and you'll have the killer, she told Doran. And find the Spanish Lady and you'll find him. As the questions continued, Louise spun new stories, often contradicting her earlier tales. She invented unlikely new characters, odd reasons for past actions, convoluted justifications for her illegal actions. She was a novelist, always quick to invent a new twist to a plot she had never quite thought through to its conclusion. But despite Peete's inventiveness and wondrously sincere delivery, Doran became firmly convinced that she had killed Denton. And Louise, caught up in the glow of an appreciative audience, was equally convinced that no jury would ever convict her.

Then she arrived in Los Angeles to learn from the newspapers that it was Doran who had ordered the X-rays used to determine the cause of Denton's death. Doran had outwitted her, had earned her confidence under a pretense and deceived her about his real intentions. Doran played her own game, but he played it better. Losing her composure, Louise refused to face the grand jury and was indicted for Denton's murder.

But she quickly regained her old self-assurance. In custody she provided eager newspaper readers with new and elaborate variations on her basic story. She told police that one day, while she was in her room at Denton's, she heard a shot. Racing to the kitchen, she found Denton at a table. The Spanish Woman bled from a wound in her shoulder—or maybe her chest. And a bullet was "spinning around in the sink."

Her trial convened January 21, 1921. A parade of witnesses poked gaping holes in her elaborate lies. One testified that on the night Denton was murdered, Louise had sung and danced and put flowers all around the house. Her public defender asked the jury how such an obviously refined woman as Louise could have behaved in this way with the knowledge that Denton's still-warm body lay in the cellar below. This convinced some of the spectators, and many who read the newspapers, that Louise could not possibly be the killer. It failed to convince the jury.

After deliberating four hours and casting six ballots, they found Peete guilty of murder in the first degree and sentenced her to life imprisonment. Following her suggestion, husband Richard divorced her, but remained her most loyal supporter, promising to "wait forever" for her release. In 1924, she stopped replying to his letters, refused to see him, broke all contact. He went to Tucson on business and there put a bullet through his head. Three husbands, three suicides.

During the trial, her friends Margaret and Arthur Logan looked after Betty, Louise's five-year-old daughter. And during Peete's 18 years in prison, first at San Quentin and then at the woman's prison at Tehachapi, the Logans remained convinced of her innocence. They wrote, they visited, they bestowed small gifts.

In April 1943, Louise won parole. She was somewhat heavier than she'd been in her call-girl days, but her health was good, her face unlined. She appeared far younger than her 60 years. Her probation officer, Mrs. Latham of the Parole Board, had supported her innocence during the Denton trial. Latham invited Louise to move in with her. Louise agreed. Soon the elderly Latham had a stroke. She went to a hospital where she soon died. Louise, who had taken a new name—Anna B. Lee—stole the late Latham's .32 caliber Smith & Wesson revolver. Then she inveigled an invitation to move into the Logans' comfortable Pacific Palisades home.

Arthur Logan was 74, and thought to be perhaps a little senile, though harmless. He took long daily walks, went to the post office, conversed with his neighbors at length on subjects that held his interest. Margaret Logan held a real-estate license. But this was the middle of World War

II. She worked at Douglas Aircraft as her contribution to the war effort. Louise was paid $75 a month plus room and board to look after Arthur Logan while his wife was at work.

Louise began to spin yet another web. Almost at once she began to tell people that old Arthur was crazy, dangerously crazy. He had kicked Margaret in the face, she told family members. And Louise said she herself had been so assaulted. Using this as ammunition, Louise, five weeks after she moved in, persuaded Margaret to file a court petition asserting Arthur was "mentally ill, dangerous, and insane." Arthur was committed to Patton State Hospital. He remained there for 19 days, before doctors released him to Margaret's custody. Early in 1944 Mrs. Logan left Douglas and returned to real estate.

Louise soon told Margaret Logan about the $100,000 trust fund in Denver she was about to inherit. Then Louise told her, she was interested in buying a certain Santa Monica house for $50,000. Margaret would handle the sale. There was to be a 70-day escrow, and Logan was to be co-purchaser. Logan stood to make $2,500 in commission, but had promised half to Louise. Louise announced she intended to resell the property for a profit. But first there was the matter of the $2,000 down payment.

The Bank of America turned down her application, trust fund story notwithstanding. That put the entire burden on Margaret, who had believed in Louise for nearly 20 years. She borrowed $2,000 against her own savings account, put it in the escrow account. Louise planned a trip to Denver to "collect her trust fund." Margaret bought two train tickets. Later Louise persuaded Margaret it was better if she went alone. From Denver she telephoned Margaret to ask for a loan of $300. The money was promptly wired. A few days later she returned by train.

In early May Louise met and married 65-year-old Lee Judson, a semi-retired Glendale bank messenger who had no idea "Anna B. Lee" was really the convicted murderess Louise Peete. She told Judson about her impending inheritance, but added that it might be jeopardized were it known she had married. Though it was flimsy, this fiction got Judson to keep their marriage a secret from the Logans.

And all the while Louise artfully continued to spread her lies about Arthur Logan's growing insanity. He was violent, she said. He was dangerous. He could not remember afterward the frightening things he had done. And probably Arthur's strange behavior also accounted for the small items of jewelry that Margaret noticed were missing.

In mid-May Louise got Margaret to buy two more train tickets for a June 14 Denver trip. A few days later, on May 19, Louise forged a check to herself on Margaret's account. When the Logans' bank noted the phony signature, Margaret told them Louise would repay the funds. But what had become of the Denver trust fund? There was some unexpected delay, explained Louise. Soon all would be in order. But Margaret Logan now stood to lose the $2,000 she had put in escrow. This may well have been when she began to doubt her faith in Louise. If she could forge a check, if there was no trust fund, if the stories about her husband's mental condition were lies—then Louise Peete was surely capable of other deceptions.

On May 29, 1944, almost 24 years to the day Jacob Denton was murdered, Mrs. Logan was in the act of telephoning—possibly the parole board—when Louise put a .32 caliber revolver to the back of Margaret's neck and pulled the trigger. Perhaps Louise twitched at the last moment or Logan may have moved her head, because the shot did not kill her. She died from loss of blood from the gunshot wound and from myriad wounds inflicted by repeated blows to the back of her head with the steel butt of the little gun that Louise had stolen from the late Mrs. Latham.

Louise dragged Margaret's body into the back yard, buried it in a shallow grave beneath the avocado tree, then cleaned the blood and evidence of violence from the floors and walls. And then she sang gaily, danced a happy little dance, and put bright flowers throughout the house.

On May 31 Louise cashed in the Denver train tickets and used the money to repay Margaret's bank for the forged check. She hoped this would also stop the police from investigating. Later that day Louise told Arthur Logan that Margaret had been injured in an auto accident. She was in the hospital. And that same day Louise got Arthur to help her pack Judson's bags. He helped Lee Judson move in to the Logans' home.

On June 1, Louise used the accident story to get Arthur to come along to the hospital. At the psychiatric ward of Los Angeles General Hospital, Louise said she was Arthur's nurse and his foster sister-in-law. She asserted that Arthur had become so violent she could no longer care for him, and that he had beaten and bitten his wife's face. Arthur said he couldn't remember any of that. Louise exchanged a knowing look with the doctors, told her tales, signed the papers. She left Arthur at the hospital, and four days later her was recommitted to Patton. He died there, lonely and bewildered, on December 6, 1944. Louise generously donated his body to medical science, thereby saving herself the cost of his burial. And a neighbor noted the gay flowers she put out that day: noted the chic new clothing she put on; noted the spring in her step that day, and wondered.

There remained the matter of Margaret Logan's disappearance. To the questions of Margaret's friends, neighbors and relatives, Louise had wonderfully imaginative answers. Mrs. Logan had to have plastic surgery because of Arthur's violence to her face. She was in a hospital close to the one where Arthur was staying. She had breast cancer and had gone away to Oregon. She was in a rest home, humiliated by her husband's attack and her facial disfigurement. She wasn't seeing friends or relatives until she felt well enough. It was all very believable. It was said with great conviction.

From June to December, Louise filled her days with taking over the Logans' possessions. She flim-flammed the seller of the Santa Monica house into refunding half the $2,000 Margaret had put up as earnest money. She sweet-talked the bank into taking her "X" for the "crippled" Margaret's mark on the refund check. She sold or gave away valuable items from the household: an electric mixmaster, a laundry mangle, sterling flatware, fine china, linens. She had some of Margaret's clothing altered to fit her. She took the Logan car for her own use. She appropriated the Logans' ration cards and food stamps, document that all civilians required to get food during World War II. And on December 20, 1944, she and Judson broke open the Logans' home safe. They were going through its contents when the policeman rang the doorbell.

The cop at the door was Captain Thaddeus Brown, head of LAPD homicide. Louise Peete was no stranger to him. He took her and her husband downtown to the district attorney. There Judson was shocked to learn that Anna B. Lee was the murderess Louise Peete and shocked to realize how he had been duped.

Judson was held as a material witness until January 12, when police were satisfied that the highly respected messenger was just one more innocent victim of the Louise Peete charm. The next day Judson took an elevator to the 13th floor of the Spring Arcade Building and dove head-first into the stairwell. His battered, lifeless body came to rest on the landing between floors four and five.

In April 1945, another jury listened to Louise's latest string of lies. She had not killed Margaret Logan. It was Arthur who shot her. Crazy Arthur. Louise tried to stop him but he was just too crazed. After the shooting, Arthur beat Margaret's head with a steak hammer. When she died, Louise was afraid to call the police. Surely they would not have believed *her*, a convicted murderess. So instead she cleaned up the mess, buried poor Margaret, had crazy Arthur committed, and went on about her life. That was the substance of her story. The details were involved and presented at length, with enormous verisimilitude.

But physical evidence from the Logan home contradicted all of Louise Peete's wonderful inventions. The jury was allowed to hear some of the similarities between the deaths of Denton and Margaret Logan. "Mrs. Peete, who was a Dr. Jekyll and a Mrs. Hyde, must have sat in her prison cell figuring what went wrong the first time and plotting this new crime," said Deputy District Attorney John Barnes, in his jury summation. The jury deliberated three hours, returning a verdict of guilty of murder in the first degree, without recommending mercy. Louise Peete died in the San Quentin gas chamber on April 11, 1947. Charming to the end, she spoke her last words to the warden: "Thank you for all your many kindnesses."

—MJW & KM

# 35

# ALMA RATTENBURY
## Old Enough to be His Mother

The jury prepared to file out.

"Beware that you do not convict this woman of the crime she is accused of because she is an adulteress!" The judge's final warning still rang in their ears. The fate of two people rested in their hands. Seated round the table of the jury-room a few moments after their leaving the courtroom, they earnestly weighed the facts of the case. Were the couple—George Stoner and Alma Rattenbury—guilty of the murder of Francis Mawson Rattenbury, husband of the woman standing accused before them? Or was but one of them guilty, and the other innocent of any complicity in the murder? That was what they had to decide. Piece by piece they went over the evidence that had been brought before them.

Francis Mawson Rattenbury, elderly and retired architect, residing at Villa Maderia, Manor Road, Bournemouth, was married to a woman much younger than himself—Alma Victoria Rattenbury being thirty-eight, whilst he was well over the fifty mark. In their employ was a young man, George Stoner, not yet twenty, who acted as chauffeur for them. Thus we have all the factors that go to make the eternal triangle: Stoner, young and presentable, Mr. Rattenbury, comparatively old and decrepit, and Alma Rattenbury, described as a woman utterly without moral sense.

Stoner was easily, if not willingly, seduced by this woman, who was old enough to be his mother. It could be said that she bought his affection, for squander money on him she did, buying him jewellery, clothes and presents with the money she obtained from her unsuspecting husband on numerous pretexts. But subsequent events proved that, money or no money, presents or no presents, he must have really loved the immoral creature—loved her enough to commit murder on her behalf!

In his capacity as chauffeur it was only natural for Stoner to accompany Mrs. Rattenbury on all her journeys, and make many she did. Little did people know the real purpose behind these journeys. Purporting to be visiting relatives of hers, the couple actually utilized these journeys for a far different purpose. Unable to indulge in their illicit love-making in the house, the couple spent many a week-end at various hotels in London, and other large towns, where there would be no fear of recognition. The intrigue, like so many of its kind, ended in tragedy.

The night of March 24th, 1935, saw Irene Riggs, help companion to Mrs. Rattenbury, returning to the villa from her evening out. Shortly after retiring to her room she heard her mistress calling her. On going into the lounge she found Mrs. Rattenbury leaning over her husband, who was slumped forward in one of the armchairs, with blood streaming from his head. "He's had an accident," cried Mrs. Rattenbury, "help me to get him to bed, will you!"

A doctor was summoned, and on finding that Mr. Rattenbury's condition was serious, he ordered him off to hospital, and sent for the police. They arrived to find Mrs. Rattenbury in an intoxicated condition. In answer to their question, she made a number of confused statements. To begin with she told them that she had been sitting playing cards with her husband, and had gone to bed leaving him alone in the lounge. A few minutes later she had heard a shout, and on running down to the lounge found her husband slumped forward in one of the chairs with blood pouring from his head.

She followed this with another statement in which she said:

"I know who did it . . . I did it with the mallet . . . I have hid it . . . No, my lover did it . . . I will give you ten pounds to say nothing about the whole business . . . no, I mustn't bribe you . . . I will tell you all about it in the morning—where the mallet is hid, and everything . . ." She then giggled foolishly, and went on to say that she had made a proper muddle of it, but that she would make a better job of it next time.

The police decided to wait until she was sober before questioning her again. In their search of the house they discovered a blood-stained mallet outside the front door. Morning found Mrs. Rattenbury giving them a more coherent statement.

"I was playing cards with my husband, and an argument developed in which he dared me to kill him. I then hit him with the mallet . . . I would have shot him if I had a gun."

She was immediately charged with inflicting bodily harm on her husband, and held pending trial. The case took on a more serious aspect when it became known that Mr. Rattenbury had died during the night without regaining consciousness. The charge was now altered to one of murder.

The police decided that Stoner, the chauffeur in the Rattenbury's employ, might have had a hand in the murder, and a drag net was put out for him. He was arrested alighting from a train at Bournemouth Central Station. They wasted no time in preliminaries. What did he know about the sordid affair? He confessed immediately on hearing that his mistress had been charged with the murder.

"I did it," he insisted; "she had nothing to do with it. I did the job whilst he was asleep in the armchair. I hit him with the mallet: I was outside the window, you see, when she kissed him goodnight. After she had gone upstairs I crept in through the windows which were kept unlocked. He was dozing in the chair . . . I hit him . . ."

The police now had to decide whether Stoner was shielding Mrs. Rattenbury, or whether she was shielding him. On the other hand it was also within the realm of possibility for them both to be guilty of the crime. It would have to be left to a jury to decide.

They were brought to trial at the Old Bailey, scene of many a similar drama. Both the prisoners pleaded "Not guilty." The prosecution opened their case by mentioning the illicit relation existing between Stoner and Mrs. Rattenbury. They stressed the fact that Mrs. Rattenbury had used her husband's money to buy presents for her paramour. They produced evidence to show that the pair of them were as dissolute a couple as had ever been brought to justice. They were drug addicts, licentious and depraved, living on deceit, and another man's money.

Mrs. Rattenbury visibly flinched when the prosecution demanded that she tell the court when she became Stoner's mistress. In a voice that was barely audible, she told the court that it was in the November of the previous year that she had given herself to him. The prosecution finished by claiming that the lovers were both equally guilty of the crime, having conspired to kill the elderly man, and carried out the murder between them.

The defence seized on the prosecution's statement about the prisoners' use of drugs, and claimed that the crime was not the result of two people working it out beforehand, but the result of a sudden impulse—a mad act by one under the influence of drugs.

The prosecution discounted this by bringing forward witnesses to prove that Stoner had obtained the mallet from his father's house, having borrowed it especially for the job, giving his father to understand that he was erecting a tent for the Rattenburys, and needed the mallet to drive the pegs in with.

The defence tried a different tack. What of Mrs. Rattenbury? they argued; why was she being held? There was not a shred of evidence against her, except those incoherent statements she had made to the police. Was it possible that such a frail person had sufficient strength to attack and kill her husband?

The prosecution would have none of this argument. Frail or not frail, it was their contention that Mrs. Rattenbury helped to murder her husband.

The defence then rose and reminded the jury of the Bywater-Thompson case, referring them to the doubt in the people's minds as to whether both parties had been guilty. "That must not happen here," the defence pleaded—"there must be no mistake!"

The judge, in summing up, emphasised that the law was that if two persons agree together that a felony—such a felony as 'feloniously wounding'—shall be committed on somebody, and if in the pursuance of that agreement that felonious wounding is committed by one of them, and death is caused and ensues as a result of that felonious wounding, then each of those persons is equally guilty of murder.

"It matters not by the hand of which the fatal blow was delivered," he went on to say, "and it matters not whether both of them were even present at the time . . . Members of the jury, it is not a pleasant thing to have to say what I am about to say of this woman's character; but even her own counsel said things about her which must have been very painful for her to hear—if indeed she has any moral understanding at all . . .

"It is the case of the prosecution, as I understand it, that she is a woman so lost to all sense of decency, so entirely without any morals, that she would stop at nothing to gain her ends, particularly her sexual gratification; and if that be true, then, say the prosecution, do you think that such a woman would hesitate to kill her husband? You will remember that she gave evidence herself that she was regularly committing adultery with her husband's servant. Sometimes in her own bedroom, and in that bedroom there was her child of six!

"It may be that you will say you cannot possibly feel any sympathy, you cannot have any feeling except disgust for her; but let me say this: that should not make you more ready to convict her of this crime; it should, if anything, make you less ready to accept evidence against her. If you think there can be any explanation consistent with her innocence of that crime, I know you will not let it prejudice you against her.

"Beware that you do not convict her of this crime because she is an adulteress, and an adulteress, you may think, of the most unpleasant type."

After an absence of approzimately an hour, the jury returned with their findings. They found Mrs. Rattenbury "Not guilty." She heard their verdict without the slightest sign of emotion; but when Stoner was pronounced guilty, she gave a pitiful cry, and extended her arms to him, as if to protect him, to comfort him.

On her release she was hounded by newspaper men and photographers, until it became necessary for her to seek refuge in a nursing home. The thought of her lover going to the gallows preyed on her mind, giving her no peace. Her nights, her very waking moments, were tortured by the thought of her losing him, of him going to the gallows.

A few days before Stoner was due to meet his end, a man crossing a small bridge on the outskirts of Christchurch, not far from Bournemouth, saw a well dressed woman standing on the banks of the stream that flowed beneath the bridge. He thought no more of it until the sun suddenly glinted on what she was holding to her bosom. It was a knife, and before he could cry out, or spring to prevent her, she plunged the knife into her body, and fell face forward into the water.

Springing over the bridge, he rushed to pull her out. The water flowed red where the body lay. She was dead when he pulled her out. Alma Victoria Rattenbury, unable to bear the thought of being separated from her lover, had taken her life.

The bitter irony of it all was that Stoner did not die. An appeal was made on his behalf, and was first rejected by the Lord Chief Justice on the grounds that the fact that the accused was a lad of good character, but had been corrupted by an abandoned woman old enough to be his mother, raised no question in law, nor could it be employed as a ground for an appeal.

"We have no power," said the Lord Chief Justice finally, "nor the inclination to alter the law relating to murder in this respect."

But a reprieve was granted for all that, Stoner's sentence being commuted to that of penal servitude for life. Mrs. Rattenbury died thinking that she was joining her lover. She died in vain.

—M.H.

# 36

# VERA RENCZI

## The Crypt of Dead Lovers

Born in Bucharest of fairly well-to-do parents, Vera started out with every advantage in life. She received a fine education, and from her earliest days showed promise of the great beauty which was later to prove a fatal snare to so many. Her mother died when her daughter was still a child, and her father, inheriting some property in Berkerekul, went to live there with ten-year-old Vera. Although disciplined by the several governesses employed to educate her, the child soon developed a rebellious, selfish nature that brooked no obstacle to the attainment of her desires.

Chief among those desires was the companionship of members of the opposite sex. She was scarcely ever seen about Berkerekul without the modern equivalent of a "boy friend." And as she grew in loveliness she had no difficulty in attracting youths who in the first flush of adolescence succumbed to her beauty. With an easy-going father who fondly imagined that his daughter was simply high-spirited and could do no wrong, and with governesses who were anxious to keep on the right side of both girl and father, Vera was able to do pretty much as she liked, and if what she liked was not always in her best interests it was not altogether her fault.

She had just turned fifteen when she was discovered at midnight in the dormitory of a boys' school, and this was the first of a series of indiscretions into which her waywardness led her. On several occasions she ran away with her flame of the moment, but invariably returned in a few days declaring that she had tired of her lover. In vain her father admonished her, and it must have been a great relief to him when she fell head over ears in love with a well-known business man in the town, many years her senior. He was extremely wealthy as well as handsome and he appealed to the romanticism of the fair Vera, to whom he was as greatly attracted.

From the moment of their first meeting, she became a changed person. She was now modest and subdued, sweetly content to wait upon her lover's every wish. Their marriage was one of the great social events in Berkerekul and they departed for their honeymoon in the Tyrol, with the blessings of the girl's father and the good wishes of all their friends.

Vera and her husband settled down in the vast mansion belonging to the bridegroom, and she soon became one of the most popular women in the town. She revealed great competence in handling the big household and she was a charming and lovely hostess. When, fourteen months later, a baby boy arrived on the scene, the joy of both Vera and her husband knew no bounds. The young mother devoted every waking hour to the well-being of her son, but some three months after the birth of the baby Vera appeared in the town looking distraught and sad. To friends she confided the unbelievable news that the husband, whom she "loved beyond everything" as she put it, had deserted her. "He left me without a word of warning or a single note to say why he was going or where," she tearfully told them.

The friends condoled with her, proffering the comforting opinion that the errant husband would soon return; but to this Vera smiled wanly, saying, "He'll never come back to me."

She was literally dead right, for at that very moment his body, encased in a zinc coffin, was lying in the cellar of his own mansion, the first of the thirty-five bodies to enter this domestic tomb.

A year passed in which Vera devoted all her time to the upbringing of her boy, who, as the days went by, grew into the very image of his father. To the friends who came to console her in her loneliness Vera exhibited her son, remarking proudly on his likeness to her vanished husband. "So long as I have little Karl," she would cry pathetically, "my husband will always be with me."

And then, of a sudden, Vera shed her grief and embarked on a carefree bohemian life, in which she flung convention to the winds and caused the tongue of scandal to wag in the social circles that had hitherto known her as the most circumspect of women. The night cafés of Berkerekul became her regular haunts and she was avid for the company of young men. Vera had reverted to type. One day she made it known that she had just learned her absent husband had been killed in a car accident, an announcement that paved the way for her obvious attachment to a new admirer. And just as her first marriage seemed to have had a restraining influence on her, so did her second big romance result in the taming of her unbridled passions. The object of her devotion this time was a young ne'er-do-well, Josef Renczi, whose only recommendation was that he was an Adonis of a youth, apart from which he was dissipated and profligate.

But as soon as they were man and wife, Vera settled down once more to a quiet homely existence. Not so, however, her husband, who soon tired of his young bride and began to seek his pleasures elsewhere. Vera was prepared to incur any amount of scandal in connection with her own affairs of the heart, and was ready to acknowledge she was not capable of holding her husband, but the one thing she was not prepared to tolerate was that her husband should find happiness in the arms of another. She, who knew full well the depth and extent of her own burning passion and with what unbounded generosity she could lavish it upon husband or lover, could not endure the thought of Josef yielding to the embraces of another woman. And for jealous Vera there was an easy way out of the dilemma. Beneath the château in which she lived, her former husband reposed in his little zinc sarcophagus, and in this large and secret mortuary there was plenty of accommodation for newcomers. Thus, four months after her marriage to Josef Renczi, Vera was to tell her friends that her new husband had gone "on a long journey," adding "and I don't care if I never see him again," a sentiment endorsed heartily by all who knew of Josef's philandering.

Actually the journey which Josef had taken was *not* a very long one, just down a flight of stone steps into the cellar where his forerunner lay, but it was a bourn from which there was no return.

A year later Vera announced that her second missing husband had written to say he had decided to leave her for ever. The message itself may have been false but its content was inexorably true. So once more she resumed the gay life and passed from the arms of one lover to another, with considerable, if unladylike alacrity.

Her wanton behaviour resulted in her ostracism from those circles where she had shone, but this did not worry Vera, for while she could bask in the adoration that she seemed able to inspire, she was content enough. Yet although she encouraged all comers, she was essentially monogamist in the physical relationship with her particular lover of the moment. Upon him she lavished all the passion of which she was capable, but like the black-widow spider she consumed her mate as soon as his ardours waned. For days and nights she would then sit beside him, tenderly administering the small doses of arsenic which would eventually usher him into eternity and cellar below!

One after another her lovers were enticed—and doomed—into her fatal bower. Three old retainers who believed their mistress could do no wrong accepted the presence of the various lovers as a part of the routine of life in the mansion and no suspicion was aroused in their minds by the disappearance of the visitors. That no fewer than thirty-two young men could have vanished, after visiting the house of death, without a flicker of suspicion of foul play being aroused seems wellnigh incredible.

But there is always a last time, and in this case, then, it arrived when Vera, instead of seeking a victim from the unattached males in the night haunts of Berkerekul, picked on a young banker only just married and desperately in love with his beautiful young bride. This love which he had confided to Vera seemed to act as a challenge to the Borgia of Berkerekul. She exerted all her wiles upon the young bridegroom, who, overwhelmed with her beauty and the violence of her passion, and flattered by his obvious conquest, soon became a regular visitor to the château wherein reposed so many who had made the last pilgrimage of love.

But despite the ecstasy which the bridegroom enjoyed in the arms of his mistress he soon became consumed with remorse. The illicit honeymoon was over. His own wife was going to have a baby. He must return to her and never see Vera again.

This pathetic confession was his death-warrant. Vera insisted that he come to take a farewell meal with her one evening, when they would say goodbye in each other's arms, as befitted the ending of a great romance such as theirs. The idea of this one last night of love appealed to the young man's vanity and he gladly accepted the invitation.

On the night of the last supper, Vera, ever the consummate actress, poured out wine, and holding her glass aloft drank to the happiness of "the only man I ever loved." He never responded to this cynical toast for into his glass Vera had dropped a fatal dose of arsenic, adding a grain or two of strychnine for good measure. Then she callously watched him die in agony.

That night when the household had retired, Vera gathered his body into her strong arms, carried it down into the crypt of dead lovers and carefully placed it in one of the zinc coffins, on which she inscribed the name of her latest—and as it turned out—her last victim.

It was the bride-wife of the dead man who proved to be Vera's Nemesis. When her husband failed to return from his "short business trip" she made inquiries at his office, and was stunned when she learned that there had been no such "business trip" on the day of his departure, nor indeed at any of the other times when her husband absented himself from home.

At once she went to the police, certain that her husband had fallen into the toils of some evil woman, but because she ruled out any suggestion of foul play the police could do little. She therefore took it upon herself to rescue her husband from the rival who she was convinced had taken him from her.

From inquiries among her husband's closest friends, who now had no sympathy with a man who could desert his expectant wife, she was astounded to learn about a beautiful blonde with whom her husband had been seen in a café. Again she went to the police, and this time they had no doubt as to who the "beautiful blonde" was. Vera was picked up and grilled. "Yes!" she answered without a shadow of hesitation. "He was my lover. I trusted him completely. I had no idea he was married, but when he told me, as he lay in my arms one night, that he was married to a girl he loathed and detested, I dismissed him. I told him to dress and get out . . . I have not seen him since."

A devastatingly frank but plausible story on the face of it, and if it seemed to impress the police it certainly did not convince the sorrowing wife. She went on with her own inquiries, and when she had gathered evidence about other men who had disappeared she demanded that the police search Vera's house. By now she dreaded what they might find, but was determined that no stone should be left unturned to solve the mystery of her husband's disappearance. The police took swift action. They surrounded the château and broke into the cellar. The sight was unbelievable. The vast vaulted place was bare of all furniture except for one comfortable easy chair, set in the middle of the room. Neatly arranged around the walls were thirty-five zinc coffins, each containing the body of a husband or lover, and one the body of Vera's own son.

Vera Renczi at first denied everything, but as one lover after another was traced from his home to hers, she broke down and confessed. Asked what impelled her to kill her lovers, she gave a little shrug of the shoulders, and said: "I could not bear to think that they might love another woman . . . I dare not let them go to the embraces of anyone else . . ."

"And the easy chair in the cellar?"

She smiled. "I liked to go down there in the evening

and sit among my victims gloating over their fate," she grimly replied.

"And why did you kill your son?"

"Because he threatened to expose me," was the callous answer.

Seldom has a more loathsome specimen of sub-human depravity been revealed than this figure of Vera Renczi, who slew and coffined her lovers with diabolical precision. It is not enough to say that she was a sex-crazed nymphomaniac. She was something more than this. The nymphomaniac will yield herself to the embraces of any man in her lust for sexual satisfaction without any deep attachment to any particular lover and certainly without regrets or feelings of jealousy when she loses a charmer. The nymphomaniac does not love anybody in the strict sense of the word, although she may delude her lover and even pretend to herself that she is in the throes of a grand passion. Once her desires are gratified, she can lose all further interest in her partner completely.

With Vera it was very different. The sex urge was just as great, and she could go from one lover to another almost without pause, and with equal facility after the first fiery burst of passion had lost some of its ardour. But those whom she had possessed she refused to yield to another. Her embrace was the clutch of death.

The leading psychiatrists of Europe who were called in to examine the vampire of Berkerekul were vastly intrigued by the case. To the question whether man or woman was the more cruel by nature, one of them answered, "Given a man and a woman equally devoid of moral character, I believe the woman will usually be found to be more cruel." Vera's behaviour certainly bore him out.

At the final scene of her trial she listened sullenly as

sentence of death was passed upon her, knowing full well that it would, in accordance with custom, be commuted to imprisonment for life. Scornfully she tossed her head as she vanished from public sight for ever. Still supremely beautiful, the amorous undertaker entered upon her prison term without a single expression of sorrow for all the carnage she had wrought. It was said that in jail she continued to believe herself surrounded by lovers, and that at night the prison corridors echoed with her ravings as she talked to those who had died at her hands.

She joined the considerable company of her dead lovers a few years after her conviction.

BO'D

# 37

# MADELEINE SMITH

## Having Her Own Way

---

The case of Madeleine Smith has a perennial interest for what may be termed mystery fanciers, or, in more modern slang, murder-fans.

And yet, although Madeleine Smith, an old, old woman, died many years ago in the United States, and one is now, therefore, at liberty to assert the inescapable conviction of all students of the trial that she was guilty, a certain mystery will always hang around this famous trial of 1857. But it is not a mystery of action, but of that strange thing, the human heart.

It was not Madeleine's heart which held mystery. That merely tried to hold its secrets, a very different matter. It is L'Angelier, the victim, who remains an enigma to this day.

I am aware that this statement may bring upon me the wrath of other students of this great trial, but I leave the reader who comes to this article with an open mind to judge for himself.

Madeleine Smith was the eldest daughter of a well-known Glasgow architect. Near her in age came a brother, Jack, and a sister, Bessie. There was a younger boy called James, and a little girl of twelve called Janet.

Only Janet, called by the defence, gave evidence at the trial, although Bessie was with Madeleine when L'Angelier was first introduced to her, and although Jack fetched her back from her father's country house, whither she fled after L'Angelier's death. In fact, the Smith family was protected in every way. Mr. and Mrs. Smith seemed to have taken to their bed and remained there.

L'Angelier was a penniless young clerk from Jersey, a Frenchman and a foreigner to Scottish eyes. It has always been an interesting question what the result of the trial might have been had Madeleine Smith been the friendless foreigner and the dead man the son of a wealthy and respected local family.

Yet Scottish justice is, as a rule, impartial and as good as can be found in this rough-and-ready world, and I think the answer to the undoubted bias in favour of the accused is to be found not so much in the influence of the Smith family as in the fact that L'Angelier had, after seducing Madeleine, proceeded to blackmail her and make her life a misery.

In fact, the verdict of Not Proven might be summed up as meaning: "We'll let you off this once, but don't do it again."

Madeleine Smith was born out of due time. She was beautiful in a handsome, defiant way that was not feminine enough for the period in which she lived. She was a girl of strong physical passion at a time when no woman was supposed to possess such a thing.

She was talented and capable; but arranging the flowers in her parents' home, and, if she were married, being a good housekeeper in her husband's house, was all the mental effort deemed suitable for a woman. In the late war, Madeleine Smith would have driven an ambulance or filled some organising post most admirably.

Pierre Emile L'Angelier, a peculiarly nasty little lady-killer, earning about a pound a week, may have been, and probably was, attracted by Madeleine's bright beauty as she passed about the grey Glasgow streets.

But he also knew that she came of a wealthy family and he pressed a mutual friend, a youth called Robert Baird, to introduce them. Baird asked his mother whether he might bring L'Angelier home one evening when Miss Smith was visiting the house.

But Mrs. Baird evidently thought such an acquaintance unsuitable and declined permission, and the introduction took place in the street. A clandestine acquaintance ripened between Madeleine and L'Angelier, but it was discovered by the girl's father, and Madeleine attempted to end the acquaintance in the same month that it had begun.

L'Angelier, however, was not to be shaken off, although Madeleine made another attempt to get free of him in July of 1855. Her heart was not in the business of dismissal, however, and the acquaintance continued, growing more and more intimate.

To Madeleine, L'Angelier's foreign origin, his poverty, his flowing whiskers, and his skilful love-making made of him a figure of romance. L'Angelier's mind was set from the first on marriage with this daughter of a wealthy family, and his seduction of her, if seduction it can be called when her passionate nature was more than ready to submit to him, was merely a step in his campaign.

In June of the following year Madeleine became L'Angelier's mistress. The lovers met sometimes in the woods outside her father's country house, sometimes in the house in Blythswood Square to which she used to admit him after the family were all asleep.

And during all this time a series of passionate love-letters went back and forth. He kept all of hers. She kept but one or two of his. Hers were supposed to show a shocking lack of decency, though nowadays they do not seem strange letters for a woman to have written to her lover whom she thought to marry. His show him as the unpleasing mixture of a sensualist and a preacher that he was.

The raptures of the early months began to fade for Madeleine. Her common sense told her that her father (and Mr. Smith seems to have been the very personification of the terrible Jove-like Victorian papa) would never consent to a marriage with L'Angelier.

A Mr. Minnoch, a middle-aged man of good standing and a friend of the Smith family, fell in love with her and asked for her hand. The solid comforts of Mr. Minnoch's establishment, the charm of being its mistress and a young matron, began to appeal to Madeleine, and her letters to L'Angelier grew perceptibly colder.

He took fright and began to importune her. She definitely tried to break with him, only to find that he refused to let her go, that he even threatened to show her letters—those letters which would damn her for ever in the eyes of her contemporaries—to her father.

Madeleine Smith is not a lovable character, but it is possible to sympathise with the agonies of fear, with the remorse and disgust which must have taken hold of her. She had accepted Mr. Minnoch's proposal in January, 1857, and she still could not get free of L'Angelier.

In February she told him candidly that she no longer loved him, but she could not pique him into returning her letters. She wrote to him imploringly, but to implore a blackmailer's mercy is a singularly useless proceeding.

She then asked the page boy to go to a chemist to buy her a bottle of prussic acid, saying she wanted it to whiten her hands. The chemist, very sensibly, refused to comply with her request.

She next began to write to Emile in the old strain of affection. While writing these loving epistles, making appointments for him to meet her, she was also employed in buying arsenic. She made three purchases in all, giving the usual well-worn reasons—one, the improvement of

her complexion by using the drug as a face wash, and
the other the even more hackneyed one of wishing to
destroy rats.

Her first purchase, as far as is known, was made on
February 21, and there is no doubt that L'Angelier's first
bad attack of sickness was in the morning of the 19th.
This was a strong argument in favour of her innocence.

But L'Angelier had thrice before been seized with
sickness of the same description in the houses of his
friends, and it may be that his illness of the 19th was not
due to arsenic poisoning. But she was in possession of
arsenic on the 21st, and L'Angelier was taken extremely
ill on the 22nd. Madeleine bought arsenic again on March
6 and March 18.

Madeleine tried to get him to go away to the Isle
of Wight for a holiday, but he refused to go further
than Bridge of Allan. Now she began to write to him
asking him to come and see her, using the most ardent
phrases.

The prosecution maintained that she handed him poisoned cocoa from the window of her basement bedroom
when he came there by appointment on the evening of
March 22.

But the prosecution was never able to prove this
meeting. Had they been able to do so, nothing could
have saved Madeleine Smith. L'Angelier, recalled from
Bridge of Allan by a letter—from whom the letter came
could not be proved—left his lodgings that evening in
better health, but at half-past two on Monday morning
he was ringing the bell of his lodging-house violently.

His landlady helped him to his room, and there he
vomited for about two hours. At five o'clock a doctor
was sent for, but refused to come, merely suggesting
twenty-five drops of laudanum and a mustard plaster.

The landlady continued to attend him, and he became so ill that she insisted on the doctor coming at about seven o'clock. The doctor gave him a little morphia and applied a poultice, making the sapient remark that time and quietness were required. By eleven o'clock L'Angelier was quiet enough, for he was dead.

Now the curious thing about L'Angelier's final agonies is this—although he seems to have known that he was dying, he never accused Madeleine Smith, or, indeed, mentioned her name. He did ask his landlady to send for a Miss Perry, a sentimental maiden lady, who had played the part of go-between for him and Madeleine, but by the time Miss Perry arrived he was dead.

Whether he had been going to accuse Madeleine to her we shall never know. According to Miss Perry's evidence at the trial he had said to her after his illness on February 19: "I can't think why I was so ill after taking that coffee and chocolate from her." Miss Perry understood her to mean Miss Smith.

He had added: "It is a perfect fascination, my attachment to that girl. If she were to poison me I should forgive her."

L'Angelier was an eminently practical person, and there is little doubt that he would not knowingly have taken poison from the hands of Madeleine or anyone else. And so we can be almost certain that in those last hours of agony on the morning of March 23 he realised for the first time that at least one previous attack of sickness may have been due to Madeleine's cocoa, and that the present one must have been caused by her.

If, when dying, he realised what Madeleine had done and yet refrained from naming the girl he had bullied and blackmailed, so much may, at least, be allowed to him for righteousness.

But why did this contemptible little lady-killer show such magnanimity? It was suggested, of course, by the defence that he might have taken the poison accidentally, or that some other person, not Madeleine, had murdered him, or that he had committed suicide. The last suggestion is the only one not outside of the region of possibility.

However, if he killed himself by repeated doses of that extremely painful poison, arsenic, he remains unique as a suicide. Also, it is far more in keeping with his character to blackmail Madeleine, or to go to her father and demand from him money for keeping silent.

It is, therefore, not only possible, but perhaps even probable, that a certain remorse entered his heart as he lay dying, for there seems no doubt that he knew that he was dying.

He said to his landlady: "I'm far worse than the doctor thinks." His pain and weakness must have been so intense, his knowledge that some lethal substance had been administered to him so certain, that he can have had but little hope, although he murmured: "Oh, if I could get five minutes' sleep I think I would get better."

Madeleine's name never passed his lips, nor would he give any hint as to the cause of his illness. This reticence and generosity in a man who had hitherto been completely ruthless is the most mysterious thing in the case.

There is no answer to the riddle, although it may be permitted to hope that the solution is to be found in the theory—which must always remain a theory—that regret touched his scheming little heart in his last hours.

L'Angelier's death seemed so inexplicable that an autopsy was held and more than sufficient arsenic to destroy life was found in the body. L'Angelier's effects were examined and Madeleine's letters were found.

She fled blindly and futilely to her father's country house, but came back unprotestingly with Mr. Minnoch and her brother, Jack. All thought of marriage with the respectable Mr. Minnoch was, of course, over for good; and, indeed, when that unfortunate man, who seems to have felt the discovery of her previous passion very acutely, had to give evidence against her at her trial, it is said he never looked towards her.

Yet Madeleine was worth looking at, in her full, sweeping, dark silk dress and her bonnet, which, shaped like a halo, showed the front of her sleek, dark head so that her cameo-like profile and beautiful complexion stood out unshadowed.

Rumour has it that one of the judges was peculiarly susceptible to the charms of a pretty foot and ankle, and that Madeleine sat slightly sideways in the dock, her skirt pulled up a little to display this charm, so exciting to the Victorians.

The trial was chiefly noticeable for the magnificent speeches by the Lord Advocate, for the prosecution, and the Dean of Faculty, for the defence. The latter, Lord Inglis, who was to become Lord Justice-General of Scotland, made a closing speech which has remained a model to this day.

The strength, the passion, with which he fought every inch of the ground, the brilliance of his arguments and the closeness of his reasoning, remain untouched by time. And if some of his oratory seems a trifle lush and old-fashioned, the same can be said of that of the late Marshall Hall, and still more so of the sentimental periods of Mr. Clarence Darrow, most noted defence counsel in the United States.

Three of the Dean of Faculty's strongest points were:

> *1. That the prosecution could not show that Madeleine possessed any arsenic before February 21.*
> *2. That there was no proof that L'Angelier had met Madeleine before his attacks of sickness on February 22 and March 22.*
> *3. That it might reasonably be argued that L'Angelier's death placed Madeleine in a very awkward position, as her letters would be bound to be discovered.*

There is not, perhaps, much force in the third argument. Madeleine could hardly be in a worse position than if L'Angelier fulfilled his threat of showing her letters to her father, and she may have hoped that if her lover's death passed off without comment the letters would be destroyed. They were, in any case, nearly all signed Mimi, or sometimes even Mimi L'Angelier. But the Dean of Faculty would not have found himself in nearly such a strong position when he argued that there was no meeting between the two on the crucial dates, if a little diary of L'Angelier's had been allowed to be put into evidence.

The entry for February 19 ran: "Saw Mimi a few moments. Was very ill during the night." While that for February 22 read: "Saw Mimi in drawing-room, promised me French Bible, taken very ill."

It was ruled, however, that this diary was inadmissible as evidence of a fact against the accused.

The summing up was admirably fair, but certainly it gave the prisoner the benefit of every doubt and it was, probably, a very relieved jury that returned a verdict of Not Proven.

Madeleine Smith, who had remained the calmest and most unmoved person in court throughout the trial, wrote in a letter to the matron of the prison, that she was not at all pleased with the verdict! In the same letter she complained that the feeling of the people towards her round her home was not as kindly as that of "the good people of Edinburgh" had been.

Apparently she expected to be found Not Guilty and received with acclamation. Even her excellent nervous system, however, found it impossible to bear home life after all the revelations that had been made, and she went to London alone, became a Socialist, and married, the first two steps being rare for a girl of those days, and the third something of an achievement, considering her past.

It is said, with what truth I do not know, that she made an excellent wife, and that her husband was very devoted to her, but that he never allowed her to do any cooking.

There would have been little risk, however, of Madeleine Smith attempting to kill for a second time. She was not a congenital killer, she was merely a woman who knew what she wanted and who, much rarer, knew when she had ceased to want it.

And her resolution was such that she was determined to have her way in both these matters. She was, in short, a woman born at the very worst time in the world's history for such as she; a time when women were not supposed to want much, but were also supposed to want that little long.

"I shall ever remain true to you," Madeleine had written to L'Angelier. "I think a woman who can be untrue should be banished from society."

She had the courage of her change of conviction.

FTJ

# 38

# RUTH SNYDER
## The Iron Widow

There is no very obvious connection between a wink exchanged between a pretty woman and a flirtatious young man, as they passed in the street, and the electric chair. Still, it is an interesting exercise to trace back to some apparently trivial cause a great or tragic event. And it was such an incident, casual and unpremeditated, that began for Ruth Brown Snyder the dreadful journey to the smoky cell.

Ruth Snyder had been about eighteen, a blue-eyed, blonde-haired beauty, when she married Albert Snyder, the art editor of a motor-boating magazine, whose secretary she had been.

Whatever glimpses of life and colour she had had before her marriage—and one may guess that young as she was there had been episodes—she was not of the type that settles down to a staid domesticity. In the years that followed her marriage her vitality and vivacity seem to have won her friends of both sexes. They called her "Tommy."

Snyder, himself, was thirteen years her senior, and a man of different character. "Tommy" herself has drawn the contrast. "He was just the opposite to me. I am younger and like to have a good time. He likes to stay around the house, to fix it up, and dig in the grounds, and feed the birds. I like to go to parties and dances. I like hotel life, dinners, gay affairs. He has never liked them."

To all appearances, a commonplace couple and a commonplace situation, these two people of different tastes and temperaments carried on for many years without any very serious differences showing to the world. They had a comfortable home, he had a good income, and in time a baby girl was born to them.

Snyder was an easy-going man. He was content that—within limits—she should go her way while he went his. The woman, a mixture of ice and fire, made no disclosure of her growing distaste for him. She had both character and intelligence, and was something of an actress.

There came a day when a man winked at her in the street. Quite likely other men had winked at her, and she may have responded as she did on this occasion, but they do not matter. From this incident an acquaintance sprang up, and some time afterwards she was introduced by her new friend to a man with whom he had business dealings.

This was Henry Judd Gray, a salesman of corsets, some thirty-five years old. He was a simple man, happily married, and living with his wife and child in a neat little suburban home. Probably no one like the dashing blonde had ever entered his life before.

The introduction was followed up. Presently the situation developed, and they became clandestine lovers. He had become infatuated with her. How far his passion was returned the reader must judge. She may have been deeply in love with him, or she may have been using him as a mere dupe. For behind the grim deed that was to come there was possibly a deeper, more sordid motive than that of illicit passion for this corset salesman. "Tommy" Snyder did not always wear her heart on her sleeve.

In fact, Mrs. Snyder had determined to get rid of her husband. She was tired of him—tired of even the frail bonds that his existence imposed on her. If he could die—preferably by violence, for the money to come from the insurance policy on his life was to be doubled if he met a violent end—she would be richer by some ninety thousand dollars, and free. She felt that the instrument lay to her hand. Gray the corset salesman, Gray the simpleton, Gray the plastic, was there to be moulded to her will.

When first she opened the project to him, he recoiled in horror. She was patient. Week after week, month after month, she used all the arts of sex, bent all her powers to break him to her purpose. She had accustomed him to drink, and while he was befuddled she whispered insidious and terrible urgings to him. There would be no risk. She would be free. It was all so simple. She had thought it all out.

It is always hard to believe that a pretty and attractive woman can be guilty of planned and ruthless murder. Yet criminal history has many such cases. Ruth Snyder had merely joined the infamous group which includes such women as Brinvilliers and Manning. She was a notable recruit.

Something over a year was spent in persuading Judd Gray. His scruples began to disappear. The poor weakling, at first terrified at the word murder, began to accept the idea that Albert Snyder should be put out of the way with equanimity. He was even prepared to discuss ways and means. The matter was talked over at many of their secret meetings.

A plan was at last decided upon. The imaginative mind of the woman had been at work, and she evolved a scheme that did credit to her inventive powers. It might have worked out, leaving the man and his mistress free from all suspicion had they known more about the methods of criminals and detectives than could be gained from the more melodramatic movies. The idea was to stage an attack which would look as though it had been committed by burglars. Snyder was to be killed, and his wife was to be found next day bound and helpless. Details of the plan were perfected.

One March evening, in 1927, Mr. and Mrs. Snyder, with their little nine-year-old daughter, went to a bridge party. Mrs. Snyder's mother, who lived with them, was away. Judd Gray, who already possessed a key to the house, secreted himself in the mother's apartment before their return. He was provided with a bottle of chloroform and some lengths of new picture wire. Also there was a bottle of whisky.

The stage was set for the next act of the grim tragedy. When the family returned, Snyder went immediately to bed. Mrs. Snyder gave one meaning glance into the room, where a sinister and trembling figure was waiting, and then put the child to bed, and retired to sleep with her husband.

The minutes passed slowly. She lay by his side till his breathing showed that he was safely asleep. Rising softly, she crept, in her night attire, like a modern Lady Macbeth, to where Judd Gray was waiting with tingling nerves. Into his hands she thrust a murderous sash-weight, which she had brought up from the cellar in readiness. It was now or never, she told him. There was the whisky, if his resolution needed strengthening. She, herself, did not drink. She needed no stimulant, this woman of iron.

The thing was done. The first blow struck by the unnerved Gray was so light that, although it stunned the sleeping man, it did not satisfy the woman. She seized the sash-weight, and herself wielded it. ("Infirm of purpose; give me the dagger.") Cotton wool soaked in chloroform was pressed against the unconscious victim's mouth and nose. The picture wire was bound tightly round his throat. His hands were tied behind his back.

Then, perhaps, again to the whisky bottle for Gray. There was still much to do, for all the circumstances of robbery—according to the moving pictures—had to be arranged. Finally, Mrs. Snyder was tied up, and Judd Gray stole away—back to his home in Syracuse and his sleeping wife and child.

It was little Lorraine Snyder, her small child, who found Mrs. Snyder at half-past seven the next morning lying in the passage outside her bedroom. The woman's ankles and wrists were secured with picture-wire. A neighbour, hastily called, released her, and, carrying her into the bedroom, found there the dead body of her husband. Mrs. Snyder screamed at the sight of the dead man.

There was an artistic incoherence in her story, but she had it all pat. Awakened about half-past two in the morning by some sound outside her room, she had gone to investigate. She was immediately attacked by two dark men with heavy moustaches. She fainted, and knew no more until she was found by her daughter.

To this tale she held when the police came. The hard-headed detectives from the central office, however, were more than a little doubtful. Even a hurried glance at the house had told them several things.

The thieves were supposed to have fled through a side door. The key was on the floor. Why should they have bothered to have taken it out?

Some of the rooms were in calculated disorder, and the cushions had been taken from couches and chairs and thrown about. Why, the detectives asked themselves, should professional thieves have done this? What would they expect to find under chair seats?

Snyder had been hit twice with some heavy instrument.

Why should professional thieves have worried about putting the wire round his throat? If their object had been to silence him, surely they could have made certain by striking him again with the original weapon?

It was Carey of the Homicide Bureau who noticed a small piece of soiled cotton waste caught on the dead man's moustache. He diagnosed chloroform at once, and it may be said that his opinion was later confirmed at the post-mortem. The wire, the chloroform, some heavy weapon had all played their part in the crime. Would thieves in a hurry have gone to all these pains to kill a man?

On the bed was Snyder's revolver and some cartridges. Would thieves have left them there? Nearby there was a blue handkerchief and a corner torn from an Italian newspaper. Why? The little child said that the wire about her mother's wrists was comparatively loose. Wouldn't desperate murderers have seen to it that she should have no chance to free herself? Add to this that Mrs. Snyder had told them that she lay in a dead faint from the time she was attacked till she was found by her daughter—about five hours—and it will be understood why the detectives were more than dubious about the robbery.

So it was that they took Mrs. Snyder away while the investigation of the house proceeded. The whisky which had been liberally used was found. A few questions showed that Mrs. Snyder had shown no indications of drink when she was found. Who, then, had been at the bottle? A hint was provided when a cancelled cheque signed by her was discovered. It was for two hundred dollars, was made out to H. Judd Gray, and bore his endorsement.

Clearly Mrs. Snyder had to be made to "come clean," and the American detectives used their own methods to persuade her. What those methods were is indicated by the former Deputy-Inspector Carey:

She was taken to the precinct station house, questioned by the District Attorney, and later by Police Commissioner McLaughlin. For hours she sat stolid, refusing to answer questions. She was incensed that anyone should suspect a woman of her respectability . . .

Mrs. Snyder was sitting in a small office silent and sullen. Suddenly the door opened. A young man looked in.

"Why, hello, Ruth," he smiled.

"Oh, are you—?" she started to reply, greatly surprised to see him. He whispered to her something that was never disclosed. The veil of respectability fell. The man knew a great deal of the woman's past, hidden chapters. She weakened. Her stolidity vanished. For the best part of a night she sat in that little room revealing the details of how she had murdered her husband. At first she denied that she had been aided by an accomplice. Then, finally, she admitted that a man had helped her to kill her husband.

"And is this the man?" he asked her, showing the cancelled cheque which had been cashed by H. Judd Gray.

"Yes, he helped me," she replied.

That was the beginning of the end. In a short time Gray was tracked and arrested. There was a dramatic session at police headquarters, which lasted something over six hours. According to Gray, he was subjected to an almost incessant stream of questions by detectives, and even threatened with violence, till he broke down and confessed to his part in the crime.

That their confessions had been extorted by "third degree" methods was declared by both of them at a later stage. Mrs. Snyder, indeed, repudiated many of the details she was said to have given.

It was at the trial, which lasted for nearly a fortnight, that the sobriquet "the iron widow" was fastened on Mrs. Snyder. In a black dress of fashionable cut, with dainty shoes and silk stockings, she listened, with white set face, without any change of demeanour, while the fight to save her life went on. Only on the tenth day, when her little daughter was mentioned, did her composure fail her, and she broke into tears. Gray, wretched and dejected, sat with his eyes fastened to the floor, and appeared utterly unaware of what was happening.

In the witness-chair Mrs. Snyder gave her final version of the grim business. On the night of the murder, she said, she had expected Gray to be at her home to meet her. She had found him waiting in her mother's room. When her husband had gone to bed she joined him.

"He kissed me," she said, "I felt his hands clad in rubber gloves, and asked, 'What are you going to do?' He said, 'If I do not rid myself of him to-night, I shall end the pair of us.'

"I took Gray downstairs and thought I had dissuaded him.

"I went upstairs to the bathroom, and then heard a terrific thud. I ran in and saw Gray beating my husband. I struggled to pull him off. Then I fainted. The next thing I saw was my husband huddled in a blanket."

At this point she once more gave way. Sobbing bitterly, she explained that she tried to extricate her husband from the blanket until Gray forced her away from the body.

Every device that could avert or delay justice was resorted to by the lawyers for the defence. But all efforts were in vain. The inevitable verdict was followed by the inevitable sentence. The case was carried to appeal, and the verdict was confirmed. Then, indeed, did "Tommy" Snyder, the sometime gay and debonair pleasure-seeker, the "iron woman" who had played so determined a part in her husband's murder, the blue-eyed blonde who had been so frigidly composed in court, almost give way to despair. Almost, but not quite. It had been seventeen years since a woman had been executed in New York. Surely the law would not exact the supreme penalty from her? The Governor of the State would surely exercise his prerogative of mercy.

That faint hope vanished a few days before the date fixed for the execution. Governor Smith refused to interfere. "I had hoped," he wrote, "that an appeal to the executive for clemency would disclose some facts which would justify my interference with the processes of the law, but this has not happened. I have searched in vain for any basis which my conscience, in the light of my oath of office, would approve, and on which I might temper the law with mercy."

A last desperate and dramatic effort for a respite was made by an application to a Supreme Court judge to grant an injunction delaying the execution until Mrs. Snyder had given evidence in a lawsuit arising out of her husband's insurance. This was, in fact, granted, but was overruled as illegal by the Attorney-General.

The terrible last scene was enacted on January 12, 1928. Mrs. Snyder had sent a last letter to some relatives a little before. Passages from it ran:

"I don't want anything but the simplest of everything, only I ask that Father Murphy shall say a prayer for me before I am laid away . . . I would like to have had my baby with me when the time comes. Could I ask you again, before I'm called, either to adopt Lorraine for me or else have mother adopt her. . . . This is my last letter, Andrew; bear up and help mother to bear her heavy burden . . . Remember, only the simplest burial. No Mass, no inscription, and all very plain. I want to go out of this world as I came into it, just a poor soul."

The executions were fixed to take place at Sing Sing at eleven o'clock at night. Strange to British ideas were the elaborate arrangements made for viewing and reporting the last scene. There were a number of official "witnesses," four doctors, and twenty reporters, besides the ordinary officials. At a "soft drinks" parlour, some distance from the prison, fifty telegraph wires had been installed for the use of the newspaper men.

The spectators had scarcely seated themselves at the benches provided for them in the cream-coloured room when Ruth Snyder was brought in from her cell ten feet away.

Swiftly she was strapped in the electric chair by her four guards. Her hands clenched as she cried hysterically, "Forgive them, Father, for they know not what they do."

The switch was turned on.

A minute or two later Gray was brought in. He was repeating the Beatitudes after a priest when he was electrocuted.

—G.D.

# 39

# MAGDALENA SOLIS
## The Cult of Human Sacrifice

In Yerba Buena, Tamaulipas State, Republic of Mexico, on the last day of May, 1963, some 125 miles southwest of Brownsville, Tex., a weird ritual, as old as the history of Mexico, took place.

Here in a Mexican federal farming community called Yerba Buena, deep in the rock strewn ravines of the Sierra Madre Mountains, but only 30 miles south as the crow flies of the teeming metropolis of Monterrey, Mexico, the ancient Aztec festival of the 31st of May was re-enacted in all its horror—a festival which included sacrificing a living woman to the god, *Huixtocihuatl*. Here, cut off from the world, with no electricity, no telephones, no newspapers, no roads, except a cart trail winding over the wooded slopes of the mountains to the highway a half-day's journey away, a group of simple farmers came together for the purpose of practising their religion, a cult which claimed as its aim the restoring of the true Aztec religion to the only true Mexicans—the Indians.

Police Inspector Abelardo G. Gomez from the nearby town of Villagran, a hardened, experienced veteran of many years on the rural police force, and the man who led the raid on the cultists bringing their activities to light and to a halt told me their acts exceeded in human depravity anything he'd known before in all his years as a policeman.

"The Indians are always coming up with some new kind of religion," he said. "It doesn't last long and we don't bother them if they're peaceable. This Magdalena Solis and her twin brother, Eleazar, came down here from some religious confederation in Monterrey and did pretty well for themselves. I understand they'd already established some centers of the cult to the east of Monterrey, even to the borders of Texas on the Rio Grande."

Further questioning along with a few shared bottles of Mexican *cerveza*, led Inspector Gomez to relate in detail his harrowing experience with the cultists. Here is his story:

Two years before Magdalena Solis and her twin brother, Eleazar, 16 years of age, having broken off from the Mexican Confederation of Spiritualists in Monterrey, set out traveling east and south of the city to establish several centers of their own private cult among the simple Indian folk of the desert and mountain areas. Inflamed by their successes, they came to Yerba Buena and began to attract followers. In this isolated farming community, where most of the people can neither read nor write, they found fertile soil for their diabolical ideas.

Basing their religion on the framework of old Aztec rites and rituals, dressing it up with form and ceremony learned from the Confederation in Monterrey, and adding major inventions of their own, they found little difficulty in convincing the poor farmers that they had brought with them divine authorization for their acts.

According to Inspector Gomez's description of the site and his questioning of the captured members, the cult's chief inspiration came from a weird mixture of human blood and marijuana leaves. The farmers understood little of the nature of such a concoction, but upon drinking it, apparently found for the first time an effective remedy for their boredom and hard lives.

One can well imagine the success of Magdalena and her brother, Eleazar, when once the ignorant Indian farmers had tasted this devilish brew. For the first time someone had brought them a revelation they could experience. These teenagers from Monterrey had brought them a religion that eased their burdens, at least temporarily.

With vigorous imaginations the Solis brother-sister team added to and polished the ceremonies with further revelations. Magdalena became the incarnation of a famous Mexican faith healer of the region of over 50 years ago. Eleazar became the reincarnation of St. Francis of Assisi.

The face of Inspector Gomez grew hard when he spoke of the operations of the group, as he learned it from his detailed questioning of the 40-odd farmers taken prisoners after his raid.

"The Solis twins managed to capitalize on the old Indian ancestor reverence," he said. "The 31st of May corresponds to the Aztec festival of *Huixtocihuatl*, in which a living woman always was sacrificed to the gods. They played up this business of the revival of the Aztec religion; the true religion of Mexico, they called it. When we raided the place we found their color pots and feathers where the chief priests had fixed themselves up in Aztec paints and costumes of 400 years ago."

According to information given to Inspector Gomez, conditions had been coming to a head for quite some time before the May 31st festival that exploded and brought public attention to the deeds of the cultists. Already struggles for leadership and power were beginning to raise problems. And some of the less faithful among the farmers were beginning to be restive about the tribute which was extracted from them, by force in some cases, to provide for the necessities of the leaders.

The Solis twins had ordained two farmers from the group to perform the human sacrifice rituals which had been going on for nearly a year. The brothers Santos and

Cayetano Hernandez had made the most progress under the twins' system of instruction and Cayetano had the peculiar combination of devoutness and viciousness, plus a touch of insanity, that was needed to relieve the farmers, in one way or another, of enough provisions to keep himself, his brother, and the Solis twins in comfort.

Thus on the night of May 31, according to Gomez's informants, the potion of blood and marijuana did its job as always. Cayetano had reached the point of inspiration where he was certain that gold was buried in the cave in which their meetings were held and that, with the sacrifice of a woman to *Huixtocihuatl*, he, Cayetano, would be given the knowledge of the gold's exact location. With this money they could spread the cult to other areas!

When he called for the sacrifice the meeting had progressed far enough for most of the farmers to accept anything. According to Gomez, 12 times before Cayetano had asked for a volunteer from the faithful and 12 times someone had volunteered to be sacrificed—so powerful an effect did the drugs have on them!

This time, Celina Salvana, 30, mother of two illegitimate children, came forward, slumped and submissive. Hector Solis, a native of the area and a childhood sweetheart of hers, tried to stop her.

"But she wouldn't listen to him," Gomez said. "She wanted to be sacrificed straight to a god, to live in guaranteed bliss forever."

Solis apparently had not drunk as deeply as the others. He wouldn't stand for it. Celina picked up a stone and gave it to him, begging him to use it to crush out her life. They struggled, she fell, and the others rushed in on them knocking Solis out of the way and pelting her with stones until she was senseless.

Deeper in the cave the Hernandez brothers, with

Eleazar's help, had constructed a wooden temple of four pillars and a thatched roof over a large flat stone that served as an altar. There, Cayetano and Santos quickly opened Selina's soft body and tore out her heart, to offer it, still pulsating, to *Huixtocihuatl*.

"Apparently they had the idea that *Huixtocihuatl* drew life and renewed himself and his strength from the living human heart," Inspector Gomez said. "We found where they'd burned the remains of Celina in a corner of the cave. The bones of several other bodies were there in the same place."

Solis, when he revived, started a riot, trying to kill them all with his bare hands. Then, seeing it was useless, that Celina was already dead, he left the cave and returned to his wife and four children in their mud hut at the village. As soon as it was daylight he left his hut and walked to Villagran and Inspector Gomez's headquarters.

"He gave me the names of all the members he could think of and I wrote them down," Gomez stated. "I told him to go back as if nothing had happened. Soon as I rounded up some men, I left for Yerba Buena."

But by the time Inspector Gomez arrived Solis was already dead, his throat cut by Cayetano's two-foot-long machete. The two brothers had been waiting for him at his hut.

When Gomez got to the village with half a dozen men the Hernandez brothers had gathered some of their most fanatical followers and returned to their hut on the other side of the village. Cayetano came out to meet the police, affecting an air of innocence.

"He told me he was a farmer, like all the rest," Gomez said. "He claimed to know nothing of this religion that kills people. I have not been a rural policeman for long years for nothing. I knew he was lying. I told Luis Martinez, one of my men, to take him in for questioning and I started to take the list of names out of my pocket. When Martinez stepped forward Cayetano brought out his machete fast as lightning and nearly cut Martinez's head off, killing him instantly."

At this point Gomez's face turned as hard as an old leather shoe. He fortified himself with more *cerveza* and then said, "We filled Cayetano full of lead before he got halfway back to the house. From inside Santos and the others opened fire. I had my men spread out and take cover and we systematically shot up the mud hut so that no one inside could stay alive. When we went in they were all on the floor, dead, Santos with them."

In a day's time Gomez and his men took nearly 40 prisoners, including Eleazar and Magdalena Solis. On questioning them he found the cult extended to the neighboring village of Delgado. The thing was too big for his small detachment. He sent for federal troops from Tampico to search the hills and caves of the surrounding area for other temples and to beat the bushes for the remaining members of the Yerba Buena cult who had escaped into the hills.

Gomez ordered his men to burn the thatched temple inside the cave and to carry out the bones and bury them.

"It was the worst thing I've had to deal with in all my years," he said. "After this nothing can surprise me."

Why did they do it?

The little village of Yerba Buena, cut off from the world, forgotten and by-passed by what little progress Mexico has known, was a natural for the remnants of the old Aztec ideas and culture that still linger with the people, only 400 years removed from the empire of Moctezuma in a land where time means nothing.

Perhaps some of these farmers, after drinking the vicious brew, truly believed that God revealed Himself to them. Others may have used the cult as a means of release for their frustrations and hatreds. To others perhaps the gory proceedings provided only a relief from their painful existence, their uneventful lives.

Governor Praxides Balbo of the State of Tamaulipas may have been thinking of these and other causes when, a day or two after the raid on Yerba Buena, he ordered a school built on a site near the cave "as a symbol in the fight against ignorance."

—B.S.

# 40

# EDITH THOMPSON
## Incitement to Murder?

Percy and Edith Thompson were a prosperous couple living at Ilford. Their joint income was over £10 a week, £6 of which was earned by the wife, manageress of Carlton and White's wholesale milliners in Aldersgate. They had been married six years, and for the first two years at least the marriage had been happy. There were no children. Edith said at the trial that the marriage had ceased to be happy after the first two years.

When Edith had been married six years and was twenty-eight years old, she met a ship's clerk called Freddy Bywaters at the house of her parents, the Graydons. Her sister Avis was still at home, a sufficient reason for the ship's clerk to spend some hours of his leave at the house. But Bywaters seems soon to have been attracted by the riper charms of the married sister; at any rate he accompanied the Thompsons on their annual holiday to Shanklin, and although his relations with Mr. Thompson seem never to have been cordial, he became a lodger at their house on June 18th, 1921.

It was a pleasure to Mrs. Thompson to give and to Freddy to receive from her small commands. Between the husband and wife this pleasure did not exist. On August 1st Mrs. Thompson asked her husband to get her a pin. Thompson refused, and there was a scene which culminated in Thompson throwing his wife across the room. Bywaters was present, commiserated with and comforted the wife, and the incident no doubt marked a turning point in the relations of the three of them. "Peidi," as she signed herself in the letters which she wrote to him after he returned to his ship, referred to this incident at some length when sending Freddy one of the many marked novels which might serve as a guide to them in their difficulties:

> *"The part about 'a man to lean on' is especially true. Darlint, it was that about you that first made me think of you in the way I do now. . . . Note the part, 'always think of her first, always be patient and kind, always help her in every way he can, he will have gone a long way to making her love him.'*
>
> *"Such things as wiping up, getting pins for me, etc., all counted. Do you remember the pin incident, on Aug. 1st, darlint, and the subsequent remark from him, 'You like to have some one always tacked on to you to run all your little errands.' That was it, darlint, that counted, obeying little requests—such as getting a pin, it was a novelty—he'd never done that.*
>
> *"It is the man who has no right who generally comforts the woman who has wrongs . . ."*

Four days after the incident of the pin there was another scene which culminated in Mr. Thompson ordering Bywaters out of his house. That there was intercourse between the lovers before Bywaters left may be inferred from the following passage in one of his letters:

> *"Darlint Peidi Mia—I do remember you coming to me in the little room and I think I understand what it cost you—a lot more then, darlint, than it could ever now."*

It is not easy for a husband to control the spare time of a wife earning £6 a week. Peidi and Freddy managed to see a good deal of each other in the five weeks before he rejoined his ship. From his letters it appears that parks and empty railway carriages had to do duty for "the little room."

During the next year Bywaters spent a total of eighty-four days in England in the intervals between his five voyages on the S.S. *Morea*. The lovers managed to see a good deal of each other when Bywaters was on leave, and when he was on his ship they maintained a copious correspondence, more copious on Peidi's part than on Freddy's, for while only three of Freddy's letters were preserved (she wrote to him that she always destroyed his last letter), Peidi's often express disappointment when she has returned from the post office after calling for her mail from the East.

It appears from Peidi's letters that Thompson insisted upon his rights as a husband, and when his wife made difficulties he accused her of having changed her feelings as the result of her friendship for Bywaters. How far he suspected adulterous intercourse is not clear. If he did, the effect was to make him insist upon his rights rather than to turn squeamish; and the photographs of Mrs. Thompson suggest a woman who would inflame passion rather than sentiment in men. For her part Peidi deemed it prudent to yield to her husband's embraces in order to avoid a definite breach.

It was not her plan to become the London mistress of a man eight years her junior who spent many weeks in the glamorous cities of the East. Her aim was to bind Freddy to her by at least such security as marriage could give. Moreover she was in a good job, and she liked having money to spend. Though the joint income of the

Thompsons, a childless couple, was over £500 a year, and they were of humble origin, we find Mr. Thompson, no spendthrift himself, worrying because his rates are overdue. If she got involved in a scandal she might lose her job, and Bywaters might also lose his.

In one of her quarrels with her husband she asked for divorce, but her husband refused to entertain the idea. The only other solution was murder, and she began to correspond with her lover about methods. In order to reinforce the murder pact, she set herself and Bywaters a five year term within which to compass the murder, failing which they were pledged to commit suicide together.

Her efforts were all doomed to failure. She "had the wrong porridge to-day;" then she tried something with a bitter taste, but he noticed the taste in his tea. On a page marked "Don't keep this piece," she tells Bywaters of these difficulties:

> "*Now I think whatever else I try it will still taste bitter—he will recognise it and be more suspicious still.*"

From the bitter stuff she turned to glass:

> "*I used the light bulb three times, but the third time—he found a piece—so I've given it up—until you come home.*"

In another letter she wrote:

> "*I was buoyed up with the hope of the light bulb and I used a lot—big pieces too—not powdered—and it*

*has no effect—I quite expected to be able to send that cable . . . Oh, darlint, I do feel so down and unhappy . . . Wouldn't the stuff make small pills, coated together with soap and dipped in liquorice powder—like Beechams."*

She fears that the act may later cause her lover to shrink from her:

*"This thing that I am going to do for both of us will it ever—at all, make any difference between us, darlint, do you understand what I mean. Will you ever think any the less of me—not now, I know, darlint—but later on . . . Darlint—if I thought you would I'd not do it, no not even so that we could be happy for one day, even one hour."*

But this mood did not last, and she was soon telling Bywaters that she would not let him roam the world again alone, leaving things as they were:

*"But there will be no failure this next time, darlint, there mustn't be—I'm telling you—if things are the same again then I'm going with you—wherever it is . . . You'll never leave me behind again unless things are different."*

She tried to encourage Bywaters by the example of characters in fiction who have got rid of unwanted spouses. Her favourite authors were Robert Hichens and W. B. Maxwell. Sending Freddy a copy of *Bella Donna*, she carefully copied out the headnote to the novel:

> *"It must be remembered that digitalin is a cumulative poison, and that the same dose, harmless if taken once, yet frequently repeated, becomes deadly."*

She asks Bywaters whether digitalin is any use, and at the same time draws a subtle distinction between the character of the heroine and herself:

> *"About Bella Donna—no, I don't agree with you about her, darlint—I hate her—hate to think of her—I don't think other people made her what she was—that sensual pleasure loving greedy Bella Donna was always there. If she had originally been different a good man like Nigel would have altered her, darlint—she never knew goodness as you and I know it—she was never interested in a good man or any man unless she could appease her sensual nature . . . loved and lived for his money or what it could give her. . . . Yes, she was clever—I admire her cleverness—but she was cunning, there is a difference, darlint, I don't admire that. . . . If she had loved Baroudi enough she could have gone to him—but she liked the security of being Nigel's wife—for the monetary assets it held. . . ."*

That Mrs. Thompson also liked the monetary assets is clear from other portions of the correspondence. Writing to her at Christmas Freddy says:

> *"I know all those wishes of yours will run into a deuce of a lot of money. Such items as fur coats, cars and champagne, will be very prominent on the list."*

Indeed she spent twenty-seven guineas on a fur coat,

borrowing £15 from "the account"—her personal cash account at Carlton and White's. She had her diversions while Bywaters was away, although she was unfortunate in her holiday boarding house, where drinks were not allowed to be brought in. At the Waldorf Hotel a man asked her whether she was not "Romance" who had put a notice in the personal column of a newspaper. In answer to Freddy's comments on the episode she wrote:

> *"No, I don't think the man who mistook me for 'Romance' was decent darlint, but I do think he was quite genuine in mistaking me, I don't think it was a ruse on his part."*

There was another man who took her out to lunch, and expected something in return. She accepted a box of chocolates from him under protest—they were marrons glacés. She promised Freddy that she would not cultivate the Regent Palace.

It appears from one of her letters that Bywaters was sometimes short of the money for her entertainment when he was on leave:

> *"And I haven't any money to give you," she writes, "at least not much and perhaps you haven't any. I wish you weren't going to take me out darling and even now its not too late—if you'd only tell me, be quite frank about it darlint, I'll understand—surely you know I will. I didn't intend to mention this darlint, but neither you nor I must harbour thoughts that each other doesn't know . . ."*

There was also the difficulty that Mrs. Thompson at

any rate wanted to keep their meetings secret from her husband. Once, when Thompson happened to see them together at Ilford Station, he said to his wife:

"Bywaters is not a man or else he would ask my permission to take you out."

Bywaters accepted the challenge and went to see Thompson next day, and told him that he ought to arrange for a divorce or at least a separation.

Bywaters returned from his last voyage at the end of September 1922. The lovers had one meeting in September, and a week-end intervened between their next meeting on October 2nd, for it was easier for Mrs. Thompson to meet Bywaters without her husband's knowledge on a working day. She wrote to Bywaters during the week-end:

> *"Darlingest lover, what happened last night? I don't know myself I only know how I felt—no not really how I felt but how I could feel—if time and circumstances were different. It seems like a great welling up of love—of feeling—of inertia, just as if I am wax in your hands—it's physical purely and I can't really describe it. . . . Darlingest when you are rough I go dead—try not to be, please."*

It appears that even during this week-end she submitted to her husband's embraces; at least so she tells Bywaters—perhaps to goad him to the decisive action of scotching the husband whom Bywaters later described as "several degrees lower than a snake."

The lovers met on the evening of October 2nd, and on October 3rd they had tea together at a restaurant. After tea Bywaters went to the Graydons'. Mr. Graydon had promised to get him a supply of some special tobacco, and Mrs. Graydon rallied him about a pouch which Peidi had given him.

"You have got a new pouch, Freddy. From a girl, I expect."

"Yes."

"I expect the same girl gave you that as gave you the watch?"

"Yes, the same girl gave it me."

"I know who it is, but I am not going to say. Never mind, we won't argue about it. She is one of the best."

"There is none better."

While Bywaters was basking in the benevolence of Peidi's parents, she and her husband were at the theatre. At about eleven o'clock Bywaters left the Graydons and walked to East Ham Station. He was staying with his mother at Upper Norwood, but he walked on to Ilford. He had a big knife in his overcoat pocket. About midnight he came up with the Thompsons in a dark street between Ilford Station and their house. He stabbed Thompson several times. Mrs. Thompson cried out:

"Oh, don't, don't."

Bywaters ran away. Mrs. Thompson ran on until she met people returning from a party. She said:

"Oh, my God! Will you help me; my husband is ill, he is bleeding."

They went with her and found a man lying on the pavement. Then they asked her what had happened, and she answered:

"Oh, don't ask me. I don't know. Somebody flew past, and when I turned to speak to him blood was pouring out of his mouth."

They went to fetch a doctor. There was nothing for the doctor to do except to call the police who took the corpse to the mortuary.

After throwing his knife down a drain, Bywaters made his way to his mother's house which he entered without waking her. Next morning he did some shopping with her in London. After lunch he went to the City, and about tea-time he bought an *Evening News*. It contained an account of the Ilford tragedy. Bywaters called on the Graydons and asked Mr. Graydon whether he had seen the paper, saying:

"This is a terrible thing if it is true."

Mr. Graydon said:

"I am afraid it is only too true."

Soon afterwards the police arrived and arrested Bywaters on a charge of murder. Earlier in the day Mrs. Thompson had been arrested on the same charge. On the charge sheet the indictment read:

> *"Particulars of Offence. F. E. F. Bywaters and E. J. Thompson the 4th day of October 1922, in the County of Essex, and within the jurisdiction of the Central Criminal Court murdered Percy Thompson."*

In such a case whether the accused shall be tried separately or together is within the discretion of the judge. Mr. Justice Shearman decided that they should be tried jointly.

The case for the Crown against Bywaters was only too easy. It was not disputed that Thompson had died as the result of wounds inflicted by the accused. The defence was that the wounds were inflicted in self-defence. But Bywaters had gone right out of his way at that late hour to meet the Thompsons. The judge who, on his way from Kensington to Temple Station, where East meets West, had so often got into a train labelled with the mysterious words East Ham, observed with that insight into workaday problems with which a judge will sometimes electrify the court, that the ordinary way from East Ham to Upper Norwood would be by District Railway to Victoria. Bywaters said that when he left the Graydons he was naturally thinking about Mrs. Thompson:

"I was thinking how unhappy she was, and I wished I could help her in some manner. That was the trend of my thoughts all the way to East Ham Station. When I arrived at East Ham Station I thought, 'I don't want to go home; I feel too miserable. I want to see Mrs. Thompson, I want to see if I can help her.' I turned round from East Ham Station and walked in the direction of Ilford. I knew Mr. and Mrs. Thompson would be together, and I thought perhaps if I were to see them I might make things a bit better . . . I went to see the Thompsons to come to an amicable understanding for a separation or divorce. I had no previous intention at all of going to Ilford that night. It kind of came across me all of a sudden.

"I arrived at Ilford Station and crossed over the railway bridge. When I got into Belgrave Road I walked for some time, and some distance ahead I saw Mr. and Mrs. Thompson, their backs turned to me. They were walking along Belgrave Road towards Kensington Gardens (East), and Mrs. Thompson was on the inside of the pavement. I overtook them and pushed Mrs. Thompson with my right hand, like that. With my left hand I held Thompson and caught him by the back of his coat and pushed him along the street, swinging him round. After I swung him round I said to him, 'Why don't you get a divorce or separation, you cad?'"

In answer to counsel's question he continued:

"My hands were by my side; I had let go of him. He said, 'I know that is what you want, but I am not going to give it you; it would make it too pleasant for both of you. I said, 'You take a delight in making Edie's life a hell.' Then he said, 'I've got her, I'll keep her, and I'll shoot you.' As he said that he punched me in the chest with his left fist, and I said, 'Oh, will you?' and drew a knife and put it in his arm . . ."

But the evidence of the inquest doctor was that there were two stabs in the *back* of the neck over two inches deep.

Mrs. Thompson's letters had been found in Bywaters' ship's locker. The case against her was that it was she who moved the hand that struck the fatal blow. The Solicitor-General said: "If Mrs. Thompson incited Bywaters to murder Thompson, and if, in consequence of that incitement, Bywaters did murder Thompson, Mrs. Thompson is guilty of murder."

The judge ruled that this was a correct statement of the law.

The case for Mrs. Thompson was that the only issue to the situation seriously contemplated in the letters was divorce, that the various references to desperate action which they contained meant the possibility of Mrs. Thompson running away from her husband, and that the ground glass and poison passages were mere play-acting by a woman who lived in an unreal world of romantic fiction. Mr. Filson Young, who has written a very lucid account of the trial, is no doubt right in saying that if the trial had taken place before the Act of 1898 which made accused persons competent to give evidence in their own defence, Mrs. Thompson would have stood a better chance of acquittal. Even as it was, he thinks that she would have done wisely to have declined to give evidence, notwithstanding such comment as the judge would be entitled to make on her failure to do so.

It is not unlikely that her counsel advised her in this sense, but she was the kind of woman who is not easily kept out of the witness-box. Having given her evidence she had to undergo cross-examination upon it. She made a bad impression by trying to explain the many references to a desperate act which she and Bywaters were planning, as merely meaning that they intended to run away together. She made the tactical mistake of throwing Bywaters, who had done his best to shield her, to the wolves. This may have told against her with the jury, although his case was so obviously desperate as to excuse her conduct in this respect.

Both the prisoners were found guilty, and they both appealed, though without success. The appeal was dismissed, and the only hope left was a successful petition for a reprieve. A leading daily newspaper shouldered this burden, and before the list closed nearly a million signatures had been obtained.

But justice took its course, and on January 9th, 1923, Bywaters walked with a firm step to the execution shed at Pentonville, while Edith Thompson was being carried to the shed at Holloway.

After the execution public emotion concentrated upon Mrs. Thompson. A famous publicist wrote that it would be the last time a woman was hanged in this country. Mr. Filson Young, who took the view that the criminal passages in her letters were mere play-acting, curiously contended that the proportion of these passages to the whole correspondence is very small. Only a few of them have been quoted here; whatever merits the passages of literary criticism and romantic love may have, the problem of murdering the husband is the *Leitmotiv* of the whole, while various passages show that the writer appreciated the risk she was running in committing such sentiments to paper.

As to the plea that she was play-acting, we must remember that she was a thoroughly business-like woman, capable of holding down a managing job in a big firm, and a woman who, in Mr. Young's words, "came constantly into contact with a large circle of acquaintances, and in the course of this independent existence had many opportunities of amusement of which it is clear that she availed herself."

—B.L.

# 41

# LA TOFFANA

## "Manna Of Saint Nicholas"

---

During the early part of the seventeenth century the southern parts of Italy, including Sicily, appear to have been infested by unscrupulous practitioners in the use of poison, and Naples became a centre for this nefarious trade. The most notorious of these criminals whose name has been left on record is the woman named Toffana, who is said to have been responsible indirectly for the deaths of hundreds of people. About 1650, when she was little more than a girl, she began her evil career in Palermo, but in 1659, during the pontificate of Alexander VII, she removed to Naples and made it the centre of her operations. Whether she herself devised the poison which is associated with her name, or whether she obtained the knowledge from a confederate, is not known. Her method was to prepare a solution and bottle it in special phials bearing the representation of some saint, generally Saint Nicholas of Bari, who was associated with a medicinal spring, the water of which had a reputation for healing. Sometimes she used other names for her poisonous solution, such as "Aquetta di Napoli," "Manna of St. Nicholas di Bari," or "Aqua Toffana." These bottles of poison were freely sold, especially to women, reputedly as a cosmetic for application to the skin to improve the complexion, for which purpose, owing to its active constituent being arsenic, it probably proved effective. Anyone in the secret could buy the poison for its supposed external application, and Toffana took care only to deal with individuals after due safeguards had been built up. She changed her abode so frequently, and adopted so many disguises, that even when suspicion actually fell upon her after many mysterious deaths, detection was rendered very difficult. She cunningly worked on the minds of her customers who were susceptible to religious or superstitious influences, and those who were unaware of the origin of her deadly solution were told it was a certain miraculous liquid supposed to ooze from the tomb of St. Nicholas, a saint of healing.

Her preparations were doubtless bought by many in good faith in the belief that the liquid had miraculous properties, but those who knew the secret, especially women, who wished to rid themselves of their husbands, often used it for criminal purposes, and it is estimated that over six hundred persons were poisoned by her preparations in Naples and Rome. Two Popes and other Church dignitaries are said to have fallen victims to the poison, and it was not until after a long career, and when Toffana had reached the age of seventy, that she was found to be the originator of these wholesale crimes. In a letter addressed to Hoffman by Garcelli, physician to the Emperor Charles VI of Austria, he informed him that being Governor of Naples at the time, he knew that the Aquetta di Napoli was the dread of every noble family in the city, and that the subject was investigated legally. He thus had the opportunity of examining all the documents, and found the poison to consist of a solution of arsenic, which was of such strength that from four to six drops in water or wine was said to kill an adult, and that it was colourless, transparent and tasteless.

When the manufacture and sale of the poison was at last traced to Toffana, she took refuge in a convent where, under the privileges of the place, she bade defiance for some time to the officers of justice, and continued to vend her solution from the very bosom of the Church until the scandal at length became too great to be tolerated. She was then dragged from her refuge and thrown into prison. A great outcry was raised by the clergy at this violation of their privileges, and the people, unwilling to be defrauded of their right to use the poison, joined in the clamour of the priests. It was only by circulating a report that she had poisoned the wells in the city, that the current of public sentiment could be turned against her. Being put to the rack she confessed her crimes, and named those who had afforded her protection. They were immediately arrested in various churches and monasteries. It was stated that the day before her last flight from justice, she had sent two boxes of her "manna" to Rome. They were found in the custom-house in that city. The archbishop still murmured at her being torn from a privileged asylum and accordingly the authorities contrived to have her strangled and thrown into the court-yard of the convent from which she had been taken in 1709. The sale of her preparations however, did not cease at her death, and, according to Keysler, who travelled in Southern Italy in the early part of the eighteenth century, the *aquetta* continued to be prepared in great quantities for some time afterwards.

There was naturally much mystery at the time as to the composition of Aqua Toffana and the most extraordinary properties were attributed to it. Its alleged effects are thus described by Behrens, a contemporary writer: "a certain indescribable change is felt in the whole body, which leads the person to complain to his physician. The physician examines and reflects, but finds no symptoms either external or internal, no vomiting, no inflammation, no fever. In short, he can only advise patience, strict regimen, and laxatives. The malady, however, creeps on, and the physician is again sent for. Still he cannot detect any symptoms of note. Meanwhile the poison takes firmer hold of the system; languor, wearisomeness, and loathing of food continue; the nobler organs gradually become torpid, and the lungs in particular at length begin to suffer. In a word, the malady from the first is incurable; the unhappy victim pines away insensibly even in the hands of the physician, and thus he is brought to a miserable end through months or years, according to his enemy's desire."

—C.J.S.T.

# 42

# MRS VERMILYA
## The Deadly Pepper Pot

The East Twenties in Chicago present one of the most interesting and diverse complexes of humanity to be found in America. Here is part of the Tenderloin; here are squalid streets lined with boarding-houses and shoddy apartment houses. Here are blacks and whites, tans and yellows, wanderers and strays from all the regions of this world.

It was in this region of contrasts—of dreams and dregs—at 415 East Twenty-ninth Street, in the fall of the year 1911, that one of the strangest of all poison mysteries was unfolded.

On the afternoon of October 23 of that year an ambulance appeared before the door. Several stretcher men mounted a flight of stairs and carried from the apartment of Mrs. Louise Vermilya, a widow, the prostrate form of Policeman Arthur T. Bissonette, who was supposed to be suffering from a severe attack of gastritis. The officer was quickly motored over to Mercy Hospital and put to bed in charge of the ordinary nurses, while Mrs. Vermilya shortly arrived, declaring that she would be present to give the patient special attention, since she was his fiancée. Doctor F. A. van Arsdale, the policeman's physician, and physicians of the hospital attended the sick man, gave him stimulants and restoratives, plied him with stomachics, and did what could be done for a man sore stricken in his alimentary tract. It was all to no avail. On the twenty-fifth Officer Bissonette died.

There is nothing strange in such a death. Men overeat, overdrink, and otherwise abuse the vital internal machinery. If nature has not specially equipped them for such outrages against their forces, by a long line of hard-living ancestry and its consequent hereditary benefits, they do not always survive the effects.

Yet this man, Bissonette, was a strong, robust fellow. His station mates knew that he did not drink. He may have had a liking for food, but was he not a healthy youngster of twenty-six, pounding a beat all day, playing hand-ball by the hour, and able to eat a raw bear if need be? Was it possible that such a man should be walking his beat on one Thursday and dead the next? Obviously it was, since the evidence was at hand—but it was strange.

Mrs. Vermilya, had she been as wise as some have made her out, would have maintained a dignified silence at this point. The doctors had certified that Bissonette had died of acute indigestion and that was final enough. The lady seemed to feel the urge for explanations. She said that Bissonette was a very heavy drinker on the sly, at home, when there was no one to observe him.

Unhappily, perhaps, men know too much about the peculiarities of these heavy solitary drinkers. Among other things, they know that the solitary lush does not rise at early hours in the morning, looking like a lily and playing hand-ball like an athlete.

There was another little matter. Bissonette was not twenty minutes dead when an undertaker, by name C. C. Boysen, appeared and claimed the corpse on behalf of the dead man's landlady and fiancée. As it turned out, a sister of the deceased had already arrived, and she vehemently opposed any such surrender of her brother's body. There came near being violence. In the end the sister triumphed.

Finally, there was a third matter to stir curiosity. Bissonette had, as already stated, been a blooming youngster of twenty-six. Mrs. Vermilya was a lady in mature life—forty-two she said. She was not one of those miraculously preserved modern women who look thirty when nearly fifty years have passed. Indeed, she was an ordinary kind of creature, whose face was actually unpleasant in some lights and positions. What was young Bissonette doing, betrothed to this faded creature?

At any rate, suspicion reached the point where Coroner Hoffman decided to act. An autopsy was begun, and Mrs. Vermilya was ordered to be detained. She was not technically arrested, mainly for the reason that she had, herself, collapsed after the death of Bissonette and the first whisper of suspicions against her. Instead of being jailed, she was put to bed in her apartment, with two policemen and a matron or nurse always present, with instructions to watch her closely against any attempt at suicide.

While the suspected woman lay there, the internal organs of the dead policeman were submitted to the State toxicologists and chemists. And while these gentlemen were busy at their slow and precise tasks, the newspapers began to clear up the externals of the story. They sent their reporters in every direction, ran down every rumour, and built up about the beleaguered landlady a most astounding story, the like of which has been told few times in the history of feminine criminality.

The woman, now known as Mrs. Louise Vermilya, had been born of farmer parents in the little country settlement of Barrington, Illinois, now no more than a suburb of Chicago. She had married, when still a slip of a girl, a farmer, Fred Brimmerkamp, much older than she, having with him children by an earlier marriage. To these, the second marriage added three more, a boy and two girls.

Some eighteen years before the present events—which would be in 1896—Fred Brimmerkamp died suddenly, apparently without having received medical attention.

Only a few months later, on February 24, 1897, Mrs. Brimmerkamp's little daughter Florence, four and one half years old, also died at the Barrington farm, after what the newspapers declared to have been a short and mysterious illness.

On November 23, 1898, Cora, the eight-year-old daughter, followed her little sister to the grave, having also been strangely attacked and surviving only a few days.

Shortly after the death of this child, Mrs. Brimmerkamp met and married Charles Vermilya, a railroad man, who also had been married before, and who brought a maturing son into the household.

In 1904, according to the information gathered by the authorities and the newspapers, Mrs. Vermilya had a quarrel with this stepson, the issue being the sale of some property belonging to the elder Vermilya, situated at Crystal Lake. The young man, then a telegrapher, twenty-three years old, died soon afterward of an illness diagnosed as heart disease.

In 1906 came another death, this time of Lillian Brimmerkamp, the daughter of the lady's first husband. She also was ill only a short time, dying of a malady that was not satisfactorily diagnosed.

In 1909 the second husband, Charles Vermilya, died of a sudden and mysterious ailment, though only fifty-nine years old and in robust health until a few days before his demise.

In 1910, Frank Brimmerkamp, the last of the accused woman's children by her first husband, died after lingering agony, but not before he had made certain bitter and suggestive statements to his fiancée.

Mrs. Vermilya now began to take in boarders, and the first of them was Richard T. Smith, an Illinois Central Railway conductor. Some said he had married the lady, although it appeared that the marriage, if there had been one, had existed without benefit of clergy. Mr. Smith departed this earth in March, 1911.

Then Patrolman Bissonette went to board in Mrs. Vermilya's little apartment, with the results already noted.

All this might not have seemed so strange, for the dread Thanatos sometimes has a way of "following fast and following faster" some afflicted family. Yet there was a matter of money involved here.

When Fred Brimmerkamp had died, he had left his widow five thousand dollars in sound insurance. Vermilya had left almost as much. Smith had left her two thousand dollars, and her stepson twelve hundred. In all, the district attorney declared, Mrs. Vermilya had benefited to the extent of about fifteen thousand dollars through the sudden deaths of these various relatives and near ones.

Lying on her bed and trying to be brave, Mrs. Vermilya issued statements. Indeed, she talked herself into more trouble than might have been brewed for her. With the policemen and a nurse always at hand, she felt the human impulse to talk to some one. She gave out statement after statement, without knowing just what she did.

Her first husband had drunk himself to death, as any one in Barrington might testify. Her second husband had been taken ill on his train, had been brought home, and tenderly nursed by her, till his death. She could readily explain why this man or that had taken out insurance in her favour. The ordinary precautions of life were being twisted into serpents to sting her. In time she would be able to explain everything. She had nothing to fear, for she had done no wrong beyond having had a lot of people die about her—a mere coincidence.

The authorities and the newspapers, however, viewed things in quite another light. To them the facts were incriminating. Here was a woman who led men into her arms and then slew them for trifling amounts of money. She had slain two husbands, her own little daughters and her own grown son out of the most sordid of motives. It may have been true that she slew all the others for their insurance money, but the filing of the will of Bissonette clearly showed that she could have had no such motive in his case. His will left most of his slender property to Miss Lydia Rivard, a farmer's daughter of Kankakee, Illinois, whom he specifically noted in the testament as his fiancée. As Mrs. Vermilya had witnessed this paper, she must have known its contents and seen clearly that she could not benefit by the policeman's death. On the other hand, the fact that she had witnessed a paper in which another woman was specially named as fiancée, and still had claimed the same relationship to that man before and after his death, gave rise to further suspicion.

Mrs. Vermilya answered that she knew all about Miss Rivard, and had met the young lady. The engagement between Policeman Bissonette and her was an old affair, and had been superseded by his troth with her. Miss Rivard denied this with some heat, but that was, after all, a woman's squabble.

On November 2, while still lying sick at home, her guardians ever at her side, Mrs. Vermilya did a strange thing. It was not then explicable, but soon showed the direction in which her mind was working. She made her will, and the newspapers of the country, which by this time were watching the Vermilya case carefully, recorded this happening at length. Even Mrs. Vermilya's faithful keepers asked her why she wanted to make a will. She returned a significant remark:

"I am suffering from the same pains the others suffered from."

Two days later this rather cryptic statement was solved.

November 4 opened with the official report of the chemists. They had found in the viscera of Policeman Bissonette no less than eight grains of white arsenic, about a teaspoonful, enough, according to text-books on toxicology, to dispatch four ordinary men.

This news was conveyed to Mrs. Vermilya that day at noon.

"Is that so?" she said calmly.

An hour later Mrs. Vermilya told her nurse, Miss Rose Wiseman, that she would like some fried eggs, several of them. Since eggs were considered excellent diet for her, the nurse hastened to prepare them, placing them on a platter with a little bread and the ordinary salt and pepper shakers. She brought these materials to the bedside. Mrs. Vermilya grinned with satisfaction, and the police, who sat by, marvelled at her composure. Then the sick woman's face changed a little. She said:

"Miss Wiseman, I never could stand black pepper. You will find white pepper in an old talcum-powder can on the second shelf in the kitchen, back in the corner. Do you mind getting it for me?"

The nurse got the can, and Mrs. Vermilya shook great quantities of the white pepper over her eggs, smacking her lips all the while, declaring that she just couldn't eat eggs without lots of white pepper. Finally she gulped down her eggs with a look of positive enjoyment.

The police guards and the nurse congratulated themselves. They had got the patient to eat at last. She was getting better, and would be able to face her accusers. Yes, the way she ate those eggs was an excellent sign.

Suddenly Mrs. Vermilya raised herself in bed in a violent convulsion, shrieked with pain, and fell back unconscious.

Suspicion at once fell upon that old talcum can. It was sent to a chemist, who reported in a few minutes that it contained black pepper and powdered white arsenic!

Amazement seized the police and the prosecutor. They had searched Mrs. Vermilya's house again and again for poison. They had taken away with them a dozen bottles from her kitchen shelf and bathroom cabinet, only to find them filled with innocuous substances. They had inquired of drug stores in Chicago and Barrington, trying to trace to Mrs. Vermilya a purchase of poison. They had failed again and again. Yet here, all this time, stood the wanted evidence in the common old talcum can.

The woman, who stood now self-accused, was violently ill. Doctors went to work on her with antidotes and emetics, and on the second day it was announced she would live.

Meanwhile the pepper shaker was becoming famous. Pictures of it were printed everywhere. It brought in a fresh bit of direct evidence. The father of Arthur Bissonette came forward, though he had previously remained in the background, grieved and depressed, to tell the district attorney of a meal he had once taken at his son's boarding place, in which the pepper shaker had figured.

He had gone to call on his son, and dinner had been served while he was there, he being invited to stay. Ham and fried eggs were served, and he thought them first-rate. The famous pepper shaker was on the table, and he had helped himself liberally. Afterward, he had left the house and been seized on the street with terrible cramps. He had gone to a drug store, got an emetic, and been relieved. He was still feeling pains and stiffness of the limbs, although that had been several weeks before the death of his son.

Another witness also came forward in the person of Miss Elizabeth Nolan, fiancée of Frank Brimmerkamp, Mrs. Vermilya's own son, who had died on October 30, 1910. Miss Nolan said that young Brimmerkamp, in the course of his last illness, had said to her on several occasions that he thought he was being poisoned, as his father had been before him. Miss Nolan had seen him refuse to drink mineral water offered to him by the accused woman. His dying words were that Mrs. Vermilya might as well call the undertaker, and have him stuck in the ground. Miss Nolan also said that her fiancé had been extremely suspicious of his mother, declaring several times that he knew his father had been poisoned. To all these Miss Nolan made solemn affidavit.

The authorities, now feeling certain that they had in their hands a murderer of the utmost skill and heartlessness, went to work feverishly to exhume the bodies of Richard Smith and Frank Brimmerkamp. The town was in a great state of excitement as to the outcome of these new analyses, and Mrs. Vermilya, as soon as she had recovered from the self-administered pepper and arsenic, also took a lively interest in the matter. She had meantime been transferred from her home to the detention hospital, where she was under close surveillance for fear of further attempts to take her life. On November 10 she was informed, as was the public, that arsenic had also been found in the bodies of Smith and Brimmerkamp, through both of whom Mrs. Vermilya had reaped insurance money.

Again Mrs. Vermilya was not disconcerted. It was strange that both these men who had died in her apartment should have been found poisoned with arsenic. Coincidence was a great thing. Maybe one of them had put the arsenic into her white pepper. How could she know?

There were a good many men and women of fair mental equipment who felt as she did. They expressed a great doubt of her guilt, a sympathy for her, and the belief that a jury would not convict her. Her attorney declared that she was an unfortunate woman, the victim of men and of circumstances, and that at the proper time her innocence would be established. It was not an especially surprising statement from a defence attorney, but an indication of the front that was being put up in the face of evidence that seemed conclusive.

The formalities, of course, went forward briskly. On November 27, the coroner's jury held Mrs. Vermilya, and on December 19 the grand jury brought in the indictment. The news of this portentous event was brought to the prisoner in jail, where she was now occupying a cell like other accused women, among them a Mrs. Quinn, who, having been charged with having shot her husband, was supposed to feel a natural kinship with the lady of the pepper shaker. Once more Mrs. Vermilya merely shrugged and said that time would vindicate her.

It happened that there were being held in the Cook County jail at this time four young roughs who had held up on the road, and beaten to death, a farmer. Their motive had been simple robbery. The scaffolding for their hanging was being erected in the jail yard. Mrs. Vermilya could hear the thudding of the hammers and the working of the saws. She knew, as all the prisoners did, that preparations were being made for a hanging, and she had been told of the crime of the four young men.

The reporters, who brought her the news of her own indictment and got her nonchalant reaction, asked her the cruel question of her feeling toward the men who were about to be hanged.

"They should be hanged," said Mrs. Vermilya crisply. "They deserve it. Only it's a shame it's so near Christmas."

The whole country, or that part of it which follows the strange and the terrible, became interested in the problem of this inscrutable woman. Psychologists and alienists were besought for opinions and gave them.

Meantime, old friends and acquaintances of Louise Wolfe Brimmerkamp Vermilya came forward to tell, in their simple way, of events in her life which they had deemed merely curious. Certainly they had never suspected them as having the least significance. One of these friends was an undertaker in Barrington.

When old Fred Brimmerkamp was still alive, and his wife's children were babies, the woman used to love to come around to the undertaker's shop and help embalm the bodies. She knew, before he did, who was dead or dying in the little settlement, and she had a strange way of intruding herself into the confidence of families where a death was expected. She would sit with the dying and watch the ebbing of life with a rapt and unflagging attention. She could watch those scenes which drive the hardest and best beloved from the bedside of the expiring—watch them without any emotion unless it was a secret pleasure.

After a death, she would appear at the undertaker's rooms and seem to delight in performing those dread offices which men must harden themselves to endure. She came and took part in the processes of preparing bodies for burial, though she usually received no pay for her work, and though she was sometimes made to feel unwelcome.

The Chicago undertaker, Boysen, who was at first suspected of having had some evil connection with the woman, although later quite cleared, had a similar story to tell. Mrs. Vermilya's mind turned about death and the dead. Her topics of conversation revolved about the matter of who might die next. She almost kept a record of the sick in her neighbourhood, and had an uncanny way of knowing where death had struck or was about to strike. She loved to spend her time in the undertaker's rooms, often doing his most disagreeable work gratis.

In other words, this woman was a necrophile. Those who care to examine examples of this kind in other lands and under other circumstances may consult the medical books, particularly Krafft-Ebbing. There is the kind of being who, because of some quirk in the brain mechanism or the nerve and gland system, reverses the usual attitude, the normal feeling, of the race, and, instead of being repelled and horrified by death and the dead, is attracted to them.

In Chicago a good many people saw through the terrible enigma of Louise Vermilya and wanted to have her tested for lunacy. Her attorney, sensing the direction of the wind, and seeing that there were certain holes in the State's case, had her brought to trial on March 7, 1912. Of the details of the trial, we need no recounting, the whole affair, except for moves of the defendant counsel, having already been told.

On April 6, a day less than a month after the opening

of the trial, the jury set to try Louise Vermilya came to a disagreement. The woman was never again haled into court to defend herself.

—E.H.S.

# 43

# LA VOISIN

## Black Mass and Murder

---

Madame de Brinvilliers achieved an undeserved reputation as one of the great poisoners of history. She was, on the contrary, an incompetent bungler as is shown by her many failures, including those twenty-six unsuccessful attempts to poison her father. The sensation caused by her arrest and execution was not because she was an adept but because she was an aristocrat—one of a class in France who were virtually above the law until the Revolution.

So in order to see her against the dark background of her time, she must be pictured as merely one of many hundreds of buyers of poison dealing with scores, perhaps hundreds, of suppliers in Paris alone. Catherine Montvoisin, better known as La Voisin, was one such poison-vendor, but she also amply qualifies as a multicide because she confessed to having arranged, among other murders, the killing of over two thousand infants, many as human sacrifices in the worship of Satan.

The black page of French history known as *L'Affaire des Poisons* would be sufficiently shocking if it stood alone as what can only be described as a murder epidemic. But it was not, in fact, an isolated phenomenon; it was merely one in a two-thousand-year sequence of similar epidemics. Nor was it, as is widely believed, the last of its kind. A twenty-year epidemic of murder came to light as recently as 1929, which lifts the subject out of the history books and into a class of crimes which we cannot be sure will not occur yet again. Which is why the subject needs to be briefly reviewed.

The earliest murder epidemic on record is mentioned by the Roman historian Livy as having occurred in that city about 200 B.C., when some hundred and ninety matrons, mostly of patrician birth, were executed for poisoning. A similar epidemic occurred in Rome a couple of centuries later when a hundred and fifty women, again mostly patricians, were executed, but their supplier, an old woman known as Locusta, so favourably impressed the Emperor Nero that he reprieved her and appointed her as a sort of Court Murderess. Other epidemics broke out from time to time, and it was not until more than fourteen hundred years later, at about the time of the Reformation, that Rome ceased to be the proud centre of both the Christian religion and the poisoning industry.

The success of the long-established Roman school of poisoning, reputedly sanctified by the patronage of Pope Alexander VI and his offspring, encouraged imitators in rival cities. A Venetian school arose, with more ambitious objectives than mere husband-slaughter, and its most prominent practitioner was a Franciscan monk, John of Ragusa, whose scale of charges for proposed diplomatic poisonings, as submitted to the Council of Ten, included 150 ducats for removing the King of Spain, and, quite cheaply but rather disloyally, a mere 100 ducats for doing the Pope. Then a Sicilian school achieved notoriety, and centred around a woman known as Toffana who supplied numerous delighted clients with a deadly fluid sometimes called "Aqua Toffana", or, for her more devout customers, "Manna di St. Nicholas di Bari". And another seventeenth-century epidemic was spread by a hag named Hieronyma Spara who sold a special brew which she called "Aquetta di Perugia".

As an indication of the scale of these epidemics, it may be noted that one Roman lady, Madame Olympia, was reputed to have killed no less than one hundred and fifty people, through whose deaths she inherited money. She bought her poisons, incidentally, from the notorious chemist Exili, who later went to Paris, where one of his pious customers eased her conscience in the confessional. As a result the Grand Penitentiary betrayed Exili to the authorities and he was imprisoned in the Bastille. He suffered for being a pioneer in days when murder by poisoning was still apt to be regarded as unusual or even reprehensible. Not many years later priests of Nôtre Dame revealed that most of the confessions made to them were of poisoning. But Exili did not waste his time in the Bastille, as we have already seen that he there met and shared his secrets with Gaudin de Sainte Croix, lover of Madame de Brinvilliers, and thus helped to spread the germs of an epidemic of which *Le Roi Soleil* himself was nearly a victim.

The central plague-spot of nearly all murder epidemics has been an evil old woman, not a leader but a supplier of poisons and adviser on their use, one who has perceived and stimulated an existing demand, greatly to her own financial advantage. In which the twentieth-century epidemic conformed to pattern. It is a pity that so little reliable information has been published about this epidemic, the reason being that efforts were made first by newspapers to distort the story and then by politicians to suppress it. It began some years before the First World War in a district in Hungary known as the Tiszazug, where a few villages are enclosed by a loop of the River Tisza. The evil genius of this epidemic was an old witch-like woman known as Auntie Fazekas, who for eighty pengö—then worth about three pounds in English money—would sell a fatal dose of what she called the "water of inheritance", which she made by stewing a few pennyworth of arsenical fly-papers. And she did a steady trade for about twenty years until in 1929 the authorities took very belated action. A preliminary batch—a mere sample—of fifty bodies were exhumed, of which no less than forty-six were found to contain arsenic. Thirty-four suspects were arrested, of whom all but three were women, and when preparations were made to exhume a further fifty bodies several women committed suicide, including Auntie Fazekas. More denunciations followed, more exhumations, more arrests, and the weary Public Prosecutor was still charging prisoners in batches twelve months later.

As practically all the accused were women, editors sent sob-sisters to the earlier trials in search of sensational stories of crimes of passion. But most of the murders had been committed from mercenary motives, and the killers were not Hungarian glamour-girls but elderly peasants with wrinkled old faces framed in rusty black head-shawls—types who were deadly but dull. Efforts to scrape passionate love-stories out of this material were unconvincing, and crowds in Court began to dwindle. And it is clear that after a few months the authorities issued directives to Hungarian newspapers to play the story down; it was beginning to spoil the reputation of the Regent, Admiral Horthy, for having re-civilized his country after the post-war Communist régime of Bela Kun. So the Tiszazug story petered out—a half-told reminder that, after two thousand years, epidemic murder is still liable to recur.

We can now see La Voisin more clearly in historical perspective, but before considering her as an individual we should try to check a contemporary estimate that she was only one of hundreds of poison-vendors of her day.

Such check is possible from the archives of the *Chambre Ardente*, a court somewhat on the lines of the earlier British Star Chamber. The French tribunal was set up to investigate poison cases only, and was presided over by the conscientious lieutenant of Paris police, de la Reynie, a man whose integrity in a corrupt age was above reproach. And the records of the *Chambre* erred, if at all, on the side of understatement, because among the individuals denounced to it many were so highly placed that their activities could not be investigated, such, for instance, as the King's evil mistress, Madame de Montespan. Ravaisson wrote: "The chief culprits belonged to the nobility or the law, and almost all of them had amongst the members of the Court friends, clients or relatives." C. J. S. Thompson wrote: "The weight of the condemnations fell almost entirely on the miserable creatures who sold the poisons—and not on those who bought and used them." In its 210 hearings, the *Chambre Ardente* considered 442 cases and ordered 367 arrests. It condemned 36 to be executed, and sent 246 to prison, exile or the galleys. So perhaps it was not very far wrong to estimate that La Voisin was only one of some hundreds of other wholesale dealers in commercialized horror and death.

La Voisin was, however, a somewhat less repulsive character than the selfish, callous, arrogant aristocrat Brinvilliers. La Voisin was a woman of the people, earning a good living in a highly-skilled trade, fond of her parents and children and, in her spare time, enjoying bawdy songs at drunken parties. All her life she provided money to support her mother. She did occasionally dish out a dose of poison herself, and it must often have been a temptation to do so when she had deadly fluids in store by the gallon. But her attitude seems to have been rather like that of an abstemious innkeeper who on rare occasions takes a sip of his own Scotch with an embarrassed wink at smiling customers in the bar.

Catherine Deshayes was born in the late sixteen-thirties, probably in 1638. Her family were so poor that at the age of nine the little girl was sent out to tell fortunes in the streets of Paris at a sou a time. She was married and just over twenty when her husband, Antoine Montvoisin, an amiable, shiftless individual, lost his job in a haber-dashery shop on the Pont Marie. So Catherine, an energetic, thrifty young French housewife, started a connection as a midwife and beauty expert to keep Antoine and their daughter Marguerite. She also worked up a business as a herbalist, and possessed a recipe for a "quintessence of hellebore which kept the Dean of Westminster alive for one hundred and sixty-six years", which suggests that she had a mail-order connection in England.

After Antoine had failed to restore the family fortunes by hawking cheap jewellery, it became clear to Catherine that she must take over the responsibilities of bread-winner. She had not lost what she called the "God-given talent" for fortune-telling of her young days, and she soon managed to expand her business to include palmistry, prophecy, astrology and similar popular and profitable side-lines. But by pretending to have extra-terrestrial influence, she was infringing the monopoly of the Church, and aroused the opposition of priests of St Vincent de Paul. So Catherine went to the Vicars-General of Paris to demand protection for her business deals. It is a measure of her character that this little plump, vulgar, bright-eyed girl in her twenties convinced the learned tribunal—the Vicars-General and several doctors of theology from the

Sorbonne—that her brand of astrology was acceptable to the Church. Having achieved which useful advertisement she went home in triumph and a borrowed coach to grapple with a greatly expanding business.

The now increasingly prosperous Montvoisin family moved to a big house standing in its own garden not far from the Porte Saint-Denis. It was in Rue Beauregard, probably No. 25, which was still standing in the nineteen-thirties. There La Voisin dealt with an unending flow of wealthy clients, who would be already waiting to consult her before she was out of bed in the morning. These would be admitted one by one, masked and trembling, to a darkened chamber where they were received by an impressive figure in an ermine-lined robe which had two hundred eagles embroidered in gold thread on its purple velvet. La Voisin gave her advice in a low, nasal, priest-like intonation, and collected for her services as much as she thought each client could afford. Thus she met many famous people, and later capitalized her new acquaintanceships. She rose ever higher in society among people who were afraid to offend her, and she sank ever lower into unspeakable evil. She attended the church of the Abbé Saint-Amour, Rector of the University of Paris, and even dined privately with him. She gave fashionable garden parties attended by highly-placed guests, and they would listen with delight to a small choice orchestra playing softly on lovely lawns, beneath which were buried the bodies of hundreds of babies who had been sacrificed to Satan.

La Voisin ran her business very economically. She would accommodate ladies who became inconveniently pregnant, and for an inclusive fee would see them through their trouble and take over the baby. Thus she built up a stock of prospective sacrifices for celebrations of the Black

Mass, which saved the cost of sending out to buy a baby for an écu from some starving subject of *Le Roi Soleil*. And when supply exceeded demand she could always thin out her stock by incinerating surplus infants in an oven she had installed in a pretty grotto in her garden. Selling poison for the removal of unwanted wives or husbands was, of course, a nice steady trade which never fell off much. But it could be made more profitable by selling a first dose of adulterated poison which merely made the victim ill. When disappointed clients rushed back with this bad news they could usually be persuaded to pay a second and higher fee for "something stronger" which completed the job satisfactorily. Some such deal may, indeed, have explained why it took Madame de Brinvilliers so long to finish off her father.

All these were easy routine tasks. The first really tricky assignment offered to La Voisin she was cautious enough to decline. She was approached by the notorious Olympe Mancini, Comtesse de Soissons, who wanted to become the King's mistress by poisoning the reigning favourite, Louise de la Vallière. La Voisin turned down this proposal and pointed out that it might greatly annoy his Majesty. But Madame de Soissons was determined. "I shall get rid of one or the other," she said firmly. "No, of both!" The probable truth of this conversation is indicated by the fact that when La Voisin revealed it under torture, Madame de Soissons did not even stay to deny it but immediately fled abroad. The incident indicates the reputation for efficiency and discretion which La Voisin had achieved in her terrible trade.

But if murdering La Vallière, and possibly the King as well, had seemed to La Voisin not merely disloyal but distinctly risky, it was quite safe later to arrange a few little ceremonies requested by Madame de Montespan, La

Vallière's successor, with the innocent object of retaining the King's affection for her. It was not only safe but easy, for all that La Voisin had to do was to select from stock a suitable baby or two, glance down her list of priests who combined public worship of God with private worship of Satan, and send for one who might be disengaged—quite often the Abbé Guiborg.

It is necessary to glance briefly at the Abbé Guiborg, not as a nauseating phenomenon but as a type of La Voisin's many priestly accomplices. The Abbé was a bloated old man, aged about seventy when he was finally arrested, whose repulsive mauve face was covered with a network of tiny blue veins. He was either one-eyed or had such an appalling squint that one eye-pupil was almost invisible. He had held a number of public and private ecclesiastical offices, and when he was arrested he was sacristan of St Marcel at Saint-Denis and was also attached to the parish church of Vannes. He was a skilled distiller of poisons, and had invented a novel and popular fluid which must have brightened up many a premature death-bed, as its victims were supposed to die of excessive laughter. Out of his spare-time earnings he maintained several mistresses, and kept down the housekeeping expenses by using as human sacrifices some of the many children they bore him. One of these women bore him seven babies, giving birth to one under a hedge and another in a disused dungeon. Another girl began to weary him and he tried to poison her so that he could have her sticks of furniture. Another useful contact, the niece of conscientious André Guillaume, the public executioner, bore him several children of whom he disposed in infancy.

A full description of the Black Masses recited by the Abbé Guiborg and his like over the nude bodies of ambitious ladies of the aristocracy would be unprintable. Such ceremonies were not novelties but were manifestations of the hopes and fears felt by primitive minds towards powers of evil long before they were ever felt towards powers of good. For even the Old Testament Jehovah was a God of wrath and vengeance whom men feared and flattered and tried to bribe, but could not love. Briefly, the Black Mass was a Christian service in reverse, with obscene embellishments. The priest had to have been ordained; the book of blasphemous prayers was bound in human skin; the incense stank evilly; the "holy water" was urine; the Host had been stolen from a church and defiled with filth; the offering was a living baptized baby, usually flung aside or into a furnace after its blood had been drained into a stolen chalice. Some details of the rites were so horrifying that at one such ceremony a young girl brought in to assist as one of the naked servers at the altar died of fright and had to be hastily buried. And all this nauseating nonsense would be in support of some such prayer as that of Madame de Montespan: "I . . . implore that the love of the King and Monseigneur the Dauphin may still be mine; may the Queen be barren; may the King leave bed and board for me . . ." and so on.

It has been necessary to hint at these horrors because we are trying to glimpse the mind of La Voisin, one of many who employed such priests, who organized such rites, who bought and sold babies for such purposes. As a wife and a mother, what, it is reasonable to enquire, was she like at home?

Even in that hellish house in the Rue Beauregard there were the touches of macabre absurdity which so often mercifully brighten up the bloody background of a multicide. In this case it was provided by Antoine

Montvoisin, a character so shadowy and unimportant that he is only once mentioned by name in all the records of the *Chambre Ardente*. He seems to have been not merely too shiftless to maintain his family, but too foolish about money to have been trusted with any but small sums. So he became a sort of reluctantly tolerated odd-job man, running errands and collecting herbs, and occasionally making feeble sneers at the solemn obscenities going on around him, like some pimply City office-boy mimicking the managing director. Antoine's life was not, on the whole, uneventful. One of his wife's many lovers once nearly bit his nose off; another beat him up so savagely that he was left for dead; and another tried to cast a spell on him with a decaying sheep's heart. He was in great pain after that ceremony, but when La Voisin heard what had happened she rushed to the nearest church, confessed her sins, received absolution and went happily home to a now restored and smiling hubby.

Family ties were considerably stronger, in fact, in the Montvoisin establishment than among, say, the aristocratic Brinvilliers. In moments of irritation La Voisin might, of course, pop some poison into Antoine's wine or soup, just as another sort of wife might slam the kitchen door in a temper; but perhaps she quite liked having him around to give the house an air of respectability because he always survived. She probably knew the exact dose to produce effects which would be punitive but something short of fatal, and she may have regretted giving him one awful brew which left him with hiccoughs which he did not shake off until a couple of years later. Quite soon after La Voisin died swearing at the stake, the shadowy Antoine died too, and we shall never know whether it was because his heart was broken in his bereavement or because his limbs were broken in the torture chamber.

· The eldest daughter Marguerite, who was actually Antoine's child, helps to build up the picture of her unspeakable mother's establishment. Marguerite seems to have been a dutiful and sensible girl. She knew all that was going on, of course, and once or twice assisted at a Black Mass. But such things had been familiar to her all her life, and her attitude was probably similar to that of a poulterer's daughter allowed as a special treat to watch Daddy kill a chicken. She was loyal to her parents, never betrayed her mother, and nursed her father devotedly when he was ill. She bore a child by a married neighbour, which was hardly a matter for comment in such a *milieu*, and had the good sense to send it away to be brought up in the country, thus avoiding the risk of its getting mixed up with Mummy's sacrificial waiting-list.

There were also in the house other children of La Voisin by other fathers, for she was never short of lovers. And although we do not know much about the children it will help to fill in our picture if we glance at the fathers. One was the King's architect, Fauchet, who wisely brought a snack in his pocket when invited to dine with his mistress; there was Denis Poculot, a coiner; and the Vicomte de Cousserans, a coiner too and also an alchemist; there was André Guillaume, the God-fearing executioner; there was the Comte de Labartie, quite charming, but he would keep trying to poison poor Antoine; there was Latour who knocked her ·about; and Lesage who swindled her, which was worse. There were others too, but perhaps these few provide a sufficient glimpse of the love-life of La Voisin.

The beginning of the end came at a jolly little witches' dinner party given during the last week of 1678 by La Vigoureux, with La Bosse as an honoured guest. Both of these ladies were friends of La Voisin and in the same line of business. Having drunk more wine than was good for her, La Bosse became alcoholically boastful, and although it was distinctly bad form to talk shop in her profession, she announced that after another three poisonings she could afford to retire. A male guest present happened to repeat the joke later to a friend; and the friend happened to be the detective Desgrez who had so cleverly caught Madame de Brinvilliers. Desgrez sent an *agent provocateur* round to La Bosse who sold her some poison. By 4 January 1679, La Bosse and La Vigoureux were in Vincennes prison being closely questioned and everybody whose name they mentioned was arrested and questioned too. From the number and rank of the suspects it soon became clear that La Bosse's tipsy jest had uncovered a state of affairs too big and important for Desgrez, or even de la Reynie himself, to handle. The King was informed and the *Chambre Ardente* was set up. On Sunday morning, 13 March 1679, Desgrez arrested La Voisin as she emerged from church at peace with God after attending Mass. Antoine was arrested at home later that day—perhaps he enjoyed his Sunday dinner better when he stayed at home to cook it himself.

Months passed during which many more people went into prison and some came out—to the cemetery or the Place de Grève. Madame Brunet, a poisoner, was hanged and burned; a poison-vendor, La Cheron, suffered the same fate; La Vigoureux was tortured so severely that she died in the chamber; La Bosse, who had started all this fuss by having one over the eight, was burned alive. But La Voisin lived on, and Paris wondered why. Madame de Sévigné wrote: "Everyone is on tip-toe, sending for news and going from house to house to pick it up." What Paris did not know was that King Louis XIV, eager sponsor of the *Chambre*

*Ardente*, had changed his tactics and was busy trying to sabotage it.

What was happening behind the scenes was that the vast foul Paris underworld of defilement and death was being exposed too relentlessly under honest de la Reynie's merciless interrogations. There were unsuccessful plots to assassinate him. And there were numerous rumours that these exposures of Court life would lead to revolution, perhaps even to invasion when other countries realized that France beneath the brittle glamour was such a feeble, festering muck-heap. The *Chambre Ardente* and its literal witch-hunts had to be played down, and was never even mentioned by the official *Gazette de France*. The two-faced King helped high-born evil-doers to escape abroad; he suppressed confessions implicating his foul mistress, Madame de Montespan; he could hardly avoid agreeing that La Voisin be tortured to make her talk, but hints from high quarters were conveyed to the officials concerned that for the time being they need not be too rough with her. The former bare-footed fortune-telling beggar-girl had become a factor in State policy.

Eleven months passed and by then the smoke had blown away—the smoke from women screaming at the stake and the smoke from burned confessions inconvenient to *Le Roi Soleil*. It became safe at last to finish off La Voisin, and she was tried and condemned to be burned to death. But first it was usual to try a little preliminary torture, in case a condemned person's memory had been faulty on any small point. So La Voisin suffered four six-hour periods in the torture chamber between 19 and 21 February 1680, but revealed nothing that much mattered excepting about people already condemned. Officially she was given eight wedges of "the Boot", which was supposed to reach the limit of human endurance and should have crushed her plump legs to pulp. But according to de la Reynie the torture was still not properly applied, and not long afterwards La Voisin was back in her cell singing obscene songs and refusing to see a confessor.

On 23 February she went out to execution, roughly shoving aside a priest who held a crucifix towards her. At the stake she kept trying to kick the straw away, and as the flames blazed up "she swore a great deal" wrote Madame de Sévigné. A priest stated that La Voisin's last words were, "I cannot suffer too greatly for all I have done", which seems a highly improbable remark from such a tough character. But the priest was naturally anxious to report some trace of contrition, and may have misconstrued unfamiliar words she was bawling at him as she burned. Madame de Sévigné's story sounds the more likely.

—G.D.

# 44

# DOROTHEA WADDINGHAM
## The Nightmare Nurse

On the 12th January, 1935, Mrs. Baguely and her daughter, Ada, moved in from Burton Joyce to Nottingham. Mrs. Baguely was eighty-seven years old and Ada Baguely was fifty. Both ladies were in poor health and the reason for their change of residence was their inability to manage a house between them. The old lady was too frail to do anything for herself, and her daughter was a cripple, with a long history of ill-health. They came into the city to live in a nursing home, run by a lady of many names, but at that time operating as "Nurse Sullivan", a widow, who had received some training as a nurse at Burton-on-Trent Infirmary.

The agreed terms were thirty shillings per week each, which, perhaps, was an indication of the kind of "nursing home" it was. The two ladies lived mainly on the income from eight cottages which had been left to Ada by her father.

In February 1935 a cousin, Lawrence Baguely, visited the home to satisfy himself that his relatives were comfortable. It was not quite as he could have wished, but at the price they were paying it was not too bad, and they seemed happy enough.

The "nurse" introduced herself as Nurse Waddingham, not as Sullivan, and told Mr. Baguely that she wasn't satisfied with the amount of money she was receiving, because they caused her considerably more work than she had anticipated and, furthermore, when she had taken them in she had believed them to be poor people who could not afford any more. She told a very good story, but Mr. Baguely pointed out to her that, while they owned a certain amount of cottage property, the rents were small and formed practically their sole income.

Nurse Waddingham then suggested that the two ladies should make over their capital to her, and in return she would keep them as long as they lived. This was not a scheme which appealed to Lawrence Baguely and he would not agree to use his influence with the ladies in persuading them to agree to such a proposal.

Nurse Waddingham had already complained to the manager of the Netherfield branch of the Midland Bank when he had called on 27th January to interview Ada Baguely about her affairs. She had made the same suggestion of transferring the property to her name, but the bank official's reaction was unfavourable and he would have nothing to do with the matter. This had angered Nurse Waddingham and, later, to a Mrs. Wood she had said that if the women did not make over their property to her they would have to go to the Poor Law Institution in Nottingham.

The tenant of the premises was Joseph Sullivan, with whom Nurse Waddingham was living. Early in March, Sullivan called on Messrs. Kirkland and Lane, solicitors, of Southwell, and was seen by one of the partners, Mr. Lane, who had acted for Ada Baguely and her mother for many years. Sullivan told the solicitor that Ada Baguely wished to make a will and that it should be drawn up in favour of Nurse Waddingham and himself. In return, there would be an agreement that Miss Baguely and her mother should remain at the nursing home for the remainder of their lives.

Mr. Lane strongly advised against such a will and Sullivan left the office a disappointed man, a fact which he took little trouble to conceal.

In May, Ada Baguely wrote to Mr. Lane and asked him to visit her at Devon Drive, the nursing home. She seemed so set on making the will that the solicitor had no option but to agree. A will was drawn up in favour of Sullivan and Nurse Waddingham. Dr. G. H. H. Manfield and Mr. B. C. Fernihough, an insurance official, were named as the executors, an honour which neither gentleman knew had been conferred upon him.

The will was dated 7th May, 1935, and witnessed by T. B. Daft, a somewhat appropriate name under the circumstances. It was in favour of Dorothy Nancy Waddingham and Ronald Joseph Sullivan.

In April, Sullivan had gone to the Midland Bank, Netherfield, with a letter signed by Ada Baguely, requesting the bank to hand over to Sullivan certain scripts standing in her name. The manager refused point-blank to do any such thing, no doubt remembering the unfavourable impression he had received when he had called at Devon Drive the previous January. Bank officials do not reach the rank of manager without being extremely shrewd and experienced gentlemen.

On 20th April, the solicitor, Mr. Lane, received a letter signed by Ada Baguely, but written by Sullivan, asking him to bring her bank passbook and conversion bonds to his Nottingham office, where Sullivan would call and collect them. Sullivan called the same day and was given scripts to the value of £150, all the script which stood in Ada Baguely's name.

In June, Mrs. Baguely died; the death certificate, signed by Dr. G. H. H. Manfield, showed the cause of death as cardi-vascular degeneration. After the death of her mother, Ada Baguely's health rapidly became worse and she was practically bedridden. On 11th September she died, from a stroke, and the death certificate showed that as the cause of death.

On 12th September, Dr. Cyril Banks, Medical Officer of Health for the City of Nottingham, contacted the Chief Constable regarding an application for cremation. In his official capacity the M.O.H. is required to agree before any cremation may take place. This particular application raised his suspicion, and small wonder, too. The letter purported to be signed by the person whom it was sought to cremate, an extraordinary document which read:

> "To Dr. Manfield,
> I desire to be cremated at my death, for health's sake. And it is my wish to remain with Nurse and my last wish is my relatives shall not know of my death.
>> Signed,
>> Ada Baguely.
> Witness, R. J. Sullivan."

When the Chief Constable, Captain Athelstan Popkiss, saw the letter he was in entire agreement with the Medical Officer of Health, that it cried aloud for investigation.

The letter was passed to the Nottingham City Coroner and police investigation began forthwith. In a very short time the detective officers had uncovered a sorry story indeed, one which was to lead to a charge of murder.

Nurse "Waddingham" was identified as Nancy Leech, alias Sullivan, alias Chandler and other names. She told the police that at 7.30 p.m. on 10th September, Ada Baguely had complained of feeling very ill. But she had been like this for the past month and Nurse Waddingham was not unduly alarmed at her condition. At 2 a.m. she had visited her patient again and found her unable to speak, although her eyes were open. She noticed a twitch on her left side and stayed with her for a while. Afterwards she and Sullivan visited Ada a number of times during the night and by 9 a.m. Nurse Waddingham was sufficiently anxious to send for Dr. Manfield. However, he was not at his surgery and she failed to contact him. Ada died an hour later.

The police investigation built up such a case against Sullivan and Waddingham that at the inquest the coroner's jury returned a verdict that "Ada Louisa Baguely was murdered by Dorothea Nancy Waddingham and Ronald Joseph Sullivan."

Waddingham and Sullivan were arrested and formally charged with murder.

They came up for trial at the Nottingham Assizes on 25th February, 1936, before Mr. Justice Goddard. They pleaded "Not Guilty". Shortly after the case for the Crown had been presented to the jury, and before Waddingham went into the box to give evidence on her own behalf, Mr. Justice Goddard dismissed Sullivan from the case. In his opinion there was not enough evidence to justify the charge being retained against Sullivan. So Sullivan was discharged and the case proceeded against Waddingham alone.

Medical evidence of the post-mortem examination was given. In Ada Baguely's stomach had been found 2.59 grains of morphine and 3.192 grains in her other organs. The minimum known fatal dose was only .25 of a grain, although the generally accepted fatal dose was 1 grain. Cremation would, of course, have totally destroyed this evidence.

Dr. Frank Jacob, who had attended Ada Baguely for over twenty years prior to her coming to the nursing home, stated that she was suffering from progressive disseminated sclerosis. On 27th August he had visited her and in his opinion her expectation of life at that time was from one to three years. There was nothing to suggest that she was in any immediate danger of death.

Waddingham had not been very happy about Dr. Frank Jacob. Perhaps she thought he knew too much. On 18th May, a niece of Mrs. Baguely, Mrs. Ayres, had called at the nursing home to see Ada Baguely. In the course of conversation she was told by Waddingham that she and Sullivan had taken over control of Ada and that she had made a will in their favour. Mrs. Ayres was a little worried by this information as she was not favourably impressed by either of them. She made it her business to ask Ada Baguely, in the presence of Waddingham, if she was in contact with Lawrence Baguely, and if he came to see her. To this Ada had replied, "No, we don't want to see him."

Waddingham had said then: "He is too interfering. He has been to Dr. Jacob to try and get him to say that Ada is mentally unfit to attend to her affairs." Waddingham had, in a later conversation, said that relatives could write to Ada if they wished, but that all letters would be opened and if they were not approved they would not be given to Miss Baguely.

When Lawrence Baguely had visited the nursing home on 7th April he had been informed by Sullivan that mother and daughter were out and in addition they had no wish to see him. Not believing this, he had then written Ada Baguely a letter. To this he was surprised, and doubtless hurt, to receive the following reply:

> *"Dear Lawrence,*
> *I received your letter and can see by the letter you are still in Scotland, but I don't like you saying what you did about Joe, as he is kind itself to me and my*

*mother and he is the only one what done anything for us all through our trouble and he is very upset about it. I am sorry to say that mother is very ill indeed and it is through all this worrying and talking that done it. So, would you mind sending your bill along as I want to settle everything up, as you no need to worry about me as I am quite all right and comfortable, and quite able to manage my own affairs as the solicitors have got everything in hand and want me to get all my bills so I can settle up."*

This letter was itself poor repayment to a man who had been so anxious about his relatives. But it was the postscript which carried the sting. This was written in Sullivan's hand, and read:

*"I should like to know what you mean about that chap you call Joe. If you ever cross my path you will know what that means. There is always straightforwardness carried on here, mark my words, we know what you have been trying to do, but if you are not careful you will regret it, so keep your eyes open in future and Miss Baguely is quite aware that I am writing this."*

Joe, of course, was Sullivan. It is little wonder that Mr. Baguely went to consult Dr. Jacob after receiving such a letter.

Counsel for the Prosecution dealt with the cremation letter, that fatal document which had brought all this to public light. He pointed out to the jury that the original letter had ended with the word "Nurse", and that the words "and my last wish is my relatives shall not know of my death" had been added later. The space between "Nurse" and Ada Baguely's signature had not been adequate and the writing had perforce to be a little crushed.

Sullivan's explanation, given to a police officer, was that the letter had been written by him at Miss Baguely's request and that after he had written "I desire to be cremated at my death for health's sake and it is my wish to remain with Nurse," he had written the word "Signed", but that when Miss Baguely saw it she had said: "I do not want any of my relatives to know of my death. I should very much like you to put that in, if you can get it in that small space." He had accordingly added that and Miss Baguely had then signed the letter.

Dr. Manfield, to whom the letter was addressed, had never seen it until after Ada's death, when he was then shown it by Sullivan. But Waddingham had told Dr. Manfield before Ada's death that Ada wished to be cremated and had asked him how to go about it. To which he had replied, "As Ada is under your care, I advise you to get her to write a letter desiring cremation."

Waddingham elected to give evidence on her own behalf. On 24th September, 1935, she had made a statement to the police that she had never given Ada Baguely morphia and that she had never had any in the nursing home. She said: "The only morphia I have had in the house was for Mrs. Kemp, who was a patient with me, and Dr. Manfield used to give me two, sometimes four, tablets, which I used to inject at night at eight o'clock. Mrs. Kemp died on 26th February, 1935, and I had none of these tablets left two days before she died. Dr. Manfield also left some tablets for Mrs. Harewood, also a patient of mine, which I believe were morphia. But they did not suit her and Dr. Manfield took them away. Miss Baguely made a will in favour of me and Sullivan, and I wish she had not. I think it is the will that is causing all the upset."

In her evidence Waddingham stated that on 27th August she had told Dr. Manfield of her patient's increasing pain and he had promised to prescribe a more effective medicine and had given her the prescription. In addition, on that same day, he had given her (Waddingham) six tablets to be given to Ada if the pain increased, but he had not said what the tablets were.

She said that on 2nd September the doctor had given her four more of the same tablets, which he had taken from his jacket pocket. By the 6th September she decided that the new medicine was not doing any good and she gave Ada two of the tablets that the doctor had left with her on the 2nd. She had followed these with two more on each day after, because the pain was so severe. After Ada had died she had thrown away the medicine glass and all the things which the patient had been using because she "did not fancy them".

Dr. Manfield's evidence was in sharp conflict with that of Nurse Waddingham and he denied most of the statements she had made about him.

The judge dealt with this very fully when he made his summing-up. He said that the jury had to consider three things: had the Crown proved that the prisoner administered that poisonous drug to Ada Baguely; if it had, had it proved that the drug was feloniously administered; and did Ada's death result therefrom?

The prisoner's case was this: "True, I administered what I believed to be morphia and what I do not dispute was morphia, but I gave it in the exercise of the discretion given me by the doctor, who himself left in my care ten tablets to be administered at my discretion, and I administered them. I have done nothing wrong."

The judge went on to say that there had been acute conflict of evidence between Dr. Manfield and the prisoner as to the administration of morphia and it seemed to him therefore that the jury must give considerable weight to the visit made by Dr. Frank Jacob at the end of the third week of August, because the first time that it was suggested that morphia was mentioned, or that any question of morphia arose between her and Dr. Manfield, according to the prisoner's own account, was on 27th August. Had any great change taken place between Dr. Jacob's visit and Dr. Manfield's visit?

Why was it that by 27th August there had been such a change in the condition as to make the administration of morphia necessary, a narcotic which was given to make that class of pain bearable which would otherwise be unbearable?

The prisoner stated that on 27th August Dr. Manfield gave her six tablets which she knew to be morphia. Dr. Manfield had denied this, saying that there was nothing in the patient's condition which would have led him to leave morphia for her. If the jury accepted Dr. Jacob's evidence they might think it exceedingly difficult to believe that such a change had taken place in the woman's condition since his visit a week previously, and that it would ever enter the mind of the doctor that morphia might be administered.

On the vital day, 10th September, according to Waddingham, she had given Ada Baguely a meal consisting of pork, baked potatoes, kidney beans, and two portions of fruit pie.

"Would anybody," asked Mr. Justice Goddard, "using their own common sense, think that anybody in their senses would give a woman who had been suffering from such severe abdominal pains that morphia had been given for three nights, pork, baked potatoes, fruit pie, during the day? It seems to me an astonishing meal to give any invalid whose pains had been so great for three nights that morphia had been administered. Is it true that she had such a meal? We have only the prisoner's word for it. If it be true that she had it, will you, members of the jury, believe the story that she was suffering from acute abdominal pain on days before and had had to have morphia for that reason? If it is not true, is it put forward as a possible reason why Ada died?"

Dr. Manfield had certified that Ada Baguely died of a stroke. Of this the judge said that the doctor proved to be wrong, but no blame could be attached to him. When a person died of a stroke a doctor could only act on what he was told. Dr. Manfield had been told by the prisoner that Ada had suffered from strokes before.

Nurse Waddingham was found "Guilty" and she was duly sentenced to death.

She appealed, and on 30th March the case came before the Court of Criminal Appeal. The ground of appeal was a familiar one which had come before the Court on many occasions. The complaint was that Mr. Justice Goddard had put the case to the jury on the basis that their verdict must be one of guilty of murder or an acquittal. It was agreed that the question of manslaughter had not been put forward by the defence, but it was contended that there was sufficient evidence to warrant the judge leaving that issue to the jury, and the possibility of an alternative verdict of guilty of manslaughter should have been left in.

The Lord Chief Justice, giving judgment, said that however diseased Ada Baguely might have been, morphia must have been the cause of her death. The prisoner had made a statement to the police that she had never given any morphia to Miss Baguely and had never had any in the house. In a subsequent effort to explain this statement she had said that she meant she had never given any morphia except on doctor's orders and that the doctor told her to say nothing about the morphia. That was emphatically denied by the doctor. The case for the appellant ultimately was that she had administered morphia according to the directions of the doctor, who had left it in her hands for that purpose. That statement the doctor wholly traversed.

The judge, in a most careful summing-up, presented the facts of the case and began by directing with great emphasis the attention of the jury to various matters which seemed to speak loudly in the appellant's favour. When dealing with the cause of death he had exhibited the evidence on the one side and the other with perfect fairness.

The only complaint with regard to the summing-up was that the judge omitted to tell the jury that they might, if they thought fit, find a verdict of manslaughter. He certainly gave no such direction to the jury, but told them in the clearest and simplest terms that the issue was one of murder or no murder.

The law on this point is perfectly clear. It was stated in Rex v. Thorpe:

"If there is no evidence on which a verdict of man-slaughter can properly be found, it is the duty of the judge not to leave the question of manslaughter to the jury, but if there is evidence, it is the duty of the judge to leave the question to the jury, notwithstanding that it has not been raised by the defence and is inconsistent with the defence which is raised."

The Lord Chief Justice went on to say:

"It was said in the present case that it was the duty of

the judge to leave the question to the jury, but that was the judge's duty if there were evidence which warranted such a verdict. In the opinion of this Court there is not a tittle of evidence in the present case to warrant such a verdict. The argument of Counsel for the appellant really amounted to the contention that the judge, exercising a scientific imagination, ought to have conjectured that the jury might conceivably invent a new case which was not supported by a tittle of evidence. The law was not so absurd as that.

"There was no evidence here on which any reasonable man could find a verdict of manslaughter and the judge was right in not bewildering the minds of the jury with so false an issue. The appeal must therefore be dismissed."

Nancy Leech, alias Dorothy Waddingham, alias Chandler, had gambled with her life and lost. It is a story of low cunning, greed, and stupidity, but one which might well have had a different ending. But for the alertness of the Medical Officer of Health and the prompt action of the Chief Constable of Nottingham, Ada Baguely's murder might never have been recognized as such.

From the moment she discovered that these two helpless women possessed some money, although it was little enough for the risk, she determined to grab it for herself. When all else failed she resorted to morphia.

Mrs. Baguely may have died a natural death, she was very old and frail, and the question did not arise, but beyond any shadow of doubt her daughter was killed by morphia administered by the hand of her murderer. The doctor, in all good faith, signed a death certificate stating another and natural cause of death. On the evidence he had he was quite justified in so doing.

This was nearly the perfect murder, but not quite. Over-anxiety on the part of Nurse Waddingham to hide the evidence of her crime led to the writing of that cremation letter, a fatal mistake, an over-elaboration which led straight to the gallows.

Yet many police officers of long experience hold the view that perfect murders are committed with much greater frequency than is ever supposed by the public. Death certificates signed by unsuspecting doctors are the assassins' passport to freedom, and more victims. In some cases the same doctor has been involved in a whole series of murders by poisoning without the least suspicion that he was being hoodwinked by a murderer. It is a sobering thought indeed.

—T.C.H.J.

# 45

# JEANNE WEBER
## A Killer of Children

One of the most extraordinary, because so unexpected, of these female killers is Madame Jeanne Weber, née Moulinet, of whose childish victims we are assured of at least seven, although there must have been others unknown to us. Her long and successful career was based largely on luck and could not possibly be repeated today, although even so recently as 1906, the doctors in the case appear to have been even greater fools than most doctors appear in early trials when society, as yet, could not bring itself to believe that these delicate creatures could be homicidal. Also, she operated with such success largely because she operated at first within the family; and although few members of most families have any illusions about one another's baseness, they would often prefer to suffer even a murderer or murderess to live than to truckle under the disgrace of having police and public prying into their affairs. Besides, it is almost impossible to believe that anybody whom you know intimately can be a murderer—a drunkard, a thief, a bully, a bore, an adulterer, a forger or an incendiary, yes! even these and many other eccentricities can be accepted; but surely, that man or woman with whom you have sat at table and laughed and quarrelled and played games, even made love, cannot be a killer? not really one of those practically mythical monsters who give salt to our breakfasts on Sunday in the newspapers? It was this natural human failing, this deliberate family refusal to open one's eyes to the truth, which not only protected Jeanne but gave her the opportunities of continuing her chosen career.

The drama properly opens on March 2, 1905, although it is more than likely that other little corpses lay already buried in the past. On this March day, Jeanne called on her sister-in-law, Madame Pierre Weber, and volunteered to look after the woman's two children while the mother went to the public wash-house, that same wash-house in which Zola's Gervase fought her heroic battle with Virginie in *L'Assommoir*. Within an hour or two of her scrubbing the family clouts, she was called home by a friend with the news that her daughter, Georgette, was in convulsions. On reaching home, she found the child lying red-faced on the bed, breathing jerkily. Jeanne stood beside the bed, one hand, under the bedclothes, on the child's chest. Soon the mother had little Georgette smiling again, out of bed, away from Jeanne, and on her lap. Then she hurried back to finish her washing and Jeanne took up the child once more. Georgette was dead before Madame Weber returned again.

It was a neighbour, watching with the open eyes of a suspicious friend untouched by family loyalties, who noted strange markings on Georgette's throat and who pointed them out to the father. He said he would do something about it, but doubtless with indignation he silently dismissed the woman's base suspicions of anyone in the family. The child was buried, and nine days later, her sister, little Suzanne, also died with a purple face. Again was Jeanne alone with the child and again the same shrewd neighbour noticed the tell-tale markings around the throat—a long bruise under a scarf that had been wound about it. This time the doctor was notified and he summoned the police. But the police took no action and without protest Suzanne was buried.

Two weeks later, on March 25, infant mortality again appeared in the Weber family group. Madame Leon Weber's seven-months-old Germaine was left in Jeanne's care while Madame Leon went shopping. Luckily, the woman's mother was in the apartment upstairs, and hearing the baby scream, she hurried down to find Germaine with the same symptoms as her departed cousins and, of course, with Jeanne at her side. Frustrated for the moment by this interference, Jeanne waited until after lunch when she asked her sister-in-law, back from shopping and appallingly unsuspicious after her baby's recent escape, to buy her some cheese, as she didn't feel well enough to go out at the moment. Madame Leon returned just in time to save her child who lay in convulsions, and with Jeanne's hand pressed on her chest. Jeanne, however, did not intend to be cheated of her pleasure for the second time. The following day, back to the attack she went and again she persuaded her sister-in-law to do her shopping for her. Now, determined not to be baulked, she acted expeditiously and when the mother came back, her child was on the point of coughing to death. This third interruption was too exasperating for the murderess to tolerate. Only after a fight was the mother able to drag her from the bed; then she rushed for salts and vinegar as possible restoratives. Again was Jeanne alone with the baby; and when the mother and a friend returned, Germaine at last lay dead.

Suspicion must have been beginning to sprout even in these simple folk and Jeanne attempted to stifle it as efficiently as she had stifled the babies—or, more probably, the joy to be found in killing the helpless had grown uncontrollable—for that night her own seven-year-old son died in almost the same way as the others. Perhaps the pleasures of killing had become an obsession that ousted mother-love and thought of retribution. Alone with her own little Marcel, Jeanne stretched out her hands . . .

She was a drunkard, and drink can lessen the will. In that lies its danger. What is long controlled may take the opportunity to escape into action when the drunkard is—to use that old and excellent phrase—'disguised in liquor'. In Jeanne's life we can follow the slow growth towards murder and trace it back to its sources; and drink became to her a refuge, blotting away memory while fostering resentments. But the resentments were what turned her to drink: drink did not breed the resentments; therefore it cannot be blamed for the killings any more than a doubtful book can be blamed for the harlot's life.

The deaths of her own children had first set Jeanne on the road to murdering other women's children. One of eight born in semi-poverty, the daughter of a fisherman in a small French village, she had left home at the age of fourteen to earn her living as a servant. After her going, the family never saw or heard of her again until she had made her name notorious. No sign was there of the future murderess in the obedient little servant; and soon she began a wandering existence, shifting from job to job in a hopeless search for the perfect job, until she reached Paris and married Marcel Weber. Now followed a few years of happiness. It would have seemed then that the discontented girl would settle into a commonplace wife; and as one need not doubt she would have done had her two daughters not died, leaving her with an only son. At this disaster, Jeanne took to drinking. Happiness fled with those deaths and there is no reason whatever to believe that she had murdered these children. Only, after this cruelty from heaven, she looked with hating eyes on life, intent upon revenge, her rancorous jealousies of luckier mothers heated by wine and raw spirits—it is the era, remember, of Zola's mighty *L'Assommoir*—and she was remarked on as often falling into melancholy fits of brooding. And in these fits, brooding on God's injustice, she saw her sisters-in-law fat and happy mothers with their babies. Therefore those babes of theirs had to die.

Revenge first provoked pleasure in the deed. After having begun to kill, the impulse to kill again became overpowering until Jeanne had to feel and watch even her own son under her hand. Beyond all control had now become this terrible itch; and when Madame Charles Weber arrived from Charenton to visit her relations and brought with her her ten-months-old Maurice, Jeanne set again to work. While lunching with Madame Charles and Madame Pierre, she sent Madame Pierre to buy some wine and Madame Charles to buy her some needles. Once she was alone with the child, Jeanne became busy; and the doctor, summoned by the child's hysterical mother, noticed blackish markings around the throat.

Now could the family no longer hide from the truth. The coincidence of so many infants' deaths occurring only when Jeanne was alone with the children made them wonder whether she might not be a murderess. Even the doctor became suspicious. He sent the dead body to a hospital that a post-mortem might determine the cause of death.

Jeanne was arrested and on January 29, 1906, she stood her trial, only to be acquitted because of the footling medical evidence. The bodies of the other two children, Georgette and Suzanne, had been exhumed and examined. Yet in the witness-stand the doctor, the expert witness, airily dismissed the possibility of there having been any murder. He was an important man in his profession, a professor of the faculty of medicine in

Paris, but he scoffed away the idea that these children could have been strangled. Altogether, seventeen other doctors also swore that they could find no proofs of murder; and amidst applause from the court, Jeanne was unloosed, her husband leaping over benches to clasp her in his arms.

"I didn't kill them," she cried to him. "Say that you believe me now!"

Even murder can grow monotonous to the reader, although never to murderer or murderess, when it repeats itself exactly, as it usually does, the murderer being very conservative and distrustful of new methods of work. Nevertheless, we must follow Jeanne to her own terrible end, so perfect a specimen is she of this type of killer.

Next she appears as a housekeeper the following year at Chambon in the family of the Bavouzets who had three children, two girls and a boy. The boy, aged seven, died, and Jeanne grumbled at the doctor because, had he come earlier, she said, he might have saved the child; and when the doctor remarked on the curious fact that the boy was wearing a clean nightgown which had obviously not been slept in, Jeanne confessed that she had taken away the soiled one because the boy had vomited while dying. Suspecting the truth, the doctor reported to the police; and again Jeanne stood her trial; and again was she freed, thanks to the conflicting medical evidence.

A certain philanthropic M. Blonjean had been so touched by her martyrdom that he set her in a child-murderess's paradise, in a children's infirmary, where she was surrounded by tempting subjects, like a vixen in a chicken-run. Soon out of a job she was again, having been caught just in time with her hands around a child's throat. For the sake of the infirmary's reputation, the sentimental good man hushed the scandal, nobody liking to confess that, when *compos mentis*, he had appointed such a notorious woman to such a post.

One cannot believe that the pleasures of killing were waning, but, most likely, Jeanne missed the éclat of a trial and resented being pushed out like this in disgrace without any extra renown. For she went to the police, and, cunningly, confessed to only the killing of the Webers' children. Having been acquitted of these crimes, she knew that she could not be tried for them again. So she opened her mouth and had the self-glorious satisfaction of confession, realizing before her enemies, the police, that urge which is always pressing behind the murderer's teeth, the need to purge the soul and to relive and exult in brute achievements. Only after such a catharsis can he throw off Christian's burden and walk with angels and trumpets into paradise.

"I want to confess," Jeanne told the police; but she did not fully confess. Just as the drunkard, in remorse, will swear never to drink again even while he has a bottle concealed in the wardrobe, Jeanne relieved her mind and relived her acts by telling how she had slain her three nieces and nephew; beyond that, she would not talk. When the police pressed for details about later victims, she withdrew; she had not murdered them, she said. Hyde had returned to reject the miserable Jekyll, and Jeanne defied all questioning. Thus was her conflict resolved for a time: her guilt had been expressed, expiated and her conscience cleansed.

Now she was able to begin again.

In company with a young cement-worker, she travelled about the country until they reached Commercy and here her companion left her. Jeanne had noticed the landlady's little son and her desires itched alive again. Pleading that she had a fiendishly jealous husband who, should she sleep alone, would be certain to accuse her of infidelity, she asked if she might have the boy to sleep with her.

This time she was caught beyond any possibility of rescue even by the talkative doctors in the box. A lodger at the inn heard sinister gurglings in the night and she ran into Jeanne's bedroom to find her leaning over the little boy. Help was needed from the landlord and his wife before the woman could drag the murderess from her prey.

She had enjoyed her last debauch, save for dreams, and in the asylum in which she was confined, it was noticed that she would crook her fingers around invisible throats until at last they crooked about her own and she was found dead with dried foam on her lips. Unable to find further subjects, she had been reduced to performing on herself, for we may rest assured that was definitely not suicide in a paroxysm of remorse.

Of course Jeanne was mad. Even the specialists who examined her before her first trial suspected lunacy, although they found her calm in manner and logical in speech. Once when she fainted and, on suddenly recovering, complained of giddiness, they diagnosed her condition as hysteria; but hysteria—from the Greek word for "womb"—is an elastic-sided word and can mean very much or very little. They put her neurotic behaviour down to grief at her children's deaths—here, without understanding why, doubtless they were correct—and to that pre-Freudian all-comprehensive mumbo jumbo for any woman who wasn't feeling well: "gynaecological disorders", which meant precisely nothing.

Yes, Jeanne was mad; but so are all mass-murderers when we set them beside the norm of sanity—a relative term which, for each of us, has its own moveable point—and so can be classified any genius in any form of self-expression. But what interests us in Jeanne is her inability to learn, her cravings proving stronger even than her self-protective instinct. Typical is this of these creatures of bad habits, repeating, until crushed by an outraged society, their automatic deeds as of a machine.

At least she did not bother to conceal, even from herself, that she killed for the pleasure of killing, and that is as unusual in murderesses as it is in murderers.

—P.L.

# 46

# KATE WEBSTER
## Dead Woman's Shoes

---

Kate Webster was born in Ireland, and it is obvious from her subsequent history that she must have kissed the Blarney Stone at a very early age. The agility of her tongue was only equalled by the fervidness of her imagination and powers of invention. From lying she took to stealing. The laws in Ireland are obviously stricter than ours, for we find her being sent to prison at the tender age of fourteen for larceny.

On her release she made her way to Liverpool. Sea ports are notorious for their criminal element, and Liverpool in the early 1890s was no exception to the rule. Vice and crime were rampant along the water-front. Kate took to it all like a duck taking to water. Hers was a rough, coarse beauty, which only attracted the lower types of men, and admirers she had in plenty. She led a riotous life until the age of eighteen when she was again caught stealing, and sentenced to eighteen months' imprisonment.

The eighteen months in prison must have had a sobering effect on her, for on coming out of prison she actually took up honest employment. But this was not to last long. Within a few months she was in trouble again—trouble of a different nature this time. An illegitimate child was the outcome of her escapade. Motherhood, however, did not serve as a steadying influence in her case. She was, in fact, heard to remark that it would be an excellent joke if she abandoned her tiny offspring on some doorstep, with a note pinned to its breast stating that the father was a certain Mr. Harris, the town's most prominent and highly respected citizen.

The records show that she did not carry out her threat to desert the child, and in the six years that followed they gypsied all over the country, living on scraps and the proceeds of her petty thieving. What happened to the child whilst she served another two sentences in prison is not known, and it can only be surmised that she left him in the tender care of one of her less disreputable friends.

The scene now shifts to Richmond where we find Kate and her little son living with a certain Mrs. Crease, and it was this same Mrs. Crease who was instrumental in getting her a position as housekeeper to an elderly little woman named Mrs. Thomas. Mrs. Crease must have given her a glowing account of Kate; either that, or Mrs. Thomas was an exceedingly trusting and kindly person, for she engaged Kate on the spot, without troubling to go into her antecedents or references.

Mrs. Thomas was a widow, but comparatively well off for all that, and lived in a nicely furnished little villa not far from the river. She was neat and tidy in her appearance and liked her house kept in the same fashion. Kate made a great show of her enthusiasm for the work, and Mrs. Thomas must have congratulated herself on her find. Kate worked and sang with a zest; her sparkling wit and lilting brogue intrigued and delighted the good lady. Kate was indeed a treasure, she thought happily.

But not for long. True to type, Kate soon tired of respectability. Her work became slovenly; she absented herself for long periods, and returned intoxicated and recalcitrant. She augmented her income by purloining various household articles and pawning them. And when Mrs. Thomas attempted to remonstrate with her, she was rewarded with a stream of abuse.

The altercations between them grew more violent as the days passed, for what Mrs. Thomas lacked in size she made up for in temper. Late one Sunday afternoon saw them almost coming to blows. Trembling with indignation, Mrs. Thomas left the house threatening to have her prosecuted. The walk to the police station must have given her sufficient time to calm down, for instead of carrying out her threat, the devout woman went to church instead.

She returned home prepared to forgive Kate, but Kate was in no mood for such pleasantries. Using all the vile names she could think of, she berated the old lady all the way up to her room. Mrs. Thomas kept her temper in check as long as was humanly possible, and then turned on her furiously. "Get out of my house, you—you harlot!" she screamed. "Get out before I have you charged for theft. If you are not out of the premises within five minutes I shall call the police!" and slamming the door of her room, she started to remove her hat and things.

"I'll show her," muttered Kate, her voice thick with hate; "call me a harlot, would she! I'll—I'll . . ." Her eyes fell on an axe lying on the kitchen floor. "I'll kill her, that's what I'll do!" and snatching the axe up, she mounted the stairs towards Mrs. Thomas's room, mouthing horrible threats and curses.

Bursting open the door she advanced on the terror-stricken old lady, axe in hand. Cowering against the wall, she attempted to plead, to reason with the mad creature facing her. The vicious grin on Kate's face only broadened, and raising the axe she struck Mrs. Thomas on the head. The blow was only a glancing one, and Mrs. Thomas, although dazed, endeavoured to push past her and so escape her horrible fate. Kate, however, forestalled her, and with a vicious push, sent her flying, head over heels down the stairs. And as she lay there seriously injured and only partially conscious, Kate seized her by the throat and throttled her. Not content with this, she proceeded to finish her off with the axe.

Covered with the blood of her victim, she entered the kitchen, and seizing a meat saw and a large knife, returned to the scene of the crime and coolly and methodically began to dismember the still warm body of her erstwhile mistress. This done, she spent the greater part of the night burning such parts of the body that could be destroyed by fire in the kitchen grate. The rest she made up into neat parcels with the intention of dropping them in the river as soon as possible. In her haste to dispose of the body, she almost forgot to remove the few pieces of jewellery that adorned the body, but she rectified the mistake in good time, and even went so far as to remove her victim's gold teeth, not because they might help to identify the body, but because she hoped to be able to pawn them at a later date. Such was the soul of Kate Webster.

Morning found her removing all traces of her crime from the stairs and the rest of the house. And such was her self-possession, that when the various tradesmen made their calls, they found nothing in her behaviour to arouse their suspicions; indeed they found her most entertaining and lively.

Her ghoulish task completed, she dressed herself in the dead woman's best clothes and jewellery, and purloining what loose cash she could find in the house, ventured out, carrying with her a large black bag. She made quite an imposing picture in all her fineries—a model of propriety, in fact—but snugly reposing in that black, shiny bag she carried was the severed head of her victim! It was her intention to dispose of it in the river when dusk came; but in the meantime her vanity prompted her to call on some friends so that she could impress them with her fine clothes and jewellery.

Her friends were indeed impressed with her finery, and over a cup of tea, Kate gave them to understand that she had come into some money and property recently. And whilst she chatted with them so freely and gaily, the black bag with its horrible contents reposed, innocently enough, at her feet. The callousness and self-possession of the woman has no equal in the annals of crime.

Her friends escorted her part of the way home, and as they drew near the river, she excused herself for a moment. When she rejoined her friends she was without her bag. "You've lost your bag," her friends exclaimed. "I left it at Mrs. Brophy's down the road," explained Kate. "The poor soul is in desperate need of some warm winter clothing and the like, so I thought I'd treat her to some." "How very kind of you," remarked her friends. Kate smirked back at them, secure in the knowledge that the bag was in actuality somewhere at the bottom of the river.

The following morning she brazenly contacted a furniture dealer and arranged for him to collect the furniture. She was disposing of the premises she explained, and wished to sell the furniture at the same time. But what Kate did not know was that the house was only rented to Mrs. Thomas, and when it came to the ears of the landlady a few mornings later, that a furniture van was outside Mrs. Thomas's place, and that the furniture was going out and not coming in, she naturally became rather suspicious as to the intentions of her tenant, and immediately hurried round there.

"What's going on here?" she demanded, confronting Kate.

"And what business is that of yours?" retorted Kate.

"I happen to be the landlady, that's what, and I want to know why Mrs. Thomas is moving out without giving notice?"

Kate was at a loss for words for a moment. This was an eventuality she had certainly not prepared for. "I—er . . ." she stuttered: "Mrs. Thomas is not . . . er . . . moving—she's just changing the furniture, that's all."

"Where is she?" demanded the landlady, not at all satisfied with the explanation. "I want to speak to her."

"She's out," muttered Kate, edging away from the door.

"Then I'll call again," snorted the other, "and in the meantime that furniture had better go back into the house. Nothing is to leave the premises, you understand; not until I've seen Mrs. Thomas herself!"

Kate waited for her irate form to disappear out of sight, and hurriedly made herself scarce, taking with her what valuables she could lay her hands on. She had already taken the precaution of spreading the rumour that she and Mrs. Thomas were going on a visit to Scotland; and when the landlady returned to find no trace of them, she informed the police, who immediately contacted their colleagues up North, requesting word of Kate's arrival.

Whilst her movements were being tracked, numerous gruesome discoveries were made in the river at Richmond. Boxes and parcels containing human remains were washed up at various points; but it was not until Kate was arrested in Ireland, wearing her late mistress's clothing, that the police connected the disappearance of Mrs. Thomas with the remains found in the river.

Kate had cunningly returned to the place of her birth in the hopes that the police would tire of their search for her in Scotland and drop the whole matter. She might have indeed escaped detection had she not been foolish enough to enter into correspondence with one of her paramours in Richmond. He was heard boasting of his acquaintanceship with the wanted woman in a tavern, and was immediately brought in for questioning.

Kate made a great show of innocence on her arrest, pretending to know nothing of her mistress's whereabouts or fate. The clothing and jewellery, she insisted, were a parting gift from Mrs. Thomas. They had parted on the best of terms, and nothing the police could say could shake her story.

On being confronted with her paramour, she immediately accused the befuddled fool of having committed the crime. Unfortunately for her, he proved that he was out of London at the time of the murder. In that case, declared Kate, the inveterate liar that she was, it was another of her friends who perpetrated the deed—none other than the husband of the woman she called on before disposing of the black bag. Lying statement after lying statement followed, only to be refuted time and time again.

She was brought to trial at the Old Bailey, where she again reiterated her belief that it was one of her paramours who murdered her mistress. She had quarrelled with one of them, she explained innocently, and he, mistaking her mistress for her, had killed the old woman. On finding out his mistake, he had disposed of the remains in the river. Where was she when this took place? Oh, she was out at the time visiting some friends, and had returned to find her lover already dismembering the body. What was her lover's name, and where was he to be found? She didn't know.

The judge and jury had no difficulty in dismissing her entire testimony as pure invention, and a verdict of "Guilty" was brought in in record time. When asked if she had anything to say before sentence was pronounced on her, she played her last card, declaring that she was pregnant. This was soon disproved, and she was removed to Newgate prison pending her execution.

Kate still refused to believe that she was actually going to be made to pay the full penalty of the law for her crime, and continued to invent fantastic story after fantastic story as to who the real criminal was. She accused all her friends in turn, and when their numbers were exhausted, she resorted to naming anyone and everyone. Her lies and fabrications did not serve to retard the wheels of Justice in any way. She was hanged early one bright summer morning, having confessed her guilt at the last minute.

—M.H.

# 47

# ROSEMARY WEST

## Keeping It in the Family

---

### I

The woman in the dock looks unremarkable. She could be the school-dinner lady, the woman behind the supermarket checkout, the neighbour who nods and smiles when you pass her in the street. Middle-aged, shortish, bespectacled and plump, she seems absurdly out of place in the main dock of Winchester Crown Court, this massive concrete structure built for trying terrorists and other high-risk prisoners. She is Rosemary West, widow of the late Fred West, and she is charged with ten separate counts of murder. They are murders of the most cruel and sickening nature. What on earth happened?

### II

She was born in the English west-country village of Northam in November 1953. Her father, Bill Letts, was an ex-Navy man now doing low-paid casual work when he could get it and struggling to bring up his growing family. Bill was not just a strict disciplinarian: he was a domestic tyrant who beat his wife and children whenever they displeased him, and often for no apparent reason at all. Rose's brother Andrew later recalled life under their father's regime:

> *If he felt we were in bed too late, he would throw a bucket of cold water over us. He would order us to dig the garden, and that meant the whole garden. Then he*

*would inspect it like an army officer, and if he was not satisfied, we would have to do it all over again. [. . .] We were not allowed to speak and play like normal children. If we were noisy, he would go for us with a belt or chunk of wood. He would beat you black and blue until mum got in between us. Then she would get a good hiding.*

After Bill's death it emerged that at an early age he had been diagnosed as a violent schizophrenic, but he had never sought or received treatment for this condition, which caused him problems at work and ran unchecked at home, becoming increasingly savage as time went by.

Unsurprisingly his wife Daisy developed problems of her own, which reached crisis point after the birth of Andrew, her fourth child. At first it seemed like post-natal depression, but it soon developed into a fully-blown nervous breakdown and she became an out-patient of the psychiatric unit of Bideford General Hospital, where her condition was deemed so serious that she might benefit from ECT (Electro-Convulsive Therapy), in which severe electric jolts are passed through the patient's brain. She underwent this treatment six times in all while pregnant with her fifth child, born shortly afterwards: Rosemary.

Daisy doted on the new arrival, but it soon became clear that Rose was an odd baby. For hours on end she would rock herself to and fro in her cot, and if she was left in a pram her movements could propel the pram across the room. As she grew into a toddler Rose developed a habit of swinging her head from side to side, again for hours at a time, until she seemed to attain a trance-like state. Her brother and sisters considered her slow and stupid and usually left her out of their games, nicknaming her "Dozy Rosie". She was a pretty child, however, with curly brown hair and big brown eyes, and achieved something that none of the other children had managed: to make herself her father's pet and thereby avoid much of his wrath.

At school, Rose was a slow learner and developed a tendency to chubbiness which brought ill-natured teasing from the rest of the class, from whom she became isolated. She defended herself against their mockery, however, and as she progressed up the school she began bullying and tormenting younger children, seeming to relish her new image as someone not to be trifled with. By now the family had moved to Bishop's Cleeve, a village five miles from Cheltenham, where Bill was working for Smith's Industries and earning something like a decent wage. This had not improved his temper, however, and his assaults on the members of his family became even more grotesque: he would beat them with his fists, or pick up a knife—even an axe—to them, and inflicted harsh punishments on the children without rhyme or reason. Rose now had a younger brother, Graham, with whom she shared a bed. Puberty came early to Rose and she quickly became obsessed with sex, walking around the house naked and masturbating Graham, who was too young to understand what was happening. But Bill forbade her to date boys her own age and, in any case, her temperament and lumpishness deterred the local boys from taking much of an interest, and so she transferred her attention to older men. She later claimed that one of them raped her after offering her a lift in his car.

In January 1968, when Rose was fourteen, a fifteen-year-old girl named Mary Bastholm disappeared in nearby Gloucester. She had been waiting at a bus stop with a Monopoly set under her arm, on the way to visit her boyfriend. All that the police found at the bus stop were a few pieces from the Monopoly set. She had worked as a waitress at the Pop-Inn café, where one of the regular customers was a young workman called Fred West. The disappearance was thought to be linked to several rapes in the area, and a massive police search was launched. Rose and other local girls began to fear for their safety, but the investigation drew a complete blank.

A year later, Daisy had finally had enough of Bill and went to live with her married daughter Glenys, taking Rose with her. Freed from her father's restraints, Rose now went out a great deal and carried on affairs with several men, most of them a good deal older than she was. She sometimes worked for Glenys's husband Jim, running a roadside snack-bar which was often closed when Jim returned to it in the evening, with Rose emerging in a rather bedraggled state from one of the parked lorries. Jim claimed that Rose had once even tried to seduce him. Exactly what prompted Rose to go back to her father is not clear even now, and it surprised all the family, but after a few months back she went. There were rumours of an incestuous relationship, and at one stage the local social services became involved at Rose's request, but the precise nature of these events is not known.

One thing that is known is that Bill had been nagging Rose to get a proper job, and—again to the family's surprise—she did, as a waitress at a tea shop in Cheltenham. After work, no doubt with the memory of Mary Bastholm in mind, she usually avoided waiting at the lonely bus stop and went instead to the central bus station. It was here, in the summer of 1969, that she met Fred West.

## III

The Wests were a family of farm labourers who had lived in and around the Herefordshire village of Much Marcle for generations. Fred was born in 1941. The previous year his mother—also called Daisy—had given birth to a daughter, but the baby had died when it was only a few days old. Fred was a beautiful baby with blond hair and large blue eyes; he quickly became his mother's pet and remained so despite the arrival of six more children over the next ten years. Fred's father, Walter, was a stern man and conditions in their tiny cottage were cramped and impoverished as the family grew during the Second World War, but Fred seems to have got on reasonably well with his father, even looking up to him as a role model. Fred later claimed that his father had sexually abused the female children, on the principle that "I created you, so I can do what I like with you", but this is unsubstantiated.

As Fred grew older his blond hair turned into a brown, curly mop, and his features coarsened. His wide mouth opened to reveal a gap between large, usually dirty, teeth, and his build was short and bandy. He was sometimes taken for a gypsy or even a half-caste boy, though there is apparently no gypsy or Negro blood in the West lineage. He too was a lacklustre student and so unruly that he was frequently caned for his misdemeanours—which often brought Daisy clumping down the road to rebuke the teacher who had dared to strike her beloved boy. This did nothing for Fred's reputation with the other kids. He left school at fifteen and started work as a farm hand, like most of the male Wests before him.

Fred's earliest sexual experiences took place in the fields and meadows surrounding the village with any girl who was game, whatever her age or looks: "We used to dive in the hay, take pot luck and go for it," he remarked later. The other farm-workers found Fred a dull, uncommunicative youth who only came to leering life when a girl walked down the lane. By 1957, the older West boys were seeking their evening entertainment in Ledbury, the nearby market town which boasted a cinema, a milk bar, a youth club and a fish-and-chip shop. Fred cleaned himself up for these trips and became a persistent chatter-up of girls, some of whom found him attractive though others were repelled by his crude talk and aggressive manner. Fred himself was greatly impressed by some of the older boys who bowled into the town square on motorcycles, and he wanted one. After a battle with his mother he eventually got a mauve 125-c.c. James bike and for a while he cut a dash in Ledbury, but it was not long before he was involved in a collision with a girl on a bicycle on a lonely lane; she suffered only minor injuries, but Fred was knocked unconscious and remained in a coma for a week, from which he eventually emerged ("like coming back from the dead") to find that he had many broken bones, including a broken leg which necessitated callipers and a metal shoe, and which left him with a permanent limp. He later claimed that the injuries to his skull had resulted in a steel plate being fitted to it, but that may have been another of his stories. What is certain is that after this head injury his behaviour became even more erratic. The bike was sold.

He had became bored and restless at home, but the summer of 1960 was enlivened when he met a pretty girl from Scotland who was staying with relatives nearby. Catherine Bernadette Costello, nicknamed Rena and often called Reen, was at this stage even more of a handful than Fred. At the age of sixteen she was a practised thief who had frequently been in trouble with the Glasgow police and had spent a period in an approved school. Rena was probably the first girl that Fred had met who was not disgusted by his crude ways, and they soon became inseparable, Rena even tattooed Fred's name onto her arm, using a needle dipped in Indian ink, but the relatives with whom she was staying soon put a stop to these antics, and after a short stay in a flat in Ledbury Rena was obliged to return to Scotland.

For Fred this meant a return to the youth club and badgering the local talent. With one girl he went too far when he chased her half-way up a fire escape and stuck his hand up her skirt. Angrily she turned and hit him, causing him to fall head-first to the concrete floor below. Again he was knocked unconscious, this time for twenty-four hours. His moods and tempers grew still worse.

Early in 1961, Fred and a friend stole a watch-strap and some cigarette cases from a shop in Ledbury, and were apprehended with the stolen goods in Fred's pocket. This led to Fred's first court appearance, where he and his accomplice were fined £4 each. A few weeks later and seemingly out of the blue, Fred was arrested and charged with having sex with a thirteen-year-old girl (Fred was now nineteen), who was now pregnant. Fred was indignant and unrepentant ("Well, doesn't every one do it"), and although he was jailed briefly while bail was arranged he suffered no further punishment, for when the case came to trial the girl refused to give evidence and it was dropped. In the meantime there had been other arrests for theft, and one former girlfriend claims that Fred raped her at this time.

In the summer of 1962, Rena Costello reappeared. She had left Scotland and got herself a job as a waitress in Ledbury. In the intervening period she had not been idle. At the age of sixteen she had taken up prostitution in the streets around Glasgow Central Station and been arrested several times for importuning; she had been convicted of attempted burglary and spent seventeen months in a Borstal, being released just before her eighteenth birthday; she had then tried to get away from her life of crime by starting training to be a nurse, but had soon been arrested and convicted once again for theft; and, last but not least, she had dyed her hair peroxide blonde and become pregnant from a casual liaison with an Asian bus driver. She and Fred immediately took up where they had left off.

The Wests scarcely approved—they had thrown Fred out the year before because they felt shamed by his behaviour, but after a few weeks they had relented and taken him back: this was probably the last straw—so Fred and Rena married secretly in a Register Office and moved immediately to Scotland. Rena's baby was born in March 1963 and named Charmaine. Since Fred was all too obviously not the baby's father, they said that Rena's own baby had been born dead and that they had adopted a mixed-race child.

To describe the marriage of Fred and Rena as tempestuous is to put it mildly. There were many other women in this complicated ménage, and Rena had other lovers besides Fred, but one name came to figure more prominently than the others in this story: that of Anna McFall, another Glasgow girl with a troubled home life who found a haven at Fred and Rena's flat and became infatuated with Fred.

Fred got a job driving an ice-cream van, which he evidently enjoyed and which gave him endless opportunities to meet young women. By now he had started spinning unlikely, boastful yarns about himself, but since he seemed amiable and funny and carried a supply of sweets to dole out free to regular customers he made many conquests. This did not curb his sexual demands on Rena however, which were usually brief and brutal, and which she came to resent. Nonetheless, she became pregnant by Fred, and in 1964 bore him a daughter whom they called Anna Marie.

Fred doted on the new baby, and for a while things seemed to be settling down to some sort of pattern. Fred even got himself an allotment, where he spent a great deal of time when he was not doing his ice-cream round, but although he carefully weeded and raked the soil there didn't seem to be much in the way of crops: just a row of them down one side of the plot. When people remarked on this he would say that he was preparing the rest for "something special". Then there was an accident with the ice-cream van. With children constantly clustering round the vans such mishaps were not uncommon, but the boy that Fred knocked over was killed. There were no charges, but Fred felt that the atmosphere had soured and he feared reprisals, so he decided to get out of Glasgow and back to Much Marcle. Rena was unwilling to go with him at first, so Fred took the children back to the family cottage, where he had to sleep on a couch in the front room, but after a while Rena did follow him, and they set up home in a caravan park not far away. Fred got a job in an abattoir—a portent, perhaps, of things to come—but the relationship was no more stable than before with Rena frequently going back to Glasgow, and on one of her trips she brought back with her Anna McFall.

A curious phase now began, with three women (Anna's friend, Isa, had come with her) and two children with Fred in this tiny caravan, and tensions soon appeared. The women were often left to their own devices while Fred drove the carcass-wagon around, and two of them had to sleep as best they could on the tiny couch in the caravan's lounge area. Rena soon decided that she wanted to return to Glasgow and to take the children with her, but Fred would not part with them so she went alone, returning a few weeks later to find Fred and Anna living as a couple.

Rena was outraged, and spitefully stole some of Anna's belongings. She stole from other women too, but these thefts were reported and Rena fled back to Scotland to try and avoid arrest. The Gloucestershire police sent Constable Helen Savage to fetch Rena, and she listened to Rena's tale of woe on the way back: it was the first she had heard of Fred West, but not the last.

Rena was put on probation for three years, and Anna McFall became pregnant by Fred. Anna wanted Fred to divorce Rena and marry her. Fred did not want to lose the existing children nor for Rena to find out about this new pregnancy. It was a complicated situation, with Fred under pressure from all sides . . .

Anna McFall disappeared from the caravan site in July 1967. There was a police inquiry in the course of which Fred was questioned, but she was not traced and no charges were brought. There were several other violent assaults on young women in Gloucestershire around this time, and a fifteen-year-old boy named Robin Holt who had been seen with Fred from time to time was found hanged in a barn; pornographic magazines were found near him, with nooses drawn around the necks of the models.

Shortly after Anna's disappearance Fred got a new job as a labourer on the night shift at a local mill and moved to another caravan site. Rena moved back in with him, and was soon earning extra money as a prostitute. People in neighbouring caravans said that they saw Fred sexually fondling Charmaine, now a toddler. Fred also reverted to his old thieving ways, and changed jobs several times. He was working as a delivery driver for a local bakery when Mary Bastholm vanished from the bus stop in Gloucester, and when he picked up Rose at the bus station.

## IV

They were soon chatting, and when Fred discovered that Rose lived in Bishop's Cleeve, only a short walk from the caravan site where he lived with Rena, they started travelling back there together, and soon began dating. It was not long before Rena walked out on him again, and for a time Fred shared his caravan with a pot-smoking hippy couple, but they became alarmed when Fred started boasting of his prowess as an abortionist and showed them Polaroid photos he had taken of his "clients". They called the police and again questions were asked, but the photos were not illegal in themselves and again no action was taken. The hippies moved on.

That left Fred trying to look after the two children, Charmaine and Anna Marie, on his own, and it was probably the plight of the children that brought Rose to the caravan. A letter from Rose to Fred from this time has survived:

*Dear Fred,*

*I am glad you came to see me. Last night made me realize we are two people, not two soft chairs to be sat on. [ . . .] about us meeting this week, it could be Sunday afternoon. I will have to get Lynda to say I am going out with her. You know we won't be able to meet so often, that's why I can't get the idea out of my head that you are going with someone else. [ . . .] You told my aunt about Rena. But what about telling me the whole story even if it takes all day. I love you, Fred, but if anything goes wrong it will be the end of both of us for good. We will have to go far away where nobody knows us.*

*I will always love you.*

*Rose*

Rose's caution was justified, for when her father Bill discovered that she was sleeping with Fred in the caravan he kicked up a fuss with the social services and personally threatened Fred, and Rose was taken into care—then Fred went to prison for various thefts and for failing to pay the fines for previous convictions, and the children were also taken into care while he served his sentence.

On 29th November, 1969, Rose was sixteen and could no longer be detained by social services. Shortly afterwards she packed her bags and announced that she was going to live with Fred, who had just been released from prison and who had collected Charmaine and Anna Marie on his way home. Rose—little more than a child herself—looked after them as best she could amid the squalor, and the children were frequently sent to live with foster parents. Rena reappeared at this point demanding custody of them, and perhaps met Rose for the first time (Rose would later claim that she never met Rena), but Rena's bid was unsuccessful and she went back to Glasgow. Rose soon found that she was pregnant herself, and Fred, deciding that a caravan was no place for a growing family, found a ground-floor flat that they could rent in Gloucester.

Rose gave birth to a daughter in October 1970, and brought her back to the flat in Midland Road. She was named Heather. Fred worked at various jobs but was soon in trouble with the police again, for theft and a forged tax disk on his car. This time he was sentenced to three months in prison, leaving Rose to look after the three children on her own. She soon began to feel the strain, often taking it out on the two older children, especially Charmaine, now eight, whom she found disobedient and surly. Neighbours said that they had seen Charmaine tied up in Rose's kitchen, and later Charmaine was taken to the local hospital with an injury to her ankle. It was a bleak Christmas for all of them and it looked like being a dismal new year.

The following spring Charmaine went missing. Rose told people that Rena had been to collect her. This was untrue, and it was only a matter of time before Rena herself would come looking for Charmaine, and indeed in August Rena appeared in Much Marcle asking about her daughter. The Wests referred her to Fred, now out of jail, who after some stalling said that he would take her to see her Charmaine. Rena climbed into Fred's car and was not seen again.

Rose, meanwhile, was discovering the delights of prostitution. This had probably started when she was living with Fred in the caravan, taking up where Rena had left off, but from the flat in Midland Road she threw herself into it with great enthusiasm. Gloucester had a sizeable population of West Indians, and West Indian men comprised a large proportion of Rose's clients, though she went with them for pleasure as often as for money. Fred liked to watch, and made a peephole in the door. As sexually obsessed as he was, Fred was personally not much interested in "straight" sex, and there was no tenderness in his own lovemaking—if such it could be called. A fuck from Fred usually lasted less than a minute. For him, sexual excitement meant bondage, acts of sadism or lesbianism: the kinky stuff. Between them, Fred and Rose soon assembled a large collection of dildoes, vibrators, handcuffs, chains and all the rest of the paraphernalia, and Fred took nude photos of Rose which he placed in local magazines for "swingers".

Later that year, Fred and Rose became friendly with a new neighbour, Elizabeth Agius, who sometimes acted as babysitter for them. When Fred and Rose returned home on one such occasion Mrs Agius asked them where they had been, and their answer shocked her: they had been cruising around looking for young girls, hopefully virgins, they cheerfully admitted. Fred said that with Rose in the car a young woman would be more likely to accept a lift, then they could see if she fancied coming to work as a prostitute with Rose. Mrs Agius assumed that they were kidding, but later she was propositioned by both Fred and Rose, and subsequently claimed that on one occasion they had drugged and raped her.

Although Fred's marriage to Rena had never been officially ended Fred and Rose got married in January 1972, and six months later Rose had another daughter by Fred, whom they named May. May West, ha ha. Like most young marrieds, the Wests now decided that they needed a house of their own, and they found one at 25 Cromwell Street, Gloucester.

## V

The area had seen better days and the semi-detached three-storey house was not much to look at, but inside it was surprisingly spacious and it had a long strip of garden, a garage, an attic and a good-sized cellar. Little Anna Marie could not believe that they had it all to themselves, and they didn't for very long as they soon took in lodgers to help pay for it all. The male students must have thought they had landed on their feet when they found that their pretty nineteen-year-old landlady was often willing to jump into bed with them. Elizabeth Agius called by, and Fred showed her round the property, telling her that he was going to turn the cellar into a place for Rose to entertain her clients; either that, or he would soundproof it and use it as his own private torture chamber. What a bullshitter, she thought.

In the event he did the latter, (Rose was allocated the

front room for her activities), and the torture chamber's first victim was Anna Marie, then aged eight, who later said that her father and Rose told her that they were going to help her by making sure that when she was old enough she would be able to satisfy and keep her husband, and that she was lucky to have such thoughtful parents. They then undressed and gagged her, and Rose sat on the girl's face while Fred bound her arms, forced open her legs and raped her. The pain was excruciating. Rose, she said, "was laughing, smirking and saying to me it was for my own good and to stop being silly". Anna Marie couldn't attend school for several days afterwards, and was threatened with a beating if she ever told what had happened.

Once they had settled in, Fred and Rose resumed their pick-ups—for what they had told Mrs Agius had been the simple truth, or some of it. One of the young women that they picked up was seventeen-year-old Caroline Owens, who regularly hitchhiked through Gloucester to visit her boyfriend. She trusted Fred and Rose and told them that she was unhappy at home with her parents, and this produced an invitation to come and live with the Wests at Cromwell Street as their nanny. Caroline would be paid £3 per week, and given a lift home every Tuesday. After discussing it with her parents she accepted Fred and Rose's offer, and moved in the following week. She shared a bedrom with Anna Marie who, she noticed, seemed uneasy in the presence of her parents.

Fred and Rose soon began to shock Caroline with their frank sex talk, especially Fred's yarns about carrying out abortions, and she was astounded to learn that Anna Marie had already lost her virginity—penetrated by the handlebar of a bicycle during a fall, Fred quickly added. Rose was attracted to Caroline and made advances while Fred was out at work. When Caroline realized what she had got into she politely announced that she had had second thoughts about the job and was leaving, but Fred and Rose were not going to let her get away so easily and planned her abduction; they knew her weekly routine, and when they stopped to offer her a lift as they had done before she accepted it gratefully enough. Fred followed the usual route for a while, then turned off the road and stopped the car; Rose started groping Caroline and when she protested Fred turned round and punched her senseless. She was bound and gagged, then taken back to one of the upstairs rooms at 25 Cromwell Street, where her clothes were removed. Rose then started touching, kissing and feeling her up, then held her legs apart while Fred beat her genitals with his leather belt; Rose then performed cunnilingus on her while Fred had sex with Rose from behind. When Rose left the room Fred furtively raped Caroline.

She was left bound and helpless while Fred and Rose slept. In the morning a visitor arrived at the front door, and she tried to make herself heard. She did not succeed, but later Fred was furious with her, snarling, "I'll keep you in the cellar and let my black friends have you, and when we're finished we'll kill you and bury you under the paving stones of Gloucester." Later, Fred was remorseful and said that the whole thing had been Rose's idea, and all done for Rose's pleasure. Would Caroline consider coming back to work for them? She realized that her only hope of escape was to pretend to agree to this astonishing proposal, and managed to slip away later that day. When her mother saw her bruises, she wrung the truth from her and called the police.

The case was heard in January, 1973. Fred was thirty-one and by now an old hand at court procedure. Rose was nineteen, and had just discovered that she was pregnant again. During the hearing Caroline's statements were steadily undermined by the defence until it almost appeared that she had been a willing partner in a harmless bit of fun. Fred casually admitted the charges, but adopted his usual attitude of "So what if I did?". The Wests were fined £25 on each of four charges, and that was the end of the matter. When Caroline heard the verdict it made her feel worthless. At least she was alive, however. Another young woman who came to look after the West children, Lynda Gough, was not seen again. When her mother called at No. 25 to ask after her daughter, Rose told her some vague story about Lynda going off to Weston-Super-Mare, where Mrs Gough then went to make further enquiries. Nothing came of this and the matter was not reported to the police, even though Mrs Gough had noticed that when Rose answered the door to her she was wearing Lynda's slippers.

## VI

The Wests continued to live at 25 Cromwell Street for the next twenty years, and the account that follows must necessarily be a somewhat compressed one. Outwardly, they seemed to the casual glance like any other large working-class family, with Fred bustling about his various jobs—he was always an energetic, even obsessive, worker—and Rose at home looking after her large and still-growing family. She gave birth to her first male child, Stephen, in August, and for the next five years the household comprised Fred, Rose, Anna Marie, Heather, May and Stephen, plus a succession of lodgers.

Fred worked as a jobbing builder and general handyman, and when he wasn't doing these things for other people he was doing them at home. He started by excavating the cellar, which was prone to flooding, deepening the floor and shifting tons of earth by hand until an adult could stand in it. Next he demolished the garage to make way for a new bathroom and a kitchen extension, often working late into the night as he built the walls and laid the concrete floors. The neighbours became used to hearing the sounds of banging and crashing at all hours. The bathroom was finished in time for the arrival of Stephen. The house, at first rented but soon mortgaged, became Fred's pride and joy, and the fact that he stole most of the materials for these improvements from building sites in and around Gloucester no doubt added to his delight in it, since they hadn't cost him anything.

The lodgers in the upper rooms came and went, as lodgers will. The police tried to interview as many as possible of them during the course of their later investigations, and tracked down 150 of them: by no means all. Most of the early lodgers were male and, this being the hippy era, the walls and ceilings of the upstairs rooms were soon daubed with psychedelic colours (which Rose loathed) and the floors spread with mattresses to accommodate a constant stream of visitors and girl-friends. The police were frequent callers too, sometimes investigating drug offences committed by the lodgers and frequently harrying Fred about his constant thieving and fencing, but never suspecting any more serious offences. Fred was no-one's idea of a standard landlord. Although older than his tenants and about as unhip as as it was possible to be (Fred rarely touched alcohol, let alone drugs), he liked to chat with the lodgers, and was in and out of their rooms at all hours of the day and night, rambling on about this and that. What he particularly liked to talk about was, of course, sex: had they had any lately, what was it like, when were they going to have it again . . .? The ones who were offended by this sort of stuff—another odd feature of the

West household was that there were no locks on any of the toilet or bathroom doors—presumably moved on fairly quickly, but most of them seemed to take it in good part, or were too stoned to take much notice.

Rose had not liked the idea of taking in lodgers in the first place, feeling that they would disturb the family's privacy, and although she was friendly enough with most of them she came to resent the constant comings and goings (there could be as many as thirty people in the house on any one night), and came to favour single young women as tenants, preferably unattached ones with no close family ties. They were less troublesome, she felt. One such was Juanita Mott, a teenager from a broken home who came to Cromwell Street in search of a cheap room and who lived there on and off between 1973 and 1975, getting to know Fred and Rose well. She was living with a friend just outside Gloucester when she disappeared. She often went into Gloucester at weekends, hitching a lift on the B 4215—the main route from Much Marcle to the city, which Fred often travelled—and this is what she intended to do on 12th April, 1975. No-one reported her as a missing person, and no inquiries were made as to her whereabouts. She was eighteen when she vanished.

The front room was the one set aside for Rose's own little business. It was Rose's "special room", which had its own separate bell beside the front gate, where she entertained her male friends and clients, some of whom came in response to ads like this one in a local contact mag:

SEXY HOUSEWIFE NEEDS IT
DEEP AND HARD FROM V.W.E.
MALE WHILE HUSBAND WATCHES.
COLOUREDS WELCOME.

In the jargon of this subculture V.W.E. meant "very well-endowed". (In the porn mags and videos—the really heavy ones dealing with bondage and torture, which Fred and Rose now collected avidly—there was another, more obscure abbreviation: S.D.F. It stands for "Slowly Dying Females".) Fred liked to listen as well as to watch, and in addition to making a peephole in the door he rigged up hidden microphones so that he could listen to, and later record, the sounds that emanated from Rose's room, and he liked Rose to make as much noise as possible. She obliged with cries and moans, and the sort of talk that they had picked up from their mags and vids. "Give it to me, big boy." Stuff like that. Later, Fred said that Rose liked to be treated rough ("Rose didn't want the gentle part of it. She wanted some big nigger to throw her down and fucking bang on top of her, and treat her like a dog . . . 'I don't want none of that soppy shit,' she said, 'I want fucking, not fucking about with . . .'; I'd come home from work and she'd sit deliberately on the edge of the settee with her legs wide open and say 'Look at that . . . I bet you wish you had something that could fill that.' "), but as time went by her own cruel streak emerged more strongly. At one stage she would wear a huge weightlifter's belt—the dominatrix look—but it was not just for show: she liked to wet it (to make it sting more) and administer a thrashing to partners both willing and unwilling. Perhaps it was Dozy Rosie's revenge against the world that had mocked and abused her.

For ten solid years, from 1974 to 1984, Fred worked for Gloucester Wagon Works, ten minutes away on the other side of the park, a company which amongst other things made the shells for the trains and carriages of London Undergound. If you've travelled by tube in the last twenty-five years you've probably ridden on some of Fred's handiwork. His main job was drilling holes. He continued his building work and home improvements in the evenings and at weekends. One of the unofficial perks of Fred's regular job was that little bits of metalwork could be done when nobody was looking, and smuggled home. Most of the workers went in for things like hanging baskets and garden gates. Fred had two wrought-iron signs made, which perhaps symbolized the outer and inner manifestations of his home: the first read "25 Cromwell Street" in pretty painted scrollwork and this he attached to the outside wall beside the front door, while the second, similar in style, which he nailed to the top of the four-poster bed that he constructed in Rose's room, read "Cunt".

Another of the Wests' lodgers was Shirley Robinson, aged eighteen when she moved in with them. A former prostitute with bisexual tastes, she was soon having sexual relations with both Fred and Rose and, at a time when Rose was pregnant with the child of one of her black clients, Shirley became pregnant by Fred. Never jealous of Rose's sexual adventures, Fred was delighted at the prospect of Rose presenting him with a mixed-race addition to the family and rather flattered at the thought of having impregnated Shirley, but then Shirley seemed to be showing signs of wishing to displace Rose in the household . . . It was the the Rena/Anna McFall scenario all over again, and Fred did not like confrontations. Rose gave birth to baby Tara in December, 1977, and seven months later Shirley Robinson, by then very heavily pregnant, disappeared. Nobody reported her missing and there was no investigation, despite her imminent maternity. Rose was seen shortly afterwards sorting though her clothes, and made a false claim for maternity benefit in Shirley's name which was investigated by the Department of Health and Social Security, who were told that Shirley had gone off to live in Germany. The matter was not pursued.

Other lodgers had a better time. One of them, when she was questioned by the police later, said that the period when she lived with the Wests was the happiest of her life, and she never once suspected that any sinister events were taking place there.

Young girls constantly came to Cromwell Street. Fred began to hang around Jordan's Brook House, a local home for delinquent girls, some of whom he befriended and invited home for soft drinks and snacks. There, Rose would listen sympathetically to their problems—after all, she had been in care herself—and soon the girls were saying that 25 Cromwell Street was a good place to hang out. One of them, a troubled teenager whose name has never been revealed, (in court later she was known as Miss A), ran away from Jordan's Brook in 1976 and sought refuge at No. 25, where she felt that they—especially Rose—understood and cared about her. According to Miss A's later account, Rose welcomed her in and settled her in the lounge, but when she went to the toilet Rose followed her, and she heard Rose and Fred whispering outside the bathroom door. When she emerged, Rose bundled her into a room where she was astonished to see Fred with two naked girls, one blonde and aged about fourteen and the other dark and only a little older. There was a home-made cat-o'-nine-tails on the wall, and the room was adorned with pictures of bestiality. Rose unfastened Miss A's dress, saying that they were "all girls together", then performed a striptease for Fred. She then took a vibrator and, asking Fred, "Are you enjoying this now?", buggered Miss A with it so violently that she screamed, then Fred buggered her. She was then bound with parcel tape and flung face-down onto the bed, where she felt her nipples being painfully twisted and a female hand with long pointed fingernails penetrate her vagina. She heard Rose saying, "This is fun! It's great!", then she was buggered again with some implement, and finally fucked by Fred. By the time they had finished it was mid-afternoon, and Miss A was left to clean herself up as best she could and make her own way back to Jordan's Brook. She was barefoot, bleeding internally and highly distressed, but felt that she could tell no-one of her ordeal. A few weeks later she made her way back towards Cromwell Street carrying matches and a can of petrol, but when she got there she found that she couldn't go close to the house, and dumped the can.

The dark girl in the room had probably been Anna Marie, Fred's daughter by Rena, who had been the first victim of Fred's torture-chamber and who was now aged twelve, though she looked older. Since childhood she had been constantly abused by both her father and Rose. According to her own account, Fred regularly fucked her, telling her, "I made you. You are my flesh and blood. I am entitled to touch you," and when Rose was displeased with her or in one of her moods she would pull her hair, beat her, tie her up or tape up her mouth. On one occasion when the younger children were playing with finger-paint, Rose stripped off Anna Marie's clothes and got them to daub it all over her naked body, then Rose joined in; she forced Anna Marie onto all fours, then on her back wrote "BLACK HOLE" with an arrow pointing down to her anus, and made her stay like that until Fred got home. Everybody thought it was highly amusing, except Anna Marie. There were more vicious assaults, too. In 1978 Anna Marie was taken to hospital with lacerations like stab wounds to her ankles, similar to the ones that Charmaine had received years earlier. Fred and Rose had also turned her into a child prostitute, forcing her to have sex

with some of Rose's clients and, according to Caroline
Owens, dressing her up and taking her out to the local
clubs and bars, getting her drunk and trawling for business. Things came to a head in 1979, when Fred made
Anna Marie pregnant. The previous year Rose had been
pregnant herself with a baby that they named Louise. No-
one knew whether or not Fred was the father of that one.

Meanwhile, yet another fugitive from Jordan's Brook
arrived at the house. Alison Chambers had been placed
there because she kept running away from an unhappy
home. Sensitive though wilful, Alison liked to write poetry
and draw pictures of the farmhouse where she dreamed of
living: pursuits for which she was teased unmercifully by the
other girls, who despised such evidence of an inner life. She
nonetheless joined the circle of girls who hung out at 25
Cromwell Street, where Fred and Rose made special efforts
to befriend her. They gave her presents, and began weaving
a fantasy designed especially for her: they actually owned a
farm just like the one in her pictures, they said, and when
she was seventeen and could legally leave Jordan's Brook
they would take her there, and she could spend as much time
as she liked lying on the grass and writing her poems. They
even showed her a picture of the farm, which turned out to
have been taken from an estate agent's brochure. Alison
was completely taken in by this and seemed to be utterly
infatuated with Fred, so in August 1979, four weeks before
her seventeenth birthday, she absconded from the home and
moved into No. 25. From there she wrote to her mother that
she was now living with the Wests:

> *a very homely family . . . I look after their five children*
> *and do some of the housework. They have a child the*
> *same age as me who accepts me as a big sister and we*
> *get on great.*

She vanished soon after writing this. When friends began asking after her, the Wests first told them that she was living on their farm, then that she had gone to stay with relatives. Her disappearance was reported to the police, but since she was no longer in care they considered her to be no longer at risk, and no further inquiries were made.

Anna Marie's incestuously-conceived baby developed in her fallopian tube, and her pregnancy had to be terminated. Soon afterwards, at the age of fifteen and with premonitions that something dreadful was going to happen on her sixteenth birthday if she remained, she left Cromwell Street and went to live with friends on the other side of Gloucester. Her place in the household was filled by another baby, a second son for Fred and Rose, whom they named Barry.

Fred decided to convert part of the back garden into a patio, and laid coloured paving-stones over the area nearest the house.

## VII

The next one in line for Fred and Rose's special attentions was Heather, now approaching puberty. She had grown into a slim, thoughtful girl who was doing well at school. Fred couldn't stand her, and the lodgers couldn't fail to notice that he was consistently unpleasant to her, calling her abusive names, telling her that she was ugly, and beating her—though that did not stop him fondling her and using her for sex. She fought and protested all the way, and started dreaming of the day when she could get away, writing the letters FODIWL all over her exercise books and personal possessions like a mantra: "Forest of Dean I will live". She began smoking and drinking, was caught shoplifting, and tried to run away from home but was returned to No. 25, and it seemed that she was just going to have to bide her time until she was old enough to leave. In 1987, at the age of sixteen, she left school and started writing off for jobs, and her hopes were raised when the possibility came up of a summer job working at a holiday camp in Devon, then dashed when at the last minute it fell through. She was on the dole, hanging about the house and in extremely low spirits, but she probably made a bad mistake when she told a friend of the abuse that she was receiving at home. When she abruptly disappeared, Fred told the other children: "A girl picked her up in a Mini, and she's gone to work at the holiday camp." Apparently there had been a phone call to say that the job was available after all. Fred then announced that he was thinking of making a fish-pond in the back garden, and asked his son Steve to help him dig a hole for it. A couple of days later Steve noticed that it had been filled in.

Rose, meanwhile, had given birth to two more daughters: Rosemary junior in 1982, and Lucyanna in 1983, both from West Indian fathers. She now had seven children to look after, and they often received random beatings as the strain began to tell. Fred decided to ease matters by converting the cellar into a bedroom for the younger children, who were being packed into the attic "like battery chickens" as one visitor described it, and he set about reconcreting the cellar floor. When it was done, it restored the top of the house to the adults, where Fred made spy-holes in all the bedrooms and converted the first floor into a cross between a club and a brothel. There was a fully-stocked bar decorated in "Jungle" style, presumably to try and appeal to Rose's black clientele, a fitted kitchen, a TV and music system, comfortable chairs and a sofa. They called it the Black Magic Bar, and the curtains were always kept drawn. It also featured a vast collection of pornography which included about 200 videos, some of them illegal imports dealing with bondage, cruelty and fetishism of the kind where the participants are usually clad in restraining outfits, gas-masks and the like, while other tapes were home-made. Fred had acquired a good-quality video camera on hire purchase, and both Fred and Rose made extensive use of it. Sometimes Fred filmed Rose having sex with other men or masturbating herself, while Rose sometimes set up the camera on a tripod and filmed herself doing these things and others. One tape showed Fred lying on his back while Rose pissed all over him. These they shared with visitors to the Black Magic Bar, who were recruited from ads in contact magazines, photographs passed around the local pubs and clubs, and of course Rose's already extensive range of contacts. In the now-available attic Rose and Fred hoarded every letter and photograph they received, and Rose kept a detailed log of her activities and clients which Fred delighted in reading.

They were always trying to inveigle others into these activities. One witness to the Wests' lifestyle during the late 1980s was Kathryn Halliday, a bisexual woman of thirty whom Fred invited back to No. 25 to meet "my missus." She was lonely and accepted, and when asked if she wanted to watch a video from the Black Magic Bar collection said that she'd prefer something straight, and was shocked when Fred's idea of straight turned out to be a violent piece of porn involving bondage and beating. Rose began fondling her, and she thought that this was leading to a bout of tender lesbian lovemaking, but things soon got rough; "It wasn't really human contact that Rose wanted," she observed later; "She liked pain. I wouldn't call it making love."

Kathryn nonetheless became a regular visitor to the Wests'—she was on the dole, for one thing, and was glad of the free meals—where she generally ended up in bed with Rose, whom she found insatiable ("She wanted orgasms all the time, like a machine"), but she grew worried as things became more violent. She was tied up and beaten by both Fred and Rose, and Rose asked how she would feel "if we left you all day and just came back and tormented you every so often?", and they showed her a secret closet where they kept bondage outfits and masks, which she noticed were creased and worn, though the suits were obviously too small for Rose, who was now quite stout. Kathryn was particularly scared by the masks: "You couldn't breathe very well if you put them on. There were no holes in some of them, just black masks with zips." When during one sex session Rose held a pillow on Kathryn's face and cut her while she was restrained, Kathryn decided that things had gone far enough, and stopped going to No. 25. When she ran into Fred and Rose afterwards, they ignored her. Later, she said, "They played with me and the idea that I was frightened. They got their thing from seeing other people frightened." She considered Rose stupid and Fred pathetic, and in her opinion Rose was definitely the dominant partner. Against this, a piece of paper was later found which read, in Rose's hand:

> *I, Rose, will do exactly what I am told, when I am told, without questions, without losing my temper, for a period of three months from the end of my next period, as I think I owe this to Fred.*

She signed this "R.P. West", and Fred countersigned it. Whether this meant that she was going to be more subservient after a particularly bossy spell or whether it is was just part of the general master-slave shenanigans is not clear. The document is undated.

The children were aware of some of Rose's activities upstairs, and Steve once received a severe beating when some porn mags went missing from the Black Magic Bar, although it turned out to be Heather who had taken them, to show her schoolfriends. Even downstairs Rose seldom wore knickers, and one of Fred's little habits was to thrust his hand up her skirt then wave his fingers under the children's noses, saying "Smell that—that's your mother." They also knew—how could they not?—that Fred had been fucking Anna Marie and, after she and Heather had gone, it was May's turn to be the nearest object of Fred's sexual attentions . . .

And so it went on, for a little while longer.

## VII

Whether Fred and Rose were cunning or simply lucky to have carried on this appalling way of life for so long is a moot point, but in the spring of 1992 their luck—if that's what it was—began to run out. One of the schoolgirls that had fallen into their clutches told her best friend that she had been raped by Fred West, with Rose helping him, and the friend went and reported it to the police. As chance would have it, the case was assigned to Hazel Savage, now a Detective Constable—the policewoman who had accompanied Rena Costello back from Scotland to face charges of theft a quarter of a century earlier, and who recalled the name Fred West from what Rena had told her about his sexual perversions then. Had the case been given to anyone else the Wests might have bluffed and blustered their way out of it in their usual way, but DC Savage not only had a good memory she was also perceptive and extremely persistent.

In August, police arrived at 25 Cromwell Street with a warrant to search for pornography and evidence of child abuse. They found huge quantities of the former, which they carted off, and on the evidence of what they learned they arrested Fred for the rape and sodomy of a minor. The younger children were taken and put into care, and with Fred in jail and the police asking very awkward questions Rose attempted suicide with an overdose of pills. Her son Stephen found her and resuscitated her. Rose was then arrested for assisting in the rape of a minor. In jail awaiting trial she binged on sweets and chocolate, and watched endless Walt Disney videos. Fred was also feeling depressed and sorry for himself, but the case against him and Rose collapsed when the two key witnesses decided that they wouldn't testify. It seemed that the West luck was holding out for the moment. They all returned home, most of the porn was destroyed, and for a while life returned to something like normal.

But DC Savage was not going to leave them alone. During the course of the investigation she had interviewed members and friends of the West family, and when she had talked to Anna Marie, now living with her boyfriend on the other side of town and preferring to be called Anne Marie, she heard how as a little girl she had been abused and raped in the cellar torture-chamber, and of the continual abuse in the years that followed. Anne Marie also voiced her suspicions about Charmaine, whom Hazel Savage had of course known years earlier, and there were also the disappearances of Rena and Heather to ponder. She soon heard the rumours about Heather being buried under the patio, which had become a family joke, and she—alone amongst her colleagues—took them seriously. She discovered that Heather's tax and medical records were blank for the previous four years, which meant that Heather had not been employed, had not claimed any social security, and had not visited a doctor in Britain during that time: either she had abruptly left the country or she was dead. DC Savage also wondered what on earth had become of Rena.

It took a great deal of persuasion over a period of several months before the police would start digging, since police funds then as now were scanty and such operations are immensely expensive, not to mention the compensation to be paid if nothing is found, but on 24th February, 1994, the police arrived at 25 Cromwell Street with a warrant to search the house and garden for the remains of Heather West.

Fred was out when they arrived, working on a job twenty miles away. Rose told Steve to phone him, but he could not be reached on his mobile so Steve left a message with his employer. Fred got the message ("Ring Rose") a short time later, phoned her, heard the alarming news ("You'd better get back home. They're going to dig up the garden, looking for Heather."), and could have got back to Cromwell Street within half an hour or so—but it was nearly *four* hours before he appeared, during which time the police had begun lifting the paving-slabs of Fred's patio, ready to begin digging in earnest the following day. What Fred did in those four hours has been a matter of much speculation. Did he use the time to scurry about removing evidence from other places, to warn accomplices what was happening, or just to *think?* If the latter, it must have been a very fraught brainstorming session, and eventually Fred no doubt realized that if the police really were going to dig up the garden there could be no possibility of talking his way out of it this time: the game was basically up.

The story he told the police when he did return was the usual one about Heather having left home. "Lots of girls disappear," he said airily, "take a different name and go into prostitution." But, with a policeman stationed at the bottom of the garden, Fred and Rose stayed up and talked all night, and the next morning Fred gave himself up to the police and confessed to killing his daughter Heather. At the station he told how he had cut her body into three pieces: ("Three?" "A head, a body and two legs") and buried it in the back garden, insisting that Rose had known nothing at all about the murder or the burial. Twenty minutes later he was denying everything that he had just told them: "Heather's alive and well, right? She's possibly at the moment in Bahrain working for a drug cartel. She had a Mercedes, a chauffeur and a new birth certificate." The police could dig all they wanted, he added, but they wouldn't find Heather. Disentangling truth and fantasy in Fred's subsequent statements would prove nightmarish in more ways than one.

Back at No. 25, as the digging got underway, Rose was interviewed by Detective Sergeant Terence Onions (TO in the extracts that follow) who quizzed her about Heather:

*TO: Tell me when you last saw her.*
*RW: Before she left home.*
*TO: And when did she leave home?*
*RW: I don't know. A long time ago.*
*TO: Do you remember what year?*
*RW: She was almost seventeen, I know that much.*
*TO: What were the causes of her going, then?*
*RW: Lots of things, really. Mainly, I suppose, because she was unhappy.*
*TO: Was there any row before she left?*
*RW: I suppose there must have been raised voices. I don't know, I was upset. She said she didn't want to stay.*
*TO: You tried to persuade her to stay, did you?*
*RW: I said "What are you going to do?" I had a problem*

*with her because I knew what she was. That was what made it tricky with the other children. She was a lesbian, as far as I know.*

*TO: She was a very young girl. How did you know that? You had a picture in your mind of what a lesbian was like and she fitted it?*

*RW: That's right. One particular incident—her uncle was talking to her. He said to her about boyfriends or something and he said, you know, you had better watch it like, because they get up to tricky things. She said "If any boy put his hand on my knee I'd put a fucking brick over his head."*

*TO: That doesn't particularly mean she was a lesbian. What made you think she was definitely a lesbian?*

*RW: In the infants' school, she knew exactly what kind of knickers the woman teacher had on.*

*TO: It sounds as if you are annoyed.*

*RW: The only reason it annoys me is because I believe it cut off communication between me and her. Teenagers disagree with their parents. I know May is very close to her father.*

*TO: The night before, there were raised voices, and it was about that, was it? "You are a lesbian."?*

*RW: I couldn't talk to her. There was no communication. She said she would talk to her father. That was it. You can lead a horse to water but you can't make it bloody drink.*

*TO: I'm trying to find out if Heather is still alive.*

*RW: If you had any brains at all, you could. It can't be that difficult.*

*TO: We could actually pinpoint the day she went from your account. [Rose claimed that she drawn about £600 from her account to give to Heather the day before she left.] What did she take with her?*

*RW: I don't know. I wasn't there.*
*TO: Did you go and look in her bedroom?*
*RW: Yes.*
*TO: Have you seen her since?*
*RW: No.*
*TO: Have you heard from her since?*
*RW: No. She obviously doesn't want us any more, does she?*
*TO: How did she get from here?*
*RW: I don't know.*
*TO: Did you go and ask her schoolfriends? Did you ask them why she had gone?*
*RW: No.*
*TO: What inquiries have you made?*
*RW: When you have brought up a girl like that and you have done everything and then they turn round and turn their back on you, that's it. She didn't want to know me.*
*TO: Why didn't you report her to the police?*
*RW: So I have got to snitch on my own daughter?*
*TO: Why do you say snitch?*
*RW: Well, she's obviously doing what she wants to do.*
*TO: You think she's gone away to be a lesbian?*
*RW: Yes.*

The diggers found a piece of human bone in the back garden of No. 25 early the next day, but it wasn't in the place where Fred had told them that Heather was buried, so they continued digging. At last they did find Heather's remains, and two more graves under the paving-stones. The pathologist summoned by the Home Office to examine these remains was Professor Bernard Knight, whose grisly task it now was to probe the quagmire that had been Fred's patio—it had been raining solidly for hours—and try to make sense of what he found. Fortunately, Professor

Knight had no sense of smell, for each hole contained a glutinous black mess of earth mingled with decomposed human flesh and bodily organs in which bones and a few other solid items had been preserved. These were washed and taken to Gloucester police headquarters in dustbins, where it quickly became clear to Professor Knight that none of the skeletons was complete: small bones from the fingers of each one were missing, as were some of the kneecaps, toes and other small bones. The remains that had been buried furthest from the house were soon identified as belonging to Heather West.

The media now realized that something extraordinary was going on at 25 Cromwell Street, and from here on every new development received massive press and television coverage.

Fred, still being held at the police station, now gave his version of what had happened. He had got into a row with Heather, had slapped her for her insolence and grasped her throat to stop her mocking him: "I just wanted to shake her, or wanted to take that smirk off her face." He must have held her too hard, he went on, because she turned blue and stopped breathing. He tried to revive her, but he didn't have the training, so he dragged her over to the bathtub and ran cold water over her, but it was no use: she was dead. He took off her clothes, lifted her body out of the bath and dried it, then tried to put it in the large dustbin, but it was too large to fit in. He then moved the body back to the bathtub, where he knew he would have to make her smaller—but first he strangled her with a pair of tights to make quite sure that she was dead: "I didn't want to touch her while she was alive. I mean, if I'd have started cutting her leg or her throat and she'd have suddenly come alive . . ." He had also closed Heather's eyes before dismembering her: "If somebody's sat there looking at you, you're not going to use a knife on that person, are you?" Cutting off her head was the worst part, he continued—it made a "horrible noise, like scrunching"—but once it was off he started on her legs, twisting her foot until he heard "one almighty crack and the leg come loose, like." When he had finished hacking he was able to fit the separate pieces of his daughter comfortably into a bin-liner. Later, when the rest of the family were asleep, he buried it in the garden. He still insisted that Rose had known nothing about it.

Rose was arrested the next day and DS Onions interviewed her again. At first he did not tell her that Fred had confessed to killing Heather:

> *TO: What about her leaving? Were you there when she left? Did you have any conversation about her leaving?*
> *RW: I must have.*
> *TO: At what stage did you know she was leaving?*
> *RW: She had had a job offer in Devon somewhere.*
> *TO: Was it her decision to leave, initially, and how long before she left had she made the decision to leave?*
> *RW: Members of the family believe she had it planned for quite a while.*
> *TO: Did she go with anybody?*
> *RW: I can't remember.*
> *TO: This is your own eldest child.*
> *RW: Yes.*
> *TO: So it was quite a traumatic event?*
> *RW: That's right.*
> *TO: You have never done anything to find out where she might be?*
> *RW: Nothing. As far as I'm concerned she left home of her own accord.*
> *TO: Why do you think you've been arrested today? For*

> *the most grave of offences. There has been a major development this morning. Fred has confessed to mur-dering Heather.*
>
> *RW:* What? *[—Those who have heard this tape say that this was an untranscribable cry, somewhere be-tween a shout and a moan.] So you know where she is?*
>
> *TO: He has told us where she is.*
>
> *RW: So she is* dead, *is that right?*
>
> *TO: Fred has confessed to murdering Heather.*
>
> *RW: What?*
>
> *TO: And that automatically implicates you.*
>
> *RW (crying): Why does it automatically implicate me?*
>
> *TO: Our suspicions are aroused that you are implicated in it.*

Fred was now growing loquacious. Of the two other bodies buried under the patio he said that one was Shirley Robinson, the bisexual lodger that he had impregnated. He couldn't recall the name of the other girl—she was just "Shirley's mate"—but she was the one buried near the bathroom wall. Rose, released on bail, watched glumly as the police broadened their search to the whole of the area at the rear of the house, and it was not long before more remains were found. It was now decided that the search be extended to the floors of the house itself, and Rose was moved to a police safe-house a few miles outside Gloucester. This was wired so that any incriminating re-marks she made could be recorded, but in the weeks that she spent there and in other such houses she said nothing at all to implicate herself in the killings. Meanwhile, a new line of investigation was now opened, into the disappear-ances of Fred's first wife Rena and her child Charmaine.

In custody Fred continued to talk, and now he con-firmed that he had buried girls in the cellar, too. As the layers of concrete were smashed and removed, three sets of bones were revealed in the cellar and three more under the concrete floor of the kitchen extension. The police made a list of every young female known to have disappeared from the area in the previous thirty years, and tried to fit names to the remains. Fred was helpful up to a point, but said that he could not remember all their names or exactly what he had done with each of them. After much painstaking work the identification exercise was successful, however, and eventually names were fitted to all the remains. Some of them—Lynda Gough, Juanita Mott, Shirley Robinson, Alison Chambers and of course Heather— were names already associated with the Wests, but who were Carol Ann Cooper, Thérèse Siegenthaler, Shirley Hubbard and Lucy Partington? This account of them will again have to be brief.

Carol Ann Cooper was fifteen when she disappeared in 1973. After an evening out in Worcester her boyfriend took her to the bus stop, and when they had said their goodbyes she climbed aboard the bus that would take her to her grandmother's, where she planned to spend the weekend. She was not seen again. What happened to her after that is not known, but when her remains were unearthed from beneath the cellar floor at Cromwell Street there were remnants of surgical tape bound around her head, and pieces of cord and twisted cloth around her arms.

Thérèse Siegenthaler and Shirley Hubbard both vanished during the course of 1974. Thérèse, then aged twenty-one, was a Swiss student studying sociology in London, and in April was hitchhiking to North Wales, where she intended to catch a ferry to Ireland to meet up with a friend there. En route she vanished. Shirley was a pretty, rather rebellious girl of fifteen, originally from

Birmingham but in November 1974 living with foster-parents in Droitwich. She had been dating a boy that she had met at a fairground, and was supposed to be catching a bus to meet him, but Shirley was not on the bus she had said she would get, nor the one after . . . and she was not seen or heard from again. The remains of both girls were found beneath Fred West's cellar floor. Shirley Hubbard's skull was encased in parcel tape, with a plastic breathing-tube inserted through a hole to what was left of her mouth.

Lucy Partington was a university student from a good family (one of her cousins was the writer Martin Amis, with whom she had played when they were both children), who in late 1974 was spending the Christmas holiday at her mother's house in Gretton, near Cheltenham. She spent the day after Boxing Day visiting a disabled friend, leaving to catch a bus home late in the evening. Fred must have picked her up (maybe with Rose too, since it seems unlikely that Lucy would have accepted a lift from a man on his own), and she was taken back to Cromwell Street. Perhaps she was knocked out and abducted like Caroline Owens, and perhaps she and these other girls underwent the same sort of treatment. At any rate, no more was heard of her until her remains were discovered beneath the cellar floor twenty years later. Lucy was no drifter, and in her case there was a major police enquiry, but since there was no reason to look for her at the Wests' it produced no results. The investigations of 1994 revealed two particularly unpleasant facts, however: one was that in addition to the usual finger- and toe-bones one of Lucy's shoulder-blades (a difficult bone to sever) was missing from her remains, and the other was that a whole week after the date of her disappearance Fred West rushed to the casualty unit of the local hospital with a severe laceration to his right hand: exactly the sort of wound that someone might receive when trying hack off an awkward bone with a kitchen-knife. It is possible that Lucy was killed immediately after being abducted and that Fred waited a week before carving up her corpse, but it is also possible that her ordeal lasted for this length of time: an appalling thought, for her and all these girls. SDF, slow death of females.

And what about Charmaine? She had disappeared before the Wests moved to Cromwell Street, and Fred now said that he had buried her in the back garden of the flat they had previously rented in Midland Road. By a curious chance he had been called back there in 1976 to build a kitchen extension on the very spot where she was buried, and this had enabled him to lay a concrete floor over the whole area. The police now dug this up and found Charmaine's bones where Fred had told them they would. Her limbs had been severed, and no clothing was found in her grave. Fred said that he had killed Charmaine himself, without Rose's knowledge—but wasn't he in prison when Charmaine had vanished?

Fred also confessed to murdering Rena Costello, and said that she was not buried in Cromwell Street but in a field near Much Marcle. He said that Anna McFall was also buried nearby, though for some reason he would not admit to killing her. He was taken to the area and he pointed to spots in two adjacent fields. Fred's talk, wild and fantastic as it often was, became even more bizarre as these interviews progressed—he now claimed to be a chum of the pop singer Lulu, for instance—but the police decided that it would be worth excavating at least part of the fields to which Fred had taken them, and in due course the remains of Rena and Anna were found there in deep graves. Both bodies had been dismembered in what became Fred's usual manner, although these were presumably two of his earlier efforts—or three, in fact, as the skeleton of Anna and Fred's unborn baby was found interred alongside Anna's severed corpse. Anna's wrists had been tied with some kind of cord. Fred lead the police to other places too, but his accounts of these were vague and seemed not to warrant their digging elsewhere. Since Anna had disappeared in 1967, two years before Fred had met Rose, it now became clear that, whatever Rose's role in subsequent events, Fred was already a murderer when he picked her up at the bus station in Gloucester.

Fred said that he knew nothing about the disappearance of Mary Bastholme, the waitress at the Pop-Inn (her body has never subsequently been found), and if his Glasgow allotment had been used for any sinister purpose that was also going to remain a secret since it had long ago been obliterated by the construction of Junction 22 of the M8 motorway, but on the murders that had taken place at 25 Cromwell Street he was frankness itself. He had picked up the girls at various places, he said, and had had relationships with them—he always firmly denied rape—and had only killed them when they had demanded money and threatened to tell Rose. He spoke almost casually about his sexual fetishes. He said that he had cut off the girls' heads to make sure that they were dead and that he cut off their legs to make them easier to bury, but he wouldn't say why all those small bones were missing from the remains, nor why some of the heads had been bound with tape. Rose had never been present when he had strangled these girls, he insisted, and had known nothing of his butchery and grave-digging.

Unsurprisingly, the police found this difficult to believe. While Fred talked they worked hard to discover the extent of Rose's involvement in these horrific events, and as they interviewed members of her family, friends and neighbours, and some of Rose's clients they soon learned of the sadistic nature of her sexuality, and perhaps to get her into full custody they brought charges against her for assisting in the rape of an eleven-year-old girl by a sixty-seven-year old black man (a second man was also charged a few days later), and for assaulting a small boy at 25 Cromwell Street on her own, both crimes going back to the mid-1970s. These charges were indeed sufficient to put Rose behind bars for the first time in her life, and she was moved to Pucklechurch Prison, near Bristol, where she was questioned more closely about the murders, particularly those of her daughter Heather and of Lynda Gough, the young woman who had succeeded Caroline Owens as the Wests' live-in nanny. She was questioned forty-seven times in all, but of the murders would only say "I'm innocent". She was very soon charged with Lynda Gough's murder, however—wearing Lynda's slippers when she answered the door to Lynda's mother had been a bad mistake—and more charges would follow.

Fred and Rose met again in June, when they were jointly charged at Gloucester Magistrates Court with nine counts of murder, one for each of the bodies unearthed at Cromwell Street, with Fred facing two additional charges for the murders of Rena and Charmaine. Interestingly, Rose was not deemed to be implicated in Charmaine's murder at this stage. They had to stand together in the dock, but when Fred laid his hand gently on Rose's shoulder she shrank from him, and avoided him as they were both lead away. Rose said later that having to stand next to Fred had made her feel sick. For Fred, Rose's rejection was devastating, and when he was returned to prison he found himself marking time; he had given 108 hours' worth of interviews to the police, and there was still a great deal more that could be told—about the sexual torture of the victims, for instance, and about all those missing bones—but for the moment the detectives seemed to have lost interest in him, so Fred filled in the time by drawing, writing and chatting with his son Steve, to whom he said that Rose seemed to be trying to break up the family. They met once more at a remand appearance in December. Fred had been warned that Rose wouldn't speak to him, and in court they were separated by two policewomen. Rose glanced at Fred just once.

Fred's case was hopeless, as it had been ever since the police had started digging at No. 25, but he had obviously found a purpose for himself in trying to shield Rose, perhaps even felt a little noble about the sacrifice he was trying to make on her behalf, but with Rose now alienated all this crumbled, and on New Year's morning Fred plaited together some strips of material that he had secretly collected in his cell, and hanged himself.

## IX

That left Rose to face the music by herself. Many wondered how any case against her could now proceed in view of the lack of direct evidence, since there was not one witness who could claim to have seen Rose kill, dismember or bury anyone, not one scrap of forensic evidence to link her with any of the crimes, and the one person who definitely knew all about the murders had consistently told the police that Rose had known nothing about them. "She *must* have known" was the overriding feeling, but it still came as a shock when she was charged on *ten* separate counts of murder: the murders of Charmaine, Lynda Gough, Carol Cooper, Lucy Partington, Thérèse Siegenthaler, Shirley Hubbard, Juanita Mott, Shirley Robinson, Alison Chambers and Heather. The task of the prosecution was to create a web of circumstantial evidence from which Rose could not escape. The difficult job of the defence was to argue that evidence of Rose's sexual activities and other crimes ("similar events", in legalese) did not necessarily make her a murderer, and that no matter how repellent her life may have been each separate charge of murder had to be proved beyond reasonable doubt.

Her trial began on 3rd October, 1995. It was keenly anticipated by the media, and there was the usual feeding frenzy among the more salacious newspapers to acquire the rights to the "stories" of the principal witnesses: a bugbear of modern high-profile cases like this one, and a cause for concern since witnesses with cash on their minds may be tempted to liven up their stories to make them more ratings-worthy, or even to falsify their evidence to try and secure the convictions without which their stories would be unpublishable and therefore worthless. The defence, lead by Richard Ferguson QC, made objections to the trial going ahead on these grounds, but presiding judge Mr Justice Mantell dismissed any suggestion that these goings-on and the massive press coverage that had already taken place might be prejudicial to a fair hearing, and Rose's trial proceeded.

After the preliminaries the prosecution, lead by Brian Leverson QC, questioned a string of witnesses about Rose's sexual assaults on young women. Caroline Owens [Raine?] told of her abduction and abuse. The woman known as Miss A related her pathetic story. A man named Arthur Dobbs said that ten years earlier he had replied to an ad in a contact magazine and met "Mandy", who turned out to be Rose, and become one of her regulars; she had once told him that Fred was having sex with the children, and he had tipped off social services about it. Kathryn Halliday told of the beatings and the bondage gear. Then Anne Marie was called to give evidence. She was in a highly apprehensive state, and spoke in a monotone with long pauses between her statements, frequently breaking down as she told of the sexual abuse that started when she was eight, of the repeated beatings and rapes, and of the threats that kept her silent for so long. She had tried to kill herself when she learned that Fred had hung himself in prison, and after this gruelling session in court Anne Marie tried it again, but was revived and eventually able to continue her testimony. She then told for the first time how Fred had made her pregnant when she was fifteen.

Professor Knight told the jury of the recovery of the human remains from Cromwell Street, and showed them photographs of the bones and the instruments of torture, including one of Shirley Hubbard's skull with the masking tape and the breathing-tube still in place. The jury were then told how the remains had been identified. The court then listened to tapes of the police interviews with both Fred and Rose.

On 30th October Rose herself took the stand. Most people had thought that she would not testify—she was not obliged to—because of the poor impression she might make, and because of the risks that went with cross-examination, but she insisted on doing so. She was dressed almost like a schoolgirl, in a white blouse and black jacket, a long dark-green skirt and low black shoes, and made the bad impression that her counsel had feared. To begin with she sought to blame her parents for abandoning her (which wasn't quite what had happened), and of Fred she said, "He promised me the world. He promised me everything. Because I was so young I fell for his lies." She insisted that she loved all her children, and of Heather said "I loved her very, very, very much." Of her sexual habits she said that she enjoyed sex with other women because it was "warmer . . . closer", but the court saw flashes of her temper when she was asked about Caroline Owens.

She was on the stand again the following day and fared even worse, giving versions of events that were obviously untrue and frequently contradicting herself—and all this was in response to questions from her own defence. Brian Leverson's cross-examination, when it came, provoked a few exchanges:

> *BL: You abused that girl [Charmaine], didn't you?*
> *RW: Not to the extent that you would like to think I have.*
> *BL: You tied her arms?*
> *RW: No sir.*
> *BL: Tied her to the bed?*
> *RW: No sir.*
> *BL: You beat her?*
> *RW: No sir.*
> *BL: You killed her and kept the body for Fred to bury . . . and from that moment on you were tied together for ever.*

But mostly Rose now just claimed that she didn't know, couldn't remember, and blamed Fred for everything:

> *It's all very well for someone to say I did this or did that, because I'm the one now in the spotlight. Fred West is dead and I've got to take responsibility for what he's done.*

The defence called witnesses to try and show that Fred was quite capable of making sexual attacks on his own, and the court was played tapes of Fred's confessions, again at Rose's own insistence since she wanted everyone to hear Fred owning up to all the murders and saying time and again that she had known nothing about them, but the prosecution had little difficulty in discrediting Fred's confessions on the grounds that they too were self-contradictory and often plainly fantasy.

One of the prosecution's key witnesses was a woman named Janet Leach. She had been Fred's "appropriate adult", a voluntary worker who had been assigned as a sort of companion for Fred while he was being interviewed, and who had frequently visited him when he was in custody. She now told the court that what Fred had said to the police and what he had told her privately were two very different things; to her he said that Rose was the killer, and that he was protecting her; what's more, there had been other people involved, including Rose's father Bill (who had died in 1979), some coloured men, and another person unnameable for legal reasons. It had not all happened at Cromwell Street, either: there was this disused farmhouse . . . Then Mrs Leach was taken ill and it was some days before she could take the stand again, during which time it emerged that she too had made a deal with a newspaper.

In his summary, Brian Leverson described Rose as the "strategist" and the dominant partner. "The evidence that Rosemary West knew nothing is not worthy of belief," he said. Richard Ferguson in turn stressed that the evidence pointed only to Fred. The judge's summing-up took three days. Amongst many other things he told the jury that Rose did not need to have strangled anyone with her own hands to be guilty of murder. If it had been committed as part of a "joint plan" she was just as guilty. The jury took very little time to find Rose guilty on all ten counts, and the judge sentenced her to life imprisonment for each one.

Shortly afterwards, in the clubs and pubs a song began doing the rounds. Sung to the tune of Village People's hit

"Go West", which had recently been revived by The Pet Shop Boys, one verse ran:

> *Rose West*
> *You will never get out now*
> *Rose West*
> *Serves you right, you fat cow*
> *Rose West*
> *You won't see daylight again*
> *Rose West*
> *And you won't be a Dame*

## X

There are still many unanswered questions about what happened inside 25 Cromwell Street. The bones missing from the skeletons have lead to speculation that they might have been removed as grisly souvenirs—the toe- and finger-bones might have been made into necklaces or ornaments for the Black Magic room, for instance—and there have even been suggestions of cannibalism. The pattern of the murders as it unfolded during the investigation has also prompted speculation about how many *more* there might have been, since after the spate of killings and burials between 1973 and 1975 there appears to have been a gap until the murders of Shirley Robinson and Alison Chambers in 1978–9, and then an even longer gap until Heather's death in 1987. Did the slaughter just stop for years at a time or, with the cellar and kitchen floors concreted over and the garden rapidly filling up, did Fred find somewhere else to dispose of the bodies? After all, he had buried Rena and Anna McFall in the countryside years before, and nobody had discovered their graves until he pointed them out. There is also the fact that sexual-compulsive serial killers don't usually take seven-year breaks from their activities. So was there any truth in the persistent rumour about a *farmhouse* somewhere, and were others indeed involved besides Rose? What did Fred do during that four-hour period before he turned up to face the police? Fred himself once remarked that despite the hours of interviews the police "didn't know the half of it".

The exact nature of Rose's relationship with Fred has also been the subject of much debate. Rose's own line, once she was in custody, was that she had fallen under the influence of a bad man who had killed before he met her and who drew her into his madness: much the same argument that Myra Hindley had earlier employed about Ian Brady. *Folie à deux*. Plenty of people who knew the Wests did not see it that way at all. *Rose* was the dominant partner, they thought, and it was Fred who was hopelessly besotted with *her* and did *her* bidding; did everything just to please Rose, in fact. Several substantial books have now been written about the case, arguing the matter this way and that, and no doubt there will be more.

Finally, did Rose get a fair trial? At the time of writing, she has been in Durham Prison for six years and has recently asked to have her case reviewed by the Criminal Cases Review Commission, the body responsible for referring suspected miscarriages of justice to the Court of Appeal, on three main grounds:

1. *That under the terms of the Human Rights Act, the news coverage before her trial and the approaches made by the press to key witnesses made a fair trial impossible.*

2. *That the jury might have been misdirected by the judge.*

3. *That new evidence has emerged in the form of an album of Polaroid photographs which might indicate that Frederick West was the sole killer.*

If such photographs do exist and were suppressed at the original trial, more questions perhaps need to be asked. Concerns have also been raised about the disappearance of Caroline Owens's original statement to the police in 1973, and about whether Fred West was in or out of prison when Charmaine vanished: remember it was Fred who was originally charged with her murder, Rose only after Fred's suicide.

It is difficult to feel very much sympathy for Rosemary West. Sexually abusing children and young people for one's own sadistic sexual gratification is perhaps the most sickening of all crimes, and when such activities become central to a whole way of life that continues for decades, and which taint and destroy many other lives, the reaction of most people is one of mingled anger and revulsion. Even so, anyone charged with *any* crime deserves a fair trial. There are probably many reasons why Rose West ought to be behind bars, but there are also a few nagging feelings that she may have got more than even she deserves.

—R.G.J

# 48

# DR ZEO ZOE WILKINS

## The Vampire of Kansas City

It was a strange premonition of death which came to Dr. Zeo Zoe Wilkins some forty-eight hours before she was discovered with a knife in her throat. Amidst a scene of wildest disorder she lay dead in the sumptuous office in Kansas City, from which she ran her osteopathic business.

Just two days before an assassin's hand struck her down, Zeo told Mrs. Eva Grundy, a patient and friend, "I have but forty-eight hours to live."

Almost to the very hour her prophecy came true.

Prior to that she had confided to her attorney, Jesse James, "At least four persons have threatened to get me . . . I'm worried—terribly afraid." And well she might be, for murder, suicides and the wrecks of human lives and fortunes had been the milestones of her life; indeed she had been guilty of pretty well every crime in the calendar.

The tragic discovery was made by Mrs. G. L. Palmer when she made a personal call upon the osteopath. She noticed that newspapers lying in the porch of the premises had not been taken in for two or three days, and that uncollected letters were poking out from the over-filled letter-box. To repeated knocking she obtained no reply, so Mrs. Palmer got a little boy to clamber through a side window. He soon came out, a look of terror on his face as he cried, "She's dead—she's been killed—there's blood all over the place."

When the police forced the door and entered the room which had been used as a consulting room, they found Zeo

Wilkins lying on the floor in a welter of blood. A great hole had been burned in the thick pile of the Turkish rug on which lay the body, clearly indicating that the murderer had tried to set fire to the place in order to destroy traces of his crime. There was evidence too that the dead woman had put up a terrific fight for life. Her gown was torn to shreds, and her injuries indicated that great violence must have been used. In addition to the wound in her throat her neck and forehead had been bruised and lacerated. The room was strewn with papers, and every drawer had been thoroughly ransacked.

Who had murdered Dr. Zeo Zoe Wilkins? And why?

Those were the two questions to which the police tried to find answers. Three people were suspect! Charles Wilkins, a brother of the victim, B. F. Tarpley one of her patients, and Dillard Davis, the coloured janitor in the home of the dead woman. They were all subjected to the fiercest grilling and proved innocent, so to this day the murder of the osteopath remains shrouded in mystery.

Not so the lurid story of her life, for the glare of publicity which was concentrated on her death revealed the hideous spectres of her past in all their revolting details.

It was perhaps an unlucky omen that she should have been the thirteenth child of her parents who lived in the little township of Lamar, Montana, U.S.A. They were humble in circumstances, dealing in butter and eggs, yet they managed to scrape up enough to send fifteen-year old Zeo to the School of Osteopathy at Kirkville, in the same state. They did not know that their daughter had decided on osteopathy as a profession, simply because it would be the means of putting her in touch with men and women of wealth—particularly men. She wrote to a schoolgirl friend that she intended to use her beauty to this end.

Thus early she had decided on a vampire career, and how utterly and unscrupulously she carried out her plans will be seen. She did in fact become one of the best known feminine practitioners of the science, and, because she was a woman, and a very beautiful woman at that, she gathered around her a clientele of wealthy patients among whom the male sex predominated.

Of Junoesque figure, with a wealth of crisp curly hair and a pair of dark flashing eyes, she had a striking appearance, and from the very outset of her career Zeo Wilkins cashed in on her physical charms.

In a way she was a female Jekyll and Hyde, for in a diary which she wrote even before she began her studies, she described her two personalities. "Helen was the better self," she confessed in this document, "Zeo the evil. My family always liked Helen the better but Zeo developed so readily that I soon grew too fond of her and Helen found less and less favour in my mind," an illuminating admission you may think in view of subsequent developments.

At the school of Osteopathy, Zeo applied herself to her studies with zest for she had determined to make a success of her career. One of her fellow students chanced to be Richard Dryer, the son of a prominent banker in Montana. "I intend to marry him," wrote Zeo to her girl friend at Lamar. "I shall get enough money to finance my start in osteopathy and then divorce him," which was further early evidence of her cold and calculating mind.

She carried out her intention, and the young man had scarcely got to know his bride upon whom he had settled a large sum of money, when she blandly told him that she was going to divorce him and return to school to continue her studies. She was as good as her word. Some weeks later she received a heart-broken letter from the boy's father to say that his son had taken his life because of her desertion.

Displaying not the least remorse or sorrow at the tragedy she had brought about, she promptly set her cap at a young doctor, C. K. Garring, who was adding osteopathy to his other medical qualifications. As well as being captivated by Zeo's beauty, he was also impressed by the brilliance of her work, and the combination made him a ready victim to her wiles. On the very night following their graduation in 1905, they eloped and after a brief but passionate honeymoon, young Garring proudly took his wife back to San Antonio, Texas, where he lived with his extremely wealthy parents. They settled down in one of the most fashionable quarters of the town in a fine house purchased for them as a wedding present by the bridegroom's doting parents. Every luxury that her heart could desire was lavished upon Zeo, who became one of the most popular women in San Antonio social circles. Had she so desired, she could have lived a life of ease and pleasure. But the Zeo (or Hyde) in her, gradually rose to the surface. She could not resist the adulation of men, and there was one in particular who captured her imagination. They became lovers, and during one of his surreptitious visits to her, tragedy for the second time entered Zeo's life.

She was in the arms of her lover when she heard her husband's car drive up to the front of the house. Without a moment's hesitation Zeo seized a revolver, and crept downstairs into the hall to await the entrance of her husband. The moment he opened the door, she fired a fusillade of shots at him. He staggered out of the door and fell bleeding on to the lawn. In the meantime the lover made his escape.

When the police arrived, Zeo was still standing over

Garring, the smoking revolver grasped in her hand. Her husband alive, unconscious, was rushed off to hospital.

"I heard noises downstairs and saw a shadowy figure moving about," Zeo told the police in answer to their questions. "I thought it was a burglar and I fired."

Her plausible explanation was accepted by the police, but evidently the husband had other views. When he had recovered and was discharged from hospital, he brought an action for divorce and succeeded. In court he declared that his marriage had been "a foolish mistake", and that his young wife was "too temperamental and hot headed". An understatement one may think.

For a time Zeo faded from public sight and knowledge, until one day the newspapers came out with a sensational story of the arrest of a prominent Oklahoma banker on a charge of embezzlement. It was revealed that this elderly Romeo had fallen beneath the spell of Zeo Wilkins (she had reverted to her maiden name) and had loaded her with jewels, furs and other extravagant gifts including vast sums of money. It was only when his bank failed and he was brought to the verge of ruin, that his folly and his crime came to light. A typical entry in Zeo's diary read:- "Without a scratch of the pen I got 17,000 dollars."

The banker was sent to gaol, and Zeo turned her attentions to Leonard Smith, a druggist in Kansas City who completely lost his head when this Jezebel focussed the battery of her charms upon him. For the time being she was eschewing matrimony having found that she was able to wheedle money from her victims without becoming a bride—at any rate dispensing with the marriage ceremony.

In all, she obtained over 15,000 dollars from her lover Smith which fact was duly recorded in her diary with the brief note, "He gave me all his money and went to get more . . . poor man."

The sympathetic comment arose from the fact that her lover was accidentally shot dead during a street fracas while going to his bank for further money to squander on his beloved. In this case Zeo must be absolved from direct responsibility for her lover's tragic fate.

One would think that with all these thousands of dollars simply falling into her lap Zeo Wilkins might have concentrated on her osteopathic career, and left romance behind for a time. But she was a girl of great ambition, and was determined that once she *did* start it would be on such spectacular lines and on such a sumptuous scale that only the wealthiest patrons would seek her services.

It was through her picture appearing in the newspapers as a result of her connection with the banker in Oklahoma that Zeo entered the matrimonial stakes for the third time. In Oklahoma City lived a prosperous furniture dealer, Grover Burcham. He saw the photograph which was published, and—like countless others who are drawn to anybody achieving notoriety—he wrote to her. Zeo made discreet enquiries ere committing herself, and having discovered that the writer was a man of repute and substance, she replied to his letter and Cupid took charge.

They were married and again a long and happy union might have ensued but for the wanton extravagance of Zeo. There appears to have been a certain amount of mutual affection but her spendthrift ways would have ruined any man no matter how wealthy. Only a few years after their marriage Zeo awakened one morning to find her husband gone. He had risen, packed a few things and disappeared without a word or note by way of explanation. This was a reversal of the usual procedure with a vengeance since it was Zeo, who, as a rule, performed the deserting act. She could not understand it, but was forced to the conclusion that her wild extravagance must have been partly the cause when she discovered that her husband had sold his business, realised all his available assets, and taken practically every dollar he could lay his hands on, leaving her stranded.

Of course, Zeo was not without money, for she took good care that wherever she happened to be somebody would be around to provide her with considerably more than the bare necessities of life. A couple of weeks went by, and the deserted wife was just making up her mind about her next move and her next victim, when there came a brief note from the missing Burcham. "Join me at Houston, Texas," it said. "Say nothing to anyone as to my whereabouts."

Her immediate problem thus solved, Zeo blithely set out to rejoin her husband. He was living in a nicely furnished house on the outskirts of town, and clasped her fondly in his arms when she arrived.

"You nearly broke me," he told his wife. "I just had to get away before I got into trouble. But I missed you darling—and I simply had to send for you." For a few months Zeo tried to restrain her extravagance, but eventually she broke out again, and it was not long before her infatuated husband found himself up against the old problem of finding enough money to satisfy the inordinate demands of his wife.

The climax came one night when the Houston police shot and killed a robber whom they caught red-handed in the process of burgling a mansion in the town. The intruder had put up a stiff fight until a bullet found its mark. It was Burcham! He had resorted to crime in order to keep his wife in luxury. Zeo was arrested in the belief that she had been at least the instigator, if not an actual partner in her husband's crimes. For *crimes* it was, as a search of the home in which they lived made clear. The fine clothes and furs which had bedecked the statuesque figure of Zeo, as well as the costly furnishings which had decorated their love nest, were either the proceeds of burglaries far and near, or else had been bought with stolen money.

Although Zeo pretended to be greatly upset and protested her innocence about her husband's activities, there can be no doubt that it was she who had driven him to crime. At the same time it must be admitted that she did genuinely grieve the loss of this husband—probably the only man of whom she was ever really fond.

The police could do nothing to her, and to get away from the scene of her sorrow she journeyed to Colorado Springs, the playground of the idle rich. Among the visitors there, was seventy-two-year-old Thomas W. Cunningham, a retired millionaire banker who cast an appreciative if rheumy eye upon the physical charms of the alluring widow Zeo. It was the first time for twenty-five years that this aged Romeo had taken a holiday from his native Joplin in Montana where he owned a big estate.

Zeo was quick to notice the ardent glances the old man cast upon her figure as she disported herself in the sunshine, clad in the latest fashion beach wear. She made discreet enquires and from the moment she learned his identity, old man Cunningham became her target. She displayed tender solicitude towards him, and acted the old man's darling to such effect that before a month had passed, the banker was begging her to become his wife. Zeo though not eager for matrimony, had nothing against wifehood provided its dividends were substantial.

She first made sure that there was to be no slip betwixt cup and lip so to speak, and even before their marriage she succeeded in obtaining from her lover, dollars to the equivalent of £80,000.

This nice cash-down advance payment was sufficient to convince the insatiable Zeo that this elderly bridegroom was a most attractive investment. Coyly she professed that her love for him was growing, and he could name the happy day. So December and May were married at Colorado Springs, and as a further token of his love, the husband—President of Joplin's most prosperous bank, bear in mind—promptly gave Zeo 300,000 dollars worth of bank stock which she as promptly sold for the equivalent of £60,000. He also settled upon her certain landed property of which he was possessed. Their honeymoon over, the bride thought she would like to visit Chicago before settling down in Joplin.

Motor-cars, town and country homes, jewellery of immense value, these were the offerings which Cunningham laid upon the altar of love and in return his goddess did not stint him the kisses he craved. But alas! his dreams of love were soon destined to turn into nightmares.

The first shattering blow to the romance came when a Mrs. Tabitha Taylor, seventy-year-old housekeeper of Mr. Cunningham, declaring that she was his common law wife, brought an action against Zeo for alienation of the old man's affections. She had tended him for twenty-five years, she averred. Then, Joplin friends of the aged bridegroom brought an action for the annulment of the marriage on the grounds of the old man's insanity. They even went so far as to kidnap him, snatching him from the very arms of his young bride while the trial of the action was pending.

Once away from the wiles of Zeo, and back again in

Joplin Mr. Cunningham had leisure to repent his hasty marriage, and he consented to divorce proceedings being instituted. Zeo also compromised and consented to yielding up all her husband's property with the exception of assets to the value of £60,000. All in all, her net total of £120,000 was generous compensation for a few months of married life to an old dotard.

And among the tangible assets included in the settlement was an exceptionally handsome young man, Albert Marksheffel, who had been employed by the Cunninghams as chauffeur. Handsome Albert had qualifications beyond those necessary to a driver-mechanic and often when Mr. Cunningham was enjoying his afternoon siesta, Zeo and Albert would enjoy the intimate delights of each other's company. To put it plainly they became lovers and Albert was already earmarked as husband number five when the brief—but profitable—encounter with Banker Cunningham came to an end.

This time, however, Zeo had picked a partner who was less amenable to her whims than her previous husbands or lovers. Albert was unable to give her anything but love, so it fell to Zeo to provide the material things of life and this she did with unwanted profligacy.

She embarked on an orgy of spending, and opened a banking account for her husband with £5,000 to his credit. They occupied a fine house in Colorado, and she set him up in a motor business. In return, he fulfilled the role of a spouse without the rapturous adoration that she had known from all her other men. There were no extravagant presents from him, not even a few flowers on occasion, and Zeo loved flowers.

Once she lay in bed for three days pretending to be ill, in order to arouse some sympathy in her husband's heart. But all in vain! From her "sick-bed" she demanded flowers and she wept when he refused even a posy. Then Zeo staged a macabre scene to shake him out of his indifference.

One night when Albert returned home from the garage he found a bow of black crepe tied round the knocker of the front door. His heart missed a beat! Was Zeo really ill after all? Had something terrible happened to her? Yes! he was shaken all right, and his feet could not carry him quickly enough up the stairs to his wife's bedroom. As he got to the door he noticed the sickly sweet odour of some disinfectant. All was silent within. He called her name but there was no answer. Almost fearing to turn the handle of the door he paused for some seconds before he pushed it open and took a frightened glance towards the bed. He nearly dropped in his tracks at what he saw. The blinds were drawn and in the dim light of four flickering candles, two at each end of the bed, lay Zeo her face white with the pallor of death, her lovely body shrouded with a sheet.

With slow faltering steps, and with horror gripping his very soul, the stricken husband made his way towards the bed to look down upon all that was mortal of his wife, or so he thought. As he approached the lids of her eyes flickered upwards, and she gazed at him with reproach. And then her body rose from its recumbent position, her outstretched hand pointed towards him, and her croaking voice echoed his name.

Poor Albert! He simply fell flat on his face in a dead faint while Zeo wiped the chalk-like powder from her face. It had taught him a lesson however, and he never ceased to bring her flowers—even without her asking—for the rest of their married life. But their married life didn't last long.

It was in 1917 that they were married, and in 1919 Zeo obtained a divorce from her husband. It must be a matter for conjecture as to which of the pair was the most relieved by the dissolution.

Following her divorce from Marksheffel, Zeo embarked with zeal on her osteopathic career. She opened her fabulous surgery in Kansas City, where with one or two love affairs mingled with business, she carried on a lucrative practice.

Her "manipulative surgery" was not the only activity in which she indulged however. After her death the police discovered documents which proved that many of her patients, whose trust she had gained, had been cleverly blackmailed by the resourceful Dr. Zeo Zoe Wilkins, the name by which she was professionally known. Some of her victims had been her lovers and as such—her slaves. She wormed from them guilty secrets which gave her the power to levy tribute upon them under pain of exposure.

By way of variant too, her osteopathic skill provided an ample if sinister cloak for carrying out abortions on wealthy women anxious to avoid motherhood, who thus also became prey to her blackmailing wiles. And if this was not enough, drug-peddling was another side line which Zeo added to her shameful accomplishments.

Perhaps hidden deep somewhere in these nefarious exploits there is the clue to the murder of this fickle, fascinating and vile woman. But it has never been found. The secret is locked in the dead black heart of the Vampire of Kansas City.

—B.O'D

# 49

# AILEEN CAROL WUORNOS
## "Digging Up Bones"

Troy Burress had a routine enough day ahead of him when he set off last August in his van to deliver sausages around his usual sales patch in the tranquil horse-breeding countryside of central Florida. But with one more call to make that afternoon, he disappeared. His empty truck was found the next day. There was no sign of 50-year-old Burress until nearly a week later when picnickers stumbled across a man's badly decomposed body along a desolate dirt-track on the edge of the Ocala National Forest.

For local detectives, Burress's death might have been a routine investigation, were it not for the disturbing fact that the bodies of middle-aged men, all of them travelling through the state, most of them blue-collar workers, had been turning up in the area since the previous December, at a rate of about one a month. Some were clothed, others naked. All had been shot several times with a small-calibre revolver and all were found dumped in remote spots near a major road, their vehicles missing or abandoned a few miles away.

By the time a sixth and a seventh body—a 56-year-old ex-police chief and a 60-year-old truck driver—were found, the notion that a serial killer was on the loose was rapidly gaining currency.

Nevertheless, it was a startling announcement that detectives made when they revealed that they believed one or two women were responsible for the homicides, shooting the seven motorists in the past year, most of them along the Interstate route 75 which bisects Florida.

Within a few months they had arrested Aileen Carol Wuornos, 34, charged her with the murder of Troy Burress and two other victims, 51-year-old electronics repair-man Richard Mallory and 56-year-old ex-police chief Charles Humphreys, and publicly linked her to four other murders. She confessed to the killings, telling police how she shot Humphreys seven times, including once in the head, "to put him out of his misery". Her former lesbian lover of six years, Tyria Moore, 28, who was in protective custody, became the star prosecution witness against Wuornos.

Police named Wuornos as a suspect for the murders only a few weeks before her arrest in January 1991. It was not until the autumn that they had begun even to link the chain of roadside killings, and to believe that they were hunting a woman, or a pair of women. Leads appeared that pointed to the same two women being seen near the spots where the bodies or cars were found. In November 1990, the police issued sketches of a stocky woman wearing a cap (Wuornos), and a younger, slimmer woman with what looked like a tattoo on her arm (Moore). Hundreds of leads then began pouring in—most importantly, from a woman who recognised the faces as those of two women she'd seen walking away from a grey Pontiac Sunbird, which they had crashed near her house in Orange Springs. That car, detectives knew, belonged to Peter Siems, a 65-year-old evangelical missionary who went missing in June 1990 on his way through Florida to visit relatives. At last, they were getting warm. They picked up Moore, who agreed to testify against her ex-lover, then shadowed Wuornos in the hope that she would lead them to more evidence. She didn't; Siems's body has still to be found.

By this time, the police had begun to change their minds about the motive for the murders. With the discovery of each body, shot and stripped of cash and personal belongings, investigators repeatedly suggested robbery as a motive. Once they had tracked down Wuornos, that theory evaporated; she is, according to Captain Steve Binegar, who led the hunt, "a killer who robs, rather than a robber who kills".

Not only was Moore aware of the murders, but it was claimed Wuornos had given her jewellery she'd taken from some of the men. Other belongings linking Wuornos to all the victims had been found in her suitcase.

The day before Wuornos was charged, police divers trawled the bottom of Rose Bay, a few hundred yards from a motel room that Wuornos had been renting, and came up with a .22-calibre handgun, along with a torch and gun belonging to the last victim, a 60-year-old truck driver, Gino Antonio.

When police picked Wuornos up in January 1991, she was sleeping rough on a dirty yellow car seat in the front porch of the Last Resort, a biker bar in the small, straggly town of Orange Springs near Florida's east coast, not far from where Mallory's body was found. It was, perhaps, the nearest place Wuornos had to a home. Married for a month at twenty, gaoled for three years for armed robbery at 24, Wuornos has spent most of her life on the move or on the run. A full-time drifter and part-time prostitute, she seems to pick up and drop pseudonyms—Susan, Lori, Lee, Sandra, Cammie—as regularly as odd jobs, waitressing, labouring and housekeeping.

Russell Armstrong, a local lawyer who defended Wuornos on the armed robbery charge, has painted a picture of a "disturbed" and "confused" woman, an alcoholic and drug addict with good reasons to dislike men:

she told him that she had been raped "numerous times" by men who picked her up as she hitch-hiked across the country.

At the Last Resort she seems to have lived on the margins of the bar's closely woven and profoundly macho biker culture. It seems an improbable haunt for a woman who the police describe as a man-hater, its ceilings festooned with a collection of knickers and bras, its walls papered with centre-fold spreads. But something about the place, where the garden is landscaped with a lined metal coffin and a tree hung with nine motor bikes, clearly appealed to her. She'd come here, sometimes with Moore, to drink beer, shoot pool and play the juke-box, usually her favourite number, "Digging Up Bones" by Randy Travis. Most of the time she kept herself to herself, but when she got drunk, she could be loud and foul-mouthed, directing her abuse at the mostly male regulars. "She was not," as the bar's owner, Al Bulling, put it, "the kind of girl you would take home to mother."

An elderly couple who ran a restaurant nearby also recalled Wuornos and Moore, who briefly rented a room from them. The women rarely left the room, only going out in the morning to buy coffee and a local paper, and appearing in the restaurant only when it was empty to eat their usual meal of chicken paprika and beer.

The media's first glimpse of Wuornos came when she appeared in court for the first time. She seemed relaxed, waving and smiling at reporters and chatting brightly to her lawyer.

Even at the time detectives arrested Wuornos, they remained puzzled as to precisely why she may have killed these men. But there was no shortage of speculation. There's been a theory that the whole escapade was a kind of "team sport" between Wuornos and Moore. Dr. James Fox, a criminologist and co-author of *Mass Murder: America's Growing Menace* (Berkeley Publishing Group), suggests the killings satisfy a need for power and dominance which typifies the serial killer.

But it is still unclear exactly how Wuornos would have been able to lure victims to their deaths. Though empty condom wrappers were found in some of the cars, detectives are still not convinced that the men picked Wuornos up for sex. It has been suggested that she may have left the wrappers simply to sully her victims' reputations. It's more likely, police have said, that she posed as a motorist in distress or as a hitch-hiker. But even then, it seems strange that these men—one an ex-police chief, another a former sheriff's deputy—could have been caught so far off-guard.

But caught, it seems, they were, by a woman who was tried and convicted, receiving multiple death penalty sentences and is currently on death row, earning herself a very rare distinction—women mass murderers are extremely thin on the ground. America has boasted a few in the recent past: Mary Beth Tinning, Jenene Jones, Gwendolyn Graham and Catherine Wood were all convicted of serial murders in the 1980s. Tinning, from New York, murdered seven of her infant children over a number of years; Jones, a Texan paediatric nurse, killed several of her charges; Graham and Wood were lovers from Michigan who went on a murder spree as part of a love pact.

Yet even in this exclusive company, it seems Wuornos could be unusual in that she reportedly behaves more like a classic male serial killer, tracking down strangers, while female killers tend to pick victims they know. Women also tend to favour poison or suffocation. With the possibility of an appeal, it is certain that Aileen Carol Wuornos will continue to add still more pages to this chapter in America's criminal history books.

—C.B-J.

# Sources and Acknowledgements

Andrew Ewart on Agrippina, from *The World's Wickedest Women* (London: Odhams, 1964), copyright © 1964 by Andrew Ewart, reprinted by permission of the publishers. Arthur Lambton on Maria Manning and Mrs. Pearcey, from *Thou Shalt Do No Murder* (London: Hurst & Blackett, Ltd, n.d.). Brian Lunn on Edith Thompson, from *The Fifty Most Amazing Crimes of the Last 100 Years*, ed. J.M. Parrish and John R. Crossland (London: Odhams Press Ltd, 1936), reprinted by permission of the publishers. Bernard O'Donnel on Mary Ann Cotton, from *Should Women Hang?* (London: W.H. Allen, 1956), copyright © 1956 by Bernard O'Donnell; on Vera Renczi, from *The World's Worst Women* (London: W.H. Allen, 1953), copyright © 1953 by Bernard O'Donnell; both reprinted bu permission of Virgin Publishing Ltd. Bill Starr on Magdalena Solis, from *Strange Fate*, ed. Curtis and Mary Fuller (New York: Popular Library, 1965), copyright © 1963 by Clark Publishing Company. Carys Bowen-Jones on Aileen Mary Wuornos, from *Marie Claire*, August, 1991, copyright © 1991 by Carys Bowen-Jones, reprinted by permission of the author. C.E. Maine on Myra Hindley, from *50 True Tales of Terror*, ed. John Canning (London: Souvenir Press Ltd, 1972), copyright © 1972 by Century

Books Ltd, reprinted by permission of the publishers. C.J.S. Thompson on Madame La Farge, from *Poison Romances and Poison Mysteries* (London: Routledge, 1899); and on La Toffana, from *Poisons and Poisoners* (London: Harold Shaylor, 1931). Charles Kingston on Christiana Edmunds, from *Law-Breakers* (London: John Lane, n.d.). Dorothy Dunbar on Lizzie Borden, from *Blood in the parlour* (London, 1964), reprinted by permission of Oak Tree Publications Ltd. Edward S. Radin on Winnie Ruth Judd, from *Crimes of Passion* (New York: Popular Library, 1954), copyright © 1953 by Edward S. Radin, reprinted by permission of the publishers. Edward H. Smith on Mrs. Vermilya, from *Famous American Poison Mysteries* (London: Hurst & Blackett, Ltd, n.d.). Edmund Pearson on Kate Bender, from *Murder at Smutty Nose* (New York: The Sun Dial Press, Inc., 1938). Ellery Queen on Martha Beck, from *Deadlier Than The Male* (London: Corgi, 1966), copyright © 1964 by The Estate of Ellery Queen, reprinted by permission of A.M. Heath & Co., Ltd and Scott Meredith Literary Agency. Elizabeth Villiers on Mrs. Bravo, from *Riddles of Crime* (London: T. Werner Laurie Ltd, 1928). F. Tennyson Jesse on Madeleine Smith, from *Great Unsolved Crimes* (London: Hutchinson, n.d.), reprinted by permission of the Estate of F. Tennyson Jesse. Grierson Dickson on Madame de Brinvilliers and La Voisin, from *Murder by Numbers* (London: Robert Hale Ltd, 1958), copyright © 1958 by Grierson Dickson, reprinted by permission of the publishers. George Dilnot on Ruth Snyder, from *Rogues' March* (London: Geoffrey Bles, 1934). Judge Gerald Sparrow on Madame Fahmy, from *Crimes of Passion* (London: Arthur Barker Ltd, 1973), copyright © 1973 by Gerald Sparrow, reprinted by permission of the publishers. H.M. Walbrook on Adelaide Bartlett, from *Murder and Murder*

on Countess Bathory, from *Perverse Crimes in History* (New York: The Julian Press, Inc., 1963), copyright © 1963 by R.E.L. Masters and Eduard Lea, reprinted by permission of the publishers. Richard Glyn Jones on Rose West, *Keeping It in the Family*, copyright © 2002 Richard Glyn Jones. Rupert Furneaux on Elvira Barney and Ruth Ellis, from *They Died By The Gun* (London: Herbert Jenkins, 1962), copyright © 1962 by Rupert Furneaux, reprinted by permission of the publishers. T.C.H. Jacobs on Charlotte Bryant, Mrs. Donald and Dorothea Waddingham, from *Pageant of Murder* (London: Stanley Paul & Co., Ltd, 1956). Tom Gurr and H.H. Cox on Pauline Parker and Juliet Hume, from *Famous Australian Crimes* (London: Muller, 1958), copyright © 1957 by Tom Gurr and H.H. Cox, reprinted by permission of the publishers.

While every effort has been made to trace authors, publishers and copyright-holders in a few cases this has proved impossible; the publishing editor, c/o Constable & Robinson, would be glad to hear from any such parties so that any omissions can be rectified in future editions of this book.